ARROWSTORM

ARROWSTORM

The World of the Archer in the Hundred Years War

Richard Wadge

The History Press

First published in 2007
This edition first published in 2009
Reprinted 2013

The History Press
The Mill, Brimscombe Port
Stroud, Gloucestershire, GL5 2QG
www.thehistorypress.co.uk

British Library Cataloguing in Publication Data.
A catalogue record for this book is available from the British Library.

ISBN 978 0 7524 4951 7

Typesetting and origination by The History Press

Contents

Acknowledgements

My lifelong interest in history led me to discover archery in the early 1990s. This book emerged from the combination of these two pursuits. I have known many archers over the years who have been generous with their time and opinions. Brian Annetts, Trevor Green and the late Margaret Tyson gave me generous advice and encouragement when I started archery. Steve Stratton has endured my historical musings, and helped me to think more clearly on several issues. He and Mark Stretton also cheerfully donned their fifteenth-century garb to appear in this book. Pip Bickerstaffe asked some of the questions which this book attempts to answer. Thanks to all my fellow archers, particularly the members of the Pickwicks Pepperpots.

My parents encouraged my study of history, particularly by supporting my postgraduate studies at Leeds University. Discussions with other history lovers have helped to keep the subject alive for me. Shaun Barrington and Tom Chidlaw of Spellmount have provided valuable advice from their experience as publishers. While researching the book the good humoured expertise of the staff at the Bodleian Library in Oxford made my task so much easier.

Finally, there is an incalculable debt to my family. My children provided a captive audience for historical storytelling at home and abroad. Eleanor has supported and encouraged me throughout the writing of this book without complaint and listened to me expound on medieval archery at all sorts of times. Grateful thanks to you all.

Introduction

Stories of the triumphs of the medieval English archer are widely known; how the bluff, no-nonsense English yeoman defeated armies of arrogant, aristocratic enemies. While there is some truth and great drama in these stories, they do not give us any idea why these men spent countless hours over many years practising archery so that they could be part of the English armies in the later Middle Ages.

This book is a history of the people who were involved in medieval archery, either militarily or in allied economic and manufacturing activities between roughly 1300 and 1550. The actions of kings and nobles, the events of the great battles are a part of this; they provide a structure. But this is not a conventional military history, an account of strategy, campaigns and battles. It is in part a history of military logistics in the modern sense of organizing supplies, but the scope is wider than just military matters. The main focus is on the ordinary people and how and why they took part in the great events of their time. This is not a chronological history, but instead a series of studies of related topics, which build together to produce an outline of the world of the medieval English and Welsh archers, and the economic framework that supported archery at the time.

Before delving into the world of the medieval archer it is necessary to outline briefly the social and economic conditions of the period. Medieval men and women were not greatly different to us in many ways, except that they lived in a smaller world than we do. A holiday might have meant a trip to the nearest big town or city to enjoy the religious parades or plays, no farther. One great difference between their lives and ours was the immediacy of death. While medical care was more competent in the Middle Ages than we sometimes think, life was much more precarious, even without war or major pandemics. Another fundamental difference was that active religious belief, or at least practice, was universal. The imminence of death was not the only reason for devotion. Church attendance was compulsory, which helped to make religious practice an integral part of life.

This investigation will include an analysis of how willing men were to become soldiers, how many of the archers became professional soldiers, and what was in it for them. In part this is revealed by a consideration of how English armies were raised and organised. Unfortunately, there is no personal narrative by an archer of the period to rival, say, Benjamin Harris's account of being a rifleman in the Napoleonic wars, so we can only get a general picture of what motivated men to serve as archers. The one account that I am aware of is by Peter Bassett and Christopher Hanson, who both began as archers but later served as men at arms, and covers service between 1415 and 1429. This is fairly brief – valuable since the authors were participants in the events themselves – but it gives no insight into them as individuals and their feelings about military service.[1] While it may not be possible to know the archers as individuals, it is possible to gain insights into their reasons for undertaking military service by looking at the opportunities and rewards available to them.

It is not just the ordinary people that we know little about as individuals; personal accounts of life in this period by noblemen and merchants are scarce. The chronicles of the churchmen provide vital, if not unbiased, narratives, but almost all of these give little consideration to the life and feelings of the ordinary people. The author of *Gesta Henrici Quinti*, a chaplain in the royal household, provides an important eyewitness account of the whole Agincourt campaign. While his purpose was to bear witness to the nobility and excellence of Henry V, he makes passing comments about the way he and others felt on the campaign, which gives a limited insight into the feelings of the archers. Because of this lack of personal accounts and a general lack of interest in the doings of ordinary men and women in the histories and chronicles, the main sources used must be administrative records. Occasionally, accounting records list rewards and pensions given to archers, which afford some clues to motivation. As well as records of the Royal household, there are customs and tax records, and administrative records of major cities such as London and York, which allow some understanding of local involvement in both war and the archery industry.

When a country makes a sustained military effort over several generations, as happened with England in the period of what we now call the Hundred Years War, an arms industry is born and grows. The second part of the book provides an account of the economic and manufacturing developments that underlay the military activity. It gives an idea of the dedicated trading networks that grew across Europe, as well as the economic developments within England that arose to meet the need for the regular supply of military archery equipment. This specialization was typical of the arms industries of Europe in the Middle Ages; though England developed an industry making the best military archery equipment in Western Europe using imported resources, but deliberately no export trade. The armourers of Milan and Southern Germany developed the reputation of producing the finest armour based on local raw materials, and exported their goods.

This sustained war effort put a strain on the economic and social development of England. Yet the mass of the population in the last quarter of the fourteenth century and most of the fifteenth century enjoyed a better quality of life. This seems paradoxical, when the English kings of the time were continually struggling to finance their wars. It has been estimated that in periods of heightened military activity – the 1340s and from 1415 to the end of the 1420s – perhaps 10% of the male population was directly involved in the war [2] and an undetermined number of women and children were part of the supply industries, with the concomitant commitment of money and material. This level of investment of capital, materials and people must have been a problem in the decades after the major outbreaks of plague, when labour was at a premium.

Throughout this period, England as a country covered much the same geographic area as it does currently. The king of England was crowned in a religious ceremony, and was regarded as being divinely anointed. This did not give him absolute powers; he had to take notice of Parliament, which gained influence through the period because of its tax levying powers. More importantly, as Richard II discovered, the king had to keep a good working relationship with a majority of the established magnates to be effective. Although the thirteenth to the sixteenth centuries saw many political disturbances, including popular uprisings, royal depositions and a significant number of battles between the king and his magnates, England did not suffer from the sustained instability that afflicted France for example, where princely nobles feuded almost constantly for the throne. The exception was the Wars of the Roses from 1455 to 1487, but even this period included about 20 years of peace (interrupted by fighting in 1469 to 1471) under Edward IV and Richard III. There was no attempt by any English magnates to break free from England, in the way that the Dukes of Burgundy effectively managed to do in France in the fifteenth century.

While the people living in the towns and villages of England seem to have thought of themselves as English in a broad sense, local and regional identities were emphasised by quite significant differences in the English spoken in different counties. Though by the end of the 14th century English had just about ousted French everywhere. Scotland was an independent kingdom with its own divisions and foreign alliances. There was regular warfare between the English and the Scots throughout the period, though after Edward I's reign the English kings made no sustained attempt to conquer Scotland, but rather tried to maintain some level of dominance through politics and periodic bloody battles. By the fourteenth century, Wales, which for much of the medieval period had been a collection of principalities and lordships, had been conquered, but was not fully integrated into England. The Welsh were not universally hostile to the English Crown, a number fought in Edward I's armies of conquest, and significant numbers fought in the English armies of the fourteenth and fifteenth centuries. Cornwall, while politically integrated into England as a Dukedom, was differentiated from England by its language and culture. The English kings claimed overlordship of Ireland, and some of the magnates also held substantial estates in Ireland. The reality of these claims fluctuated.

The period of the Hundred Years War is one of great change. The Black Death, one of the greatest catastrophes of world history, descended. This on its own would have brought about change in the societies of western Europe: but this was also a period of chronic warfare. In this book there will be some account of the changes that may have arisen in English society through the sustained involvement in military archery.

References to money paid as wages, won as spoils or paid for the purchase of bows and arrows, are common within. All these prices are in English pounds sterling, twenty shillings to the pound, twelve pence to the shilling. The complication when assessing medieval prices and wages is not converting medieval shillings and pence to modern pounds and pence, but relating the converted figures to the cost of living, and so giving a realistic figure in terms of days or weeks worked. An outline is provided showing what the money earned by the archers could buy, including some tables of medieval comparative values, so that the reader can make the same estimations of value that the archer himself might have done, when he thought about how profitable his service was going to be. Any medieval weights and measures mentioned are converted into their Imperial equivalents.

Sometimes we can get a glimpse into the life of an individual, but in the end we cannot construct a series of biographies as can be done for the knights and men at arms. We are left, in Anne Curry's words describing the victory at Agincourt, with '...the faceless majority of Henry's archers.'[3] While we may never know much about them as individuals, I hope that this account will leave an idea of their motivation, perhaps some glimpses of the sort of personalities involved. Of course much of this is an interpretation of fragmentary historical data, the story no more than a reasonable likelihood. As Francis Pryor pointed out, 'History is personal, not absolute, and there is no such thing as absolute historical truth'.[4]

NOTES

1 Rowe, B J H A Contemporary account of the 100 years War from 1415–29. *English Historical Review* 1926. p.504-13.

2 Postan, M M (1964). The Costs of the Hundred Years War. *Past and Present.* 27 p.36.

3 Curry, A (2005). *Agincourt: a New History*. Stroud, Tempus Publishing. p.192.

4 Pryor, F (2005). *Britain AD.* London. p.235.

What was Life like in England in the Fourteenth and Fifteenth Centuries?

The men and women of Medieval England no doubt had very similar hopes and fears for themselves and their families as we do today, but they lived in a very different world. So before giving an account of the activities of the archers, bowyers, fletchers, stringers and merchants involved, we need a basic outline of the circumstances under which they lived. How many people lived in England; how long did they live for; how healthy were they; how and where did they live?

The nearest thing to a census in medieval England was the Domesday Book, which has enabled historians to estimate a population of c.2.2 million in 1086[1]. As we move forward from this date, it is easier to describe, and to some extent explain, trends in the population than it is to provide exact numbers. By the early part of the fourteenth century, there had been a steady rise in the population from the Domesday baseline until it reached at least 5 million[2]. What is significant in this rise is that 'The growth in population in the twelfth and thirteenth centuries was largely the result of increases in the number of peasants.'[3] These peasants tended to live in nuclear families of two generations, with family size limited in the poorer households by lower fertility and higher child mortality.[4] Despite the struggle for subsistence that affected a noticeable proportion of the population, this population increase suggests that in these two centuries there were few bad harvests, and few significant epidemics, a circumstance which was to change markedly in the fourteenth century.

The first disaster in the fourteenth century was the Great Famine of 1315-22. This began with a poor harvest in 1314, with the harvests in the next two years being worse, if anything, largely because of heavy and persistent rain. Although the harvest of 1317 was better, there was another poor one in 1321. Things were no better for livestock farming; there was disease in sheep in 1315-6 and a 'murrain' affecting cattle in 1319-21. It has been estimated that about 10% of the population died as a result of this famine.[5] Contemporary accounts strongly imply that not all these people died of starvation, since the better-off peasants, the clergy and gentry also died in higher than usual numbers. Diseases such as pneumonia and typhus would thrive among the famished, particularly given the wet weather for two years, and these would spread to the more affluent. However, conditions improved over the next two decades, and the population probably began to increase once more. By the 1340s, Edward III was able to raise large armies, in fact the army that landed in Normandy in July 1346 for what would become the Crecy/Calais campaign, was the largest transported to France at one time during the entire Middle Ages.[6] He had his most dramatic successes in his wars against the French in these years, something that would not have been possible if the population at large was weakened by starvation and disease. But any recovery there was came to an abrupt end.

The Black Death, which affected the British Isles between 1348 and 1350, was a disaster on a scale that is difficult to comprehend today. It seems that it was either septicaemic or pneumonic plague, so that it was spread not only by the flea of the black rat, but to some extent from person to person as well.[7] As a result, it is estimated that about 45% of the population died. The death toll was spread remarkably evenly across the country, although some manors suffered much less than others and some groups of people suffered less than others. In general, the clergy suffered badly, particularly the parish priests, although the higher clergy escaped much more lightly. Perhaps it is not surprising that the nobility seemed to escape the worst of the Black Death, one study showing them suffering a death rate of only 13%, about one third of the average for the population as a whole.[8] But what helped to make a remarkably rapid recovery possible – at least in social and economic terms – was the different death rate between different age groups. It seems probable that while between 40% and 45% of young people in their twenties died, as many as 60% of the elderly died. This awful statistic means that there were plenty of economic opportunities for the survivors to better themselves.

The Black Death was the first great outbreak of the plague in the period, and it became endemic, there were outbreaks with grim regularity. The outbreak of 1361 was particularly cruel, known as the *pestis puerorum*, the children's plague, it killed high numbers of the children of the survivors of the Black Death, regardless of social group. Somehow, people held society together. After this the plague did not necessarily strike nationwide, outbreaks could occur at a regional level through the rest of fourteenth century, and in the fifteenth and sixteenth centuries. But it was not the only disease that caused epidemics in these centuries. The chroniclers' accounts of the epidemic of 1473 make it likely that dysentery was the problem, while the 'sweating sickness' of 1485 was perhaps influenza.

The population stabilised at its new level, maybe about two and a half million, over the next 150 years or so, but quite why puzzles historians. Despite the standard of living for the survivors improving markedly, there does not seem to have been the trend towards earlier marriage and larger families that happened in parts of Europe. As Dyer puts it, 'an English family culture had emerged which prevented population growth.' He notes that through the late fourteenth century and into the fifteenth century, direct father-to-son inheritance of landholdings declined in some areas, and when there was direct

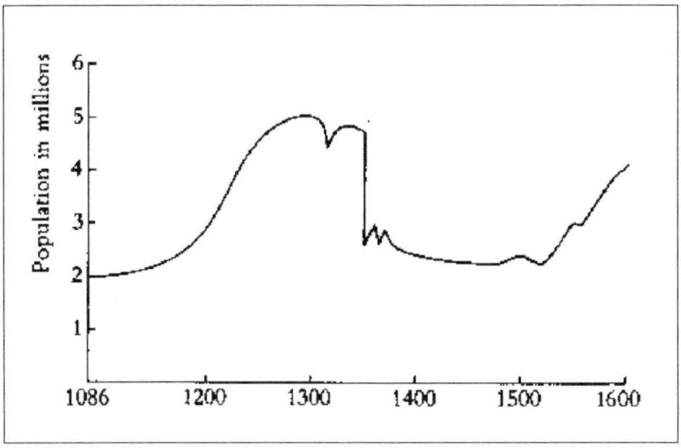

Population of England 1086–1600. Diagram derived from Dyer, C (1989) *Standards of Living in the Later Middle Ages*, p. 4.

inheritance the sons sold up and moved much more frequently than before the Black Death. Even where people continued to live on their agricultural holdings, they seemed to be more determined to move between villages. He describes it as 'a restless and rather unstable society with its lack of kin solidarities and with a reduction in family support.'[9]

The reduction in population resulting from these large scale outbreaks of pestilence led to the widening of work opportunities for women and young people. But it did this without shaking the fundamental male dominance of society. Women in medieval England had always worked in less financially rewarding work, such as making up sheaves at harvest time, or spinning in support of the cloth industry. In the times of labour scarcity they were able to improve the pay they received for their traditional work, and move into better paid craftwork such as weaving or metalworking. There are more examples from the second half of the fourteenth century onwards of women taking over the business on their husband's death. It is probable that women in towns had more opportunities, both for huckstering victuals and working in support of craftsmen. Whatever their skill and competence, women in most cases could become neither formal apprentices, nor members of the craft misteries. The improvement in women's earning capacity made them more self-sufficient and gave them more freedom of choice about marriage and remarriage.

One sign of the improvement in living standards was that the mass of the peasantry began to live in better housing. Throughout this period in England and Wales there was a slow trend towards the living spaces of humans and animals being in separate, commonly conjoined, buildings, rather than sharing the same living space. While there are some examples of peasants building new houses for themselves or members of their families in the first half of the fourteenth century, these efforts became widespread in the late fourteenth century, with a real concentration of activity between 1440 and 1520, according to dendrochronology.[10] The cruck houses that they built at this time in the Midlands and some of the northern counties gave them considerable living space, and sometimes included two storeys at one end of the building. The quality of the construction work is shown by the number of these houses that have survived to become highly sought-after properties today.

How did the Black Death affect urban life? By the 1340s about 15% of the English population lived in towns and cities.[11] After the plague, the expansion of towns tended to cease, and indeed a number went into steep decline. This may well not have been a direct consequence of the Black Death, since places such as Boston, Grimsby or Winchester had begun to decline before the cull. One of the consequences of the plague was that there were very few of the rural population who did not have a chance of getting an adequate landholding or wage labour to support themselves. So a combination of a stable rural population and there being sufficient economic opportunities for it to support itself in the countryside limited immigration to the towns. Some contemporary accounts recorded the view that rural life was healthier than urban, which may have helped to curb any drift to the towns.[12] The health problems in larger towns and cities included high population density, inefficient sewerage and waste disposal and limited access to clean drinking water, all exacerbated by people living very closely with domestic animals. This provided an environment for disease to spread rapidly. While rural dwellers might also live in close proximity to animals, it was not such an unrelieved closeness. Finally, at times of economic hardship, the rural population had better opportunities for subsistence activities.[13]

Life expectancy in medieval England was affected by social standing, but less than might be expected. The nobility tended to suffer less from the plague because they did not live so close to the black rats and their fleas, but the gentry and the clergy seem to have died at a rate quite close to that of the mass of the population. There is no evidence of life expectancy being higher in some regions than others; although it is probable that life expectancy in the Northern Marches was lower in the periods of persistent military activity. Life expectancy in towns would almost certainly be lower than that in rural areas. The relative deadliness of urban living was not really resolved until the Victorian era. Childhood, especially early childhood, was the time of highest mortality for both sexes, while adult women also suffered significant mortality as a result of childbearing.

Period	Group	Life expectancy
Late 14th century	Essex Peasants	42 years at age 12
Early 15th Century	Essex Peasants	39 years at age 12
Early 15th Century	Monks of Westminster	29–30 years at age 20
Late 15th century	Essex Peasants	36 years at age 12
Late 15th century	Monks of Westminster	20 years at age 20[14]

Dyer found that peasants in Worcestershire could expect to live to much the same age as the Essex peasants at similar dates. While this sample is very brief, it shows that, despite fatal epidemic disease being fairly frequent, the majority of the English population who lived outside towns might reasonably expect to reach 50 years old, at least if they survived childhood. It also suggests that living in privileged conditions like the monks did not guarantee long life.

The discovery of the Towton war grave in 1996 has given us information about the ages of about 38 men involved in military service. The ages ranged from four who were between 16 and 20, to three who were over 46 years old. The average age of the group was about 30. This average age is higher than that found in some nineteenth-century war graves, and data from the Korean and Vietnam wars.[15] While the Towton grave provides a relatively small sample, there is no reason to believe it is misleading, that it is a grave of second class conscripts, a group of older men scraped together to fill the battle lines. Indeed, of 28 skulls studied from the grave, nine were considered to show traces of well healed wounds, suggesting they belonged to experienced soldiers.[16] It is important to remember that fighting in a medieval battle line required stamina, strength and agility. Considering the age range of this group we can assume that men in their forties in the fifteenth century considered themselves fit enough to undertake this dangerous activity. Eighty-eight of the skeletons that have been recovered from the *Mary Rose* are complete enough to allow their age in 1545 to be estimated. The average age of these probably falls in the mid 20s, with about 20% being 18 or younger,[17] a marked reduction in age in comparison with the Towton group.

Apart from life expectancy, what can we glean about general health?[18] Any comments made about the health of the people of medieval England will tend to underestimate the real level of illness because we only have skeletons to work from, and bones do not always show traces of serious illnesses. Also, any figures will be more accurate with regard to adults since disproportionately few child skeletons survive. The average height of men in the Middle Ages is about 170.6 cm or 5ft. 7in, slightly more than that of later centuries. The Towton group have an average height of 171.6 cm or 5ft $7^1/_2$ in., reflecting either the bias of a small sample, or a preference for recruiting bigger men for military service (although two of the 37 individuals identified were 162.5 cm or 5ft. 4in at most). The *Mary Rose* men show a very similar range of heights, with a smaller percentage of the taller men (5 ft 10 or more) than the Towton group, and their average is perhaps half an inch shorter. As regards dental health, perhaps one in four people in this period had a dental abscess and one in two a tooth with a cavity.[19] Osteoarthritis was quite common among men, particularly in the upper body joints, reflecting the physical nature of life. Interestingly, the vertebral columns of the Towton men show a much higher incidence of changes linked to joint disease than those from other medieval cemeteries such as Wharram Percy.[20] While sustained military practice could cause these changes, we cannot draw any firm conclusion. In general there are few signs of sustained malnutrition in the surviving skeletons, although there are signs of periods of poor nutrition in the development of many. Given that the diet of most of the population was defined by what was available in the particular seasons, and that many of the methods of storing food reduced the nutritional value, this is not surprising. Roberts and Cox suggest that that many of the less well-off might have suffered from vitamin deficiencies by the end of the winter,[21] which would have the most obvious effects on growing children. The individuals in the Towton war grave show signs of this sort of deficiency; 32% showed evidence of iron deficiency, probably in childhood. Clearly they had matured into healthy adults, since this didn't prevent them from having an active life subsequently.

Serfdom is a dominant feature of rural life from the Norman Conquest to the middle of the fifteenth century. There can be no doubt that serfdom could be oppressive and was an unfree state in law, but it was not slavery. The major difference between free and unfree tenants was that unfree tenants were under the jurisdiction of the manorial courts of their landlords in most matters, rather than the royal courts. Unfree tenants could be pursued by their landlords if they left their holdings without permission. Besides paying rents and entry fines (paid to take on a tenancy) the unfree tenants had to ask permission of their landlords when they wished to marry, inherit their tenures and marry off their children, and pay them dues for the 'privilege'. They also owed labour dues to their landlords, which were usually well defined in both legal agreements and custom and practice. These latter were possibly the source of most dispute and resentment at local level, since, given the cycle of life in the countryside, they tended to fall most heavily on tenants when their own farming required most of their time.

It would be quite wrong to think that all unfree tenants were living in grinding poverty; many tenants held enough land to feed their families and have a surplus to sell. Equally, it would be a mistake to think of social and economic practices in medieval England as the same throughout the country. Firstly, while unfree tenure was present in all the English counties, the proportion of this type of tenancy varied, with it accounting for a little more than half the tenures in the northern and eastern counties, but a higher proportion in the midland and southern shires. Secondly, the burden of labour dues varied, often from landlord to landlord within a shire. One must not assume that serfs were poor peasants, struggling to make a living among their free neighbours. This was particularly true after the Black Death, in 1381 William Smith of Ingatestone for example, owned six cattle, five calves and some pigs, while being a tenant of sufficient land to maintain himself and his beasts.[22] However, there was another side to the duties of, and opportunities for, the unfree peasantry: military service, particularly through the array system, which will be outlined later. The men were expected to have arms, however simple, in their houses, and to make themselves available for military service at the king's command.

The fifteenth century eventually saw the demise of serfdom, with the Black Death probably being the major factor. As previously noted, the population of England rose steadily until the first decades of the fourteenth century and this led to land hunger. This benefited landlords: they could increase entry fines and rents, knowing there were more potential tenants than landholdings; they could encourage the clearance of forest and marginal land to bring it into cultivation and so have more paying tenants; they could start to commute labour services for cash payments, knowing that there was plenty of labour to be hired from those who did not have enough land to live off. The other advantage of commuting labour services was that it saved the landlords the trouble of getting their recalcitrant tenants to perform these services. As a result, commutation was widespread.

After the Black Death, potential tenants and labourers were scarce, so that the balance of power between them and the landlords swung in their favour. Tenants could refuse high entry fines and rents and go to a landlord who offered them a better financial deal. This could also lead to them losing their servile status, since the new landlord would either not know or not care about it. At the same time, wage labourers looked for work from whoever paid the best wages. While the landlords could do little about the decline in their rental income when there was a real shortage of prospective tenants, they and other employers tried to do something about wages. Landlords tried to reinstate labour services from their tenants to solve their labour problems. However, since the main enforcers of this were the Reeves, who were usually part of the village community themselves, this reversal was not generally successful. As part of the efforts by the employers of wage labour, whether landlords, merchants or guildsmen, to regain their control of the labour market, they used their strong representation in the Parliamentary Commons to encourage and support the passing of the Statute of Labourers in 1351. This attempted to set wages at pre-Black Death levels, limit the right of wage earners to pick and choose the work they took on, and penalised both those who sought and those who paid higher wages.[23] The court records, unsurprisingly, contain more cases of men and women being charged with asking for or receiving higher wages than the Statute allowed, than cases brought against those who paid the higher wages. This repressive Statute was one of the causes of the Peasants' Revolt in 1381, which, although unsuccessful in the short term, emphasised to the governing classes that the broad population of the South East and East Anglia at least would not quietly accept oppressive economic and social control.

Edward I completed the military conquest of Wales, a process started very soon after the Norman Conquest.[24] Because this was such a long, drawn-out process, some parts of Wales, much of the south and Flintshire for example, were under English lords for much longer than the heartlands of North Wales. In addition, Welsh princes and nobles periodically allied themselves with the English kings. So there might be a revolt by some Welsh at the same time as other Welsh gentry and archers were serving in the English king's army, as happened during Glyndwr's revolt in the early fifteenth century.

The power of the great English Lords, particularly within their estates, was considerable, and no English king could afford to attack or discount these men as a group. Inevitably, individuals fell out with the king periodically, sometimes fatally, as did Henry Percy in 1403. The rising power within the political structure throughout the period was Parliament, and especially the Commons, with their power over the granting of taxes. Although this sounds potentially damaging to the cohesion of the kingdom, the King's administration through the Sheriffs and the King's Justices helped to counteract the tendency. Though not in accordance with the classic model, it was an early example of the separation of powers within the state that Montesquieu recognised in Great Britain 300 years later, and recommended.

Religion was an integral part of medieval life. Besides the descriptions of archers praying and seeking blessing before battle that suggest this was deep seated, the Church also ensured that the people had at least one day's rest a week. This was expressed in a prohibition against working on Sundays to allow church attendance. There was also a large number of religious festivals and holidays that gave medieval men and women rest from their labours, between forty and fifty a year in addition to Sundays in the fourteenth century. These festivals were not imposed on the people by the church, but enjoyed and promoted by them through parades and play cycles.[25] Between the Black Death and the Reformation, people in both town and country celebrated these festivals with increasingly complex and lavish displays. England rivalled Italy in its piety in the fourteenth and fifteenth centuries; it is very easy for the many sons of the Reformation in Northern and Western Europe (and the US) today to misapprehend this: England did not stand apart from Catholic Europe, it was central to it. In the words of Peter Ackroyd in his fascinating book, *Albion: The Origins of the English Imagination*, 'Life was only the beginning, not the end, of existence and thus could be celebrated or scorned as one station along the holy way.'[26] A fine outlook for a military archer.

NOTES

1 Dyer, C (2003). *Making a Living in the Middle Ages: The People of Britain 850–1520*. London. Penguin. p 95

2 Dyer, C (2003) op cit p.233

3 Dyer, C (2003) op cit p.155

4 Roberts, C and Cox M (2003). *Health and Disease in Britain*. Stroud. Sutton Publishing. p.225

5 Dyer, C (1989). *Standards of Living in the Later Middle Ages*. Cambridge University Press. p.267

6 Ayton, A and Preston, P (2005). *The Battle of Crecy 1346*. Woodbridge, Boydell Press. p.15
7 Platt, C (1997) *King Death; the Black Death and its Aftermath in Late Medieval England*. London, UCL Press. p.33
8 Platt, C (1997) op cit pp.49-50
9 Dyer, C (2003) p.277
10 Dyer, C (2003) p.356
11 Ayton, A and Preston, P (2005) op cit p.217n
12 Platt, C (1997) op cit p.33
13 Roberts, C and Cox, M. (2003) op cit p.235
14 Figures from Dyer, C (2003) p.275
15 Fiorato, V, Boylston, A and Knusel, C (editors) (2000). *Blood Red Roses. The Archaeology of a Mass Grave from the Battle of Towton AD 1461*. Oxford. Oxbow Books p.52-3
16 Fiorato, V, Boylston, A and Knusel, C editors, op cit p.94
17 Stirland, A J (2005) *The Men of the Mary Rose*. Stroud. Sutton Publishing. p.81-2
18 These comments owe much to Roberts, C and Cox, M. (2003)
19 Roberts, C and Cox, M. (2003) p.265
20 Fiorato, V, Boylston, A and Knusel, C editors (2000), p.67-8
21 Roberts, C and Cox, M. (2003) p.248
22 Dyer, C (2003) p.288
23 Dyer, C (2003) p.283
24 It is probably more accurate to say that the process was started by the English kings of Wessex, but they seemed unable to hold significant areas of Welsh territory in any sustained way, merely exercising some level of overlordship at times.
25 For more about these festivals, and what is often called the ritual year, Hutton, R (1996) *The Rise and Fall of Merry England*. Oxford University Press, is a good survey for the end of the period covered in this book.
26 Ackroyd, P (2002). *Albion: The Origins of the English Imagination*. London. Chatto & Windus p.124

Part 1

How and Why Men became Military Archers

Introduction

The ways in which the English armies were raised throughout the time of the Hundred Years War (and some of the subsequent campaigns of the late fifteenth and early sixteenth centuries, which could seem like continuations of it) can reveal motivation for military service. While this section will concentrate on service in English armies, it will also include a brief survey of English archers serving foreign employers.

In some ways it is misleading to call many of the armies English, since they always included a number of French, Flemings and Germans as men at arms, as well as large numbers of Welshmen serving as archers and infantry. In the fifteenth century the armies even included small but noticeable numbers of French archers. These armies were English because they served the king of England and his interests, and their ultimate paymaster was the royal administration.

Most of these armies were not led by the king or a royal prince, or even directly recruited by a member of the royal family. In practical terms they were employed by their commanders, who could be one of the great nobles of the realm, or just as likely a knight or man at arms. This gave the archers a lot of choice about who they worked with, where, and for how long.

Increasingly, the archers became professional soldiers for a longer or shorter part of their working lives commensurate with the rewards archery provided, making it sometimes a worthwhile career choice. After an account of the potential scale of these rewards, there is a brief attempt here to indicate what an archer's income from war might have been worth in the fourteenth and fifteenth centuries. This will show how the archers themselves might have weighed up the rewards of military service, and give an idea of what they might have bought with their military wages.

How were Armies Raised?

The renowned military archers of medieval England and Wales became a major part of armies of the time through an established but evolving system for raising these forces. By the time of Edward III, the English king could only wage war if he, and the purpose of the war, had some measure of support from the people at large. While the king could call on the magnates and those knights and others who held property or position directly from him for military service on occasion, these men would still expect some kind of pay and expenses. If he was planning any sustained military endeavour he needed the compliance of the Commons in Parliament, and the taxpaying population at large. The heart of the matter was not necessarily money; rather, could the king raise sufficient willing, competent soldiers to wage war successfully? It is this question of willingness to serve that colours any account of how medieval English armies were raised. This is all the more significant since a high proportion of the population in the fourteenth century were classified as serfs, legally defined as unfree. The nature of serfdom was touched on in the previous chapter; it was a matter of which courts individuals could use and did not imply that they were the property of their lord or without individual rights. The serfs, in common with the other social groups in medieval English society, owed a duty to their communities and their lords, and ultimately to the king, and could reasonably be expected to do military service. This was a clear legal duty, which could be enforced with penalties including fines and even the threat of forfeiture,[1] and was the basis of raising of armies at this time.

In England, this duty can be traced back to Anglo-Saxon times, with service in the Fyrd. There has been sustained academic debate about the continuity of the Fyrd tradition into post-Conquest England, and the consensus is that the Norman and Plantagenet kings exploited the tradition. These kings described and developed this duty of military service in the Assizes of Arms and Statutes associated with them. These divided the male population aged between 15 and 60 into groups defined by financial status. Members of each group were expected to serve in person, armed to the appropriate standard for the group. The English kings were thus sufficiently confident in the stability of the broad population of England to require their subjects to have arms in their houses and be competent in their use. English law encouraged a wide range of men to try to develop the skills necessary for military service.

These military duties as laid down in the Assize of Arms of 1230 begin to include the development of military archery. This Assize stated '... he who has goods to the value of 20/- shall have a bow and arrows, unless he lives in our forest, if he lives in our forest and has goods to the value of 20/- he shall have an axe or a spear.'[2] This was expanded in the Assizes of 1242 and 1253 until the Statute of Winchester of 1285, which was for the most part a revision of these earlier Assizes of Arms, consolidated these developments.[3] The Statute laid down what type of soldier each man should serve as, and the weapons that he should have in his house. Later generations looked back to it as the measure of legitimacy with regard to the demands for compulsory military service made by their kings.

Given the scale of his military activities, Edward I might have been expected to have brought about major changes to the recruiting system in England, but this was not the case. His main contribution was a pragmatic one, extending the paying of royal wages for arrayed troops so that they received them from when they reached the place of muster.[4] His concern was to get predictable numbers of troops to where he needed them on time, and payment of wages from arrival helped. The real developments in the system were brought about by his father, Henry III, a much less successful military figure. Firstly, in 1230 he extended the duty of military service to include the unfree, and divided freemen and town burghers into two wealth categories, those holding 40/- of goods and those holding 20/-.[5] In doing this he widened the pool of potential fighting men considerably, which contributed to the effective development of the English army over the next two centuries. Secondly, his Assize of Arms of 1242 brought about changes in the types of arms the various financial groups should hold, and, most importantly for the purposes of this book, recognised the importance of the bow and allocated it to those holding land worth more than 40/-. The main regulations of the Statute of Winchester were:

> Every man between fifteen years and sixty years shall be assessed and sworn to armour according to the quantity of their lands and goods; that is to wit from £15 land or 40 marks goods a hauberk, sword, knife and a horse: £10 lands or 20 marks goods a hauberk, sword and a knife: and from 40/- land and more unto 100/- of lands sword, bow and arrow and a knife: and he that hath less than 40/- yearly shall be sworn to keep gisarmes, knives and other less weapons: and he that hath less than 20 marks in goods shall have swords, knives and other less weapons: and all others that may shall have bows and arrows out of the Forest and in the forest bows and boults.[6] And that view of armour [a view of arms in the records discussed below] be made every year two times.[7]

The Statute of Winchester is the final stage in the transformation of the purpose of the Assizes of Arms. In 1181 the purpose was as much concerned with local law and order, by insuring that law abiding men were well armed, as it was with providing a pool of potential soldiers. By 1285 this had changed and the Assize had become a key part of the English military system, aiming to ensure that the Commissioners of Array had a large number of men with military equipment to select armies from.

Edward III followed the traditions of his grandfather Edward I, and his father, Edward II in abandoning the demand for unpaid compulsory military service for infantry serving outside England. Edward I, and less successfully Edward II, had made extensive use of the feudal system to raise armies for their campaigns. In doing this they put particular pressure on those wealthy enough to be eligible to be knights, and antagonised the mass of the population with the financial demands of equipping and paying the armies. All classes of soldier served without royal pay in England, relying on their own or their community's resources, but once they crossed to Wales, Scotland, or went further afield, they could claim pay. The first Parliament of Edward III's reign in 1327 discussed the matter at length and petitioned the King not to follow his forbears' practices, including that of expecting the city or county to pay arrayed troops' wages or food costs outside the county boundaries. A consensus arose in the following years such that conscripted men could only be required to serve without royal pay in the case of foreign invasion, and even then only with the consent of Parliament. But if they were paid by the king then they were expected to serve wherever they were sent.[8] It is clear that Parliament felt that this agreement was not always followed by the king and his officials since 'in 1384 the Commons requested that Edward III's ordinance against military service outside counties at other than the King's cost be observed.'[9] The request may not have been heeded, since in 1386 the orders for the array of archers from twenty-three counties specifically said that the '...archers should be brought to London at the cost of the county...'[10] In this struggle over who should pay the travel expenses to the muster point, it was the archers who lost out, since they had to live without pay until the argument was settled.

The real change in the system for raising armies was the rapid development of the use of indentures to raise companies of soldiers. As paid service in English armies of the period became the norm, there was a tendency towards the recruitment of smaller armies than had been the case in Edward I and II's reigns,[11] inevitable anyway because of the Black Death.

THE OWNERSHIP OF ARMS AND THE DEVELOPMENT OF ARCHERY SKILLS

It is difficult to estimate how rapidly archery skills developed, and how widely they spread over the country. The Norman kings and magnates soon came to use Welsh archers, exploiting their existing military archery skills. It seems that men of the English shires had not developed similar skills to any comparable extent until the thirteenth century. There were clear exceptions among particular occupational groups, such as foresters and parkers, who relied on archery skills as part of their day-to-day work. Archery skills had certainly developed in the northern counties by 1244, when a writ summoning infantry from these areas specified that they be arrayed with bows and arrows.[12] In 1260 Hugh Bigod The Justiciar and Philip Bassett were ordered to raise men armed with bows and arrows from Kent and bring them to the king at Dover.[13] In 1266 '300 of the best archers from the Weald' were arrayed for coastal defence duties.[14] In 1274 we have an early example of a group of archers in the service of a nobleman, in this case John de Warenne, Earl of Surrey, being used to promote his interests against another landholder. Surrey was authorised to raise '...200 good archers at our cost...'[15] to serve the king, under Surrey's command. Eight years later Edward I is having to order the Sheriff of Sussex to remove 'the men of John de Warenne, Earl of Surrey, archers and other armed men...' from Robert Aguilon's manor.[16] In 1277 Edward I had a bodyguard of 100 Macclesfield archers. In 1298 Robert of Werdale, described as an archer, was admitted to the Register of the Freemen of York.[17] By becoming a Freeman, probably by paying a fee, Robert was able to pursue his trade in the city. The question is, what trade did he pursue? Since he was a professional archer, he may have been in York taking employment as a paid substitute at times of array, if so it is perhaps surprising that he registered as a Freeman. Alternatively, he may have been working as a professional archer involved in teaching and training the citizens in archery for both peace and war, which could well have necessitated him becoming a Freeman. However this is all speculation, the only certainty is the presence of a professional archer in York at this date.

Some insight into the spread of military archery skills among the English male population at large can be gained from the records of the Views of Arms. One from Reading in 1311 recorded at least 276 men, but only 41 had bows and arrows (barely 15%), the majority had just axes and knives. Another at Bridport in 1319 recorded about 180 men, none of whom had bows.[18] In the 1330s the percentages of bowmen recorded in both Norfolk and Middlesex were also negligible.[19] But archery skills seem to have been more prevalent in the northern counties. The West Riding of Yorkshire alone provided 359 foot archers and some mounted archers in 1334, and Lancashire provided 232 mounted archers and 653 foot archers in 1335.[20] In both cases this was for Scottish expeditions. The figures from these two counties and London, in contrast to the much lower ones from some of the more southern counties, help to explain how Edward III was able to raise at least 5000 archers through the array system and have another 2800 or so mounted archers serving largely in retinues in 1346 for his army in northern France. He had at least 1000 archers serving in Aquitaine, which still left enough archers in England for them to make a battle-winning contribution at the Battle of Neville's Cross.

The records of a View of Arms held at Norwich in 1355 gives us an idea of the proportion practising archery in a city.[21] Medieval cities in the British Isles were fairly small and more closely linked to the surrounding agricultural areas in the Middle Ages then is the case now. This lists the men who responded to the Justices calling out of the men of the city aged between 16 and 60 to discover the number available for military service and their level of arms.

Leet of Norwich	Men with full armour	Accompanying these	Men with half armour	Archers	Unarmoured men
Conesford	13	3 archers	19	6	100
Bostrode (a sub leet)					80
Mancroft	43	5 archers 2 armed men	23	57	c.90
Wymer	58	23 archers 9 armed men	14	46	c.210.
Total	**114**	**31 archers** **11 armed men**	**56**	**109**	**c.480**

- A Leet was a division of Norwich like a ward in other cities.
- Full armour was usually a helmet with aventail, plate and mail on upper body and arms.
- A number of the men in full armour brought other fighting men with them (third column).
- Half armour was usually mail, breast plate and a helmet with aventail.
- Archers brought bows and arrows, all had knives and many had swords. The number of arrows they had is not specified.
- The unarmoured men brought a variety of weapons, All had a knife and cudgel, while about a third also brought a sword, axe or spear as well.
- A number of the armoured men, half armoured men and archers also brought servants.
- In Wymer Leet Geoffrey de Hapton, serving as an armoured man, brought his brother Stephen as an archer, and the archers included two bowyers, two fletchers and a smith.

There were 801 men who responded to the summons, of which 140, or 17.5%, were archers. Perhaps more surprising is that 170, or just over 21%, had their own armour. Since the View of Arms record doesn't include any references to horses these men may have been showing their availability to serve as men at arms, or in the category of armoured men (armoured infantry, superseded by the men at arms who fought on foot in the English tactical system), a deployment rarely used in Edward III's armies serving in France.

These figures are post-Black Death, and so these are the sort of the numbers of men who would be potentially available for service for the rest of the fourteenth and much of the fifteenth century, given the relative stability of the population figures for the period as noted in the previous chapter.

Despite the proportion of Norwich men who had bows, Edward III's armies of the 1340s, whether made up of arrayed or indentured men, were raised disproportionately from the counties. Townspeople represented about 15 % of the population of England at this time, but not of the armies.[22] However, it is likely that these figures are on the low side since there may have been some evasion of the View, and there were almost certainly a number of Norwich men, mainly archers no doubt, serving in retinues at the time. So it is difficult to draw a clear conclusion about any positive effect that Edward III's successful campaigns may have had on the number of men practising archery with a view to undertaking military service, although these figures for archers are noticeably higher than those from Reading noted above.

So what can we say about the number of reasonably competent archers in England in the 1330s and 40s, before Edward III's successes encouraged men to practise their martial skills? Despite the encouragement contained in the Statute of Winchester, relatively few men with landholdings valued at less than 40/- seem to have taken up the bow, in the southern counties at least. It seems that archers were not as freely available in this period as might be thought, but that those there were took their military duty seriously, as is shown by the numbers involved in the campaigns of 1346–7.

The Statutes and Assizes of Arms included the expectation, not always explicit, that men would practise with their weapons. Legal obligation and a sense of duty to the community alone were probably not an adequate explanation of why men practised archery consistently over a number of years so that they could sign up as an archer. The various other motivations and pressures that worked on men to encourage them to serve as military archers are explored in later chapters, particularly the rewards. However, by the 1360s the king's government felt that this assumption that men practised archery needed strengthening by legal obligation and started to issue a sequence of statutes compelling archery practice (see *Professionals, Volunteers and Conscripts*). You can't practise without a bow. The evidence as to how many men observed their legal duty to keep bows and arrows in their houses in the thirteenth and early fourteenth centuries before the stimulus provided by Edward III's victories is patchy. The records of the criminal hearings provide some evidence of men owning bows. However, it is very unusual for the court records to include any description of either the bows or the arrows, so we don't know if the crimes were committed using military type equipment or that more suited to hunting or practice. The records of the Derbyshire Eyre of 1281 included three murders committed using arrows. In only one case, that wherein Walter of Oxford shot Richard of Charleton in the stomach with an arrow killing him instantly, do the records clearly state shot, in the other two cases it just says killed with an arrow, which could mean stabbed with it.[23] In all three cases the perpetrators fled, so they were declared outlaw and their goods were seized. While the record makes no mention of any land they may have held, the value of their chattels suggests that two of them were no more than middling peasants at best. This is very much in line with the provisions of the Assizes of Arms in force at the time. There are accounts from the court records for most forests and deer parks of poachers regularly using bows and arrows, but not to the exclusion of other weapons and techniques. A later clue comes in an incident during the Peasants' Revolt of 1381: the rebels, many of whom were Londoners, destroyed John of Gaunt's palace of the Savoy and its contents. 'They seized one of his most precious vestments, which we call a "jakke", and placed it on a lance to be used as a target for their arrows.'[24]

COMMISSIONS OF ARRAY

The English kings used two major recruitment methods in this period; Commissions of Array and the issue of Indentures. Commissions of Array developed in Edward I's reign. In 1277 the sheriffs had the responsibility of raising infantry for the campaigns in Wales, but by 1282 Edward had begun to appoint special Commissioners for the purpose.[25] The Commissioners of Array were usually local knights appointed in each county when the King needed to raise an army. Their job was to select the most suitable men aged between 16 and 60 for military service to fill a quota specified in their summons. Despite being supervised to some degree by the King's officials '...it would be an error to infer that the procedures adopted and standards of fitness and skill looked for were uniform.'[26] The commissioners were instructed to:

- Choose, test and array a certain number of men
- Clothe them
- Equip them
- (In some instances) provide them with mounts
- Pay them (to a limited extent)
- Send them under a leader to a given place, or hold them in readiness awaiting further instructions.[27]

In the counties the selection process would be managed by allocating a share of the county's quota to be raised from each hundred. It seems that within the hundreds, the village communities managed the selection. They would do this from volunteers, from an element of family compulsion, (a family would, for example, send a younger son), and from hiring men willing to serve. The hirelings might be outsiders, but could easily be members of the local group of landless labourers taking the duty on to earn a wage. However they were picked, they would be sent to the county muster for the Commissioners to assess. In cities and towns a similar approach was taken. When London was expected to raise 80 archers in 1345, the responsibility was shared out among the 24 city wards, with each ward alderman selecting and equipping the men from his ward. The involvement of local officials in what looks like a very devolved system made it more likely that the King would get the troops he needed.

For both city and county levies, part of the Commissioners' duty would be to make sure that the men were reasonably able with the bow. However, it is clear that the system was open to manipulation and corruption from the start. The Arrayers themselves were often corrupt, and local communities would deliberately send unfit men or not equip their men so that they had to be equipped at the Sheriffs' expense. In 1315 John Botetourt complained that that the men that the Arrayers had recruited for him were 'feeble chaps, not properly dressed, and lacking bows and arrows.'[28] This poor performance by the Arrayers may have been influenced by the disaster at Bannockburn the year before and popular indifference to Edward II's military plans. The Mayor and Aldermen of the City of London were in trouble with Edward III in 1337 for being slow in arraying archers and sending men of poor physique to serve, so that he had to instruct them to select 200 'from among the strongest and healthiest men in the City.'[29] (Appendix 1 lists the men selected to meet this order and one from the following year.) The Arrayers could also misuse their powers to extort money. In 1341, Edward III, when trying to raise forces for both Scottish and Breton expeditions, had to reprimand the arrayers of Kent: '... yet the electors and arrayers, not considering the danger to the realm, have acted carelessly sending few and feeble archers, and the arrayers and the late sheriff have extorted money for their own use divers sums from the men of the county in the name of wages.[30] Copies of this were also sent to the Sheriffs of 21 other counties, either as a warning or as an early example of 'name and shame'. The Black Death of course made the Arrayers task more difficult by reducing the pool of suitable men by nearly half. This and the increasing development of indentured retinues led the Commissioners of Rutland in the 1350s to complain that all the able-bodied men had been recruited by local magnates.[31]

The Black Prince had quasi-regal powers in the lands that made up the Palatinate Earldom of Cheshire, which allowed him to use the array system to raise significant bodies of archers and spearmen, both English and Welsh. In 1346 he ordered the Sheriff of Flint to raise 200 men, half archers, half spearmen, from his lands in Flint; in 1347, 300 were raised and again, half were archers.[32] These orders instructed the officials to 'choose and make trial of' the men, so clearly there was some testing of both skill at arms and general fitness required. Also in 1346, the Lieutenant of the Justice of Chester was ordered to 'choose, make a trial of and array 300 archers from Cheshire and Flint and furnish them with bows, arrows and other arms.' There is a follow-up order that 100 of the best of the 300 are to be given a uniform and sent to the Prince at Sandwich.[33] Interestingly, there is hardly any evidence of his raising bodies of archers from the Duchy of Cornwall, his other great landholding in Britain. Though there are two cases where the Prince uses Cornish archers to protect his interests, rather than serve in his army. In 1347 the Sheriff of Cornwall is ordered to raise an escort of archers to accompany a shipment of wine from Cornwall to Calais, and in the same year John de Movorom is ordered to hire sufficient ships to take the Prince's tin from Cornwall to Flanders and find archers to guard them.[34] The orders do not make it clear whether these men are hired or arrayed.

In the last three decades of the fourteenth century there were fairly regular commissions of array to raise both men at arms and archers for coastal defence. The common approach taken was to call on those shires in the Midlands and south which were under very little direct threat from the French and their Castilian naval allies to send men to support the areas under threat. So in 1371, 10 counties were asked to array 200 men at arms and 400 archers for the defence of the Isle of White; and another three counties, plus Gloucestershire (which appears in both lists) to find 80 men at arms and 190 archers to protect the Southampton area.[35] The threat to the south coast continued throughout Richard II's reign, so that he had to issue frequent commissions to raise forces to deal with it. This sort of service could have been viewed as easy money for six months of doing very little; certainly there is little evidence of it causing widespread discontent. There is some evidence that the response to these sorts of summons was patchy, and desertion would be easy.

The officials issuing these commissions seem to have been aware of the shortage of labour in this post-Black Death period, and the dangers of arraying men who were needed to work on the land. In 1373, when arraying 400 of the 'best and bravest archers' from five shires in the North of England they specifically exempted from service 'those going to their own ploughs or the ploughs of others.'[36]

The matter of when the king should start to pay the wages of arrayed men arose again in 1386, when archers were arrayed and sent London to defend against a possible invasion threat. The Commissioners of Array for Staffordshire, Derbyshire and Devon were ordered to pay the men of their counties three weeks wages at 6d per day to cover their time in attending the king.[37] The archers should have been paid something before they set out so that they had money for food and lodgings, and the king sent them home before they caused trouble. Whether this was incompetence, corruption (in that the wages would have been levied on those who did not serve), or an attempt to get the king to pay the wages in line with earlier royal practice, despite his orders that the counties should pay, we do not know. An obvious case of corruption occurred in 1418 when the king's tenants at Kidwelly petitioned the king about the actions of his receiver, Hugh Edon, who seemed to be acting as an Arrayer. The king was raising an army for the siege of Rouen, and Edon told four men that they were selected as men at arms, and another five that they were to be archers. He added that the prospective men at arms could gain exemption if they paid 16s 8d and the archers 6s 8d. Now, buying exemptions or sending substitutes was part of the system, but since Edon had selected a 70-year-old, the tenants quite reasonably felt that this looked like extortion.[38] It could be interpreted as an indirect military tax, since exemptions from array could be bought legitimately. In 1359 the citizens of London paid £500 in lieu of service of 150 mounted archers.[39]

In general, the Commissioners recruited between half and two-thirds of the men expected of them.[40] Although there were exceptions; in 1338 contingents from 18 shires gathered at Norwich and came to 90% of the totals specified in the writs for the Arrays. Less surprising perhaps is the 100% response from eight shires where records survive to orders for reinforcements issued in July 1346. While these orders went out before the success at Crecy, word of the booty available in France could have spread by then. The problem with Commissions of Array was their lack of efficiency and reliability, even at a time when governments could not expect a high response to their demands. As Sumption points out, 'Nevertheless, the results were impressive by the low standards of medieval governments.'[41] An idea of the number of men that the array system could raise over a period can be found in the surviving abstracts of Walter Wetwang's accounts for the Crecy–Calais campaign, which suggest that there were up to 15,000 foot archers serving in the campaign, the great majority of whom would be arrayed men.[42] More specific, if slightly confusing figures are found in one of the abstracts, which lists 10,806 archers from the counties, 5,443 'other English soldiers/archers' and 364 hobelars and archers from different cities.[43] In both these cases, not all the men were serving at the same time.

Curry suggests that shire levies had not been used for service abroad since the 1350s.[44] However, it is difficult to be precise, since there are records from the early 1360s requiring 19 counties to array 940 archers in total for service in Gascony.[45] Although the Array system was superseded as the method of raising armies for service abroad, it continued to be used throughout the period to bring together county and city contingents for service in defence of the kingdom's boundaries, and to counter rebellion. But the situation is not always straightforward, particularly in Cheshire, which was part of the inheritance of the king throughout this period. In 1399 Richard II gave a group of Cheshire knights and squires a commission to raise troops for service in Ireland. The commission specified that they should raise 80 of the best archers in the hundred of Northwich from those aged between 16 and 60, these to be paid 6d per day.[46] Service in Ireland may well not have counted as service abroad, since the English kings regarded themselves as Lords of Ireland, therefore, using the array system was quite appropriate, since the purpose of the campaign would be to defend English sovereignty against rebellion and foreign invasion. Henry V issued commissions of array in 1415 when he was preparing for the Agincourt campaign, but it seems probable that the prime purpose may not have been to recruit men to the army for that campaign. The Commissioners of Array for most counties included at least one knight or esquire who held an indenture to serve, so the array system may have been used as a way of them raising recruits for their retinues. However, Curry feels that it was more likely that '…the arrays were carried out to ensure that sound national defence was in place before the king left the country.'[47] Henry would have been keenly aware of this need since North Wales was still very tense after Glyndwr's revolt, and Scotland always needed watching.

Having said this, Wales, Cheshire and Lancashire differed from other parts of the country in that they were all part of the inheritance of the Crown and so men owed a personal loyalty to Henry V. So the army for the Agincourt campaign included specialist companies of archers from these three areas. But it would be wrong to think that the Crown had a monopoly of recruitment in these areas. In 1415 the Earl of Arundel, who held lands on the upper Dee and around Oswestry and Chirk, raised 22 men at arms and 30 archers from his estates, including at least eight archers from Cheshire.[48] These men were raised by Arundel to satisfy the indenture he had agreed. This demonstrates that in the fifteenth century there were competing demands on the populace for military service: the landlord raising men to meet his service commitments to the Crown; the Crown raising men directly for indentured service; and the Crown raising forces by array for home defence (in theory at least). The array system remained in use until it was replaced in 1572 with Trained Bands which were raised in a very similar way by the Lords Lieutenant of the Counties.

There was another type of archers' service which, while raised by an array-like method, overlapped in purpose with the activities of garrisons raised by indentures. This was the raising of groups of archers to guard a city or be part of the watch. In 1370, in response to reports of galleys carrying armed men being sighted off the mouth of the Thames, the Mayor and Aldermen of London ordered a night watch of 40 men at arms and 60 archers to be mounted at Billingsgate and the Tower. These men were drawn from the misteries and companies on a daily rota, with the Bowyers, Girdlers, Spurriers and Tawyers being on duty on Mondays.[49] In 1460, concerned by the turbulence that we know as the Wars of the Roses, the Mayor and aldermen of Hull organised archers to guard the wharfs because that side of the city was unprotected.[50] In 1518 there is a record of the contributions which the London Livery companies were to make to the watch. In the case of the Bowyers and Fletchers companies, they each had to provide and equip four archers.[51] While there is no information about who actually did this service, it seems more likely that it would be servants of guild members, or hired men, rather than the members themselves.

Once they had been raised, the contingents needed to be equipped and organised. In the fourteenth century the issue of clothing was part of the responsibility of the Commissioners of Array. Usually they provided a coat and hood or sometimes a piece of cloth for the archer to make his own. This seems to have amounted to a uniform for the county or city's contingent since the Commissioners were instructed that the men raised '...should be uniformly clothed (*de una secta vestitos*).'[52] The most well known example is the Black Prince who ordered the issue of green and white short coats and hats to archers in 1346, and later, cloth (usually two ells) for the archer to make his own uniform. This clothing went to the Cheshire archers, and to the men from Flint when they were serving the Prince. In 1345 the archers raised in London were given coats and hoods made in red and white stripes. In 1342 the Earl of Arundel issued red and white cloth to his Welsh troops, and in 1355 the archers of Norwich used the same colours.[53] The provision of uniforms by particular cities or counties for their contingents seems to become much less common as the fourteenth century progressed. They were replaced by plain coats or gambesons displaying the cross of St. George, and probably some would wear the livery badge of the retinue leader by the end of the century. These modes of dress overlapped for a while.

In 1355 the Black Prince declared that everyone in his army campaigning in Languedoc should wear St. George's cross, but in 1359 he issued an order to his officials in Cheshire that they were to buy sufficient green and white cloth to provide 400 arrayed archers with short coats and hats.[54] No doubt there was a problem in Languedoc, with a mix of Gascon, English and Welsh troops in his army, of recognising friend from foe, since French would be a common language in both the Prince's and his opponents' armies, so a uniform was very necessary. The largely English and Welsh armies that operated in northern and central France at this time would not have had this problem, although the English royal family and nobility would still tend to be French speaking. Certainly the St. George's cross has become the normal uniform device for English armies by 1385, when Richard II's Ordinances of war specify that 'everyone of whatever estate ... shall bear a large sign of the arms of St. George before and another behind.'[55] This seems to establish a uniform for the majority of soldiers, including all the archers, although many no doubt also wore the livery badges of their retinue leaders. Although this ordinance says of whatever estate, no doubt the armigerous classes managed to keep their own arms on display while wearing a St. George's cross.

In 1359 there are two sets of orders for the arraying of archers for service in France that are quite specific as to the level of equipment that the Arrayers of each county are to provide at the county's expense. The first order was issued in January to 28 counties south of the Trent, to raise just over 2,700 archers. The Arrayers were instructed that, having selected the best and strongest archers, they were to issue them with a suit of clothes, a bow, arrows, a knife (cutellis) and other suitable arms.[56] The king started to pay the men when they left the county on their way to him. The second set of orders issued in August of the same year is very unusual because it is for the arraying of 910 mounted archers from 27 counties. The Arrayers were to provide the same level of equipment as in the previous order and ensure that the horses, which the archers seem to be expected to provide themselves, were suitable and properly equipped at the county's expense.[57] There are a few earlier orders for raising mounted archers through the array system, usually for service in Scotland, like that of December 1355 to the Arrayers of Staffordshire asking them to provide 100 mounted archers.[58]

The final expense that fell upon the towns and counties was the provision of limited wages and supplies for the troops that the Commissioners had selected. By Edward III's reign the home communities were only expected to pay the troops until they crossed the county boundary, when the King took on the responsibility.[59]

While the array system stopped being used directly to raise armies for foreign service in the fourteenth century, it remained important for the raising of troops for home defence and peacekeeping. In part it may have been revitalised by the need to resist French raids on the South coast in the early 1450s, and it is clear that Henry VI was able to use the array system in the later 1450s.[60] How much he, or any of the great lords, was able to use it to raise armies for actual combat in the Wars of the Roses is unclear. When Henry VI issued writs for nearly 13,000 archers to be arrayed from the counties and major cities of England in 1457, this was more a demonstration of the royal power to maintain the peace than to raise forces to fight against his Yorkist cousins.[61] His successor, or usurper, Edward IV, made a similar use of the array system in 1464 when he issued orders, admittedly on a smaller scale, to the sheriffs of 16 counties that all men between 16 and 60 (the Statute of Winchester is still the basic law in these matters) should be ready at a day's notice to follow the king.[62] But by the late fifteenth century the system was in decline, since in 1509 Henry VII ordered its thorough overhaul.

INDENTURED SERVICE

When the king was planning a campaign throughout this period, increasingly he would issue indentures to raise forces. Normally these were contracts made between the Crown and a military leader, such as a peer, knight or gentleman, wherein it was agreed that the leader would provide a given number of soldiers of specified types as his retinue. Individuals also indented directly with the king for their own individual service, although this was less usual, and probably unpopular with the royal officials, since they had to do the same amount of work for an individual as they would for a captain bringing forty men. The indentures also specified the muster point and date, the maximum period of service (the king could declare the campaign over at an earlier point), the wage rates and the conditions of service, for example the rules for dividing up booty or ransoming prisoners. In addition to a daily pay rate, a recompense – a 'regard' – would be specified for all men at arms, whether peer or gentleman. This had developed by the 1370s as a fixed payment towards the expense of providing warhorses, and replaced a cumbersome compensation system paid if horses were lost on campaign. The retinue was mustered and inspected at an agreed date and place; the men were counted and checked to ensure that they were equipped to the standard specified in the indenture. At this point any variations between the indenture and the men mustered were noted.

The use of indentures became significant in the 1330s, 'furnishing not only the entire cavalry but a good proportion of the mounted archers as well, about half in the army of 1335, rather more in the smaller and more specialised field forces of the following years.'[63] The indenture system gave the Crown much more control over the timetable of the campaign; for instance, most indentures for the Agincourt campaign were sealed on 29th April 1415, when the retinue leaders would receive the first quarter's pay for their retinue. The indenture system used to build up an army was a pyramid structure. The king, or leader of the whole expedition, agrees indentures with a considerable number of others for them to provide specified numbers and types of soldier. Some of these would bring large contingents, often built up through a system of sub indentures, while others would bring a few men, or even just themselves. In the Agincourt campaign for example, 320 men indented to serve, some as joint leaders, while others, including 34 archers, indented for their own service alone.[64] Anne Curry notes that what was unusual about the army of 1415 was the large number of men (including archers) who indented directly with the Crown.[65] Although the array system continued to be used to raise troops to guard against and repel invasions of England, indentures were also used in the fifteenth century to raise forces to campaign against the Welsh and Scots. An example of this use of indentured forces is found in 1402 when Sir John de Poole and Sir William Stanley made a joint indenture to serve Henry Percy, Hotspur, with 24 lances and 48 archers.[66] This appears to have been a temporary arrangement rather than part of a tradition of service with the Percys.

From the 1330s to the end of the 1350s the great majority of archers in indentured retinues were mounted archers receiving 6d per day, twice the foot archers' rate. These indentured archers would be expected to come to the muster point fully equipped with their arms, and horses would either be personal property, or belong to the magnate in whose retinue they served. The higher pay rate reflected the greater outlay necessary to pass muster as a mounted archer; a hackney alone would have cost about 20/-. This meant that the majority of mounted archers at this early period would be yeomen, landholders making up perhaps the top quarter of the peasantry.

However, once the wage rate for all archers was set at 6d per day in the late fourteenth century this assumption is no longer valid. Ayton considers that 'Mounted archers were admittedly a heterogeneous body of men, perhaps increasingly so as their numbers expanded in the later fourteenth century and the fifteenth century, but many were of yeoman stock.'[67]

Throughout the period the way the retinues were built up through sub indentures varied, sometimes the sub retinues came together from the main retinue leader's estates, neighbours and clients, others seemed to be scratch groups of professional soldiers. So that in 1345 at least half of Sir James Audley's retinue of 80 men came from '...gentry families and tenantry close to the Audley lands.'[68] Sir Robert Morley's retinue in the Crecy campaign contained at least fifteen men, mostly serving as mounted archers, from his family's home territory. Some of the archers in the Earl of Huntingdon's retinue in the same campaign were also recruited from his tenants, including six men from Worfield, namely William and Richard Gravenore, Henry Gold, Richard Smyth, William Hockoumbe and John Tybynton.[69] We do not know the population of Worfield at the time, but six men seems a substantial contribution. Examples of the second kind of group include Sir John Strother's retinue of 30 men at arms and 30 archers put together in 1374 to serve under the command of the Earl of March.[70] It seems that Strother did not have these men as a standing company, but that he had to employ them after he had sealed his indenture, and received the first instalment of the pay. From the sub indentures that have survived, each for a man at arms accompanied by an unnamed archer, he seems to have relied on the reservoir of unemployed fighting men that collected around London to do this. The problem with this was that he had no real idea of the reliability of the men he was employing, so he did two things to protect himself from default. Firstly, to ensure that the men were properly mounted and equipped, he put in a clause stipulating that horse and man should 'both [be] well enough arrayed that Sir John would not suffer any loss or reproach at his muster.'[71] Secondly, some of his sub indentures included an obligation by a pledge or guarantor, who would be liable to pay between twice and four times as much as Strother had paid the man at arms in the first instalment of his pay if the man at arms did not appear at the muster. Two of these guarantors at least were citizens of London. What is noticeable from these indentures is that the archers were still nameless, despite their military importance. This might be because they were not directly employed by Strother, but were employed by the individual man at arms to provide part of the service that he was indenting for, effectively adding another layer to the employment structure of the retinue.

This explanation is supported by the sub indentures issued by Sir Hugh Hastings in 1380. We know that Sir Hugh campaigned regularly in the 1370s and 80s, but for only one of his campaign, that with Thomas Earl of Buckingham to Brittany, do we have information about the make-up of his retinue. He issued 24 sub indentures, and relied heavily on the men at arms taking up these indentures to recruit the archers he required.[72] His reliance was not misplaced, since he had four more archers at muster than he had indented for.

Although the Array system could provide a high proportion of the men needed on occasion as recorded above, the indenture system was superior in that it reliably delivered the required numbers of men, properly equipped. It also led to a significant increase in the professionalism of the fighting men, indeed Sumption feels that this was noticeable even by the 1330s, writing that the system '… was one reason for the noticeable improvement in the fighting quality of infantry as well as cavalry.'[73] In the 1330s and 1340s there is evidence of competition between the two systems of raising troops. In 1338 the Mayor, Aldermen and Commonality of London sent a letter to the king, probably to explain their slow response to his request for men, saying that many of the men they had chosen for the king's expedition '… declared that they were about to cross the sea with the king in the suite of divers magnates who hired them for wages.'[74] As a result they had to choose another company of 100 men. A little later in the fourteenth century the great landholders like John of Gaunt seem to have combined the two systems, using the array system as a way of raising troops, particularly archers, to enlarge their retinues to wartime strength.

Another aspect of indentured service was garrison service in the various castles of the nobility in England. The nature of this service varied from basic custodianship, guard duty, in times of peace, to real war service at other times, or in Wales or the Northern borders. Throughout the period it seems reasonable to regard the men in these garrisons largely as members of the Lord's household, rather than feudal levies, and thus as professional soldiers. In 1313–14 Thomas Earl of Lancaster had a garrison of six archers at Kenilworth, and in 1401 there was a guard of archers from the Duchy of Lancaster at Kidwelly Castle.[75] The garrison of Berwick on Tweed included 42 archers (just over 30% of the total garrison) in 1339-40 and 35 (over 35%) in 1341.[76] In 1400 the garrisons of the northern marches and the castles of Berwick, Roxborough, Carlisle, Herbotill, Jedworth and Norham included 1400 archers, all paid for by the Crown.[77] At the same time all the Welsh castles seem to have had substantial garrisons. We have figures from 1402 listing 1070 archers serving in sixteen castles, from Neath in the south to Denbigh in the north.[78] These two records show the opportunities available for archers to be professionals even in times of relative peace between England and France. In 1411 records survive for 600 archers in royal pay who served in Wales between July 1410 and April 1411 at least.[79] It is likely that the majority were English because of Glyndwr's activities at the time. Yet by 1415, while the king, many of the militarily active magnates and large numbers of fighting men were away in France, the garrisons of many of the major welsh castles were small, despite Owen Glyndwr's recent revolt. Carreg Cennan, Whitecastle, Grosmont and Skenfrith had only six archers each, Hay had eight while Kidwelly and Brecon had twelve. Clearly it was considered that the Welsh were at peace, and of course some were taking part in the expedition themselves, Davy Gam of Brecon serving with three archers for example.[80] At the same time, the garrison of Berwick on Tweed consisted of 10 men at arms and 20 archers in the castle and 40 men at arms and 80 archers in the town, indicating its importance to the English king.[81] But, since the pay for these archers was only 4d per day, why did they do it rather than serve abroad, in either the field armies or in garrisons, since both were paid at standard Crown rates in the 1420s and 1430s? It is probable that garrison duty in Wales and Scotland included board and lodgings (as did such duty in France on occasion) and it is also quite possible that garrison duty was a form of pension for older archers. But the Scots border was not controlled by garrisons alone in 1415, more mobile companies were maintained under John Neville in the West March and under John Mirbury and Thomas Straung based at Northwall. Both these companies were indentured retinues made up of 60 men at arms and 120 archers paid at the standard Crown rate, necessary no doubt to persuade some good men not to go to France.[82]

Another aspect of service as guards of English borders and property which relied on the availability of professional soldiers was the protection of merchant ships. While the sailors often had access to stores of weapons to defend their ships, the defence did not wholly rely on the sailors, since there are records of small groups of archers being employed to guard ships in this period. One example occurred in 1403 when the Mayor of Southampton and others merchants employed men at arms and archers to protect the wine ships on their voyage to Bordeaux from attack by Breton freebooters.[83]

From Henry V's time to the end of the Hundred Years War in 1453 the English armies, particularly in Northern France, were often hired in annual indentures, normally renewed year on year. These forces were effectively the first English standing army largely recruited from a well-established community of professional soldiers of all types. They were still structured in retinues employed through their captain. However, this did not mean that the individual retinues became permanent forces of fixed size. Their presence depended on the willingness of the leader to continue to take up the indenture, some, like John Talbot Earl of Shrewsbury, agreeing indentures over a 25-year period, albeit not in every year. The size of the retinue depended on the terms of the indenture. While most of the captains would have a number of men at arms and archers they worked with regularly, they may have had to employ others, probably from a pool of experienced men in England and Normandy, less well known to them personally, on occasions when the indenture specified a large number of men. The muster records for this period list thousands of men who served in the English armies for greater or lesser periods. The majority are listed by name, although there are a number who are listed by nicknames, concealing their true identity. These men may be criminals or deserters from other companies hiding themselves, or they may show attempts by captains to hide a shortfall in numbers and so ensure that they get paid as much as possible. An early example of this is found in a muster roll for the Earl of Salisbury's retinue for 1424.[84]

In the years 1418–22 Henry V made substantial, successful efforts to conquer northern France. This began a change in the nature of military service in the English armies, with an increasing proportion of men being committed to garrison service. Between 1418 and 1420 between a quarter and a third of Henry's men seem to have been part of garrisons.[85] After Henry V's reign, there were no more large expeditionary forces into northern France from England, and the English leaders such as the Duke of Bedford or Earl of Shrewsbury had to rely on the garrisons, a few small field armies based in the major garrisons, and relatively small forces of reinforcement from England to hold the increasingly effective French forces at bay. From the early 1420s onwards, a pool of ex soldiers could be found in Normandy, who could be recruited as necessary to reinforce the standing forces.[86] Another development at this time was the increased use of the 'great indenture', wherein a military leader, commonly one of the magnates such as Salisbury, contracted with the Crown to raise the whole force that was required in a given year. This made matters simpler for the royal administration, since they only had to deal with one man for the force's pay, rather than a group of indenture holders. It was the holder of the 'great indenture' that had the problems of ensuring the soldiers got their due pay, and that he had the necessary records to claim his money from the Crown. Holders of 'great indentures' were often allowed to substitute fighting men of one sort for another, most commonly archers for the increasingly hard to find men at arms. However, when substitution occurred, it was common for two or three times as many archers to be employed, than the number of men at arms who were being replaced; the Earl of Salisbury's army of 1428 being a case in point.[87] This is a clear demonstration of a widespread enthusiasm among English and Welsh men to serve as archers in France.

As mentioned above, by 1430, military activity had become more static, concentrating on holding garrisoned towns and castles to control the land around. As a result, retinues tended to be based in one area for periods of time to fulfil garrison duties and local patrols. The latter included police activities, putting down the bands of brigands often made up of deserters from the armies of both sides as well as those impoverished by the persistent warfare of the period. Some of these brigands were regarded by the local French population as being resistance fighters against the English invaders.[88] While the activities of these brigands never reached the scale of the lawlessness seen in France in the 1350s and early 1360s, they still threatened the profitability of local trade and the more isolated landholdings. One example of these policing activities can be found in a pay record from December 1425, when Richard Vean and 15 archers received their pay for their service over the previous months, getting rid of brigands.[89] While field armies were still hired in most years, they would be augmented with contingents from the garrison retinues, when a major leader needed to put together a force for a more mobile operation. As a result, the English government became concerned that retinues and garrisons might contain too many Frenchmen, concerned more with protecting their homes than furthering any ambitions of the English Crown. So, in 1430, the rules for retinues were changed: 'Under these (new rules written into indentures of September of that year) all archers were to be English, Irish, Welsh or Gascon subjects of King Henry.'[90] However, by 1434 one-eighth of the entire retinue could be French, and we start seeing a small number of French archers listed. An example of archers from outside these designated areas serving in a retinue can be found in the records of John Talbot's retinues between 1439 and 1441, when three Frenchmen, Jean de Mantes, Jean de Meaux and Jean du Mans, served as archers.[91]

This was nothing new in the English armies, which had often used 'foreign' archers, as what the Romans would have called auxiliaries. The use of Welsh archers in the Norman conquest of parts of Ireland is well known, as is Edward I's use of them in his conquest of Wales. A later example can be found in Ireland in 1361, when Lionel, Duke of Clarence went there as the King's Lieutenant. He took English troops with him but also employed Irish soldiers, including archers, since there is a record of Donald Gall being paid 4d per day to lead Irish troops, the bulk of whom were 208 foot archers, who were paid 2d per day.[92] The English archers that Clarence brought with him, 360 from Lancashire, would be receiving 3d per day.

Towards the end of English rule over Normandy the individual retinues making up forces which served there could be made up of several nationalities. One example of this is found in a muster roll of 1450 written in French for the retinue of Jehan d'Estouville, seigneur of Torcy in Normandy, which consisted of 6 men at arms and 15 archers.[93]

Name	Possible English form	Probable nationality
Men at arms		
Jehan d'Estouville		French?
Jehan de Pierrecourt		French
Jehan Becquet	John Beckett	English?
Hutin de Quebieifray		French
Gieffroy de Puchot		French
Jehan Criquet	John Cricket	English
Archers		
Le barbret Gaimain	Bearded? Gaimain[94]	French?
Jehan le Fauconier	John the Falconer	French?

Jehan le Queux	John the Cook	French?
Jehan Thomas	John Thomas	English or Welsh
Le grant Pierre	Big Peter	Impossible to know
Jehan de Caux	John of Caux	French?
Colinet de La Mare	Colinet of the Sea	French?
Colin Hout	Colin Howe?	English
Thomas de Gouldon	Thomas of Goulton? (N. Yorks)	English
Fremmot de Grantvilliers	Fremmot of Grantvilliers	French
Regnant le Charpentier	Regnant the Carpenter	French
Robin Fleurence	Robin Florence	English
Thomas Amadoc	Thomas ap Madoc	Welsh
Jehan Beachamp	John Beauchamp	English
Jehan Lucas	John Lucas	English

Looking at their names it seems that the archers in this retinue are a very mixed bag. If we were looking at a purely English list of this date we would have to be careful of assuming that occupational names such as falconer and cook mean that their holders followed those occupations. I am uncertain of the French practice regarding family names among the sub gentry classes but there is no reason to assume that they are radically different from the English. So while three of them may have occupational names (falconer, cook and carpenter), we cannot assume that they lived in d'Estouville's estates. At least four seem likely to have been French. Half are clearly English or Welsh, presumably professional soldiers, while two seem to be hiding their identities with nicknames (Gaimain and Big Peter). D'Estouville's retinue looks like a company pulled together by a captain to meet an indenture, one that contained a lot of professionals serving an employer almost as mercenaries, rather than an established company raised largely within a particular landholding, who served their liege lord.

The indenture holder had the responsibility for ensuring that his men were equipped to the correct level. This was checked on by the officials administering the muster both at the start of the indenture term, and at the subsequent musters approving payment of the later pay instalments to the retinue leader. Two examples from companies serving in English-administered Normandy in the fifteenth century give us an idea of the equipment the mainly professional archers of the time had. One from St. Lô in 1429 listed the archers as having 'arcq [bows], trousse [a sheaf of arrows], palletocq [probably cloaks] swords, daggers and [being] sufficiently mounted.' Another from Pont d'Ouve in late 1431 lists the archers as having swords, blouquiers (bucklers), pallotes (cloaks), cappelines (helmets that protected the neck – probably another word for a sallet), arcs (bows) trousse de flesches (sheaves of arrows) and also as sufficiently mounted.[95] The differences in these muster records, particularly the lack of helmets and bucklers in the St. Lô record make it seem either that the officials were inconsistent in their recording, or that a bow, a sheaf of arrows, a sword and a horse were the minimum equipment in official eyes for a serving archer. The evidence is that the officials were fairly precise and recorded what they saw, so the latter seems more likely, and that the Pont d'Ouve company was a particularly well equipped one. One sub indenture of 1440 itemises the archers' equipment with unusual precision. In it Sir James Ormand indented with James Strickland for service in France. Strickland was to serve as a man at arms '...with 6 archers in his company all on horsebak and wele chosen men...and all the seid archers specially to have good Jakks of defence, salades, swerdes and sheves of xl arwes atte lest ...'[96] (This would be relatively expensive for Strickland to provide, so we can assume that he and his archers were a band of professionals, each with their own equipment).

The practice of the leaders of indentured retinues of issuing their men with either a livery badge or a uniform points to one basic problem with indentured troops in the later fifteenth century. There always was an inherent danger in the indentured retinue system that the individual fighting men might be more loyal to their employer, especially if the employer was a powerful landed nobleman, than to the Crown. This was a problem in France when the Kings made peace, and companies of soldiers, unemployed as a result, either fought for themselves or became mercenaries. In England, when the Hundred Years War ended in defeat, the indentured men could concentrate on their lord's quarrels rather than their king's. This is despite indentures containing clauses such as'...to do him service during the same time in peace and war before all other persons, except our sovereign lord king Edward IV'.[97] An idea of the scale of this threat can be gleaned from Sir William Stanley's meeting with Henry Tudor before the battle of Bosworth; Sir William had 3000 retainers with him in red coats, wearing hart's head badges.[98]

OWNERSHIP OF THE BOW INCREASES

Earlier in this chapter we gave some of the figures for the number of men who responded to a summons to a muster, or a view of arms, at Bridport in 1319, and the weapons they brought. The men brought no bows with them. We get a very different picture from a muster recorded in 1457 at Bridport.[99] This roll results from Parliament allowing commissions of array in response to a French raid on Sandwich, showing that the array system remained the normal method of raising forces to counter foreign threats to the homeland at this later date. Although, since the Wars of the Roses were underway, the Lancastrians may well have been trying to take advantage of the system to raise forces for their own partisan needs. The scale of the response to the summons at Bridport, 197 men and four women, shows that people still had a sense of duty in these circumstances. These men and women were expected to bring their weapons to the muster, but not all those who had weapons did, and a number are recorded as being ordered to bring particular equipment to be viewed at a later date. 82 (41%) of them (including 2 of the women) are listed as bringing no weapons at all, while some brought more than one set of weapons or equipment. Some 114 (58%) of them brought bows, including the other two women. The rest of their equipment included 69 (34%) with swords, 21 (10%) with glaives (probably what we would call a bill now) or pollaxes, 74 (37%) with salets and 67 (33%) with jacks. This is a remarkable difference from the view of arms noted earlier, when 180 men were recorded, but none with bows. If we look for men who brought to the muster the equipment listed above in the pay records and Strickland's indenture, as the basic equipment for an archer, we find that 40 (20%) men brought it and another 19 (10%) are listed as having it but needing to bring some items to be viewed later.

This muster roll records the consequences of four generations of English people living with regular opportunities for paid military service, predominantly as archers. Compared with the View of Arms record from Norwich in the 1350s quoted above, which showed 60% bringing no arms, the ownership of arms seems more common. Only 17.5% of the Norwich men are recorded as archers, whereas over half of the Bridport men (and women) had bows and arrows. Full armour is much less common at Bridport, there only being two sets, compared with 14% of the citizens of Norwich who had full harness. This in part reflects the increased cost of a set of very ordinary full plate armour in the 1450s compared with a mixed mail and plate harness in the 1350s. It may reflect local economic and social circumstances, but I think it more likely that it indicates a change in military aspiration. Men wanted to serve as archers, not full time maybe, but it was a worthwhile part of their working life. Given the date of this muster roll, it is possible that some of the men who brought what seems to have been the full equipment for a military archer were veterans of the French wars. Richardson comments on the number of pavises (23) that were listed in roll (it is not surprising that nearly all had to be seen later since they were cumbersome). These are usually associated with crossbowmen, but there is evidence of them being used by English archers when attacking fortifications. In the ordinances for his 1425 campaign in northern France, Thomas Montagu, Earl of Salisbury ordered that every other yeoman in his army should have a 'pavey' to provide cover for the other yeoman to use their bows.[100] So, it is possible that these pavises are also remnants of the equipment of professional soldiers. However, the appearance of pavises at Bridport does not mean that all those who brought them to the View of Arms were professional soldiers. Since a pavise is a cumbersome piece of kit, it would have been just the sort of thing that returning soldiers would abandon on a ship, or as soon as they landed.

THE END OF MILITARY ARCHERY

Henry VIII raised one of the largest and best equipped armies that ever left England when he invaded France in 1513. Although he had re-enacted the Statute of Winchester early in his reign, he also ordered arms on a scale that suggested that his officers expected to have to re equip most of the men. Whether this was based on a realistic appreciation of the quality of military equipment men had in their homes by this date, or Henry's determination that his army would be the best equipped come what may, is uncertain. By this date the proportion of archers to other types of troops had changed in comparison with ratios found in the armies of the Hundred Years War. While the proportion of archers had increased throughout the fourteenth and first half of the fifteenth centuries, Henry's army shows signs of more nearly resembling the make-up of the contemporaneous continental armies, both in the kinds of troops and also in the development of the English tactical system away from its 'classical' form as used in the earlier wars with France and Scotland.[101] The category of men at arms was replaced with armoured cavalry and some light cavalry, both of whom fought on horseback. The core of the infantry battle lines were billmen, men of similar social standing to those who served as archers. While it did not take as much practice to be an able billman as it did to become an archer, these men were not unskilled.[102] They often served in similar numbers to the archers in Henry VIII's armies. Companies of handgunners became more common.

There were, however, two expeditions in 1511 that consisted mainly of archers. Sir Edward Poyning successfully led about 1500 archers in support of Margaret of Savoy in Flanders, while Lord Darcy led a similar number to support Ferdinand of Aragon in a planned campaign against the Moors in North Africa. This latter effort collapsed in disarray as Ferdinand changed his mind about whom he wished to fight.[103] Another company showing a massive preponderance of archers over other troops was one recorded in Portsmouth on its way to Brittany in 1512. This was made up of two knights, eight men at arms, twelve demilances (lightly armoured cavalry), two trumpets and 349 archers.[104] In all three cases, these men were surely viewed as specialist companies of archers going to support other forces.

Thirty years later Henry had became embroiled in war with both Scotland and France again. While the Scottish threat was rebuffed at the battle of Solway Moss in 1542, peace did not come immediately and military activity continued, with the Scots winning at Ancrum Moor in 1545. Peace was finally agreed the following year. The English armies in these campaigns show further evidence of the steady decline of the significance of military archery. The retinues that were part of the army that went to France included:

- The Earl of Suffolk :- 100 horsemen, 100 archers, 300 billmen.
- Bishop of Westminster:- 100 men including 30 principal archers.
- Lord Wryothesley :- 40 horsemen, 50 archers, 40 pikemen, 50 billmen and 20 with demihakes (handguns).
- Sir Thomas Wryothesley :- 10 horsemen, 10 mounted archers, 40 archers, 40 billmen; and the following men raised by others but under his command: 20 archers and 20 billmen plus 10 archers from the forest of Southbere.
- Earl of Arundel :- 300 principal archers, 200 mean archers, 500 principal billmen, 200 mean billmen, 106 household servants.[105]

The trend is not only for archers to make up less than half the infantry, but for missile troops in general to make up less than half. So it was not just a case of gunpowder weapons replacing the bow, it was a change in tactics, with more men armed with staff weapons – pikes and bills commonly in English armies – showing the influence of the tactics used by the Swiss and Landsknecht mercenary infantry.

The ranking of both the archers and the billmen in Arundel's retinue is interesting. It has usually been taken to mean that principal archers were better bowmen than the mean archers, which is not gainsaid by the billmen being classified in the same way. However, the classification could also refer to levels of equipment, with the principals having better or more equipment, and so be more able to take their place in the front lines of battle. All the men were not necessarily professional soldiers, although a man of Arundel's standing could perhaps have attracted 800 professionals.

Whether the decline of English military archery was driven from above, by the King and his officers wanting modern kinds of troops, or by the people themselves, who practised archery less because there seemed to be fewer employment opportunities to use it, has been argued over at great length. It is fair to regard the reign of Henry VIII as marking the end of the dominance of military archery. This did not come about through a deliberate decision by Henry and his government, despite their willingness to spend lavishly on new weaponry to match the armies of Europe, nor did it happen overnight. Indeed, throughout his reign Henry and the state encouraged archery both commercially and legislatively. But they were also responsible for significant skill developments among the English firearms manufacturers and English artillerymen.[106] However much Henry himself may have appreciated English archery, and wanted to maintain the tradition, he was a pragmatist in military matters (something he most certainly was not in foreign policy overall), determined that his armies should be able to hold their own in Europe.

NOTES

1 The aging Edward I made this threat in writs issued in 1300, reflecting his determination to raise enough knights and men at arms for his Scottish wars. For more on this see chapter 6 of Powicke, M. (1962) *Military Obligation in Medieval England*, Oxford, Clarendon Press.
2 Calendar of Close Rolls (*CCR*) London, HMSO, 1900-63. 1230 p.398.
3 Powicke, M (1962) p.119.
4 Powicke, M (1962) p.124.
5 Powicke, M (1962) p.85-6.
6 The slightly unclear division seems to mean that only crossbows could be owned by forest dwellers. Presumably the idea behind it is that because the cost of a crossbow would limit them to the middling levels of the community, who could be trusted not to misuse them. Any study of forest law court records shows that the middling men poached like the rest.
7 *Statutes of the Realm vol. 1*. London 1735 p.97-8.
8 Sumption, J (1990). *The Hundred Years War vol 1: Trial by Battle*. London, Faber. p.65.
9 Powicke, M (1962) p.216.
10 *CCR 1386* p.187.
11 Edward I's army for the conquest of Wales in 1277 was about 15,000 foot and may be 1000 horse, mainly armoured knights. A conservative estimate of the strength of Edward II's army at Bannockburn is over 2000 heavy cavalry and about 15,500 foot. (He called for c.21,000 to be arrayed but this is a likely number for those who marched into Scotland.)
12 Powicke, M (1962) p.90.
13 *CCR 1260* p.283.
14 *CCR 1264* p.360.
15 *CCR 1266* p.191.
16 *CCR 1274* p.116.
17 Collins, F (editor) (1897). *Register of the Freemen of the City of York: Vol. 1:* 1272-1558 Publications of the Surtees Society 96.
18 Powicke, M (1962) p.164.
19 Ayton, A and Preston, P (2005) p.222.
20 Prince, A E (1931). *Strength of English armies in the reign of Edward III*. English Historical Review xlvi 1931. p.355 and p.357.
21 Hudson, W (1900). *The Norwich Militia in the Fourteenth Century*. Norfolk and Norwich. Archaeological Society. vol. XIV p.263-320.
22 Ayton, A. Comment in a lecture at National Army Museum 22nd Oct. 2005.
23 Hopkinson, A M (editor) (2000). *The Rolls of the Derbyshire Eyre*. Derbyshire Record Society vol. XXVII p.165.
24 *Historia Anglicana* quoted in Dunn, A (2002). The *Great Rising of 1381*. Stroud. Tempus Publishing. p.86.
25 Prestwich, M (1996). *Armies and Warfare in the Middle Ages: the English Experience*. New Haven. Yale University Press. p.123.

26 Hewitt, H.J. (1966). *The Organization of War under Edward III*. Manchester University Press. p.36.
27 List derived from Hewitt, H.J (1966) op cit p.37.
28 Prestwich, M (1996) p.124.
29 Sharpe R R (1899-1912) (editor). *Calendar of the letter books of the City of London* (*CLBCL*) book F. London HMSO p.10.
30 *CCR 1341* p.369.
31 Prestwich, M (1996) p.124.
32 *The Register of Edward the Black Prince (BPR) pt.1*. London HMSO 1930-33 pp.14, 78.
33 *BPR* pt.1 p.7 and p.13-4.
34 *BPR* pt.2 p.87 and p.66.
35 Calendar of the Patent Rolls (*CPR*) London, HMSO, 1893-1916. 1370–74 p.102
36 *CPR* 1370–74 p.339.
37 *CCR* 1386 p.193-4.
38 Curry, A. (2005). *Agincourt; a New History*. Stroud. Tempus Publishing. p.61.
39 Hewitt, H.J (1966) p.38.
40 Both Ayton and Preston, P (2005) p.185 and Sumption, J (1990) p.64 suggest this proportion.
41 Sumption, J. (1990) p.64.
42 Ayton, A and Preston, P (2005) p.232.
43 Ayton, A and Preston, P (2005) p.240.
44 Curry, A (2005) p.61.
45 Wrottesley, C (1887) *Collections for a History of Staffordshire vol. 8*. London. p.108-9.
46 Driver, J.T. (1971) *Cheshire in the later Middle Ages 1399–1450*. Chester. p.7-8.
47 Curry, A (2005) p.61.
48 Driver, JT (1971) p.12.
49 Oxley, J E (1968). *The Fletchers and Longbowstring Makers of London*. London. Worshipful Company of Fletchers. p.13.
50 Gillett, E and MacMahon, K A (1980). *A History of Hull*. Hull University Press. p.65.
51 Unwin, G (1938). *Gilds and Companies of London*. London, George Allen and Unwin. p.371.
52 Ayton A and Preston P (2005) p.186.
53 Morgan, P J (1987). War *and Society in Medieval Cheshire 1277–1403*. Manchester University Press. p.104-5.
54 *BPR* pt.3 p.349.
55 Keen, M (1995). Richard II's Ordinances of War. *Rulers and Ruled in Late Medieval England* edited by Archer, R E and Walker, S. London, Hambledon Press. p.40.
56 Rymer, T (editor) (1800). *Foedera, conventiones, litterae. vol.3 pt.1* London p.415.
57 Rymer, T (1800) vol.3 pt.1 p.440.
58 Wrottesley, C (1887) p.97.
59 Sumption J (1990) p.65.

60 Goodman, A (2005). *The Wars of the Roses: the Soldier's Experience*. Stroud. Tempus Publishing, p.123.
61 *CPR* 1452-61 p.406-10.
62 Goodman, A (1981). *The Wars of the Roses: Military Activity and English Society*. London. Routledge and Kegan Paul, p.141.
63 Sumption J (1990) p.182.
64 Curry A (2005 p.63.
65 Curry, A (2000). The *Battle of Agincourt; Sources and Interpretations*. Woodbridge. Boydell Press, p.421.
66 Driver, J T (1971) p.10.
67 Ayton, A (1994). *Knights and Warhorses*. Woodbridge. Boydell Press, p.15-16
68 Ayton, A and Preston, P (2005) p176-7.
69 Ayton, A and Preston, P (2005) p.224.
70 Walker, S (1985). *Profit and Loss in the Hundred Years War*. Bulletin of the Institute of Historical Studies v.58.
71 Walker, S. (1985).
72 Goodman, A (1980). *Military sub contracts of Sir Hugh Hastings 1380*. English Historical Review xcv p.117
73 Sumption J (1990) p.182.
74 *CLBCL* Book F p.25.
75 Somerville, R (1953). History *of the Duchy of Lancaster, vol. 1 1265–1603*. London p.80 and p.169 respectively.
76 Ayton, A (1994). p.168.
77 *Proceedings and Ordinances of the Privy Council (POPC)* (1834-7) London. vol.1 p.125.
78 *POPC* vol.2 p.68-9.
79 *POPC* vol.2 p.18.
80 Curry, A (2005) p.62.
81 All information on garrisons from Somerville, R. (1953) p.183.
82 *POPC* vol. 2 p.179-80.
83 Willis Chapman, A B (1912). *The Black Book of Southampton*. Southampton, p.17n.
84 Newhall, R A (1940). *Muster and Review; a problem of English military administration 1420–40*. Cambridge Mass., Harvard University Press p.14n.
85 Newhall, R A (1924). *English Conquest of Normandy 1416–1424*. New Haven, Yale University Press. p.206-16.
86 Curry, A (1994). English armies in the fifteenth century. *Arms, Armies and Fortifications in the Hundred Years War*. edited by A Curry and M Hughes. Woodbridge. Boydell Press. p.48.
87 Curry, A (1994) p.46.
88 Allmand, C (1997). *Henry V*. New Haven Yale University Press. p.192.
89 Newhall, R A (1940) p.25n.
90 Newhall, R A (1940) p.119.
91 Pollard, A J (1983). John *Talbot and the War in France 1427–53*. London, Royal Historical Society. p.74.
92 Prince, A E (1931) p.369.

93 Stevenson, J (1861-4). *Letters and Papers Illustrative of the Wars of the English in France in the Reign of King Henry VI.* London. vol 1 p.311-14.

94 It is very difficult to translate this nickname with any confidence, although barbet meaning bearded was current in the fifteenth century.

95 Newhall, R A (1940) p.33.

96 Newhall, R A (1940) p.32.

97 Driver, J T (1971) p.16.

98 Driver, J T (1971) p.19-20.

99 Richardson, T (1998). *The Bridport muster Roll of 1457* p.46-52 in the Royal Armouries Yearbook 2 1997. Royal Armouries Museum, Leeds.

100 Warner, M (1998). *Chivalry in Action: Thomas Montagu and the War in France, 1417–28.* Nottingham Medieval Studies. XLII. p.146-73.

101 Battle lines formed of blocks (battles) of dismounted knights and men at arms with larger numbers of archers on the wings, between the blocks of men at arms and almost certainly as a skirmish line in front of them. Ratio between men at arms and archers varied as discussed in Appendix 2.

102 See Brown T (1997). *English Martial Arts.* Hockwold cum Wilton. Anglo Saxon Books, which gives an account of the practice necessary to use a bill well.

103 Cruickshank C G (1969). *Army Royal: Henry VIII's Invasion of France 1513.* Oxford, Clarendon Press, pp.3-4.

104 *Letters and Papers Foreign and Domestic.1509-19* vol.1 pt.1. p.583.

105 *Letters and Papers Foreign and Domestic.* vol.19 pt.1 p.149-50.

106 See Cruickshank C G (1969) for a more substantial discussion of these points.

Professionals, Volunteers and Conscripts

When the English kings raised their armies, they were able to rely on the population at large being broadly willing to serve. There is no sense of large numbers of men feeling they had been pressganged, and indeed by the mid fourteenth century Parliament had gained some control over the authorization of summons for military service. No doubt the men summoned grumbled, as soldiers always do, but they had put in the effort practising their archery skills to a level that meant that they could be employed.

How much choice did men have about archery practice? Before 1363 custom and duty seems to have been viewed as being sufficient motivation for men to practice. But in June of that year orders were sent to all the sheriffs of England that they should make the following proclamation:

> That every able bodied man on feast days when he has leisure shall in his sports use bows and arrows, pellets or bolts, and shall learn and practice the art of shooting, forbidding all and singular on pain of imprisonment to attend or meddle with hurling of stones, loggats or quoits, handball, football, club ball. cambuc, cock fighting or other vain games of no value; as the people of this realm noble and simple, used heretofore to practice the said art in their sports, whence by God's help came forth honour to the kingdom and advantage to the king in his actions of war, and now the said art is almost wholly disused, and the people indulge in the games aforesaid and other dishonest and unthrifty games, whereby the realm is like to be kept without archers.[1]

The authors of this proclamation specifically mention pellets and bolts because men living within the bounds of the royal forests were only allowed these, effectively blunt arrows, to prevent poaching. It is also more open about the economic class of men who should practise than the later statutes.

The sentiments of this proclamation were reiterated in 1388, but with an interesting emphasis on the wage earning part of the English population: 'No servant of husbandry, labourer, servant, artificer or victualler shall carry swords or daggers except in times of war… But such labourers and servants shall have bow and arrows and use the same on Sundays and Holydays and leave all playing at tennis or football and other games called coits, dice, casting of stones and other such importunate games.'[2] Sheriffs, Mayors, Bailiffs and Constables were to have powers of arrest to enforce this.

Henry IV also felt that servants and labourers playing 'importunate games' rather than practising archery was a problem. He issued an order in 1410 that all servants and labourers were to have bows and arrows and to use them on Sundays and feast days, and should leave off other games such as Coites, Dise and Kayles.[3] These two statutes are interesting in their emphasis on the wage earner, rather than the land and property holder. This is actually a clarification of the earlier statutes, reflecting changes in English society after the Black Death, rather than a radical extension of the burden of prospective military service. It may have contributed to the confusion that has developed in the use of the term yeoman, which had a range of meanings including being a term for a servant as well as occurring in the phrase 'yeoman archer' without implying servitude.

Statutes on this theme were not reissued for half a century, despite the decline of English interests in France, partly because of the increasing professionalization of the English armies at this time, meaning that men practised so that they could take up a military career. It may also reflect an increasing fatigue with the endless French wars, even in the royal administration.

The proportion of archers in the armies increased between the 1420s and 1450s, although the armies themselves were not usually as large as those raised by Henry V. Despite having raised maybe 9000 archers in 1475 for his invasion of France and sending another 2000 to Brittany,[4] by 1477 Edward IV was persuaded of the need to make another attempt to limit men's choice of recreation: 'No persone should use any unlawfull pleys as dise, coytes foteball and like pleys but that every persone mighty and able in bodie shuld use his bowe.' This was again enforced with the threats of imprisonment and fines.[5]

In 1503-4 a slightly surprising statute was made forbidding the use of crossbows because the practice was reducing the level of longbow archery skills.[6] This is odd because of Henry VII's earlier regulation of the price of bows. It is difficult to believe that crossbows were a cheap option when buying archery equipment. Henry concentrated on diplomacy rather than military adventures, so there may have been less incentive for men to put in the long periods of practice necessary if they were going to use the warbow effectively. Crossbows were very practical for defending one's property or more lawless activities, since they could be carried loaded and used in confined spaces, so Henry's statute may have had several aims.

Henry VIII's solution to the perceived problem of a decline in the number of competent archers available to serve him in his armies was much more all encompassing than those of his predecessors. His statute of 1511-12 covered both the practice of archery and the supply of bows.[7] He partially re-enacted the Statute of Winchester with regard to archery, laying down that men under the age of 60 'do use and exercyse shotyng in longbows' and that each should 'have a bowe and arrows redy continually in his house to use himself'. To ensure the development of archery among the young every child (no gender specified) aged between seven and 17 was to have a bow and two arrows and at age 17 youths were to have a bow and four arrows. To make it easier for people to practise Justices of the Peace (JPs) were to ensure that butts were made in every city, town and place. In this statute Henry was probably trying to codify what he thought had been the good habits of the 'golden age' of English archery under Edward III and Henry V. It seems almost an outburst of nostalgia.

It was thirty years before Henry considered the state of English archery again. In 1541-2 looking at the resources necessary to repel the French and Scottish threats, he passed another statute to both promote archery and encourage the supply of bows. This act reiterates the provisions of the 1511-12 act about the practice of archery and the provision of butts. But it is even more prescriptive than the earlier act about the type of practice and the ownership of bows. Firstly it laid down the type of shooting to be practised:

> Be it further enacted by aucthoritie aforesaide that noe man under the age of 24 yeres shall shoote at any standinge prick excepte it be at a Rover wherat he shall change at every shoote his marke, upon for every shoote doinge the contrarie 4d. And that noe person above the age of 24 yeres shall shoote at any marke of 11 score yards or under with any prickeshafte or fleight.

All these statutes show a repeated concern about the Englishman's waning interest in developing his archery skills. But it is difficult to view them as a sustained effort by the kings of England to maintain a pool of practised archers, since the statutes were issued at irregular intervals. Not surprisingly, these statutes were often issued at times when the king was preparing for, or considering, war, and after a period of relative peace. It is difficult to be certain how big a problem recruiting competent archers was; a contemporary account suggests that Edward IV's army of 1475 contained many inexperienced or unskilled men when it states 'these were not the Englishmen of his father's day and the former wars with France.'[8] So his statute of 1477 looks like a reaction to this problem. But at other times, such as Edward III's reign, the issue of such a statute is surprising, given the English military successes of the preceding years, and the encouragement these must have given men thinking of a military career. There may be an authoritarian, 'killjoy' element in some of these statutes, a concern with keeping the lower orders of society usefully employed. (Recounting the provisions of these statutes has disrupted the chronology of this account somewhat, but this was necessary in order to show some of the governmental thinking and official anxiety underlying the English medieval military system.)

Large groups of Englishmen may have willing enough to do their military duty for their king and country, but there was still some concern that the obligation to provide military service at the king's will had become oppressive. Edward III had been able to expand this obligation, most notably in 1344, because he was able to provide profitable military successes in return. But by 1352 the Parliamentary Commons had successfully petitioned the king to the effect that no one should be obliged to undertake service without the consent of parliament. This petition probably reflected the views of most of the middling men who made up much of the Commons. The 1344 assessment of service obligation expanded the categories of service and level of equipment required, and these changes and their costs fell most heavily on this group.

Desertion is some measure of willingness to serve, but not all deserters can be seen as unwilling conscripts. The cases of desertion outlined below make it clear that some deserters never really had any intention to serve; they were only interested in making what they could out of the recruitment system by deserting as soon as they received their first instalment of pay. Desertion rates were also influenced by where the men were expected to serve; it was easier to desert if you were going to serve in Wales or Scotland than if you were serving abroad. This tendency was exacerbated when popular opinion about the campaign or the king was low. We can see this in Edward I's late campaigns in Scotland, when something like war weariness seems to have set in, and from Edward II's 1322 campaign, when his poor reputation, particularly after Bannockburn, was the problem. The summons to join his army was no more popular when he needed to campaign in France in 1325, since desertion was a major problem when he tried to levy forces for service in Gascony.[9]

It seems that the medieval officials defined desertion as leaving service after being arrayed or mustered in the case of indentured service, that is, after the men received the first instalment of their pay and livery if appropriate; or leaving service before they were formally released, which could mean they lost some pay. The detection of deserters depended on the vigilance of the local officials in the cities and towns, particularly the mayors and the sheriffs. Occasionally these officials could be over-zealous, as in 1346, when the Sheriff of Shropshire arrested six men for desertion who had served as archers in the Earl of Huntingdon's retinue. The Earl had to write to the Sheriff asking for their release, since he and his retinue had returned from France with permission part way through the campaign. The array system of recruitment, with men being recruited and mustered in or near their communities and then marched to the embarkation ports, allowed plenty of opportunities to desert before leaving the country.

Once the army left England, men leaving the army before being officially discharged became the problem. The Cheshire archer John Jodrell left the army when the campaign had finished but without official leave and so was counted as a deserter. However, he was back for the next year's campaign, and subsequent ones, so can reasonably be viewed as a willing recruit who just didn't want to hang about in Bordeaux with no opportunity to make good money. This problem certainly affected the Black Prince's forces in Gascony. In March 1356 the Prince issued writs to the Lieutenant Justice and Chamberlain of Chester naming 43 archers who had returned without licence (although five of the names were noted as having licences).[10] These men were to have their goods distrained until they returned to Gascony, a humane sanction compared with later penalties for desertion. Others were common or garden deserters: after the Poitiers campaign, fourteen Cheshire archers were indicted for taking cloth and wages from the Black Prince. These fourteen included one rogue who managed to desert twice in the same year![11]

A variation on this was fraud. There is an example from 1355, when some archers being arrayed for service against the Scots bribed the bailiffs of the West Derby wapentake and managed to join up twice. As a result they took a first instalment of wages both for service with the king and for service in the Duke of Lancaster's retinue, (they seem to have lived on his estates). Clearly they believed they were on to a good thing, because they then refused to attend the muster at Newcastle in either company.[12] Another deceit was practised in London in 1338; the Mayor and Aldermen asked the king how they should deal with men who told the arrayers they were leaving the city in a magnate's retinue, but later returned to the city without a leave of absence.[13] Clearly the Mayor and Aldermen felt that some men were trying to avoid military service by exploiting the lack of local coordination between the two methods of raising armies. It is difficult to discover the scale of desertion between muster and embarkation, but there is no doubt that it was a problem with troops raised through the array system.

In the Earldom of Chester the array system worked slightly differently, since the Earl himself, the Black Prince in the 1340s to 1370s, ordered the array. So men were not only meeting a community obligation for military service, but a duty to their lord. This must have improved both the efficiency of the system and the desertion rate in the county. Occasionally in the Black Prince's orders, we find a clear statement that men are to be arrayed from among his tenants, particularly among the Welsh of Flint.[14]

Occasionally, men had pressing personal reasons for being unwilling to serve as an archer. One such was John Clerk of Brundelegh who was arrayed as an archer in Cheshire in 1359. He successfully petitioned the Black Prince to be removed from the list of archers because he ' …has so many enemies among the said archers that he has grave fears for his life if he be detailed to go in their company'.[15]

The indenture system was not immune from the problems of desertion either. There are two sets of orders relating to an expedition in 1380, which seems to have been made up entirely of indentured retinues. The first set of orders deals with lawlessness by members of the retinues, and the second set with desertion. Orders were sent to the bailiffs of Maidstone, Rochester and Newington and the Constable of Aylesford to arrest and imprison any deserters they find in their towns since '...the king has learned that a great number so retained marched to the sea coast, and after receiving wages have departed to the said town, taking no heed to sail and delaying the expedition.'[16] Later, in 1380, there is another set of orders to the mayors and bailiffs of Southampton, Sandwich, Dover, Plymouth, Dartmouth, Falmouth, Fowey, Exeter and Bristol ordering them to detain men at arms and archers who '...having received his wages have without licence withdrawn and returned to England.'[17] These problems fit both definitions of desertion, and this raises questions about the nature of the retinues involved. Many retinues were made up of men with personal or geographic links to the retinue leaders and to each other, and with a level of professionalism built up over a series of campaigns, and it seems unlikely, given these bonds of loyalty, that they would suffer from desertion on such a scale as to prompt such orders. But it is possible in 1380 that there were more 'scratch' retinues, like Sir John Strother's noted above, at a time when the campaigning was less successful, and so less profitable. There are other cases where service in Richard's reign does not seem to have been popular, since there is an order of 1387 to the Mayor and Sheriffs of London to proclaim '...that all men at arms, armed men, archers, seamen and others retained to sail with Richard Earl of Arundel his admiral shall hasten to Sandwich.'[18] If any remained two days after the proclamation they were to be arrested. This could be a warning order to remind the men that they must not stay in London carousing their pay away, or it could reflect a continuing concern about the likelihood of desertion, as in 1380.

An intriguing insight into desertion comes from John of Gaunt's expedition to Spain in 1386-7. His army was an indentured force, with a large number of men from his extensive estates, but the expedition was underfinanced by Parliament. By 1387, this, combined with the problems of disease and the need to extend the period of the indentures, was leading to desertions, '...which he [John of Gaunt] condoned after only a few weeks in the field.'[19] How should this be interpreted? Technically, if the term of the indenture had expired, men leaving Spain were not deserting, but the accepted understanding of what should happen at the end of an indenture was no doubt different. It sounds like a dispirited, pragmatic reaction to an insoluble problem: Gaunt couldn't pay his men, there was little opportunity for them to gain from booty because there was so little campaigning, so he might as well be magnanimous.

The problem of desertion from retinues was particularly acute, unsurprisingly, when the war was going badly. In 1439, the Commons petitioned the king to deal with the problem of deserters.[20] Towards the end of the Hundred Years War there is evidence of soldiers in indentured retinues being unwilling to serve. The Duke of Somerset's expedition to Gascony in 1443 was plagued with problems. Among them was the behaviour of some of the soldiers who deceived the commissioners for musters by giving false names and appearing more than once in the muster lists using different names.[21] Their intent was either to get more than one first instalment of pay at the time of muster, or to conceal their true identity to give themselves a better chance of getting away with taking the first payment and then deserting.

Reports of successful campaigns had the opposite effect and encouraged recruitment. Taking Cheshire as an example, at least 247 archers campaigned in 1415, a muster role for 1417 lists 439 archers as arrayed, while there were more arrays in Cheshire, Lancashire and North Wales in 1420-422. These included the raising of 181 archers in 1420 from Cheshire alone.[22] Despite these impressive figures for mustering men and getting them into service from counties with an enthusiastic military tradition, that enthusiasm could quickly wane, particularly among garrison troops who had little to do and little chance to gain from booty and ransoms. While there is evidence of concern about desertion in 1421, by 1429 it had become such a problem that guards were posted at the French ports to prevent soldiers crossing to England before they had finished their contract.[23]

Royal service in general also suffered from desertion, not just military service. Henry V had to issue orders for the arrest of carpenters who had been employed to work on the king's ships in Southampton, who left after having received an instalment of their pay.[24] These men were probably employed in the same way as bowyers and fletchers were at various times (see *The Manufacture of Bows and Arrows*), in that royal officials engaged them directly. These men were taking advantage of the royal employment system, rather than evading conscripted work.

It is tempting to assume that the men serving in the indentured retinues did so because they had chosen to be soldiers, and so all them should be regarded as willing volunteers. But, looking at the retinues of the major magnates, things are not so clear cut, since a good number of the men in their military retinues were also members of their households, with peacetime roles within them. Were they primarily employed as archers with household jobs as sinecures, or conversely, in various roles in the household with the expectation of military service as a secondary obligation? In the army of 1415, some archers can be identified as having a peacetime role as a servant in their retinue leader's household. One example is the retinue of John Mowbray, the Earl Marshal. Given his status as Earl Marshal, the military role must have been more important. The household duties were probably a screen to allow Mowbray to retain professional archers without unsettling the king by making it obvious he had a substantial peacetime military following.

In 1439 the muster rolls for the Earl of Huntingdon's expedition, the *sagittarii comitis* (archers of the Earl) included Robert of Bows, Thomas of Hall, Laurence of Bakehouse, William of Buttery and John of Stable.[25] The description of these men as 'archers of the Earl' again suggests that archery was their prime duty, and household responsibilities were secondary, designed to keep them out of mischief in peacetime. From about 1340 onwards, men must have known that if they worked in their lord's household, they would be expected to fight for him, if physically able and militarily competent. No doubt a lord would encourage military practice, and make equipment available to his men.

Tenancy also brought obligations as already noted. As the retinue system developed, large landholders seem to have used something like the royal array system within their estates as a way of expanding their household companies, which in peacetime might only consist of their servants and major tenants, into a larger campaign retinue. Willingness to serve is difficult to estimate, since an individual would feel peer pressure from his neighbours, as well as pressure to serve his landlord. Tenants may well have felt that military service was part of their obligations, which could be informal as well as part of a feudal relationship, owed in return for the landholder's support at other times. There are a number of examples of magnates relying on their tenants. In the 1370s John of Gaunt called up 10 men at arms and 60 archers from his Knaresborough estates, and a total of 98 men at arms from all his holdings.[26] In the last decade of the fourteenth century, the Earl of Shrewsbury recruited 16 men from his lordship of Painswick to serve 'beyond the sea in the king's war'.[27]

Even the king relied on this sort of personal obligation occasionally, as happened in 1400 for the first campaign of Henry IV's reign against Scotland. Henry called upon the men who had a personal bond with him, which included all the great magnates, many of whom had felt a common interest with him, when, as Duke of Lancaster, he revolted against King Richard II to recover his estates and standing within the baronage of England. There was also a broad group of knights, esquires and gentry who felt they owed a duty to the king. They demonstrated this loyalty by bringing an army of about 1770 men at arms and 11,310 archers to the muster point at Newcastle in that year.[28] What was particularly impressive was the loyalty shown by Henry's own Duchy of Lancaster, which provided at a conservative estimate 3500 men, of whom about 3300 were archers. This army was definitely not raised using the array system, so that any pressure on the men from their own communities to serve would have been informal. Indeed, Brown notes that members of the county establishment such as sheriffs, Justices of the Peace or Members of Parliament were conspicuous by their absence from the army.[29] There was no emergency when this army was raised, since the Scots were not ravaging the northern marches. The size of the army demonstrates that a large number of ordinary men felt both a loyalty to their immediate lords, and a willingness to undertake military service.

In the fifteenth century there was a substantial number of ordinary men who were willing to serve as archers. In 1415, when Henry V was raising his army for what we now know as the Agincourt campaign, a number of magnates brought in retinues that contained noticeably more archers than they had indented for. John Mowbray, Earl Marshal, Earl of Nottingham and Norfolk signed an indenture to provide a retinue made up of himself, four knights, 45 men at arms and 150 archers. He actually delivered himself, two knights and 32 esquires; these men in turn brought with them 12 men at arms and 133 archers. He also had 38 archers serving as individuals, a state of affairs found elsewhere in this army, since the Crown had also issued indentures directly to individual archers.[30] This over-recruitment is remarkable, and surely demonstrates the attractiveness of serving in France. Henry had not yet established his glittering military reputation, despite his valour at Shrewsbury and dogged campaigning in Wales.

After Agincourt it is much easier to understand the enthusiasm to come forward to serve as an archer, as happened in 1418, when Henry V was raising an army to invade France. From a limited number of cases where it is possible to compare the indentures with the muster rolls showing the men who actually served, it can be seen that 10 out the 18 companies contained more men than specified in the indenture, while only three contained less. But it is the kind of extra men that is significant: 161 archers and only five men at arms.[31] This is the clearest sign that Henry V's reputation as a successful leader had resonated with those who would serve as archers. It is less sure that the same was true with the better off, who would have to invest more in their equipment to serve as men at arms. However, even in this time of great success for the English armies in France (and considerable profit for the common soldier), some grumbled either because they felt that they had had to serve for too long, or because siege and garrison service was not to their liking. One of them, John Feelde, wrote to a friend in 1419 lamenting the dishonesty of the French and wishing he 'may come sone oute of thys unlusty soundyours lyf yn to the lyf of Englond.'[32] Signs of this war weariness, brought on by hard and sustained campaigning, continue until Henry's death in 1422, although it limited the recruitment of men at arms much more than archers.

At the end of the Hundred Years War, even a renowned commander like John Talbot could have trouble raising forces. In 1452 it seems that the veterans of Normandy were reluctant to serve in Gascony.[33] Many of these men were professional soldiers, and since they had little chance of employment in Normandy by this date, they were either demoralised by defeat, or, accurately as it turned out, felt that the English position in Gascony was a lost cause. While Talbot was able to employ some experienced soldiers, he also raised troops from among his tenants. It is probable that some of these men had previous military experience, but that soldiering was not their main occupation. This practice of both the king and the magnates of relying on men who have a personal obligation to them for military support becomes very apparent at certain moments during the Wars of the Roses. In 1460, for example, after Edward Earl of March had won the battle of Mortimer's Cross, his reputation soared so that '... the larger part of the army which had followed him to London was comprised of Yorkist servants and retainers, who had come at their own expense.'[34]

Henry VIII benefited from a number of factors when recruiting his army in 1513. Firstly, he was popular, being young, handsome, physically imposing and energetic, making a strong contrast with his rather austere father. Secondly, men always seemed more willing to serve in armies led by the king himself. Finally, a campaign against the old enemy France offered the chance to revive the 'golden age' of English military adventures under Edward III and Henry V.

LOYALTY

Loyalty to a particular Lord or to a locality or a community has already been discussed in general terms, and had long been an important factor in military recruitment. At the beginning of the period under consideration, the raising of feudal levies depended on this loyalty and sense of duty to a considerable degree. The English medieval military system never seemed to have relied on compulsion alone. There is evidence from many wars since the Middle Ages that compliance often arises from a sense of duty and a desire not to let down friends or the local community, and the men of the Middle Ages felt no differently. As the fourteenth century progressed this loyalty became much more focussed. The Black Prince, John of Gaunt, Richard II, Henry V, and John Mowbray all recruited from their lordships. Evidence from Cheshire demonstrates this particularly clearly. Henry V was both Earl of Cheshire and Duke of Lancaster, so there were large companies of archers from both counties listed in the Agincourt Roll. With the development of the indentured retinue, first loyalty would be to your immediate employer and your colleagues. This was not a problem during the Hundred Years War but a strength, when indentured retinues were often banded together to form English armies fighting in the name of the king of England. But it became a serious problem by the time of the Wars of the Roses, when the competing magnates all claimed to be fighting for whoever they considered to be the legitimate king.

Certain commanders built up a reputation that attracted recruits. Henry Duke of Lancaster in the mid fourteenth century had the reputation that he '…took little or nothing for himself when a town was sacked.'[35] This reputation would add to the loyalty he could expect from the men living in his extensive estates, so that he could consistently raise large retinues of competent men with personal ties to himself. Sir John Chandos and Thomas Dagworth had the reputation of being successful captains. Leaders of this type would be likely to attract men at arms and archers who were planning to become professional soldiers, and who would have high hopes of making some money to cover their own equipment costs.

The majority of campaigns were not short, sharp and decisive. 'Men often served for long periods, through hard winters in constant discomfort.'[36] This was particularly true of the campaigns in Scotland and those in France between about 1420 and 1450. The Agincourt campaign was an exception, being both short and decisive, albeit in poor weather. The numbers of men who served regularly in the longer, gruelling campaigns shows the level of professionalism and loyalty to comrades and leaders felt by the individual archers and men at arms.

TRAINING AND PRACTICE AT ARMS

The whole array system was based on the assumption that men would be serving in person. Instructions to the Arrayers in Cheshire emphasise that after men have been chosen, they are to be 'made trial of' before finally being put on the list of archers.[37] Clearly a test of archery skills was made, only practical if men had trained for some time. By the 1340s substitution became common, and accepted by the Crown as a probably beneficial practice since it allowed the raising of money from those wishing to avoid service and hopefully ensured competent, willing recruits among the substitutes, although there are complaints at this time of arrayed archers being 'feeble men', as noted above. It is clear that Edward III became concerned about the level of competence among arrayed troops because he issued the orders banning football and other distracting sports. But that may not have been the only motivation. The orders against these sports were issued after the Black Death, at a time when the governing classes as represented by the Crown and Parliament were making a broad effort to control the mass of the population. The Statute of Labourers, controlling wage rates and more importantly the attempt to limit the rights of wage labourers to choose their work, together with the regulations issued to control prices, were all part of this effort. So it is possible to see these orders against football and other sports as part of the larger effort to restore the 'golden age' that existed before the Black Death, when ordinary men and women were more biddable, and concentrated on fulfilling their duties towards the ruling classes.

There is no evidence that arrayed men were put through drill or training in large groups at Views of Arms or at any other time. Common sense suggests that once mustered and on campaign there must have been some training so that the archers worked together in large groups. But the whole array system depended on competent individuals presenting themselves, so the selection process concentrated on testing the individual's skill as an archer, not his ability to work as part of a military unit. Though as several authors have observed, a number of agricultural tasks relied on a man being able to work as part of a team, and this co-operative approach would naturally transfer to military practice.

Another method of training men for war was a kind of unofficial apprenticeship. There are cases where an archer has the same family name as a man at arms in a retinue, which could mean that they were a younger brother or cousin gaining military experience. An early example of this comes from the records of a View of Arms held at Norwich in 1355.[38] In one of the divisions of the city, Geoffrey de Hapton came to the View equipped as an armoured man and brought his brother Stephen as an archer. Stephen was not present in his own right as an archer, but was attached to Geoffrey as part of his contribution.

The indenture system by its very nature relied on the availability of willing, competent fighting men, which stimulated the growth in numbers of professional archers and men at arms. Newcomers to the profession would have developed their skills in the archery practice enjoined on all Englishmen. Once they were members of a retinue, practice would have been part of their working life. A major difference between a newly recruited English archer in the fourteenth and fifteenth centuries and a newly recruited soldier in the nineteenth and twentieth centuries is that the archer would be competent in the use of his main weapon, because of legally required practice in 'civilian' life. The historian of the reign of Louis XI, Philippe de Commyne (1447-1511) comments, when discussing the English archers in Charles the Bold's armies: 'Those who had never had a day's experience of their job are more valuable than those who are well trained, this is the opinion of the English who are the world's best archers.'[39] He was not suggesting that a man need not have practised archery to be useful, but that because of the training regime laid down in Charles' military ordinances, archers need not have had previous military training or experience.

CAREER SOLDIERS

The development of retinues led to the professionalizing of military service at all levels. While knights had always been professional fighting men, the specification of periods of service and wages in the indentures changed the structure of their services. For men at arms and archers the mixed retinue provided the opportunity for them to become professional soldiers. In the 1330s and 40s there is solid evidence that men at arms, whether of knightly status or not, often served the same retinue leader, alongside a company of colleagues with whom they had served before. In the Earl of Northampton's retinue for the Crecy campaign, of 72 individuals identified, 31 had served with him in Brittany in 1345, and 20 had been with him at Sluys in 1340. Groups like these may have made up a whole, small retinue, or have been a sub retinue in a large one. It is not surprising that the men making up these small companies often lived close to, or held land near each other. 'Retinues exhibited a striking degree of cohesion, based on continuity of service and networks of individual relationships.' (Ayton.)[40] Unfortunately there is very little evidence for continuity of archers' service at this early date, though: 'We can assume that such relationships extended to archers, many of whom were recruited in "mixed" companies and probably served alongside men at arms in the field.'[41] The Royal Household, being better documented, does provide an example. Records for 1334-5 mention twenty men serving as archers in the Household, three of whom, John Chester, Nicholas Holford and John Pulford, are still serving ten years later, and one of them, John Pulford, is recorded as an archer of the king's household in the Crecy campaign. This is an early example of archers serving as career soldiers. In the Crecy army it is possible that William Warde and Richard Whet were such. Both served on behalf of landholders who wished to avoid carrying out their military assessment in person.[42] No doubt there were more whose names we have yet to discover.

For some recruits, archery skills were an integral part of their job, such as foresters and parkers. It is likely that these would serve in retinues rather than county levies, since they were already servants of a larger scale landholder, often a member of the royal family since the largest forests were the property of the King, or the Earl of Chester (usually the eldest son of the monarch). In 1346, just after Crecy, the Black Prince instructs Robert, Parker of Berkhamsted, John de Cestre (from his name a Cheshire man using his skills for his lord away from home, perhaps the same 'John Chester' as recorded in 1334–5), Parker of Byfleet and Ranlyn, Parker of Watlington to '...choose in those parts six good companion archers, the best [they] can find, and come with them with all speed to Dover.'[43] These skilled archers were relatively rare in the army of this campaign, but from a military point of view they would provide a useful number of 'sharp shooters'. This was a two-way process, not only were parkers and foresters sought after as military archers, but military archers would be appointed to these jobs after service.

Archers could be both loyal to their employer or his cause, and professional. Examples can be found from among the famous, or in contemporary eyes, infamous, Cheshire archers of Richard II's personal retinue. John Winnington, who was a relative of one of the knights involved in the revolt against Henry IV, became one of Richard's archers in 1397, and he showed his loyalty to his master's cause by joining Hotspur's army in 1403 and fighting at Shrewsbury.[44] Another example, this time of a man who probably did not have Winnington's social status, was William of Edgesley. He joined Richard II's retinue of archers in 1398. He was probably hit harder than Winnington by the unemployment that followed Richard's deposition in 1400, since his inquisition post mortem shows him to be landless but owning two cows and an acre of oats.[45] He also joined the rebellion in 1403, and fell at the battle of Shrewsbury in Hotspur's army.

In contrast, some of the Cheshire archers were either less loyal to a lost cause or forgiven and allowed to prove their loyalty to the new king by following their profession. A muster of Cheshire archers serving the king in France two decades after Richard's death (Richard II died in 1400) still lists about 24 members of his retinue on active service.[46] The youngest age that anyone would have been indentured into Richard II's retinue would have been 16, and no doubt many were older, so we can be certain that the average age of this group in 1420 was above 36.

During the campaigns of Henry V the majority of archers are professionals for the first time. Muster rolls from Cheshire demonstrate this, with many of the names in the 1417 roll appearing in the 1419–20 rolls. We also see siblings or generations within families committing themselves to service as archers. In the 1417 Cheshire roll there are five men with the same surname (Roneworth) in the list of those serving from the Macclesfield hundred.[47] While indentures had often been issued for a year's service before this time, in practice, as the Agincourt campaign demonstrates, actual service would be for a shorter period. The forces of the English Crown in Normandy from about 1420 onwards effectively became a standing army with annual indentures, meaning just that. An early example of this trend is the indenture of 1424 between John Duke of Bedford, Regent of France and Sir John Fastolf, who was Grand Master of the Household in France, whereby Fastolf provided 80 men at arms and 250 archers for a year's service.[48] A J Pollard points out that in 1436 there were 38 separate garrisons, and an additional nine personal retinues, and that the indentures of service for all were renewed annually. 'The bulk of the standing army was made up of soldiers who had made their career in the ranks or even settled in the duchy. Native-born Normans and other nationals were also recruited to the army, although it was laid down that no more than an eighth of the establishment of any force should be "foreigners".'[49] Career soldiers are found in the Towton war grave, though not all were archers. Nine of them have '…well healed cranial trauma that most likely resulted from previous battles or armed conflict.'[50] The average age of this group is 34.

With the final defeat of the long English endeavours in France in 1453, a generation of professionals needed employment. The dynastic struggles that we now call the Wars of the Roses both provided employment for the soldiers and were stimulated by the availability of numbers of idle and experienced fighting men.

Military professionalism did have a significant effect on the outcome of actions. While the English and Welsh archers played an important role in the storming of Caen in 1346, this was an example of raw courage and fighting spirit rather than the vision and determination of professional soldiers. In contrast, Sir Thomas Dagworth's epic fight at St. Pol de Leon in the same year, where, with about 80 men at arms and 100 archers he defeated a much larger French force in a day-long battle, was won by the professional skills and attitude of his soldiers, many of whom were in his personal retinue.

As has already been noted, in general, the English armies used in the fifteenth century were smaller, and made up largely of professional soldiers. In 1421 the Duke of Clarence impetuously attacked a Franco-Scottish force at Bauge with a force made up almost entirely of knights and men at arms. He was killed along with most of his men. The Earl of Salisbury was left the task of trying to extricate the remainder of the English army, which contained a high proportion of archers. By taking an unexpected route back to Normandy, and tricking their way into Le Mans, Salisbury and his men limited the strategic advantage the French could gain from Clarence's folly. This was only possible because Salisbury was a highly competent commander, and his men showed great skill and determination in remaining a coherent fighting force following a significant defeat to achieve a clear objective.

PROFESSIONAL DISCIPLINE AT VERNEUIL AND ELSEWHERE

The battle of Verneuil in 1424 was perhaps as remarkable a victory as the much more famous Agincourt, but its fame has suffered because a regnant king wasn't present, and Shakespeare didn't celebrate it. Since it is less well known, and the most extensive account by Burne needs revision,[51] an account of the battle follows to demonstrate the quality of the English army that fought there.[52] In 1424 Charles VII of France built up an army of between 14,000 and 16,000 men to attempt to relieve Ivry and attack the English possessions in Normandy. This army included major landholders from Normandy who remained loyal to the French king, and about 6500 Scots, of whom something like 4000 were archers, and 2000 mercenary heavy cavalry from Lombardy. The latter were hired as part of an existing arrangement between the French Crown and Italian *Condottieri* in a deliberate attempt to nullify the impact of the English archers. At this time the armourers of Northern Italy (and Milan in particular) were the best in Europe, so these cavalrymen not only had the most advanced personal armour, their horses also had the most effective protection available. The leaders of this French force included the Count of Aumale who had used cavalry to charge down the archers at La Gravelle to defeat an English force in the previous year. Jones suggests that they had confidence that they had an army that could defeat the English, and so went looking for a fight.

The English Regent in France, John, Duke of Bedford with an army of around 8000 including some Normans and Burgundians found himself confronting this force on relatively open ground near Verneuil. He seems to have arrayed his army on foot with archers forming a front line but with more of them on the flanks than in the centre, and the men at arms ranked behind them. Because of the open ground he had ordered the archers to set up stakes for defence. The baggage was behind the English lines with a guard of perhaps 500 men, and the rear was further protected by the horses being tethered in a living wall three or four deep. Except for the use of the horses, the English battle line was very similar to that used by Bedford's brother, Henry V, at Agincourt. The French army also dismounted, except for the Lombards who formed the front line. Behind them the French and Scots seem to have formed two groups side by side, with the intention of following up the planned Italian charge and taking advantage of the disruption it would cause to the English line.

The first stage of the battle went as the French hoped. The Lombard cavalry seems to have been impervious to both the English arrows and the archers' stakes, so it pushed through the archers in the centre, and then through the English men at arms and finally chased the baggage guard away. At least 500 men fled the English army at this stage, some on horseback, since it is reported that they were robbed of their horses and armour by the local populace. The English army survived this charge because the majority of the archers moved out onto the flanks, and the men at arms lay down so the horse would ride over them and divided to channel the Lombards through their centre. The resulting two blocks seem to have rallied to the Duke of Bedford's and Earl of Salisbury's banners, and after an exhortation from Bedford, set upon the French and Scottish infantry. The English were in a desperate position, outnumbered, and in danger of being surrounded if the Lombards reformed and attacked their rear. It is likely that the English archers on the wings shot into the flanks of the advancing French and Scottish infantry, forcing these troops to bunch together as they shied away from the arrows, as happened at Agincourt. Once the melee was joined, the archers gave 'a great shout' and set to with their hand to hand weapons. The heroics of the English, particularly the men at arms, broke the French and Scottish forces, indeed the Scots were wiped out. The Lombards returned too late and were driven off. It seems that the Scots archers had no effect in the battle, apparently unable to compete with the experienced English archers. What is clear from this account is the professionalism and discipline of the English army, whose men showed experience, confidence in both themselves and their leaders, and great courage.

In 1428 it was a force under Salisbury again that had vision enough and discipline to see an opportunity to begin a successful assault on Jenville, while both their commander and the town garrison were distracted after the failure of attempts to negotiate the surrender of the town.

In these examples, archers made up the largest part of the English forces engaged, but they were effective because they were part of a balanced force, (with the possible exception of the retreat after Bauge), making up between two-thirds and three-quarters of the force. Without adequate numbers of men at arms to provide a tough core to the army that could slog it out in the melee, archers were vulnerable to attack. No amount of professionalism and personal skill and determination on the part of the lightly armoured archers could enable them to resist fully armoured men on foot or horseback without an adequate level of support from similar troops.

The career of one these professional soldiers can be traced in one of the skeletons found in the Towton war grave.[53] 'Towton 16' as he is now known is famous because of the facial reconstruction made of him for a UK television programme. He was born between 1410 and 1415, since he was estimated to be aged between 46 and 50 at the time of his death. The skeleton is that of a man about 5ft. 9in tall and well built. He shows body developments that are now recognised as arising from using the English warbow, and probable signs of a lot of horse riding. So he probably served as a mounted archer for a number of years, most likely in France in the 1430s and 1440s. At some time around 1451-3 he was seriously wounded in the face, since the skeleton has a large, well healed blade wound to the jaw. It has been estimated that this wound was received eight to ten years before death. He clearly had access to competent medical care, which may suggest that in the case of more professional companies, the captains tried to ensure that they had trustworthy surgeons available for their men, or maybe that he had risen to be a company captain himself. Given all his probable years of service, it is likely that he was the captain of a company, maybe as part of one of the larger retinues present at Towton in 1461.

HOW POPULAR WAS THE WAR WITH THE ENGLISH PEOPLE?

The relative success of the Anglo Saxon Fyrd system and the medieval Array system in raising bodies of men from whom an army could be selected suggests a widespread sense of duty. In the Welsh Marches and the northern counties of England war was a more or less seasonal pursuit, so participation was a necessity. In the period under consideration, the views of the mass of the people about the war fluctuated, depending largely on how successful the campaigns were.

One measure of willingness is how much popular or parliamentary resistance there was to levies through the array system. Even a powerful and militarily fairly successful king like Edward I had to modify his requests in 1295 and 1297 by reducing the numbers he hoped to raise, in response to objection from the classes of landholder who were being levied for service.

In the late 1330s and early 1340s Edward III waged a significant propaganda campaign at home to cultivate goodwill toward his military adventures. In the autumn of 1337, 'The gentry… and anyone else who might be thought influential were called to the county towns to hear the justice of the King's cause explained by specially appointed commissioners. For a wider public there were patriotic sermons on Sundays and feast days.'[54] In 1346, when Edward wanted to make a major military effort (what became the Crecy campaign), he initiated another major round of propaganda. There were proclamations and officially inspired sermons about the threats inherent in the French King's plans and actions.[55] While Edward avowed a political reason (his claim to the French throne) for his campaigns, he exploited other factors as well: '… a deep seated fear and hatred of the French, and later … a growing confidence and pride in England's military capability, but above all the opportunities which the war offered for personal advancement and enrichment.'[56] At other less successful times, such as the 1370s and 80s or 1430s and 40s, opposition becomes more vociferous. In the 1370s, when memories of the great successes of Edward III and Edward the Black Prince were still alive, no doubt kept fresh by grandfathers' tales, the men and women of England were less concerned with peace than the feeling that they were not getting good value for their taxes, clamouring 'for good leadership, enterprise and victory'.[57] A little later, in 1390, opinions varied. Froissart writes that among those who favoured the continuation of the war were '...the less well off knights, esquires and archers of England, who appreciated its comforts and, indeed, maintained their status through war.'[58] Against this group of vested interests, the professional soldiers supporting the war, were the landholders, merchants and townspeople who had to finance it through parliamentary grants and payments to be excused personal service. Rumours of peace continued until, in 1393, a veteran of the wars led a rebellion in Cheshire and neighbouring counties. The Duke of Lancaster repressed the uprising, and helped to ensure calm in England by employing the majority of the rebels in Aquitaine in 1394. Again we see the problems large numbers of unemployed professional and semi professional soldiers could cause for the English king.

In Richard II's reign a sense of insecurity in southern England brought about by regular raids by the Franco-Castilian fleet added to this feeling of not getting good value for the money spent on the war, and may well have been part of the motivation for the Kentish men's enthusiastic participation in the Peasants' Revolt in 1381.[59]

Henry V, by a mixture of his personal qualities, his political skills as king, and his military successes was granted very high levels of taxation by Parliament. His popularity was confirmed by the fact that these were collected from the population at large with very little complaint. But as soon as he was dead it seems a reaction against this willingness to pay set in. It wasn't that the war was suddenly going badly, although Clarence's fatal debacle at Bauge may have given a different impression. Parliament decided to act as though it believed the English Crown's grand claims to France. In 1422 Parliament reduced the wool subsidy paid by native merchants by nearly a quarter, and by so doing, transferred much more of the costs of the war onto the taxpayers in English-held France. As English fortunes in France ebbed and flowed over the next thirty years, this led to financial hardship and antagonised the local taxpayers. This was further exacerbated by a steady determination by the English taxpayers, as represented through the Parliamentary Commons, to reduce their own tax payments regardless of the situation abroad.

In Henry V's reign, the idea of the English king's rights in France, and the glory and profit that could gained by serving in the English armies in France, were kept alive by songs and ballads. Henry undoubtedly encouraged this himself through sponsoring the *Gesta Henrici Quinti*, a propagandist account of his reign that concentrated on his actions with regard to France. This was written by a royal chaplain and was presented in about 1417 to stimulate support for Henry's grand expeditions to France in that and subsequent years. The Agincourt carol was also probably composed in the royal chapel around this time.[60]

Then went our King, with all his host,
Through France, for all the Frenchman's boast;
Nor spared for dread of least nor most,
Until he came to Agincourt coast.

Then foresooth that Knight comely,
In Agincourt field he fought manly:
Through grace of God most mighty,
He had both the field and the victory.

These works may have had a limited circulation round the country at first, but the carol would have eventually spread widely through being sung in churches and monastic houses. Ballads were a more important way for the population at large to hear the story of Agincourt, the miracle of the victory, the nobility of the king, and no doubt how the bowmen of England humbled the arrogant foreigner. Unfortunately, none have survived.

Throughout this period most of the population of England, except those in the Northern Marches menaced by the Scots and those on the South coast at risk of French seaborne attack, had little direct experience of war. Most knew men from their community or extended family who had taken part in the wars, men who would have returned with tales, earnings or wounds as their luck allowed. Many others would have experience of the costs of war through paying taxes, or contributing material or labour to help meet the Crown's orders for archery equipment (described in *Equipping the Archers* later). When pollarded ash and poplar were harvested for shafts and the primary goose feathers were collected for fletchings, many people could feel they were taking part in larger matters, which, when the wars went well, would have been a source of pride.

Near the end of the Hundred Years War in 1450 there is still evidence of some enthusiasm for the conflict despite the failures. James Gresham writing to John Paston laments the fall of English Normandy, saying 'Today it is told Cherbourg is gone, and we have now not a foot of land left in Normandy.'[61] Some of the middle classes at least identified the English military effort in France as a national concern and not just as the English and French kings squabbling over dynastic matters. In the same year, Jack Cade's rebels demanded the punishment of those they held responsible for the loss of English lands in Maine, Anjou and Normandy. They saw them as traitors saying 'our true lords, knights and esquires and many a good yeoman lost and solde ere they went.'[62] While this may camouflage a political attack on some of the leading nobles, it also shows a genuine feeling of betrayal in the loss.

While the leading nobles in the king's court were obvious targets of blame for the loss of English lands in France, the tax granting (and paying) classes represented in the Parliamentary Commons also deserved a share of blame. In Henry VI's reign, they seem to have lost the will to finance the war by granting taxes on the scale necessary to maintain the English hold in northern France. Men were prepared to serve as archers in France at a time when their social betters were reluctant to grant and pay the taxes necessary to support them.

In Edward IV's reign, the English population at large, certainly those parts of it that served in parliament or were going to join an expedition as archers, were probably more enthusiastic for war against the French than the king himself. In the 1470s the Commons allocated a generous amount of money and a large army was raised. Having made these threatening preparations, Edward himself would probably have preferred to come to advantageous terms with Louis of France, but he could not for fear of 'outraging the sentiments of the rank and file of his troops. English public opinion and his own prestige demanded that he should go.'[63]

Edward IV was more vulnerable to these kinds of pressures than any of his predecessors, including even Edward II and Richard II, who were both deposed by coups, because not only did he gain the throne by deposing the ruling king, Henry VI, but he had been deposed himself in 1470. He needed to keep as many of the English as possible sympathetic and supportive. In the end, when he invaded France, he very quickly came to terms with Louis XI, receiving a pension as a result. The rank and file of his army were disgruntled by this frustration of their chances to make a profit at the expense of the French population, and about 2000 stayed in France to serve Duke Charles of Burgundy.

The successes of Edward III's reign, particularly in the 1340s and 1350s, and in the reigns of Henry V and Henry VI between about 1412 and 1429, left a powerful popular tradition, a folklore, of the pride and profit that could be gained fighting in France, particularly if the king himself was in command. Henry VIII benefited from this and was able to be selective when he was recruiting his army in 1513-14 for the expedition that led to the Battle of the Spurs. Consequently, contemporary foreign commentators remarked on the discipline, spirit and quality of the troops in this army.[64]

NOTES

1 *CCR 1363* p.534-5.
2 *Statutes of the Realm (1810–28)* London. vol. 2. p.57.
3 *Rotuli Parliamentorum 1767–77*. London, vol. 3 p.643.
4 Ross, C (1974). *Edward IV.* New Haven, Yale University Press. p.221–2.
5 *Rotuli Parliamentorum* vol. 6 p.188.
6 Statutes of the Realm. (1816) London vol. 2 p.649–50.
7 Statutes of the Realm. (1817) London vol. 3 p.25–6.
8 Philippe de Commynes quoted in Goodman, A (2005) p.95.
9 Powicke, M (1962) p.154.

10 Morgan, P J (1987) p 113.
11 Morgan, P. J (1987) p114.
12 Somerville, R (1953) p.130n.
13 *CLBCL* Book F. p.25n.
14 *BPR* pt1 p.78.
15 *BPR* pt.3 p.353.
16 *CCR* 1380 p.443.
17 *CCR* 1380 p.83.
18 *CCR* 1387 p.308.
19 Goodman, A (1992). *John of Gaunt; an Exercise in Princely Power*. Harlow. Longman, p.123.
20 Allmand C T (1973). *Society at War; the Experience of England and France during the 100 Years War*. Edinburgh, Oliver and Boyd. p.35-6.
21 Vale, M G A (1970). *English Gascony 1399–1453*. Oxford University Press. p.130.
22 Driver, J T (1971) p.15.
23 Curry, A (1979). 'The First English Standing Army' in Ross, C ed. *Patronage, Pedigree and Power in Later Medieval England*. Gloucester.
24 Barker, J (2005). *Agincourt; the King, the Campaign, the Battle*. London. Little Brown. p.95.
25 Vale, M G A (1970) p.110n.
26 Powicke, M (1962) p.215.
27 Rudder, S (1779). *A New History of Gloucestershire*. Stroud. Nonsuch Publishing, p.593–4.
28 Brown, A L (1974) The English Campaign in Scotland 1400' p. 44 in Hearder, H and Loyn H R eds. (1974) *British Government and Administration*. Cardiff. p.40–54.
29 Brown, A L (1974) p.48.
30 Curry, A (2000) p.436.
31 Newhall, R A (1924) p.193.
32 Allmand, C (1997). *Henry V*. New Haven, Yale University Press. p.130.
33 Pollard A J (1983) p.100.
34 Ross, C (1974) p.33.
35 Hewitt, H J (1966). p.31.
36 Prestwich, M (1996) p.9.
37 *BPR* pt. 1 pp.7, 14 and 78.
38 Hudson, W (1900).
39 Bartlett, C (1997). *English Longbowman 1330–1515*. Oxford, Osprey. p.31.
40 Ayton, A and Preston P (2005) p.227.
41 ibid p.227.
42 ibid p.216.
43 *BPR* pt.1 p.18.
44 McNiven, P (1975). The Men of Cheshire and the Rebellion of 1403. *Transactions of the Historical Society of Lancashire and Cheshire. Vol 129* p.11.
45 Gillespie, J L (1974). Richard II's Cheshire Archers. *Transactions of the Historical Society of Lancashire and Cheshire*. CXXV p.29.

46 Gillespie, J L (1974) p.26.
47 *Cheshire Sheaf 1903-4 vol.* 5 p. 92–3 and *Cheshire Sheaf 1906 vol. 6* p.80–91.
48 Allmand C T (1973) p.58
49 Pollard A J (1983) p.33–4.
50 Fiorato, V, Boylston, A and Knudsel, C. (editors) (2000) p.94.
51 Burne, Col. A H (1956). *The Agincourt War*. London. It remains interesting as an initial overview of the military activities between 1369 and 1453, but the detailed accounts of some of the battles must be treated with caution.
52 This account is based on Jones, M K (2002) 'The Battle of Verneuil 17th August 1424' in *War in History vol. IX* p.375–411. However I have amended his reconstruction of events since he is not entirely clear about the role of the archers in the battle given their place in the English battle line.
53 Following derived from Fiorato, V, Boylston, A and Knudsel, C. (editors). (2000).
54 Sumption, J (1990). op. cit. p.220.
55 ibid p.491.
56 Barnie, J (1974). *War in Medieval Society; Social Values and the Hundred Years War 1337–1453*. London: Weidenfeld & Nicolson p.34.
57 McKisack, M (1959). *The Fourteenth Century*. Oxford. p.253.
58 Froissart, J quoted in Allmand C T (1973) p.31.
59 This argument is put forward very clearly in Searle, E and Burghart, R (1972). Defence of England and the Peasants' Revolt *Viator 3,* p.365-89.
60 Barker, J (2005). p.380.
61 Keen, M (1989). 'The End of the Hundred Years War: Lancastrian France and Lancastrian England' p. 297. *England and her Neighbours 1066–1453*. Edited by Jones, M. and Vale, M. London, Hambledon Press.
62 Keen, M (1989) p.298.
63 Ross, C (1974) p.225.
64 Cruickshank C G (1969) Chapter 7.

Everyday Life as a Military Archer

One of the truisms about life as a soldier in any age is that most of the time the individual is going through everyday routines – practising weapon skills, marching, making and maintaining camp or finding and preparing food – anything but fighting the enemy. Actual fighting often makes up relatively little of the period of service. This was true of many of the campaigns that the archers took part in, particularly of much of the service in France in the fifteenth century in the garrison companies.

FEEDING THE ARCHERS

Once the leaders of the retinues and armies were confident that their men at muster were properly armed and equipped, they made serious efforts to ensure that they became disciplined, effective fighting forces. These efforts would be wasted if they didn't also ensure that the men were adequately fed and clothed, and could remain so.

By the fifteenth century many of the indentures for service in English-occupied France required the retinue leaders to have two months supplies of victuals at initial muster and to take responsibility for arranging supplies thereafter. Keeping the army fed became a problem in the Agincourt campaign despite Henry V's planning. While accounts may have overemphasised the victualling problems to enhance the near miraculous quality of the victory, there is no doubt that the army had problems with supplies because it was marching fast through hostile territory. If an army had to live off the land, relations with the local populace were complex to say the least, and security of foragers became a headache. Supplying food and drink was a primary respinsibility of the overall expedition commander or retinue leader. The commander was not expected to provide food and drink as part of the soldiers' payment, rather, it was his responsibility to arrange for the availability of food from local sources. Garrison troops could find themselves regularly receiving part of their pay as food and lodging, but this was not universal practice, nor was it popular with the men themselves.

In general, the Crown did not provide food for its armies; it attempted to ensure the availability of supplies, either locally or by deliveries from England, which the soldiers bought, often at a higher price than the Crown had paid. Froissart tells us in his detailed account of Edward III's 1359 campaign in France that the substantial wagon train (he says 6000 carts) brought over from England was there in part to carry provisions. Yet despite this, the army had to rely on foraging to feed itself. The need for an army on the march or making a chevauchee to forage tended to dictate the pace and, to some extent the route, the army followed. Froissart notes how the length of time the army was able to stay at particular towns varied according to the supplies of food and drink it found. In the last quarter of the fourteenth century the English garrisons in Brittany were expected to arrange their own supplies. Since they were in Brittany to support the pro-English faction in the dynastic struggle over the dukedom, the garrisons should have made commercial arrangements with local suppliers, rather than lived off the land, thereby antagonising their allies. Disciplinary ordinances issued by Richard II in 1385 and by John of Gaunt in Spain in 1386 show that soldiers were expected to pay fair prices for food from merchants and the locals. These examples all relate to armies raised mainly through the indenture system. Ensuring availability of food, rather than active provision of supplies to troops, as became normal practice in later times, was the key. When Henry V was pursuing his conquest of Normandy in 1418 there are several references to foodstuffs being made available for the troops to buy. Orders were given that grain should be brought to Conde sur Norreau, so that it could be baked into bread there and sold to the English troops besieging the place. Relying mainly on the local French peasants and merchants to make it work, the Duke of Gloucester established a market to supply the troops besieging Cherbourg. However it seems that he did not rely solely on the troops buying their own food since he also ordered his officials to obtain cattle and sheep which were then to be delivered to the army.[1] When he was besieging Rouen in 1418, Henry V showed that he understood the importance of regular supplies to the success of a major siege by issuing an order to the Mayor and Aldermen of London. In this he requested them to fill '... as many small vessels as you may goodly' and dispatch them to Harfleur from where they could sail under escort upriver to Rouen.[2] By 1419 parliament was beginning to be less enthusiastic about the costs of his war in France, and Henry made it clear to them through his Council that he had to pay his soldiers, so they in turn were able to obey his strict orders that they were to pay the local inhabitants for all the victuals they acquired.[3] Henry and his brothers were particularly determined to ensure that their men were paid so that they did not begin to live off the inhabitants of northern France, whom the kings also regarded as their subjects.

All these examples apply to what amounts to field operations, where supplies might be supplemented by foraging. In contrast, it seems likely that the basic foodstuffs for the garrison troops in France frequently had to be brought in from England, which gave them some independence from a possibly sullen if not actively hostile local population. In late 1415, for example, William Loveneye and Gerald Flore were sent to Harfleur with one quarter's wages for the garrison of 300 men at arms and 900 archers. They also took over at least 1000 quarters of oats, for which they were ordered to take payment out of the wages.[4] The oats were probably used for pottage as a basic foodstuff, although they could have been malted for brewing.

In the 1330s and 1340s, when armies were more commonly raised by array, things seem to have been no different. In 1341, while based in Flanders, Edward III's financial state was so desperate that 'only with the greatest difficulty could he lay hands on enough money to keep his archers from imminent starvation',[5] that is, pay them so that they could buy food. By 1345 Edward's financial position was so bad that 'even the archers stationed in Flanders were left to shift for themselves'.[6] This circumstance, where a commander was unable to either feed his troops or pay them regularly enough so that they could feed themselves, caused problems on a number of expeditions. The English and Gascon soldiers of Edmund of Cambridge's expedition to Spain in 1381, having endured a period of idleness with little or no pay 'considered that they had been given a free hand by Edmund to practise banditry and robbery at the expense of their allies'.[7] The same problem affected John of Gaunt's expedition in 1386–7. In neither case did the soldiers become poor fighters; it was the strategic effect of their unofficial commandeering that was the problem. This problem reoccurred in 1443 when the Duke of Somerset led an expedition to Brittany to support Duke Francis of Brittany against the king of France. Unfortunately, Somerset does not seem to have been able to maintain discipline, or was careless, since Duke Francis protested to the Privy Council that despite Somerset's soldiers being 'received as friends' by the Bretons, they had gone to live off the land, taking and pillaging Laquierche.[8]

Large-scale provision of foodstuffs was necessary when the army was being mustered in preparation for an expedition abroad, whether to France, Scotland or Ireland. Besides ensuring sufficient food at the muster point, the groups of soldiers, both indentured and arrayed, had to be fed on their way to the muster point. The English kings made significant efforts, often in response to complaints heard in Parliament, to ensure that their troops did not live off the land in their own country. In 1380 there were two orders, one to the Sheriff of Kent and the other to the Earl of Cambridge, who was both Constable of Dover Castle and Warden of the Cinque Ports. These men were ordered to proclaim in the ports, cities and towns an ordinance made in Parliament:

> …that men at arms, armed men and archers of the retinues of lords and others upon their passage over sea have lain in divers counties adjacent to the sea, and that they and their servants have by their own authority

> without payment taken, destroyed and by violence consumed all victuals needful for them and their horses and other goods and chattels of liege subjects there as well as churchmen as of others beating and maiming any lieges who complained or gain said them.[9]

This proclamation included procedures for remedy, if the men themselves refused to pay then their leaders and captains were liable, being 'bound to answer for their retinues'. It seems probable that these orders were designed to reassure the inhabitants of Kent that they had remedies against the soldiery if necessary, and to remind the captains and leaders of their own responsibilities for the discipline and care of their men. The preparations for this particular expedition seem to have been troubled; six weeks after these orders were issued, there were others to the bailiffs of Maidstone, Rochester and Newington and the Constable of Aylesford, concerning deserters.

In 1381 an order was issued intended to prevent profiteering by providers of food and lodgings on a company's route to their departure port, which may have provoked disorders of the type mentioned in the orders of the previous year. It is addressed to the sheriffs, mayors and bailiffs, ordering them '... to assign and deliver honourable lodgings and needful victuals at a reasonable price for prompt payment to Peter de Veel and Robert Passelewe, knights' [the captains of an expedition to Brittany].[10] In 1415 Henry V made efforts to ensure the food supply both at the muster point and on campaign. In an order to the Sheriff of Southampton he ordered that '...each and every one of liege subjects living there [Southampton, Winchester and all towns between and around] whom it may concern shall bake and brew.' This is a clear attempt to ensure a supply of the very basics for the collecting army. Nearly a month after this first order, Henry ordered the Sheriffs of both Southampton and Wiltshire to arrange the supply of one hundred cattle each to designated points to feed the gathering army. The lords and retinue leaders were to pay a reasonable price for these beasts.[11] The underlying principle here seems to be that the king and the leaders were expected to ensure provisions for the men once they reached the muster point. There is no clear suggestion that the men had to pay for these basics. As we noted above, there could be problems with troops seizing supplies and not paying when they were between their homes and the muster point. Henry V rapidly gained a reputation as a strict disciplinarian once in France, but this may not have been established before he left England, since some soldiers took food without payment in Warminster.[12]

More detailed accounts of the foodstuffs that might be available to archers in the personal retinue of one of the great nobles are found in two records of John, Duke of Bedford's household. These give an idea both of some of the military equipment he needed for his retinue, and also of some of the food his household would consume over the winter, particularly in the extensive festivals of the medieval Christmas festival, a time when campaigning was usually at a low level.

12th NOVEMBER 1430

100 quarters of malt [probably for brewing since two vats were also sent out]
2 pipes of ale [a pipe is about 105 gallons]
14 Banbury cheeses
600 salt fish
500 grenefish
4000 mushrooms
3 casks of sturgeon
3 casks of salmon
50 quarters of salt [most likely for preserving locally slaughtered meat]

17th NOVEMBER 1433

4600 stockfish
600 saltfish
4 casks of salmon
2 casks of eels
5 casks of porpoise
4 pipes of ale
100 quarters of barley[13]

These foodstuffs would augment some of the staples like meat and bread that could be obtained locally to supply the household. The supply of ale seems to have been a problem in Rouen, but was clearly regarded as a necessity in an English Lord's household.

In the 1430s and 1440s the surviving records give an idea of the scale of efforts made to feed the garrisons and mobile forces serving in France, necessary to maintain both morale and discipline among the English troops. In 1437, considerable quantities of wheat were sent to Calais, Guisnes and Hammes; in 1442, in response to pleas from Bayonne, 500 archers and 1000 quarters of wheat, plus fodder for the horses, were sent; while in 1443 both reinforcements and foodstuffs, including 100 pipes of beer (perhaps 10,000 gallons!), were sent in all haste to northern France.[14] All this effort was at a time when the Crown struggled to pay the soldiers regularly, and may be more evidence of the payment of a proportion of their wages in kind.[15]

If the troops were being raised for service in England, either for coastal defence or for maintenance of order in Wales or the Northern Marches, it became very important to ensure that they were either given foodstuffs or regular wages to buy them, since the king could not afford to have his soldiers living off the land in England. In 1442, when troops were being mustered on the Isle of Wight as part of plans to defend the Channel and the south coast, the king ordered both arms and foodstuffs be sent for these forces.[16]

DISCIPLINE

One of the questions that immediately comes to mind when looking at medieval English armies - and their relative impermanence - is what was the level of overall discipline and how was it enforced? Through the fourteenth century, the increasing level of professionalization helps to give some kind of answer. The retinues and their component sub units are increasingly made up of men who have worked together at other times, or at least have military experience, so will have an understanding of the need for discipline. In the reigns of Edward I and Edward III the same was also true of the arrayed troops, since the Commissions of Array were active so often that those selected to serve would have been increasingly likely to have some experience of campaigning, either personally or from friends and older relations. All this contributes towards a basic disciplinary structure in the smaller units, which could be built on in the larger battles and armies.

The large army of 1346 was officially under the disciplinary control of the Earl of Northampton as Constable of the army and the Earl of Warwick, who was Marshal. While these two no doubt set the standard, there are no surviving royal ordinances giving the rules they implemented through the commanders of the three battles fought by the army. These rules clearly existed because there was a proclamation outlining them after disorderly conduct by the infantry on landing at La Hougue.[17] Edward III seems to have used pillaging along the line of march as both a weapon of war and method of supplying his army, and, as a result it was kept under firm control. This was demonstrated when he issued an order on 14th August that there was to be no pillaging on the next day because it was the Feast of the Assumption, which seems to have been strictly obeyed.[18] Once battle was joined, keeping disciplinary control was another matter – but not impossible – since at Crecy the prohibition on looting the dead before the battle was won seems to have been strictly followed. A similar prohibition against the unauthorised crying of havoc (permission to plunder) is found in Richard II's ordinances. However on other occasions, most noticeably the storming of Caen, the commanders seemed to have had little control over the archers and Welsh infantry, whose reckless determination convinced the Earl of Warwick to commit men at arms to the attack, which succeeded, rather than call it off as the king wished. So while controlling soldiers in the heat of battle was still easier said than done, as the battles of Crecy, Agincourt and Verneuil among others proved, medieval commanders were quite capable of doing just that.

The earliest set of ordinances we have are those of Richard II issued in 1385. These are most likely based on earlier sets, possibly even those of Edward III.[19] These start off by establishing the soldiers' duty of obedience to the King, his Marshal and Constable. These three should be immediately obeyed if they ordered that an attack must be broken off, to minimise the potential dangers of uncoordinated attacks like that at Caen in 1346. Then there is a rule ordering immunity from pillage of clerics, women and unarmed labourers. This is a rule that seems more pious than realistic, although Henry V famously enforced it by hanging a church robber. Later ordinances, such as those of 1415, often contained more general rules designed to limit pillaging to finding and seizing sustenance rather than the practice of the chevauchee, which was wholesale looting. Pillaging and looting were further circumscribed by the rules that soldiers must stay with their battle, stay at their allocated quarters, mount watch and go out on patrol as their captains ordered. The penalties for breaking these last rules are interesting. A man at arms was effectively demoted by the confiscation of his horse and harness (armour, not horse trappings), while an archer lost an ear. Order was further maintained in two ways. Firstly, captains should not try to defraud the muster by mustering men that did not belong to them, nor should they try to 'poach' men from other companies to make up their own. Secondly, the pillaging of other soldiers' forage or victuals, or goods brought into the camp by merchants or local inhabitants for sale, was forbidden. The latter was vital to maintain good relations with the local population. John of Gaunt's 1386–7 expedition to Spain started well since he issued the order that goods were to be bought at the sellers' price, but as soldiers were driven to live off the land through lack of pay, relations with the locals collapsed.

The allocation of quarters could cause friction both within the army and with the locals, so only the herbergeour, a company quarters officer, was to search out and allocate quarters. While this rule was not new, in 1370 the formidable Sir Robert Knollys laid down rules to arbitrate disputes over quarters, strengthened in Richard's ordinances, perhaps because of an incident in the 1380s. As the contingents were heading to muster at Newcastle, a dispute over quarters arose during which an archer in Sir Ralph Stafford's company killed a squire of Sir John Holland. Other rules dealt with the division of spoils and the management of ransomable prisoners, both of great importance for the common soldiers. Henry V built on these ordinances, adding in rules about camp followers and 'hygiene' rules about the disposal of carrion.

In the fifteenth century in France the commanders made attempts to balance the individual soldier's interest in booty with the need to maintain military cohesion and a reserve in battle. Men held in the reserve might become discontented, feeling that their chances of taking booty or ransomable prisoners were limited by their allotted tactical role. The ordinances issued by Thomas Montagu, Earl of Salisbury, in 1425 address these issues.[20] These state that the army should be divided up into 'feliships' made up of between five and seven men. Two or three of each group would remain under their captains' standard as a reserve, and to guard booty and prisoners, while the others were engaged in the assaults and raids on enemy towns and lands. Those held back around their standards were threatened not only with the loss of their share of the day's booty, but also with the promise that the whole 'feliship' would lose all of its booty as well, if they deserted their posts. At the end of the action, booty and prisoners were to be divided equally among the group. No doubt these groups were self-selecting, with men joining groups with others from their village or area, or with old comrades. Besides the obvious military value of this rule, it must have helped develop and maintain a sense of trust and co operation among the men, who would have been serving alongside some strangers even in the same retinue. But Salisbury in his ordinances was not only concerned with ensuring the cohesion of the army and the profitability of service for the soldiers. Since his army was operating as part of an Anglo-Burgundian force, there was the danger of friendly territory being pillaged; the English men at arms and archers in the force would have struggled to differentiate a Burgundian villager from a French villager. Large-scale pillaging of friendly areas could have undermined the slightly precarious alliance. To prevent this, severe punishments were set out in the ordinances.

The English military ordinances concentrated on the organisation and discipline of the forces, and assumed that all those present were competent soldiers with a common English and Welsh background, so included little provision for drill and tactical practice. The Burgundian military ordinances of Charles the Bold issued in 1471 did include such provisions, since they applied to armies that contained a large number of mercenaries who would have needed practice to meld together into individual units and work together in larger armies. There were training instructions for the lances (the basic components of the army made up of a man at arms, his page, a swordsman, three mounted archers, a crossbowman, a handgunner and a pikeman). 'In like manner [they must exercise] the archers and their horses, to get them used to dismounting and drawing their bows.' Within each lance the man at arms' page was to hold the archers' horses while they shot.[21]

THE ARCHER'S STATUS

One of the intangibles that would have affected the everyday experience of the English military archer was the level of respect shown them by their leaders. While kings, nobles and gentry used bows and arrows themselves for sport, they believed that only hand-to-hand fighting was honourable. But the English kings were pragmatic and soon understood the vital importance of competent archers in their armies. Both the Anglo-Saxons and the Vikings had competent military archers, but did not use them in battle-winning numbers, as far as we can tell. The importance of the Welsh archers is well known; the Norman marcher lords used them in their invasion of Ireland in 1175, having learnt to appreciate their value from the receiving end. When King John issued a writ summoning all landholders of whatever level to Dover to defend against an invasion threat, he dismissed the poorly armed peasant levies, retaining '…only the knights, servientes, and freemen along with the crossbowmen and archers.'[22]

It is not easy to get an impression of how the archers' leaders and employers viewed them. Inevitably there would have been a wide variety of estimations depending on the character and social status of the leader, and the archers' method of employment. In the fourteenth century, up to about 1360, at least half of the archers were raised through the array system. Most of these men would be tenants rather than landowners, holding their land by both free and unfree tenure. The archers in indentured retinues came from three sources; the leader's own household servants, from amongst the leader's family, neighbours and tenants, and from the ranks of the professional soldiers. Respect, even friendliness, might be expected from the leaders, depending on which source. By the middle of thirteenth century, those who were expected in the Assizes of Arms to serve as men at arms (£20 landholders), and indeed some of those who qualified to be knights, worked together with those who were expected to serve as archers (£2 landholders) in the tasks of local administration and politics such as the assizes and juries. This could have allowed them to build working relationships and mutual respect.

Richard II held his Cheshire archers in high regard. This retinue was very like the Imperial Roman Praetorian Guard in that it had a military role (in Richard's Irish expedition, for example), a quasi-political enforcement utility (in overawing the high court of parliament in September 1397) and at its core the responsibilities of a bodyguard. The latter core group within the retinue was made up of 312 archers divided into seven watches, each commanded by an esquire.[23] Richard was clearly concerned about competition from other employers for the services of good archers when he was building up this retinue, because in 1397 he issued a proclamation that no archer of the county could serve another lord until 2,300 men had been chosen for his retinue.[24] Richard's high opinion of these archers was not shared the contemporary chroniclers and the interests they represented. Even chroniclers generally sympathetic to Richard condemn the behaviour of the Cheshire men. Part of this was no doubt a feeling that these men, mostly ordinary peasants and townsmen but including some minor gentry, were getting above themselves: 'These iniquitous archers, in whom, above all others, the king had confidence, even entrusting the security of his person to them, whereby most of the kingdom was treated with disdain.'[25] But it also seems these men were arrogant and aggressive, whether pursuing the king's interests or their own. One of the more moderate descriptions is of

> …men of the utmost depravity who went about doing as they wished, assaulting, beating and plundering his subjects with impunity: wherever the king went, night and day, they stood guard over him, armed as if for

> war, committing adulteries, murders and countless other crimes; yet so inordinately did the king favour them that he would not listen to anyone who complained about them, indeed he would regard such people with loathing.[26]

The criticism of Richard's archers concentrated on both their behaviour and their social status. While some of them behaved thuggishly, it was also galling that Richard was relying on provincial gentry and peasants for support, protection and for his officials, rather than the more usual and more august noble circles.

This bad reputation did not ruin the status of archers as a a group in England, so long as they were employed against foreigners. The English successes in France in both Henry V's reign and Henry VI's minority restored their reputation. By the later fifteenth century, the perception that archers were central to England's military effort was so strong within the country that, when Edward IV was making aggressive gestures towards France in the 1470s, Parliament used the archers' daily wage rate of 6d as a measure of the amount of taxation that it would grant the king to fund the war. In 1472 the Commons agreed to provide the king with sufficient to pay the wages of 13,000 archers for one year. In doing this they followed a precedent set in 1453.[27]

As the development of the use of archers in battle-winning numbers from the 1330s onwards shows, the English kings and nobles were pragmatic in their approach to war; winning was the point, chivalry came second. But there is no reference to any nobleman using a bow in war in this period; the bow was still an ignoble weapon. Members of the royal family and the nobility used bows in their great enthusiasm for hunting. The records of the royal household for July 1334 show that Edward III paid Walter Daly 10/- compensation for having broken his bow, presumably either when shooting for sport or hunting.[28] This is a very generous payment when compared with the rate the Crown paid in this period for bows being added to the royal stores in the Tower of London and other places. (see *Equipping the Archers*). In 1390 Henry Bolingbroke bought a bow for 6/8d specifically as a gift for his father, John of Gaunt.[29] John of Gaunt enjoyed hunting, and, since he was 50 at the time of the gift, it was probably a hunting bow – and one of particularly fine quality given the price. In 1393 the collectors of customs for London were ordered to allow Hugh Damery, the servant of John, Duke of Brittany, to sail to Brittany with various goods, including '... two bows and three dozen arrows for the wood.'[30] Another example of a royal archer is Edward IV, for whom 'brode arrow hedes, shotyng gloves and strengs...' were bought '...for his disport.'[31] The mention of shooting gloves to protect the royal hands is interesting. In a description of the officers of Edward IV's household and their duties, among the 24 Yeomen of the Crown was one who was 'to kepe his dogges for the bowe.'[32] Most likely these were dogs that drove game out to be shot or brought it to bay, although they may have retrieved small game shot in the wood. This practical evidence of the nobility's enthusiasm for archery is strongly supported by the two great hunting manuals of the period, Gaston Phoebus, Count of Foix's *Book of the Hunt* and Edward, Duke of York's *The Master of Game*. The Count of Foix tells us more about the use of archery in hunting. In both books bows and arrows are mentioned in the context of 'bow and stable', that is, where the game is driven towards archers standing in prepared positions, and both mention all kinds of nobles, up to and including the king, taking part.[33]

Evidence for companies of archers being led by archers is rare. There was probably one in the Crecy campaign, a company of 10 archers from Rutland led by Henry Parker,[34] apparently raised through the array system. His surname suggests that he was an archer of above average competence because of his job and so was able to lead the men by example. Edward III's army of 1359 included two such companies, one of 80 mounted archers led by John Ward, the other of 20 mounted archers led by Guy de Brian.[35] At this time mounted archers tended to be men who were making military service a career choice, even if only for a few years, rather than arrayed men. Three such companies are recorded in 1370–1, when payments to Richard Archebald, Thomas de Faryndon and John Joce are recorded as 'wages for himself and his bowmen in the war.'[36] Another can be found in 1427, when Richard Millington offered directly to the Crown to serve with two other archers at a group wage of 17d per day, presumably believing that by serving the Crown directly they would keep more of their profits from booty and ransoms.[37]

Archers most commonly served in retinues led by a man at arms or someone else of higher status. The individual archers in a retinue probably signed indentures with the leader in the same way as the 34 archers signed directly with the Crown in 1415. The command structure is complicated in the army of 1415 by the presence of specialist companies of archers like those from Cheshire and Lancashire. As Curry comments 'What we would much like to know is whether the resulting companies of archers (ie the specialist companies) were kept separate, or whether they were divided up and assigned to other retinues.'[38] The same question applies to the archers who took out indentures directly with the Crown. In larger retinues the practice seems to have been for men at arms to lead bodies of archers. 'Even within the larger retinues it was common for archers to be assigned to particular men at arms. This reflects recruitment practice, but also had implications for discipline, since the men at arms were sometimes described as "masters", appropriate when archers were also their servants.'[39] So the firm impression is that while the military value of archers was appreciated, in general they were not appointed as captains even in large retinues. It seems that selected archers were designated to lead sub groups of archers, taking on the role of vintenar, commander of twenty, a position frequently mentioned in fourteenth century commissions of array. They may not have used the formal title, and certainly didn't receive any extra pay, in line with normal fourteenth-century practice. Archers were not considered suitable to lead companies. it was felt that to lead companies of soldiers, a man needed the financial and social status that came with being a man at arms. Throughout the period there was nothing to stop an archer 'promoting' himself to man at arms just by acquiring the necessary level of equipment, particularly once the professionalization of military service got under way. (Some examples of those archers who did better themselves in the fourteenth century can be found in *The Rewards of Military Service*.)

One demonstration of the social status of archers throughout the fourteenth and fifteenth centuries is found in how they were described in official documents. The records of the army that fought the Agincourt campaign used the following terms for men at arms and archers:[40]

	Term	**Meaning**
MEN AT ARMS	Homines ad arma	Men at arms
	Lancae	Lance
	Armiger	Esquire (literally bearing heraldic arms)
	Scutifer	Esquire (literally shield bearer, ie a knight's squire)
	Gentielx	Gentlemen
ARCHERS	Sagittarii	Archer
	Valetti	(literally a varlet or servant) Yeoman – a term becoming widely used by the fifteenth century to describe the upper levels of the peasantry

For both types of soldier, the terms used for them denote either their function, or their social status. It is clear that not all men at arms had heraldic arms; Thomas Montagu, Earl of Salisbury granted arms as rewards to some of his men.[41] The use of the term yeoman is ambiguous. Besides being used to describe a social status, it also described a category of servant, as in Yeomen of the Crown, and occasionally was used to describe archers. The Earl of Salisbury used the term in his 1425 ordinances to describe ordinary soldiers, including archers.[42] This use seems to have become more common in the fifteenth century and can be found in a record from 1448 in an order authorising money for the Marquis of Dorset's expedition to France: '…wages for 1000 yemenne archers, that is to say for eche of 6d by the day…'[43] There is another example from 1459 in the accounts records of Henry VI's reign, referring to the making of 3000 sheaves of arrows 'sufficient for yomene.'[44]

Fundamentally, there are two aspects to the value placed on the archers by their employers and paymasters. One is their straightforward military value in battle; they were potential battle winners from the fourteenth to the first half of the sixteenth centuries. The second is that they were very good value for money. Throughout the period archers were paid, at best, half the daily pay of men at arms, and regularly proved to be good close quarters fighters in the line of battle. These virtues combined to encourage the kings of England and other employers to modify the ratio of archers to men at arms within their retinues. There is plenty of evidence of archers knowing their own worth, some of which have been recounted. Other examples can be found in accounts of the battles of the period where archers showed pride and initiative – not always successfully, it must be said. There is no evidence that they felt they were lowly 'battle line fodder', present to provide the nobles and gentry with an environment in which they could show off their skills, on the contrary, they knew that in battle they were as effective as any noble.

NOTES

1 Newhall. R A (1924) p.250, p.251 and p.252.
2 Allmand C T (1973) p.71.
3 Allmand, C T (1997) p.130.
4 *POPC vol.2* p.184.
5 Lucas, H S (1929). *The Low Countries and the Hundred Years War 1329–47*. Ann Arbor, University of Michigan Press. p.432.
6 Lucas, H S (1929) p.525.
7 Russell, P E (1955). *English Intervention in Spain and Portugal*. Oxford, Clarendon Press. p.319.
8 *POPC. vol.6* p.11.
9 *CCR 1380* p 388.
10 *CCR 1381* p.485.
11 Allmand C T (1973) p.69-70.
12 Curry, A (2005) p.69.
13 *CCR* 1430 p.74 and *CCR* 1433 p.267 respectively.
14 *POPC vol.5* p.80, p.205-6 and p.302 respectively.
15 There is an explicit example of men having half their wages paid in victuals in 1437. See *POPC vol.5* p.19.
16 *POPC* vol.5 p.198-9.
17 Ayton, A and Preston, P (2005). p.68.
18 Ayton, A and Preston, P (2005). p.71. Although it has been suggested recently that it was military practicality, that is the need to have the army ready for battle, that motivated this rather than piety.
19 This discussion of Richard II's ordinances is based on Keen, M in Archer, R E and Walter, S, Editors, (1995).
20 Warner, M (1998) p.146–73.
21 Vaughan, R (1973). *Charles the Bold*. London, Longmans p.210.

22 Powicke, M (1962). p.59-60.
23 For a thorough account of Richard's Cheshire archers see Gillespie, J L (1974).
24 Castor, H (2000). *The King, the Crown and the Duchy of Lancaster*. Oxford. p.11n.
25 *Vita Ricardi Secundi* quoted in Castor, H. (2000) p.13n.
26 Adam of Usk quoted in Castor, H. (2000) p.13n.
27 Ross, C (1974). p.215.
28 Ayton, A and Preston P (2005) p.352.
29 Toulmin Smith L (1894). *Expeditions to Prussia and the Holy Land made by Henry Earl of Derby*. London, Camden Society p.31.
30 *CCR* 1393 p.57.
31 Somerville, R (1953). p.235.
32 Myers, A R (editor) (1959). *The Household of Edward I*. Manchester University Press. p.116.
33 There are also references to women taking part as archers, mostly late in the period under discussion. There are a very small number of earlier manuscript pictures of women hunting with the bow.
34 Ayton, A and Preston P (2005) p.223.
35 Ayton, A (1994) p.14. Though Guy de Brian may not have been an archer; a Guy de Brienne was Admiral of the Fleet in 1370–1.
36 Devon, F (editor) (1835). *The Issue Roll of Thomas de Brantingham*. London, J. Rodwell, 1835. p.14.
37 Bennett, M J (1983). *Community, Class and Careerism*. Cambridge University Press. p.176.
38 Curry, A (2000) p.422.
39 Curry, A (2005) p.66.
40 Curry, A (2005) p.64–5.
41 Warner, M (1998) p.153–4.
42 Warner, M (1998) p.164.
43 Stevenson, J (1861-4). *Letters and Papers Illustrative of the Wars of the English in France in the Reign of King Henry VI*. London. vol.1 p.480.
44 Stevenson, J (1861–4) vol.2 p.511.

English Archery in Foreign Service

Edward III's sustained military activity from the 1330s to about 1360 firmly established him as a king of England admired both at home and abroad, in contrast to his father's troubled reign. It enabled him to pursue his dynastic ambitions in Europe. His successes greatly enhanced the military reputation of the English in Europe, and led to the development of a substantial group of men who, for some years, made soldiering their main occupation. While this was the expected profession for knights and other reasonably wealthy men, an increasing number of these men were archers from the ungenteel classes. English and Welsh archers built and maintained their reputation as potential battle winners in the fourteenth and fifteenth centuries in the service of the English kings in their foreign campaigns, including those in Scotland, which was an independent sovereign country throughout this period.

Eventually, Edward made peace with his main enemies, France and Scotland, and in his old age was disinclined to restart the wars. Nor did his successor Richard II pursue large-scale continental military adventures, and it was left to Edward's great grandson, Henry V, to resume the wars and re-establish the reputation of the English archer. This relative calm left many archers at a loose end. Throughout the fourteenth and fifteenth centuries there was concern about the threat to the peace of England that unemployed soldiers represented, so there were frequent efforts to encourage them to find service abroad. Some of the archers of course wanted to profit from the archery skills they had practised so hard to develop, so they sought employment where they could if England was at peace.

Foreign service fell into three broad types: serving as a freelance mercenary; service with allies of the English kings, encouraged or supported by them; and taking part in crusades. It will become clear in the following account that the distinctions between these three types of service were often blurred.

MERCENARY SERVICE

The involvement of English archers in mercenary activity in this period tended to be as part of a fairly well established company. In times of official peace between England and France, particularly in the later fourteenth century, companies of soldiers formed, often under the same leaders as in the king's service. There were no indentures within the company. They made their living either by becoming freebooters living off the land, commonly in France, or by taking part in campaigns on a contractual basis.

From about 1358 until the mid 1360s the 'Grand Companies' ravaged France and threatened northern Spain, Northern Italy and the borders of Imperial Germany. Many of the fighters were Gascon, but there were also large numbers of English, Bretons, Navarrese and Flemings. These 'Grand Companies' were fairly loose cooperatives, made up of smaller companies that tended to come and go as suited them. With the exception of the Company led by Robert Knollys, there were relatively few English companies within the 'Grand Companies', and English archers were not a large part of them. English soldiers, and archers in particular, seem to have found other freelance service.

At the same time, Charles, Count of Evreux, King of Navarre, whose claim to the French throne had been disallowed by the Salic Law pressed his claim for the French throne with English support. In 1358 Robert Knollys led a company of English and Bretons out of Britanny through the Loire valley, and took Auxerre in January 1359. This was definitely freebooting, since there is no evidence that Edward III was behind Knollys' expedition. Although he fought under the king of Navarre's banner, according to Froissart, Knollys said that he fought 'simply for himself'. Whatever the case, this proved to be a very profitable expedition for all concerned, the booty from Auxerre alone amounting to as much as 50,0000 moutons (about £120,800).[1]

Charles established many garrisons in Picardy and southwards into the Ile de France to encircle Paris, a number of which were largely English and had English captains. Since Edward III kept his distance politically from Charles' activities, these Englishmen were serving more as mercenaries than as forces under the direction and with the authority of the English Crown. They lived off the land rather than being paid in any regular way. Edward III made efforts to bring these Englishmen under his control in line with the Treaty of Bretigny of 1360 between England and France. The relative peace resulting from this Treaty meant that many English fighting men, not to mention Gascons and Bretons in English service, had no regular employment, which exacerbated the sufferings of the French population, who were already enduring the depredations of the Companies.

In 1362, the simmering dispute between the Counts of Armagnac and Foix broke out into open warfare. Both Counts attempted to hire the mercenary companies that were still plaguing France. Armagnac was the more successful in that he recruited a much larger army, strong in cavalry. However, the Count of Foix recruited more English troops, no doubt from unemployed men in Aquitaine, including John Amory's company and about 600 archers. These archers were probably a mixture of English archers and local men, since the Count of Foix is known to have developed a company of archers from among his own men.[2] The archers were the decisive factor at the battle of Launac, shooting into the flank of the attacking heavy cavalry in what was almost a re-enactment of Poitiers.

Edward the Black Prince's campaign in Spain in 1367 to put King Pedro back on the throne of Castile was in many ways a mercenary expedition. While a treaty between the kings of England and Castile had been signed in 1362, it is probable that the real motivations for the campaign were Edward's need for money to maintain his Principality in Aquitaine and fear of the French establishing an ally on the throne of Castile.[3] Edward built up an army of Gascons, Bretons and English, including as many as 2400 archers, in part made up of contingents led by his brother John of Gaunt and the veteran captain Sir Robert Knollys. Edward was militarily successful in his campaign, winning a victory at Najera, where the English archers devastated the light Spanish cavalry and shot the horses of the heavy Castilian cavalry. However, Edward was much less successful in both his financial aims – since King Pedro paid little of what he had promised – and his political aims, because Pedro was killed two years later. The scale of Edward's debts after this campaign makes it probable that the individual archers did quite well from this adventure. They seem to have received at least some of their pay and had opportunities to gain booty from the battlefield and share in ransoms from the large number of prisoners taken.

As the Treaty of Bretigny broke down, English military activity in France was sponsored by the king again. However, as he aged, Edward III became much more reluctant to spend money, so he looked for ways to reduce the cost to the English Crown of any fighting. He had already been accused by the French in the 1360s of encouraging English companies to serve in France as freebooters, living off the land. At that time he ordered the English companies to stop their activities, which they did. This was not a sign that he had been encouraging them, but rather that the English commanders of these largely English companies regarded Edward as their liege, and so owed him obedience. But in 1370 he saw clear financial advantages in encouraging this sort of activity, when he ordered Sir Robert Knollys to raise a force of 4000 men, half of them archers. The Crown agreed to pay Knollys' men for thirteen weeks, or for the length of time it took them to reach France after leaving their homes, whichever was the longer. Once in France they were to be self financing.

Knollys set off from Calais in a spectacular chevauchee and initially the troops achieved self sufficiency by taking booty and ransoms from towns and individuals. This wasn't just banditry, although it was necessary to provide reward for the troops; it also had the important strategic purpose of drawing French attention and efforts away from Aquitaine. The self-financing approach of the army led to disputes and mistrust between Knollys and his captains, one of whom, Sir John Minsterworth, referred to Knollys as an old brigand. As a result, despite the success it had enjoyed so far, the army fractured into its separate retinues, behaving like smaller versions of the 'Grand Companies' of earlier years. Bertrand du Guesclin was able to inflict heavy defeats on several of these small bands, but not on the troops who stayed with Sir Robert Knollys.[4] In the end Edward III's parsimony was a false economy, in that it ensured that the objective of Knollys' army was to get as much booty as possible rather than to conquer and hold land and so help to re-establish his claim to France.

At this time English professional soldiers, including archers, began to look beyond their old campaigning grounds in France for opportunities to earn a living. Italy in the last half of the fourteenth century was a geographical entity made up of warring city states, the Papal States and the kingdom of Naples. All these states needed their own armies, for self defence at the very least. The more ambitious rulers, such as those of Florence, Venice and Milan, often built up large armies to overawe the neighbouring cities and defend their interests. These armies were nearly always a combination of militias and levies from the cities themselves and mercenary companies under contract, the *Condottieri*. While the majority of the foreign troops were German, there were also Englishmen fighting there, most famously Sir John Hawkwood, who served various employers in Italy for over thirty years. Naturally, these opportunities attracted English fighting men, and their reputation would make them attractive to potential employers. The contract system worked like the English indenture system in that an agreement was made for a company of prescribed size and composition to serve under particular leaders – this is important, the employers wanted both fighting men and competent captains, some of whom actually led their employers' military efforts for the period of the contract – for a specified period at specified wages. There was a muster at the beginning of the contract where any adjustments to the terms could be made.

The White Company was the first mainly English company to appear in Italy, in 1361. Its officers included John Hawkwood (not yet knighted) and Andrew Belmont. This company brought English tactics (dismounted men at arms fighting defensively with archer support) to Italian warfare, and that peculiarly English weapon, the longbow. While Hawkwood's companies and tactics over the years became less English, he could still attract English archers, since in 1387 600 English archers made a decisive contribution to his victory in the battle of Castagnaro. However, in the long term, English archers did not have a significant effect on Italian warfare, since '…gradually their numbers declined as further recruits from the north were not forthcoming.'[5]

Hawkwood's successes led other Italian city states to try to employ English soldiers, including archers. In 1379 the rulers of Lucca permitted their agent to offer monthly rates of up to 12 florins per lance and 7 florins per archer. The agent got into hard-nosed negotiations with a company of English soldiers, who not only demanded these rates – which were generous – but additional payments at the start of the contract. The archers would receive each month the equivalent of about 19/- sterling (assuming these were Florentine florins, widely used), perhaps 20% more than a mounted archer would receive in the service of the English king.[6]

In 1388, a time of peace between England and France, the Brigade of St. George, one of the companies of mercenaries looking for employment in Italy, established their camp near Ancona. As the name suggests, it was made up of Englishmen, about 800, including about 260 archers. The Brigade's representative, Sir Robert de Felton, was negotiating service with John of Moravia, Patriarch of Aquilera.[7]

The mighty Venice needed soldiers to maintain and defend both its borders in Italy and its shipping and trading empire in the Adriatic and Eastern Mediterranean. In 1390, the Englishman John Chaplet was captain of the Venetian spears and archers in the territory of Coneglino. It is likely that these archers were Venetian militia rather than English archers.[8] In 1434 the Venetian Doge Francesco Foscari:

> ...[took] into his service Sir Walter of England, knight with 100 archers himself being included in this number, and in which he shall have two spears, they to comprise mounted bowmen, the rest of the archers to be footmen. For the two spears he is to receive the same stipend as the Doge's other men at arms, with no additional pay for himself. The foot archers to have 15 light livres each per month. The archers both mounted and on foot to have bows and all other necessary and usual weapons. These archers must be from England, Ireland or from other subjects of the king of England, and not from foreign parts. When Sir Walter has engaged them and had them reviewed in arms he shall receive two months pay.[9]

While the record does not make it clear, it is likely Sir Walter had his company ready to satisfy this contract, since finding unemployed English archers in Italy by this date would have been difficult; the heyday of the great North European mercenary companies in Italy was past. But what were these men that he did have doing in Italy? England's war with France was hot (although the English forces involved were fairly small when compared with Henry V's armies). They may have been professionals who had heard stories of the rich opportunities in Italy, or were disillusioned with the relatively unprofitable grind of service in France at this time. Significantly, these men made up a company of archers without men at arms. The Venetian Doge seemed to be hiring specialists to support his existing troops, in the same way Charles of Burgundy did in the 1470s.

The presence of English archers as mercenaries in Italy may have provided some stimulus to the Italian merchants in the development of their share of the bowstave trade. As will be made clear in a later chapter, the presence of these mercenary archers did not create the trade, since the Italians were already supplying some staves to the northern markets in the second half of the fourteenth century, but they may well have encouraged the trade's expansion.

English mercenaries could end up in unusual places, such as the Hungarian border fortress of Torcsvar (now Bran Castle in Romania) where they are recorded as part of the Garrison of Louis the Great of Hungary. These men probably included some archers.

On at least two occasions English archers are found fighting in the armies of the Flemish city states against their Burgundian overlords. In 1408 there were 100 English archers in the Liege army defeated by John the Fearless, Duke of Burgundy, at the battle of Orthee. In 1453 there were some English archers in the Ghent army that Philip the Good, John's successor, defeated at Gavere.[10] We can speculate about what motivated these men. This could have been straightforward mercenary service, the men being in Flanders at the right time. In 1408 the English king was not pursuing his French wars, and in 1453, after the defeats suffered by the English in Normandy, there may well have been English archers displaced from France, who as professional soldiers had no reason to go back to England. However, it is also possible that these men may have been more principled; in each case the Flemish cities were trying to defend their relative independence against the efforts of the Burgundian dukes to incorporate them more closely into their fiefdom.

Some Englishmen served in the Burgundian armies as individuals or as part of small groups of mercenaries, rather than in larger bodies approved by the English Crown. When John the Fearless was engaged in a civil war in France with the Armagnacs, his rivals amongst the French royal dukes, he regularly employed English mercenaries. In 1411-12 he used contingents in sporadic fighting, and in 1414 his garrisons at Soissons and Arras included many Englishmen. The mercenaries in these garrisons were effective, since Soissons was able to surrender on terms and Arras successfully resisted the Armagnac siege. There are indications that this service was not openly encouraged by the English king, one being that in 1412 the Armagnacs also used English mercenaries against Duke John. Another powerful indication is that at the same time, the Duke of Clarence, one of Henry IV's sons, took a force to France to help the Armagnacs. Unfortunately, no sooner had they arrived in France than the Armagnacs made peace with the Burgundians. This left Clarence and his men in a difficult position; they maintained their honour by marching through France to the English-held lands of Aquitaine. Once there, some of the English were offered mercenary service in Spain, and some certainly crossed the Pyrennes, since there is an account of the brave resistance of an English garrison at Balaguer in 1413.[11] But the numbers involved were small, and it seems that most of Clarence's men stayed in the service of the English king in Aquitaine, or returned home to England.

In the fifteenth century there is much less evidence of the professional companies of English and Welsh troops that made up the English armies in France going freelance. In part this was because of the strict disciplinary reputations of Henry V and the Duke of Bedford, in part because Bedford in particular understood the importance of prompt payment of wages to the maintenance of discipline. The situation deteriorated to some degree after

Bedford's death in September 1435. That year John Ap Rhys and Edmund Dardeuf led a company of 120 men in the service of Henry VI as a field force charged with containing the French based in Dieppe. By 1437 Ap Rhys and his men seem to have been acting as freelances when they billeted themselves on the town of Orbec in Normandy. The English administration could not tolerate this independent action, which most certainly would have damaged relations with the local population, and so Lord Scales was sent to forcibly expel Ap Rhys. It is unclear what happened to the survivors.

Despite their battle-winning capabilities, there is little evidence of mercenary service by English archers. There are a number of possible reasons. The need for them to be used in large numbers to be effective was one; small numbers were only effective in small battles or in garrisons. They also had to be employed by a commander who understood the tactical use of archers, not least the importance of dismounted men at arms who could form a battle line to shelter the archers. Some of those hiring mercenaries may not have wished to deal with 'non genteel' soldiers, and archers, by definition, were not genteel. As a consequence, most of the examples we find are of English company commanders being hired with their company, as was the English practice.

A late example of this can be found in the career of Lord Woodville. In 1486 he led a company including 100 archers to Spain to fight against the Moors. He and his men impressed their hosts with their doughtyness in battle and their capacity for drinking. While this expedition may have had the support of Henry VII, the one Woodville made in 1489 to Brittany most certainly did not. While Henry was negotiating peace with Charles VIII of France, Woodville went to Brittany with between 700 and 800 men, mostly archers, against Henry's express orders. The Bretons were determined to exploit the impact of having these English soldiers in their army to the maximum, and about twice as many of them put on the cross of St George as there were English archers, to disguise the relatively small size of the English contingent. It was to no avail since the Bretons were defeated by a French army at St. Aubin du Cormier. Woodville and his men were wiped out, in part because the French commanders had instructed that no quarter was to be offered the English (or the unlucky Bretons wearing the cross of St George), and in part because the French army included a contingent of Swiss mercenary infantry who rarely offered quarter in any case. This provides a clear demonstration of the vulnerability of English archers – however determined – if they were not adequately supported by other troops; a circumstance that seems to have been more likely in mercenary service.

ALLIED SERVICE

The practice of states fighting their wars by proxy, through other states or powers, in the way that the USA and USSR did in the second half of the twentieth century, is not new. There are examples from both the Greek and

Roman periods. It became relatively common in the fourteenth century, and was one of the important mechanisms whereby kings could allow ambitious subjects scope to serve both their own and their liege lords' interests.

In the 1330s and 1340s Edward III started sending companies of English soldiers abroad, and actively approved the recruitment of similar forces for foreign service, without them being under his command. The earliest example is the little army of perhaps 1500 men, more than half of whom were archers, that won the battle of Dupplin Moor in 1332, when Edward III was not prepared openly to support Edward Balliol's claim to the Scottish throne.[12] Balliol's army had formed a line on high ground at the head of a valley, with archers projecting out to the flanks and the men at arms in the centre, all dismounted. Lord Robert Bruce's army, superior in numbers but badly armoured, was all-but destroyed by the clouds of arrows that descended. Those not hit by the arrows were crushed underfoot by their own men as they converged on the centre to escape the maelstrom. The deployment of men in this way would be a feature of English victories for at least a hundred years.

Edward III also allowed and encouraged English archers to serve under Flemish captains when William van Huse and Peter van den Hovene were sent to Oudenarde to maintain security there in 1342. English archers continued to serve in Flanders in the defence of the country, under both local and English captains. In 1346, while Edward himself was marching across northern France, Henry of Flanders led an invasion force into north east France. While this force was largely made up of Flemish levies it included a small English force of 250 archers and a few men at arms under Hugh Hastings. This expedition had mixed fortunes at first under Henry's command, but, once reinforced with a few hundred Englishmen under the Earl of Warwick, it became effective and highly profitable, with the sack of Therounne and Ruhout and the devastation of the surrounding areas.

Once the military reputation of the English was established, allies of the English king would often ask for military help. This help might be asked for in a dynastic struggle, as in Portugal in the 1380s, or to maintain a hold on fiefdoms, as was the case with the Duke of Burgundy. In 1384 Jaoa, Regent of Portugal (he very soon became King) sent envoys to Richard II who eventually granted permission for them to recruit soldiers in England.[13] This recruiting went very slowly, probably raising about 800 men, mainly archers. They seem to have been difficult to discipline but were determined fighters. Not only did those who landed in Lisbon have to run the gauntlet of Castilian galleys, but the group as a whole made a useful contribution at the Battle of Alberuoga. This was mercenary service with open approval from the English Crown. These troops were often recruited by the employer through agents in England. When either the the agent or the employer had a respected military reputation, such as Charles the Bold for example, this sort of recruitment was more successful. The English kings found it useful to allow the employment of reasonable numbers of English infantry abroad throughout this period, both as part of an active foreign policy and as a way of keeping experienced fighting men occupied and keep them from threatening the peace at home.

English archers fought for Philip the Good, the third great Duke of Burgundy, but in much larger numbers against him. The reason was a complicated dynastic struggle. Jacqueline of Bavaria, married to Humphrey Duke of Gloucester, was fighting Philip of Burgundy for control of parts of the Low Countries. There were English archers in her army defeated by Philip at Brouwershaven in 1426.[14] In 1436 Duke Humphrey himself supported his wife leading a chevauchee through western Flanders, which, while it may not have advanced her cause at all, was very profitable for the soldiers involved, who returned to Calais 'laden with plunder'.[15] Philip the Good hired individual English archers such as the Richard Stanley who received payments in 1459 and served again in 1462.[16]

The last of the great Valois Dukes of Burgundy, Charles the Bold, employed more English archers than any of his three predecessors. This came about through his own military enthusiasm, lack of military employment opportunities in England and active support for his recruitment efforts by the English Crown. Charles understood English tactics, knowing that the English archers needed to be supported and protected by heavy infantry in the battle line, and he used pikemen in this role. In 1467 he was allowed to raise up to 2000 archers. By early October about 400 men had arrived in Burgundy. At the end of the month they gained high praise from Commyns when they were involved in the Battle of Brustem, where they were among the archers who fought their way into the Liegeois lines and helped Charles to defeat the army of Liege. These archers were paid 15 francs a month, about 32/-. This would certainly have drawn men to Burgundian service since it was about double the English Crown rate and the Dukes had a reputation for paying wages regularly most of the time. The level of equipment they were expected to find for Burgundian service was specified in the military ordinances Charles issued at Abbeville in 1471. These concerned the organisation of 1250 lances of the ordinance, mercenaries making up a standing army. Each lance seems to have been made up of a man at arms, his page, a swordsman and three mounted archers with a crossbowman, a handgunner and a pikeman, all on foot. The archers were expected to come to the review with a bow, two and half dozen arrows (ie a sheaf), a long two-handed sword (it is unlikely that this meant a heavy two-handed sword like the one used by the German Landsknechts, but more probably what was often called a hand and a half sword) and a dagger. At their first review they would be given a uniform coat of blue and white with a red St. Andrews cross on it.[17] This level of equipment was similar to what was expected of a professional archer in the service of the English king at the time, although the sword may be of higher standard.

Even larger numbers of English soldiers, many of whom were archers, joined Charles the Bold's army in 1475, when about 2000 remained on the continent rather than return home. They had come to France in Edward IV's invading army, and, when he made peace with the king of France, they took up employment with the Duke of Burgundy, no doubt with Edward's explicit approval. Charles had encouraged them to join his army saying '…that they might just as well stay with him and fight the French as massacre each other in England.'[18] Charles was so willing to hire English troops, particularly archers, because like the Swiss mercenaries of the time they had a reputation for being reliable and militarily effective. In 1473 at the siege of Nijmegen and in 1474 at the siege of Neuss, where about 2000 Englishmen served, mostly archers, they distinguished themselves in his service. Although you could argue that it was the mutiny by the English archers in the garrison of Nancy in October 1476, almost certainly over the lack of pay, which led to its fall. This necessitated Charles's hurried attempt to retake the city, which set the scene for the battle of Nancy in January 1477 in which he was killed. Before the disaster at Nancy the English served him well throughout 1476, despite defeats at Grandison in March and at Murten in June. In the latter battle they were among the troops that attempted to delay the flank attack by the Swiss that turned the Burgundian positions. The English archers with other Burgundian troops and some artillery tried to hold a hedge line, an echo of those tactics used by English archers in their glory days in France in the fourteenth century. They failed to hold back the determined Swiss infantry because of lack of numbers. There were at least ten companies of English archers, nominally 100-strong, in the army that besieged Nancy in the winter of 1476-7 and were destroyed in battle there.

In 1472, at the same time as a number of English archers found employ in Burgundian service, Edward IV also sent 2000 archers under a Gascon, Lord Duras, to support Duke Francis of Brittany in his struggles with the French king.[19]

The death of Charles the Bold at Nancy did not mark the end of service by English archers in Burgundian armies. Effective numbers of them continued until 1481, serving in the armies of Charles the Bold's daughter, Margaret of Burgundy, and her husband, Maximilian of Austria. A leading figure among these men was Thomas Everingham, who probably came from a gentry family in Yorkshire.[20] He served in the Burgundian armies before the battle of Nancy, and in February 1477, just a month after the disaster at Nancy, he was leading about 100 English archers in a skirmish near Crespin. The weather was poor and Jean Molinet wrote in his Chronicle that 'their arrows flew as thick as the snow was falling.'[21] He and his men continued to earn favourable reports when in the following year he led just 80 English archers in a largely Flemish force that defeated the French at Izegetem. The following year he had clearly been recruiting, since he led about 500 mainly English archers in Maximilian's army, which won a hard fought victory over the French at Guingatte. These archers must have been significant in the victory, since it was won by Maximilian's infantry after his cavalry had been defeated by the French.

Edward IV's support for Maximilian and Margaret was discreet because he did not want to jeopardise his pension from Louis of France, but in 1480 he was persuaded to show more overt support. Everingham, now Sir Thomas, and two colleagues, Sir John Middleton and Sir John Driffield, were allowed to recruit two companies of 15 men at arms and 750 archers in England. The archers were to be paid 6d per day and receive six weeks pay (£1/4/6d) before they left England. Everingham had 15 men at arms and 670 archers under his command in the Low Countries in December. Given his military experience and reputation in Burgundy's service, Everingham may have been more successful in recruiting than his colleagues. This seems to be confirmed by the fact that Middleton returned to England in March 1481 with 22 men at arms and 300 archers. However, it seems likely that the English archers deserted in some numbers because they did not find service under Maximilian attractive. Their main work was various 'police actions' overawing dissidents in the Flemish towns. By April 1481 Maximilian decided to reduce his armies, in part because he was short of money, and Everingham and 120 archers were paid off. Maximilian got good value from his English archers, but they didn't feel the same about their own rewards, despite Maximilian being a punctual paymaster. The English archers probably expected more booty and ransoms.

CRUSADING

Most of the English crusading activity in this period was in north east Europe in support of the Teutonic Knights, and varied in scale from individual knights serving for both spiritual and mercenary reasons, to large expeditions, some with royal support, such as that of Henry Bolinbroke, Duke of Lancaster in 1390. More Englishmen went on crusade in the Baltic when truces or peace treaties had been agreed in the Hundred Years War than at times of declared hostility between England and France. As a result the main periods of activity were 1347-52, 1362-8 and 1390-8, with the 1360s showing the most sustained effort. When magnates like Bolinbroke went on crusade they took a retinue just as they would when serving the English king. At least some of the retinue members were paid for their service, others served for reward in heaven. In 1390 Bolinbroke paid wages to some archers for service 'extra curia', away from the court. These include John Bodenhale, who received 23 days pay at 12d per day and John Prendergast, who received 19 days pay at 8d per day. Also, a knight, John Elman, collected wages for three unnamed archers for 21 days service at 12d per day. These wage rates are generous, compared with the Crown rates of the time, perhaps including a food and lodging allowance because the archers were serving away from the court.[22] Henry's archers proved useful, enabling an opposed crossing of the river Wilia and helping to take the civilian settlement at Vilna.

Despite such demonstrations of the power of the English bow in the hands of experienced archers the knights of the Teutonic Order did not develop a body of longbowmen, preferring instead to rely on the crossbow. This is surprising, given the Order's involvement in the trade in bowstaves and their practice of employing mercenaries.

In 1394 Pope Boniface IX urged a new crusade against the threat posed by the Ottoman Turks who were pressing toward Hungary. A magnificent army was assembled, with an English contingent initially led by the aged John of Gaunt, a large noble French contingent, and the army of King Sigismund of Hungary. The crusader army that finally faced the Ottoman army under Sultan Bayezid I at Nicopolis in 1396 contained perhaps 1000 Englishmen under John Beaufort, one of Gaunt's illegitimate sons. A good number of the English were Cheshire men who had been recruited by Gaunt to serve in Aquitaine, after they had been part of an uprising against the peace proposed between France and England in 1393, so it seems reasonable to assume they included archers. Very few of them seem to have survived the defeat – or maybe the execution of some 3000 prisoners ordered by the victorious Ottoman Sultan Bayezid I, in retaliation for the earlier massacre of prisoners of the sacked city of Rahovo by the French. Nicopolis was the last full-scale crusade of the Middle Ages.

In 1409 there are instructions to customs officials of London to allow a knight, Henry FitzHugh, to take 13 bows, 38 sheaves of arrows and six dozen bowstrings to Rhodes '...for the furnishing of the castle of Seintpier [or Saumpera, this seems to have been a new Hospitaller castle at Bodrum][23] against the Saracen enemy in those parts.'[24] This stock of equipment makes up a small balanced store with sufficient arrows and strings to suggest a serious experiment in the use of English military archery in Asia Minor. There is no surviving record of the men who were going to use these bows, but it is not unreasonable to suggest some at least were English.

It seems that crusading may have been more attractive than serving in France, since in 1429 Cardinal Beaufort raised 250 men at arms and 2000 archers who served either voluntarily or for wages in his second crusade against the Hussites. This was despite neither Convocation nor the royal council offering financial help. Indeed, the Crown was trying to recruit men at the time with limited success to support the siege of Orleans, and had to order the Cardinal that he '... ne shal in eny wyse moeve ne sture those serving in France.'[25] It seems that the spiritual rewards of crusading were very attractive, although, a further attraction, the Cardinal may have been a more reliable paymaster.

The English archers in foreign service seem to have fared no better or worse than any other class of professional soldier. They did it because the pay was good, often above English rates, and in general they served their employers well. However, unlike the other great mercenary infantry of the time, the Swiss, they did not bring about a tactical revolution. It was the long term investment in practice necessary to become an effective archer using the English bow that limited the effect it had on European tactics. Meanwhile, other people copied the Swiss in their use of mobile 'phalanxes' of infantry armed with polearms; the most effective were the Germans in their organisation of the Landsknechts – and perhaps the most tragic were the Scots under James IV in the disaster at Flodden.

NOTES

1 Sumption, J (1999). p.384
2 Strickland M and Hardy R (2005). p.245
3 Sumption, J (1999) chapter 12, for a full account of the events behind this campaign.
4 Fowler, K (2001). *Medieval Mercenaries vol. 1 The Great Companies*. Oxford, Blackwell. p.289-90
5 Mallett, M (1974). *Mercenaries and their Masters*. London, Bodley Head. p.37 and Castagnaro p.54
6 Stonor Saunders, F (2004). *Hawkwood: the Diabolical Englishman*. London. Faber & Faber, p.72-3.. Conversion based on figures on p.592–3 Sumption, J (1999)
7 *Calendar of State Papers; Venetian 1202-1509* p.31
8 *Calendar of State Papers; Venetian 1202-1509* p.32
9 *Calendar of State Papers; Venetian 1202-1509* p.64
10 Vaughan, R (1966). *John the Fearless*. London, Longman p.61 and Vaughan, R (1970). *Philip the Good*. Harlow, Longman p.329 respectively.
11 Goodman, A (2005) p.86
12 Strickland, M and Hardy, R (2005) p.182-3
13 Goodman, A (1992) p.115
14 Vaughan, R (1975). *Valois Burgundy*. London, Allen Lane. p.132
15 Vaughan R (1975) p.152–3
16 Ballard, M (1990). *An Expedition of English Archers to Liege in 1467 and the Anglo Burgundian Marriage Alliance*. Nottingham Medieval Studies. xxxiv 1990 p.154
17 Vaughan, R (1973). *Charles the Bold*. London. Longman p.206
18 Vaughan, R (1973). p.217
19 Ross, C (1974). *Edward IV*. London. p.206
20 See Meek, E L (2001). *The Career of Sir Thomas Everingham 'Knight of the North' in the Service of Maximilian Duke of Austria*. Historical Research 74
21 Meek, E L (2001). p.241
22 Toulmin-Smith, L. (1894) *Expeditions to Prussia and the Holy Land made by Henry Earl of Derby*. p.122 and p.124 respectively.
23 Lutterell, A (1998). '*English contributions to the Hospitaller Castle at Bodrum*' in Nicholson, H (editor) (1998)
24 *CCR* 1409 p.2–3
25 *POPC* vol.3 p.337

The Rewards of Military Service for Archers

The rewards archers expected for their service remained the same throughout the period. Firstly there was money from pay, the spoils of war and rewards for good service. Secondly, for the professional, career soldiers, especially from the second half of the fourteenth century onwards, military service presented opportunities for advancement, particularly if you were poor – like some of the Welsh archers for example, or a younger son who would inherit little or nothing. Thirdly, as in every era, the adventure of military service would attract some men. Finally there were legal benefits: those who had committed even serious crimes were recruited on the promise of a pardon, and men could get protection from legal action while serving in the royal armies. These various rewards were the incentives that helped to balance the demands of the Assizes of Arms and the Statute of Winchester.

RATE OF PAY

Edward I, and less successfully Edward II, had made extensive use of the feudal system to raise armies for their campaigns. In doing this they put particular pressure on those wealthy enough to be eligible to be knights and also raised large numbers of conscripted infantry. However, both realised that large numbers of infantry alone, with no real selection, was neither militarily efficient nor good value for money. In their reigns there was an increasing tendency for all classes of soldier to serve without pay in England, but to claim pay once they crossed to Wales, Scotland or further afield. The first Parliament of Edward III's reign in 1327 saw their opportunity with a new young king, and, having discussed the matter at length, petitioned the King not to follow his forbears' practice. A consensus arose in the following years that conscripted men could only be required to serve without pay in the case of foreign invasion, and with the consent of Parliament. But if they were paid then they were expected to serve wherever they were sent. However, the real change in the practice of raising armies was the rapid development of the use of indentures to raise companies of soldiers.

Some examples of the basic rates of pay for archers in this period:

Date	Leader	Pay per day	Description of service
1277	Edward I	4d	100 Archers from Macclesfield to act a royal guard. (ordinary infantry paid 2d per day)
1285	Edward I	2d	John of Helpeston, Richard of Meleford, Robert Squier, Nicholas of Selewode and William le Wilde – king's archers[1]
1296	Nicholas Fermbaud, Constable of Bristol Castle	1d	Archers guarding Welsh prisoners (crossbowmen on same duty got 3d)[2]
1334	Edward III	6d	Mounted archers from Cheshire serving as 'King's archers'[3]
1340s	Edward III & Black Prince	6d	Mounted archers
1340s	Edward III & Black Prince	3d	Foot archers[4]
1355	Black Prince	6d	300 Cheshire men 'the best and most skilful archers' (Black Prince's description to his officials) raised through the Array system
1355	Black Prince	3d	Archers from Flint[5]
1360	Edward III?	6d	John Musard, a Commissioner of Array for Staffordshire, had a receipt indented for the pay of archers[6]
1374	Earl of March	6d	Sub indentures for the employment of a man at arms and his accompanying archer[7]
1381	Sir Thomas Felton's retinue	6d	Rate calculated from subcontracting indentures[8]
1397 - 1400	Richard II	6d	Personal retinue of the King. Additional rewards included livery and grants of land or lump sums for select group within the retinue[9]
1399-1400	Duke of Lancaster	4d	Garrison of Pontefract Castle (Men at arms wages also below Crown rates at 8d)[10]
1412	Duke of Clarence	9d	Indentures paid at Gascony rate
1415	Henry V	6d	Rate for service in France
1415	Henry V	9d	Rate for service in Gascony, 'presumably higher to reflect the higher costs of provisioning in the infertile southwest'[11]

1430	Duke of Bedford?	6d	A quittance for troops based at Mante for archers described as mostly mounted[12]
1474	Sir Richard Tunstall	6d	Indenture for a year's service with 10 spears and 100 archers between Edward IV and Tunstall[13]
1512	Earl of Surrey	8d	162 archers in his retinue fighting the Scots[14]

Under Edward I the basic rate of 2d seems to have been paid to ordinary archers (such as those in the garrison of Dryslwyn Castle in 1287–8) and to selected men described as 'king's archers'.[15] The pay of the Macclesfield group is exceptional, justified by their status as a royal guard.

The rates in the first half of the fourteenth century show variation depending on the type of service: elite groups, such as the 1355 group of 300 Cheshire archers; or mounted archers such as the 1340s group, were paid more. (The Black Prince issued some orders which are unclear as to the actual rate of pay. Two orders in 1346 instruct that 100 of the best archers out of those arrayed be sent to the Prince, and while there is no indication that these men are mounted archers, they are to be paid 6d per day expenses for the march from Cheshire to the embarkation port.[16] (There is no indication as to what their wage rate was.)

The significant increase in wages around 1360 arises from a number of factors:

- The need to pay good wages after the Black Death to attract enough men.
- The change to the indenture system of recruiting, which put the burden of equipping themselves on to the men, whereas in the array system the county (the Commissioners of Array and the Sheriff in other words) equipped them.
- The increasing tendency for archers to have a horse.

For much of the period under consideration, regardless of which practice was used to raise the army, a man's service was for a particular campaign and could be quite short. Indentures specified a start date for both the service and the payment of wages to the indenture holder, and an end date, often after one year during the fifteenth century. The pay records show that the actual end date was frequently before the end of the period of service the indenture allowed. So an archer would only know the total wage he might receive when he had been discharged. The records of two of the most famous campaigns of the period give an idea of how this worked out.

The government records for the Crecy–Calais campaign of 1346–7 include various abstracts from the accounts drawn up by Walter Wetwang, Keeper of the King's Wardrobe and completed by others after his death in November 1347. The whole campaign was recorded as lasting from 4th June 1346 to

12th October 1347.[17] Unfortunately, these abstracts are only summaries of the originals and the information about the arrayed troops, which would include the majority of the archers involved in the campaign, does not even give periods of service. As a result while the maximum number of days an archer might have served is known, there is no way of knowing how many of them actually served the whole campaign. The archers of the Earl of Huntingdon's retinue, for example, were back in England after the taking of Caen, so would be paid by the Crown for about 57 days.[18] Since they had been in the army when the wealthy towns of St. Lô and Caen had been taken they would almost certainly have gained booty, and so probably felt that they had done well out of a limited period of military service. Some troops involved in this campaign were quite content with their gains from booty and ransoms, and prepared to lose some of their pay. At the beginning of a sequence of letters pursuing an archer who had left the army without licence, Edward III comments that 'men at arms, armed men and archers have returned from our army about Calais in great numbers, seditiously leaving us in danger among our enemies.'[19] Edward was overstating the case, since he had quite enough troops to pursue the siege of Calais. But it does demonstrate that some soldiers were only willing to serve for as long as it was profitable and exciting, and that they viewed sitting in siege works outside Calais as not worth their while. So the men of Edward's army, for all the technical competence with their weapons that they demonstrated throughout the campaign, lacked the level of professionalism achieved by later English armies.

The Agincourt campaign can be dated from 29th April 1415, when the majority of the indentures were sealed. The campaign was declared to have ended, from a pay point of view, on 23rd November,[20] which included time for the men to be shipped home. This means that those archers who had an indenture direct with the Crown and who served for the whole campaign could expect up to 207 days pay, £5/3/6d at 6d per day. However, since the assembly date was 1st July (ie 145 days), and nearly all archers served in companies, the normal pay for the campaign would be something like £3/12/6d, plus a few days' pay for getting to the muster point. It is likely that after the first instalment paid at the time of indenture, or muster, they received most of their pay as a lump sum after the end of the campaign. They didn't take it all home. Henry's army had reached Calais on the 29th or 30th of October, but while Henry himself and the nobles received a warm welcome from the inhabitants of Calais, it was different for the ordinary soldiers. The chronicles of Le Fevre and Waurin suggest that, despite the great victory they had won and the hardships, particularly lack of victuals, they had endured, the inhabitants of Calais would not let these men into the city for fear of losing their own food supplies. This did not stop them selling food and drink to the soldiers at inflated prices. In circumstances like this, holding prisoners in hope of ransoms was a mixed blessing for the soldiers, since the captor was responsible for the feeding, housing and general care of his prisoner. As a result there is evidence of a number of soldiers selling their prisoners to citizens of Calais and other entrepreneurs to raise immediate cash and reduce these expenses. The sale price was of course less than the potential ransom price. Some accounts suggest that Henry did not forget his men, and made every effort to get shipping for them to return to England as soon as possible to relieve their sufferings.[21]

Once the indenture system was established, it is not surprising that some of the leaders of retinues tried to make profits from the Crown payments. This development was in part because of the creation of numbers of professional soldiers who needed to maximize their incomes in wartime to live off them in times of peace. It is also a sign of military service being viewed as a business activity by men for whom it was only part of their income-earning activities. The indenture agreed by Sir John Strother in 1374 and the sub indentures he agreed with his men are an example of a very commercial approach to war. His indenture with the Earl of March was for a year's service at the normal Crown rates of the time of 12d per day for a man at arms and 6d per day for an archer, a double regard for the men at arms, and a substantial personal regard of about six times what he might have expected for Strother himself. A regard was the payment that covered a mounted man's investment in his horse and equipment, and a retinue leader's expenses. Strother then went on to ensure his profits by squeezing what he paid each man at arms and his accompanying archer. The surviving sub indentures show that he offered £40 for a year's service, whereas Crown rates would pay the man at arms and his archer £45/2/0.[22] Presumably it was the regard rather than the daily rate that was reduced. Strother went further, specifying that he would pay his men in proportion to what he received from the Earl of March. All this seems pretty hard-nosed on Strother's part. Similarly, in 1403 Sir John Bold, Captain of Conway, was paying his men at arms and archers 10d and 5d per day respectively.[23] This is either straightforward profiteering on his part, or he was treating the service as garrison duty, and reducing pay because the men were also receiving food and lodgings. In either case it couldn't continue, with Glyndwr leading the rebellious Welsh and Hotspur leading an army in revolt that ended at the battle of Shrewsbury, for Bold was paying Crown rates in the following year.

In 1439 there was shameless and widespread profiteering by retinue leaders from the wages they received for their men. The Commons petitioned the King to stop retinue leaders from making large deductions from the pay of their men while they were in England, because it left the men having to support themselves by robbery and pillage.

It is important to remember that these moneys were paid to make sure that no one was out of pocket as a result of meeting his obligations to serve and they were not meant to be a calculated commercial wage for military service. However, as has already been noted, this was a period of increasing professionalization in military service, so wages really became wages. The inadequacy of the wages paid to the magnates, bannarets, knights and men at arms leading retinues, who had higher costs from the maintenance of their personal equipment and households, became more obvious. In the case of archers, the wages were not high enough to tempt an established middling peasant to make a career change. But they were quite enough to attract men without substantial holdings, sons waiting for their inheritance, small landholders, jobbing artisans or wage labourers. They were also enough to support the development of a class of professional archers for varying periods. The financial practicality of this can be seen in the table of wages of various groups of workers on page 140. This shows that the archers' daily rate was in excess of, or at worst comparable to, craftsmen's' pay for much of the time. The archer was expected to use his wages to buy food and drink for himself, and fodder for his horse when he had one and replace his clothing if necessary. There is no evidence that he was expected to buy his own arrows on campaign. Once in service it seems from the evidence of commanders holding a reserve of bows and bowstrings that an archer could expect replacement bows and bowstrings as necessary. Arms and armour became increasingly the individual's responsibility.

Sometimes wages were increased or decreased to reflect different supply situations. In 1370–71 archers serving under Guy de Brienne, Admiral of the Fleet, were paid 5d per day 'by reason of the dearness of provisions that year.'[24] This was an increased foot archer's rate; the same document shows ordinary sailors receiving a higher than normal rate as well. In 1437 the Privy Council ordered that 3000 men, including 2500 archers be paid for six weeks service 'half in monaie and half in vitaille'.[25] While this was not common practice, by Henry VII's reign the garrison at Calais and its Pale were paid this way. In 1503–4 their pay system was changed. For some time they had been paid one third in victuals and two thirds in money, so an archer would receive about 4d per day. This was changed so that an eighteenth of their pay was deducted (defined as 40d of every £1 of one third of their pay!), presumably to cover accommodation costs.[26] So an archer would lose around 10d per month from his pay in this new arrangement. Who benefited most from this change is unclear; it made matters simpler for the royal administration on the one hand, and on the other the garrison members may have felt they got a better deal now they were individually responsible for their victuals.

These figures represent the maximum that an archer could expect, but were these expectations always met? The Kings of England almost never had enough money to support their military ambitions and so their administration took a keen interest in finding ways of reducing the costs of war. Henry IV's campaign in Scotland in 1400 is one example of how the king could get the costs of an army subsidised by the magnates and armigerous gentry. This army was unusual because it was raised by the king calling on those men who had a personal obligation to him to bring forces to muster at Newcastle, avoiding both the array *and* indenture system. In doing this

Henry followed the example of his predecessor, Richard II,[27] whom he had just deposed, alleging he was an autocrat. The army was also unusual in the ratio of men at arms to archers it contained, over six archers for every man at arms.[28] At the end of an aborted campaign, the period for which pay was due from the Crown was set at 25 days, the time between leaving and returning to Newcastle. While some company leaders such as William Lord Willoughby received 25 days pay for his men, other men seem to have received a flat rate of 20/- for men at arms and 10/- for archers (20 days pay) from John Curson, the Treasurer for Wars.[29] It is not clear how many days pay the individual men at arms and archers actually received, but even if they only got 10/- plus a few days pay for the journey to the muster point, it probably seemed quite good to most of the archers for a month's work. In the case of this particular campaign, the archers would not have had to spend much of their wages on victuals, since there is plenty of evidence of their leaders having made serious efforts to accumulate sufficient foodstuffs for the early weeks of the campaign.

The Crown was effectively receiving interest free loans from the indenture holders who brought companies to war. These men usually got paid eventually, Sir Thomas Carew, for example, was paid in arrears in 1423 for his company's service in 1417. Sometimes, desperate measures were necessary to get payment, as in 1429, when John Talbot refused to move to the rescue of Crotoy without payment of arrears.[30] Arrears arose because the Crown was slow to pay later instalments of the wages, but the indenture holders had to pay their men from their own resources to keep their service and reduce the risk of desertion. I have seen no records of archers using the courts to get delayed pay from their employers. However, in 1428 the soldiers of the garrison of Calais, which was usually about two thirds archers, sent the Treasurer of Calais and others to the Privy Council to sue (in the sense of plead rather than a legal action) for their wages.[31] As already noted, Sir John Strother insured against the likelihood of the Crown being dilatory in paying by including a stipulation in his sub indentures that he would pay his sub indenture holders only in proportion to the monies he received from his lord. Sir Hugh Hastings was either more trusting or less canny in his sub indentures since he does not seem to have covered himself.[32]

There are substantial numbers of administrative records surviving from the English administration in Normandy covering the 1420s to the end of English rule. These show that the administration expected to pay troops quarterly, and indicate that the clerks checked that the men had served as required. Before this, evidence is much patchier, although in May 1418, £26,000 was literally carted from London to Southampton, and then shipped to the king in France.[33] This seems to have been pay for the army rather than incidental royal expenses. There were nevertheless plenty of times when the commanders of English expeditions abroad ran out of money to pay their troops.

Both Henry VII in 1492 and Henry VIII in 1512 showed they were concerned that the ordinary soldier should receive his pay fully, regularly and promptly, recognising that dilatory payment could lead to discipline problems. Henry VII's statute that the captains should ' geve theym their full wages without abriggement as he shall receyve of the king for theym, except for jakettis for theym that receyve land wages, that is to say 6/8d for a yoman and 13/4d for a gentilman for an hole yere.'[34] (There is no way of knowing whether the jacket referred to was a uniform coat, or soft armour such as an arming jack or brigandine. There are references in both kings' reigns to the men being issued with uniform coats, but these prices seem high for such a garment.)

The statutes of both kings – Henry VIII copied his father's statute almost word for word – also laid down that captains were to ensure that the number of men agreed in the indentures were present, and that they were to pay their men's wages within six days of having received the money from the treasurer at war.[35]

Another way the Crown could save money was by finding excuses to reduce the daily rate paid. For the 1334 campaign in Scotland, mounted archers were paid 6d per day while in England but only 4d per day when in Scotland because they were expected to live off the land,[36] rather than purchase supplies from merchants acting as sutlers or from the local population. Most of the mounted archers raised in 1341 for service in Scotland were paid the same reduced rate, except for the elite groups of King's Archers and mounted archers from Cheshire who received the full rate of 6d.[37]

The most common way of reducing pay was to employ a very rigid mustering and accounting system, such as that recorded controlling the pay of the troops in English Normandy in the 1420s to the 1440s. Though close accounting of the availability of archers for service can be traced in the fourteenth century. In 1338–39 a company of 202 archers led by John Ward were paid for 483 days service in Flanders. Forty men had 32 days pay deducted for absence, and another eight men lost two days pay.[38] It seems these men were foot archers, so their maximum earnings from wages for this service would have been £6/0/9d at 3d per day. We do not know the circumstances of these deductions; they could arise from illness, desertion or detached service. This checking became more thorough in the fifteenth century. The officials carrying out the musters not only counted the men but checked their equipment at each muster, with the aim of either reducing or refusing the pay of any found with inadequate equipment. If a man at arms did not have a horse this was a problem, leading to reduction in pay, but it does not seem to have been one for archers who had lost their horses.[39] There is no indication as to whether the officials accepted excuses about equipment being lost in the king's service or not. But this does not seem to have been a large-scale problem anyway, in the 1420s at least, since a list of muster rolls in the records of Surreau, the Receiver General of Normandy, show only four out of 127 rolls listing anyone with equipment shortages.[40]

Another ruse for reducing the costs of the armies in Normandy was not to pay any soldiers, most commonly garrison members, who had another source of income, such as owning a shop or tavern.[41] Inevitably this led to disputes. Stephen Drop, a barber who was serving as an archer in the Rouen garrison petitioned against the non payment of his wages.[42] But for most who lived and worked in the garrison, pay was docked if they weren't present at the musters, or had any reported absences. A late example comes from the accounts of the garrison of Tombelaine, where, for the quarter December 1443 to March 1444, two archers, James Hobson and Ralph Clerc, lost three days pay for absence.[43] In some cases at least, being sick or taken prisoner did not automatically lead to loss of pay. In 1430 Geoffrey Vrecnoc, an archer at Domfront, was paid for the month of May while ill from wounds because they had been received in the king's service. A muster from Fresnay for 1433 allowed payment to an archer who was held prisoner for a short time by the enemy.[44] In modern terms these examples, like Henry V's decision to issue pay for the men who died on the march to Agincourt and in the battle, could be thought of as a form of insurance cover.

There were occasions when the the Crown or other employers paid above the standard rate to attract soldiers. Most commonly the retinue leader received an enhanced regard. When enhanced regards were paid, they were usually paid for all the men at arms in the retinue, and it would be up to the leader how much he actually passed on to the individual men at arms. There are examples of the wage rate itself being enhanced; in 1370–1 for example, the archers in the Duke of Lancaster's expedition to Gascony were paid 12d per day, rather than the standard 9d per day (pay rates were higher for service in Guienne because of the higher cost of living). In the same year archers in the Calais garrison were being paid 9d per day.[45] What necessitated such largesse is unknown. In 1415 Henry V ordered that the first instalment of pay to indenture holders be paid at the Guienne rate of 9d per day, possibly to conceal his intentions from the French, but also to attract recruits. He also arranged that if service was in France the second instalment would be reduced in order to balance the payments out to the French service rate of pay.[46]

ADDITIONAL INCOME

Service in France was particularly attractive because of the opportunities available there to make substantial extra income, from booty, ransoms and grants of land or office. When archers served in English armies commanded by the King, or the great nobles campaigning in the name of England to further or protect English interests in France, their opportunities to make money were often prescribed and proscribed by orders governing conduct on the march and in battle. Edward III ordered or encouraged his army to ravage the lands 15 to 20 miles around the line of march as they went through northern France.[47] This was not just banditry or terrorism, it was organised to collect food and fodder to support the army – clearly with success – since we have no accounts of it suffering the shortages of Henry V's army on the march to Agincourt. However, it is equally clear from the contemporary and near contemporary accounts that having foraged supplies the soldiers burnt and destroyed fields and buildings as '...a strategic device intended to intimidate the local population and provoke those in political and military authority.'[48] It also provided a kind of training, getting disparate groups of men used to working together. This was very important given that the army consisted of around 14,000 fighting men with very different experiences, some long-serving with colleagues in indentured retinues, others less experienced raised from county arrays.

In the 1340s and 50s substantial booty seemed almost guaranteed. 'Almost all the chroniclers who report the campaigns ... comment on the great fortunes to be made from the war, and much of their information must have been gleaned from the impressions of returning soldiers.'[49] Froissart comments: 'During the sack of Caen they loaded their barges with cloth, jewels, vessels of gold and silver, and many other treasures of which they had great plenty.'[50] Even Edward III commented on the scale of the booty, writing in a letter of 29th July 1346 (after the taking of St. Lô and Caen) '...many of our people have been comforted by the profits they have made.'[51] There was booty to be collected in the aftermath of victories, whether large as in Crecy, Poitiers, Agincourt and Verneuil, or small as at La Roche Derien. It is very difficult to find much information on this topic, but there is the example of John Jodrell, an archer from Cheshire, who found a silver salt cellar as part of the spoils of Poitiers, which he sold to the Black Prince for £8.[52] This was quite a bonus, representing nearly a year's pay if Jodrell was paid as a mounted archer or an elite Cheshire archer. We know the bodies were looted after the battles, in part from accounts of the difficulties the heralds had in identifying the bodies when they had lost their surcoats. Besides valuable personal property such as rings and heraldic badges, military equipment would be useful, particularly for the archers.

By the end of the fourteenth century the rules for the division of booty became standardised on what could be called 'the thirds rule'. An indenture made in 1415 between Henry V and Sir Thomas Tunstall outlines these rules:

> With reference to other profits or gains of war the lord king shall have a third part of the gains of Thomas as well as the third of a third part of the gains of the men of his retinue gained during the expedition, relating to gains of prisoners, booty, money, all gold, silver and jewels worth more than 10 marks [£6/13/-].[53]

So an archer could keep two thirds of any valuable booty or ransoms he took, and all the small stuff.

At Agincourt, while there is some conflict in the chroniclers' accounts, it seems that the archers were the most enthusiastic looters of the French dead, taking away any valuables and arms and armour. Since there is no mention of the king making any gains from his share of other soldiers' booty, it is probable that each man's loot was valued at less than 10 marks, so not much gold and silver, just pieces of equipment that might be useful. In addition, two accounts state that when Henry heard of the looting of the dead, he had it proclaimed throughout the camp that men should only take what they needed for their own use,[54] not burden themselves with extra baggage. This was prudent as the English army still had to get safely to Calais as soon as possible. Just as happened after Crecy, all surplus arms and armour were burnt on the king's orders.

This looting of the dead should be viewed against the background of what had happened on that extraordinary day, when the heavily outnumbered English army had escaped what must surely have looked to most like certain annihilation. Tito Livio in his *Vita Henrici Quinti*, points to a reason why ransom was not pursued as a potentially far more profitable option than looting:

> Considering that the English were exhausted by so long and hard a fight, and because they saw that they held so many prisoners (so many that they came to the same number as themselves), they feared that they might have to fight another battle against both the prisoners and the enemy. So they put many to death, including many rich and noble men.

The order to kill the prisoners almost certainly came from Henry himself.

Naval expeditions could be just as profitable. In 1387 Richard, Earl of Arundel led an expedition which began by winning a naval battle against a large Franco–Flemish fleet in the Channel. He captured about 50 ships, and their cargoes of wine amounted to nearly as much as was imported into England in a year.[55] Arundel then went on to land near Sluys and ravage the surrounding area for two to three weeks. On his return home it was estimated that he had seized booty worth more than the cost of the whole expedition.[56] Many contemporary chroniclers sang his praises, no doubt feeling that this was a return to the good old days of Edward III.

In his campaigns after Agincourt, having declared that he was taking control of lands belonging to him in France, Henry V was obliged to protect the population at large from being pillaged by his armies. However, because a considerable number of towns and castles resisted his claims to sovereignty even after the treaty of Troyes in 1420, there were plenty of opportunities for the archers to gain often hard earned booty and ransoms as a result of the successful series of sieges and assaults Henry led. His final siege at Meaux netted at least 124 ransom-worthy prisoners, and the town apparently contained great wealth.[57] Just rewards for the dogged efforts of 2500 or so English and Welsh soldiers who sustained a winter siege from October 1421 to a successful outcome in May 1422.

An example of small scale profits from booty is to be found in the accounts of the garrison at Tombelaine in early 1444, when Roger Mill, an archer employed by Makin of Longworth, sold a sword he had won for 37/6 shillings tournois, something like 7/6d sterling (fifteen days pay).[58] The soldiers had to be careful about getting too enthusiastic in augmenting their income. In the 1420s an archer was driving a cow into the fortress of Lupellande in Maine when his English lieutenant saw him. On being challenged, the archer said he intended to pay for it, but this was not good enough and he was ordered to make immediate payment or return it to its owner.[59] Taking cattle as booty was probably not the most straightforward way to turn a quick profit. Henry V's ordinances, which were used with some additions to govern the English forces in France up until their expulsion in the 1450s, as far as we can tell, laid down that a soldier taking cattle as booty must keep the beasts within the army and make his money by selling meat to his comrades.[60]

There was one group for whom loot was vital since it was their only source of income: the outlaws serving to gain pardon. The king paid them no wages, and they had to pay a fee to get their charter of pardon. Though one of the first proclamations of that 'bold archer' (the monk of Westminster) Henry V, at his coronation banquet no less, was that all criminals, even those who had committed treason, were to be pardoned. How many of those men would later help the new King in his unwavering assertion of his claims to sovereignty in France?

Although the English soldiers were enthusiastic collectors of booty in their French and Scottish wars, they do not seem to have behaved the same way in the English civil wars of the period. Commenting on the Wars of the Roses, 1455–87, Commynes wrote: 'The realm of England enjoys one favour above all other realms, that neither the countryside nor the people are destroyed nor are the buildings burnt or demolished.'[61] This is not to suggest that they got nothing; given the number of casualties in many of the battles, the victorious soldiers would have found plenty to loot on the dead, plus their horses and any baggage wagons they had. The ordinary soldiers had particularly good chances of significant battlefield loot in the Wars of the Roses, since, until the battles of 1469–71 at least, the order 'spare the commons and kill the nobles' was given.

The rules governing the sharing out of ransoms changed during the period, as by the fifteenth century at the latest the taker of the prisoner kept two thirds, more than in the Crecy campaign when he would have kept only half of the ransom.[62] It was still a pretty good return for an archer if he was able to find a ransomable prisoner. The exception to these rules of division was when the prisoner was '... the adversary of France, or any of his sons, nephews, uncles or cousins, or any king of any kingdom or his lieutenant ...'[63] In these cases the king would provide a reasonable compensation to the captor and hold the prisoner himself. We only know of one case of an archer, or group of archers, taking a ransomable prisoner in the Crecy/Calais campaign, and that is only because they deserted the army and took their prisoner to England. A group of archers left the English army in the Calais area and returned to Essex with the Archdeacon of Paris as a prisoner. One of them, John Ballard, seems to have sold the prisoner to the Abbot of Colchester for £50. Edward III was not pleased and ordered the Sheriff of Essex to arrest the archers, seize their goods and take the prisoner into safe keeping.[64] The archers clearly thought it was worth the risk of deserting, but Edward III was provoked both by the desertions and the attempt to cheat him out of his share of the ransom. There is no record of the fate of John Ballard and his colleagues.

In the Agincourt campaign several archers took ransomable prisoners. 'The accounts give details of the capture of prisoners because of the need to pay the king his share of the gains of war[65] … I would suggest relatively few [but] some are noted as being taken by archers.'[66] One such was Robert Sadler, an archer in Sir Thomas Chaworth's retinue, who got a ransom of £58/13/4d for his prisoner, Edrad de Droyle.[67] Others were Edmund Bland, an archer in the retinue of Michael de la Pole senior, Earl of Suffolk, who took several prisoners, and John Killebury, an archer in the retinue of Michael de la Pole junior, Earl of Suffolk, who took a single prisoner.[68] Later, another successful archer was John Flourison, who served under Richard Harper in the garrison of Tombelaine in 1443–4. Flourison received eighteen gold salus, perhaps £5/15/- from a ransom and the sale of a captured horse.[69] Unfortunately, he had to pay a third to Harper, who in turn would have had to pay a third to his lord the Duke of Somerset. But even after that, Flourison's gain was equivalent to more than 150 days pay. Here was a world grown away from the chivalric ideal of warfare between social equals held dear by many of the French knights. They could be taken prisoner by common archers. This is not to say that the archers came from the lowest and poorest classes, although some may have done, but that to many of the French nobles, peasants were an amorphous mass and beneath consideration.

The archers seemed to have to learn that taking prisoners could be more profitable than killing the French men at arms and knights to loot the bodies. Sumption observes in his account of the storming of Caen in 1346 '… the archers and the spearmen (the latter were mainly Welsh), 'gens de petite conscience' Froissart called them, were killing every man they encountered.'[70] In part this was because Caen had been taken by storm and not on terms, and the archers and spearmen had fought very hard to break in, but also it seems that they just did not realise the potential value of prisoners. Some French noblemen in Caen, including such worthies as the Count of Eu, The Constable and the Lord of Tancarville, the Chamberlain of Normandy, were very relieved to see Sir Thomas Holland and Sir Thomas Daniel and quickly made their surrenders to them, since they expected no quarter from the common soldiery.[71] This was also a feature of the battle of Crecy where very few if any prisoners were taken. None are named in any of the chronicles. This may have happened at Crecy because Edward

III issued orders that no one was to take prisoners until the battle was won, and the French, by making repeated attacks until after nightfall, made it very difficult for the soldiers to be sure when victory was achieved. The situation was different at the battles of Poitiers and at Agincourt. In the aftermath of Poitiers, English and Gascon soldiers were scurrying about trying to find valuable booty and prisoners. The Black Prince had followed his father's example and given very clear orders that no one was to take either until the battle was won. The Earl of Dammartin gave his helmet and sword to one Gascon squire as a pledge: 'He called on me to surrender, and I did so at once. I gave him my word so that he should protect me.' By surrendering a man gained the protection of his captor, presumably fearing slaughter by low-born soldiers such as archers! This first captor went off to find more prizes so Dammartin surrendered to a second Gascon, who likewise wandered off. Dammartin said he would pledge himself to anyone who could protect him, to which the second captor replied 'Protect yourself if you can.' 'Another man, who belonged to Sir John Blaunkminster, then appeared and demanded my pledge. I answered that I had already been captured by two people, but I gave him my word so that he would protect me. This man stayed with me, guarded me…'[72] Surrendering was clearly a kind of transaction. Only the noblest, such as the French king at Poitiers, could be selective about whom he surrendered to.

The problem with ransoms for the ransomer was twofold: how much of the ransom would he actually be paid; and when? The ransom of King John of France, captured at Poitiers, was set at 3 million gold ecus (worth between £450,000 and £600,000 depending on the level of debasement) in the Treaty of Bretigny in 1360.[73] By the time of his death in 1364 about half had reached England[74] So we must be cautious about the gains from ransoms. There is one, possibly pessimistic estimate, that as an average over the Hundred Years War, the captor received about one third of the amount specified in the ransom agreement.[75] The figures mentioned here follow Anne Curry's advice: 'Only the post campaign accounts can be used to prove the actual receipt of money from ransoms.'[76] The captor's financial situation was further fraught by the demands of the king. From the accounts of the Agincourt campaign we can see some captors having to enter into bonds with the king that they would pay his share of the ransom by a given date, midsummer 1416 being commonly quoted.[77] The king was not interested in whether the captor had received any or all of the ransom, just that he got his own share.

Opportunities to gain from these additional income sources were circumscribed by the strategic purpose of the campaigning and the disciplinary rules the soldiers were serving under. The campaigns of Edward III and his sons in the fourteenth century used the chevauchee as a strategic ploy. This was not just anarchic looting, but an ordered stripping of the countryside along the line of march which had a threefold purpose: to feed both men and horses; to gain profitable booty, either directly by pillaging or in ransom payments from towns and cities buying reprieve; and as a provocation to the rulers, whether in France, Scotland or elsewhere and a demonstration to the local population of the power of the English. The major drawback with the chevauchee was that it of course alienated the local population, and so did not advance the claims to kingship over the areas attacked. But for the individual soldier it was a very attractive part of war. John of Gaunt tried to tackle this problem, initially at least, in his 1386 expedition to Spain. He wanted to promote his claim to the throne of Castile and so issued strict orders to his men that when buying food and horses they must pay the vendors' price. Despite this initial attempt to inculcate fair practice the expedition soon antagonised the locals by living off the land, and by early the following year organization and discipline was falling apart through disease and lack of pay.

After the 1415 campaign culminating at Agincourt, Henry V and his brothers tried to wage a war of real conquest and land retention, and understood the need to win over the local population. As a result their troops were bound by strict disciplinary codes. This is not to say that there were no opportunities for the profits of war and mention of ransoms are prominent in surviving French records. John, Duke of Bedford as Regent of France made every effort to maintain discipline among the English troops so that the French populace would at least remain quiet, if not actively support their English rulers. In part he achieved this by adding a clause into the indentures he issued, '... binding the captain both to abstain himself and to keep his men from any and every form of pillage and oppression.'[78] The troops were further restrained from extortion by the practice of the local officials, the baillis and vicomtes, having to certify that all complaints in their areas had at least been heard, if not actually settled. Bedford also understood the vital importance of regular pay to the maintenance of order, and so did his best to ensure this. Discipline deteriorated after his death in 1435 for various reasons. The nature of the war changed after that date, in many ways reverting to the earlier style, with occasional chevauchees providing a relief from the constant small-scale fighting with French soldiers and brigands.[79] Supplying and paying the English troops was a problem at this time since the English-held estates suffered from the war and so contributed less to the cost of maintaining English Normandy. As a result the war was unpopular with English tax payers and those who held or wished to hold estates in Normandy, who felt they gained nothing for their money. But a different view was taken by the fighting men, for whom the enjoyment of regular pay plus the opportunities for plunder on raids meant that the commanders could usually get as many men as they could afford. The large majority of these were archers, as is shown by the change in the ratio between men at arms and archers to about eight archers to one man at arms after about 1430 (see appendix 2).

GRANTS OF LAND OR OFFICE

One of the early examples of an archer gaining an official position after military service is found in the Earldom of Chester. By 1360, Thomas le Parker of Denbigh was the Black Prince's Artiller in Cheshire and North Wales. He had been part of the garrison of Caernarfon Castle in 1354, where he also had some responsibility for equipment. The largest group of archers receiving grants of land or offices are drawn from those in indentured employment in Richard II's substantial personal retinue of Cheshire archers, which he built up in the last years of his reign. This group included the Yeomen of the Crown, who can be traced back to Edward III's reign, when they were recorded as the 24 foot archers of the king's bodyguard. In Edward IV's reign we have a description of the sort of men who would be appointed to this role. There are to be 24 'Yomen [sic] of the Crown, most semely persones, clenely and strongest archers, honest of condicions and of behauoure, bold men, chosen and tryed out of every lordes house in Ynglond for theyre cunyng and vertew.' Some of them have specific duties such as, 'yoman of the bowes for the king; another yoman to kepe the kinges bookes; another to kepe his dogges for the bowe', but in general they are to be present in the court to be sent on various duties, and they continue to be part of the king's bodyguard. They were paid 3d per day, clothing for winter and summer or 18/- instead, and food and lodgings in or around wherever the king was.[80] These wages don't look good when compared with military wages, but both they and the extras were guaranteed, there was much less risk and being attached to the court must have given plenty of opportunity for receiving 'goodwill payments'. These yeomen would be mature, experienced men, so gaining one of these posts was a reward for good service, and a little like receiving a pension.

Another example of a magnate rewarding an archer was in 1445 when Richard Duke of York appointed John Lane as parker of Southfrith for life, at a salary of £2 a year. It is likely that this man was the same John Lane who served as an archer in the Duke of York's retinue in 1441.[81]

After his victory at Agincourt, Henry V probably intended to distribute land among his men. In general this did not profit the archers, since many of the landholdings were held on feudal-like terms, requiring both personal military service and often the building of fortifications and raising of both men at arms and archers. Most of the grants of estates and property we can trace go to men with the economic standing to be serving as men at arms at least. This remains true for most of the settlements that took place in Normandy between about 1417 and 1435. The aim of the settlements in Normandy was to try to establish an English landowning class large enough to provide for the defence of English Normandy through feudal service, both in person and by providing troops, and paying taxes to cover the costs of defence. In 1419 John Popham was granted the fortress and seigneurie of Thorigny. Besides holding this fortress, he had to provide one man at arms and three archers 'to ride with the king in wartime at his own costs', and had a responsibility for the defence of Caen castle.[82] Robert Willoughby gained the lordship of Beaumesnil in the same year, for which he owed personal service in France with three men at arms and seven archers whenever summoned.[83] In 1421 Sir Walter Hungerford was expected to pay for five men at arms and ten archers and contribute to the garrison of Rouen Castle in return for his estates in Normandy.[84] These three men thus provided employment for at least twenty archers between them, who, initially at least, would be from England. So at this date archers tended to gain from the opportunities for military service contained in the terms of these land grants, rather than receiving actual property themselves. The most substantial issue of property grants to archers was to those who fought in the battle of Verneuil, which enjoyed great contemporary fame (see *Professionals, Volunteers or Conscripts*). In contrast to Agincourt, the surviving records make the level of rewards given to the soldiers by their grateful leaders and country clear. Firstly, special taxes were ordered in October 1424 to be levied on English-held Normandy to raise money to pay the men who fought at Verneuil, a mere two months after the battle. This tax was successfully gathered, a pointer to the efficiency of the Norman administration under the English. Secondly, it seems that nearly all those who fought in the battle received a grant of land in English-held Northern France. Archers received lands worth just over £2, while men at arms received lands worth a little over £6. And if a man proved he had fought at Verneuil, this alone was a mark of good character in subsequent dealings, an intangible gain. Even in the 1430s and 1440s the majority of archers were English-born, although a good number settled in Normandy. The settlement of archers in major centres was encouraged with small-scale grants aimed at providing the man with somewhere to live: houses in Caen, Harfleur, Honfleur and Cherbourg, for example.

Some archers received pensions. In 1370–71 Edward III paid pensions to some of his archers. John Childe received 6d per day for life 'for the good service rendered by him to the same Lord the King'. Walter Wymbyssh, an archer and a forester in the King's forest at Windsor received wages of 6d per day.[85] While not strictly a pension, the king gave him a job using his archery skills as a reward for good service. John de Norfolk, 'one of the king's bow benders', received a pension of 100/- a year for his good service.[86] Quite what his role was is unclear: did he string the king's bow when Edward went hunting? It was not the same reward as a king's archer received. In 1378, early in his reign, Richard II issued orders to the Sheriff of Southampton that he was to pay Thomas de Morton and Richard Lyons, both described as 'one of the late king's archers', 6d per day for life, as ordered by the late king.[87] A year later, John Knightyngley of Wiltshire was given the same pension for his service to both Edward III and Richard as a king's archer. An example from 1384 actually tells us the length of the archer's service. The Sheriff of Dorset was instructed to:

> ... every year pay to Richard Pupplyngton, one of the foresters of Purbyk Forest 6d per day for life as the king is informed that he has served the late king and the king more than 40 years, travelling in the late king's wars, and is one of the oldest archers of the Crown, and that he has no means of living save by the king's service, whereof the king has granted him 6d per day for life as he had in the late king's time.[88]

Given the length of service, it is likely that Pupplyngton was at Crecy, and, after years of campaigning, was given a job as forester by the king, as happened with Wymbyssh. Reflecting the change in the pay rates by the 1380s, all these pensions were at 6d per day regardless of whether the man had served as a mounted or foot archer.

Some archers must have hoped to gain a better social position through family connections, profit from service or favour from being noticed by a great lord. One such was John Ward, who was a king's archer in 1334, indeed he was a leader in the bodyguard, serving in Brittany in 1342-3 in a similar role. Then he served in the Crecy campaign as a knight with his own small company of three esquires and two mounted archers.[89] He was a career soldier who made good. The Black Prince remembered the archers serving in his campaigns in the 1350s, when he supported three of them being created Freemen of Middlewich.[90] In 1357 he rewarded one of his serfs, Reynold of Byfleet, by granting him and all his descendants free status 'for his good service in Gascony.'[91]

The most spectacular examples of men achieving social advancement from military service occurred in the fourteenth century and include three men who probably started their military careers as archers. Sir Hugh Browne was the son of a yeoman from Tushingham. Sir Nicolas Colfax seems to have started his career as an archer in the Earl of Nottingham's retinue, most likely a mounted archer, since most retinue archers then were. The most successful of all was Sir Robert Knollys, who is believed to have started as an archer and by 1369 was leading an army of 1360 men at arms and 1500 archers from Calais to Britanny.[92] All these examples come from Edward III's reign, at the beginning of the period when English archers were a dominant force in European warfare. There may well be many families, like the Jodrells (page 125), where a steady rise in status over several generations was achieved, in part at least, by military service. But after Edward III's reign there are no examples of the startling social advancement shown by Knollys or Colfax.

In the fifteenth century some archers advanced themselves by serving as men at arms, and even became officials in the English administration in Normandy. Peter Bassett was an archer in the garrison of Tombeleine in 1420; by 1429 he was serving as a man at arms in the reinforcements sent to Alencon. His colleague, Christopher Hanson, was an archer in the garrison of St. Valery in 1424; by 1434, after serving in other garrisons, he was working for Nicholas Moulineaux, the receiver for Anjou and Maine, in an administrative capacity.

LEGAL BENEFITS

Outlaws, men convicted of serious crimes, provided a ready source of recruits to the armies. Only the king could issue charters of pardon to outlaws, and this is exactly what Edward III did. Given the obvious danger of desertion, although some were pardoned in advance, men indicted of murder and other serious felonies had to wait until the services had been rendered and confirmed by the leaders in whose companies the men had served. During Edward's campaigns there were 'at least 850 charters of pardon for service in 1339–40; several hundred in 1346–7; about 140 after the Poitiers campaign … the proportion of murderers in these numbers is considerably above three quarters.'[93] The pardon system had benefits for the king as well as for the outlaw. Common practice was for the enlisted outlaw to serve without receiving pay from the king. Once his leader had attested that he had carried out the agreed service, the outlaw had to pay a fee for the pardon to be issued, a useful source of money for the king. Edward III, who, despite his successes, always seemed to be short of money, stated in a privy seal warrant he sent to the chancellor dated 8th September 1346 that such pardons were to be issued in the siege camp outside Calais so that he could then use the sealing fees 'to help to pay the wages to our troops'.'[94] Charters of pardon issued in the numbers they were during the siege of Calais, when several thousand were issued at a fee of 16s 4d (although this may have been discounted) were a very useful source of cash. The archers that received charters of pardon included William Dun of Ocle who served in the retinue of Sir Bartholomew Burgherssh senior. In 1400, when Henry IV was trying to raise troops to counter the threat of a Scottish invasion, the Justiciar of Cheshire, on behalf of the future Henry V, then Earl of Cheshire, ordered that men in gaol could be released to serve as archers.[95] There is no record of how many men benefited from this. Henry V also offered pardons for military service, sometimes in a more complex way. The Earl of Arundel dominated Shropshire in the last years of Henry IV's reign, and he and his men pursued their interests with little regard to the law. When Henry V came to the throne things changed, and the Earl of Arundel and his men were soon paying large bonds for their future good behaviour to gain pardons. Arundel's retinue at Agincourt contained six of the worst malefactors, who in turn brought sub retinues containing men serving as archers who had been indicted with them for crimes in Shropshire. These men redeemed themselves in the campaign.

Military service offered other benefits within the legal system. A soldier might be issued with a letter of protection for use in any court action while he was on service, or legal proceedings might be suspended as a reward for service. While most letters of protection were issued to the knights and men at arms, since they tended to have larger properties, archers received them as well.

WHAT WERE THE COSTS OF MILITARY SERVICE?

The duty of military service with appropriate levels of equipment that were laid on Englishmen in this period has already been outlined. This brought with it the direct costs of buying and maintaining the equipment, hiring substitutes where necessary, and the indirect costs of the commitment of time to both practice of arms and the service itself.

Assize or Date	**Economic class**	**Arms**	**Cost**
Assize of Arms 1242	40/- landholders	Bow and arrows	2/-
Stat. of Winchester 1285	40/- landholders	Bow and arrows, sword and knife	3/9d[96]
	'all others that may'	Bow and arrows	2/-[97]
1345 Sheriff of Somerset & Dorset's costs	Equipment sent to the Tower of London	Bows Arrows (per sheaf)	18d 16d[98]
We can take these costs as indication of the outlay necessary for a man in the Statute of Winchester categories mentioned above, to meet his obligations in 1345.			

The costs before 1345 seem low if every man owned a sheaf of arrows – there is no evidence from this early period of how many arrows men held or were expected to bring to a view of arms. Royal accounts from the 1280s suggest that arrows were bought in dozens rather than sheaves of 24 at this time (see below) but this does not mean that men brought a dozen to the view of arms.

One of the failings of the array system was that men did not always appear with the appropriate level of equipment, putting the cost of equipment back onto the community. This left some feeling that they paid tax three times; firstly through the tax granted by Parliament to the king, secondly by providing men, which could adversely affect the local economy and thirdly, in having to stand the cost of providing them with basic equipment. The indenture system may have come as something of a relief to many communities, since the indentures always specified that men should be appropriately equipped, whether as a man at arms or an archer, at the muster point, or their wages would not be approved. This put the costs of equipment squarely on to the man himself, or the retinue leader. This included, from the 1330s onwards, as it became the expectation that retinue archers would be mounted, a horse, usually described as a hackney. In the 1340s such a horse might cost 20/-.[99]

So a mounted archer of the 1340s paying for his own equipment to meet the standard at muster – a bow, a sheaf of arrows, a sword, a strong coat (helmets were less common among archers) and a horse – would spend at least 26/-, or 52 days wages. At this date many mounted archers were retainers of great magnates, and so would receive some regular payments in some other role for their lord; but to add to equipment on the journey from array to the king's muster was an expensive business. In 1385 the king had to order proclamations made in the East Riding of Yorkshire, Lincolnshire and Cambridgeshire to the effect that the armourers and sellers of arms and horses to the men at arms and archers on their way to London had been charging higher prices than were reasonable, and that they were to stop doing so immediately.

This order was made at a time when the royal administration was trying to control prices as part of a campaign to restrict wages. But it also expressed a concern that men might find answering the King's summons to military service too expensive, and so not comply.

A record from 1429 lists an archer's equipment at muster as a bow, a sheaf of arrows, a sword, a helmet, a buckler, a cloak and a horse,[100] an outlay of about 33/-, or 66 days pay. However, the archers in the late 1420s tended to be on annual indentures, so their equipment costs represented a much smaller proportion of the pay received from each service contract. (The military equipment prices in this comparison are derived from Crown prices given elsewhere.)

Despite the cost, some archers in the fifteenth century had the use, if not ownership, of several horses. The Duke of Suffolk's retinue in 1417 had four horses for each of the 90 archers in it. It was normal for bannerets and knights to have spare horses, since they had expensive war horses and ordinary riding horses. Men at arms were also expected to have several mounts. It is quite probable that the figures for Suffolk's retinue included at least one pack horse per archer, and perhaps the high number indicates that archers also needed a change of horses if they were to keep up with men at arms on a fast moving campaign.

Finally, there is the cost of food and drink on campaign. The king or the retinue captain did not provide victuals for all of their men all of the time at no cost to the soldiers. It has already been noted that indentures commonly put a duty on the retinue captain to have up to two months supply available at muster. In addition, commanders arranged the availability of victuals for the soldiers to purchase, so that their men were able to concentrate on their military duties and not be distracted by the need to forage for supplies. Soldiers, whether in garrisons or field armies, did not like receiving part of their pay in victuals, no doubt feeling that they could do better foraging or buying in the open market.

The money to pay for the archers' wages and equipment came from taxes, loans, rents and gifts. The mass of the population contributed through taxation, while the rich churchmen, merchants and magnates were the source of loans and gifts. How much of a burden was the taxation on the soldiers? From Edward I's time onwards, lay subsidies, a tax on moveable goods, became a major source of revenue.[101] By the end of his reign these could effectively only be granted by Parliament. These were commonly set at one-tenth in towns and one-fifteenth in the counties. The assessment of value was made by local men, who were easily persuaded to undervalue goods. In 1334 Edward III ordered a major reassessment by senior clergy and officials, whose valuation was more accurate and theoretically more even-handed.

As part of this tax reformation, payment was no longer based on individual assessment, but on the amount a community was assessed to provide. Local men apportioned this, and as a result '... it has been suggested that the wealthier payers of direct taxation were even more inclined to pass the burden on to their poorer neighbours.'[102] In addition to this direct tax was the more unpredictable exaction of purveyance and prise, the right of the king to order the seizure of necessaries, usually foodstuffs, on the understanding that compensatory payment would be made. It is immediately obvious what opportunities for oppression and corruption by the royal officials enacting purveyance this offered, and the unpopularity of the practice.

When the magnates forced Edward II to accept the Ordinances in 1311, purveyance was limited but not abolished. The Lords and Commons in Parliament approach of trying to control purveyance rather than forbid it continued in the Statutes of 1340, which were re-enacted several times in Edward III's reign. The Crown started to replace the unpopular purveyance system by issuing orders directing merchants and others to deliver foodstuffs and livestock to specific places for sale.

There is an early example in 1333, when merchants in sixteen counties were ordered to take foodstuffs to the northern ports for sale in support of Edward's Scottish expedition. Henry V also followed this practice to support his mustering army in 1415. This change reduced the unpredictable burden of purveyance on the tax payers of England, but may still have created local shortages, as did purveyance, which would lead to increased food prices. Henry VIII went back to purveyance to accumulate supplies in preparation for his invasion of France in 1513. The scale of his acquisitions was such that by January 1513 the price of meat was between two and three times higher than before.[103]

THE GAMBLE

Military service has always been a gamble, since death or disablement by disease or military action was of course an occupational hazard. Nevertheless, throughout the period from the 1340s to the 1450s the English Crown could raise as many soldiers of at least competent quality as it chose to pay for. Things could go wrong. Archers were taken prisoner on occasion, rather than killed or mutilated, but this would depend on the circumstances and the enemy being fought. The danger for the archers was that, in common with other 'common' soldiers, the victors in a battle would have no interest in capturing them because they didn't consider them ransom-worthy. In 1372, when a Castilian fleet defeated an English fleet under the Earl of Pembroke, Froissart reports that the English Lords (the retinue leaders) requested the Castilians to stop killing their men as they would pay proper ransoms for them. There are records of archers being taken captive on campaign, although there is no clear record of their fate. In 1415, on the march to Agincourt for example, Richard Tourner on 8th October and Richard Charman on 23rd October were captured.[104] Sometimes the retinue commander felt a responsibility to help his men with ransom payments. In 1360, Edward III contributed towards the ransoms of a group of his men, including the young Geoffrey Chaucer, the King's carter and his assistants, and some archers.[105] In 1374, a captain was asked for help by Walter Ferrefort, an archer in Sir John Strother's company, when he was held at the fortress of Saint Brieuc. He had stood guarantee for another man, John More, who had gone on parole to raise his own ransom of 40 gold francs (about £8 sterling).[106] More had defaulted, leaving Ferrefort to pay 120 gold francs (about £24 sterling). What is interesting is that Ferrefort did not ask his immediate master, the man at arms, William Doget, for help (who is described as 'mon cher compaignon' in the petition)[107] but his retinue leader, Sir John Strother. While More probably was a prisoner of war, since he was meant to be raising a ransom, Ferrefort was not but was held – according to his own petition bound hand and foot - until he paid his debt. We do not know if Strother helped, but he certainly had the opportunity to make sufficient profit from his indentures to do so.

Any man serving as a mounted archer was taking more of a gamble than the foot archers, since he had to invest at least 40 days pay in the horse itself, unless his employer provided horses for his men. Horses could be killed or die from disease. In most campaigns it is likely that overwork and limited feeding were the main causes of death. In 1346, after his epic fight near Saint Pol de Leon, Sir Thomas Dagworth claimed compensation for a considerable number of archers' hackneys in his accounts at the end of the campaign. This seemed reasonable since the horses had probably been killed at the battle, being used as part of the defences his men fought behind. He didn't get any, although compensation was paid for the much more expensive horses belonging to the men at arms that were lost. We do not know whether Dagworth paid for his archers' horses or not. The Agincourt campaign was hard on the horses, since once the English army left Harfleur there was little opportunity to rest them and fodder became scarce on the march. This was a grievous loss in purely logistical terms for the archers, let alone the monetary loss, having been allowed to bring only one horse to France, whereas men at arms and the higher ranks were allowed more. The consequences of this overwork of the archers' horses can be seen in the Earl of Oxford's retinue; of the 84 archers who returned to England after the battle, only 37 brought horses back.[108] In a relatively short campaign like this one, with relatively limited opportunities for booty, the loss of a horse would hit the archer's purse hard, as replacement would cost around 25% of his total campaign wages. The question was – as always in indentured retinues – how willing was the captain to help out?

The military adventures of the Jodrell family from Cheshire saw mixed fortunes. William Jodrell is the first member of the family we find in military service. By 1351 he held lands in Forest of Macclesfield and seems to have been a retainer of the Black Prince, the Earl of Cheshire, serving with him in Gascony as an archer, since a pass was issued to allow him to return to England from Bordeaux.[109] John Jodrell, also an archer, was a younger son of the family, and as such was unlikely to inherit much, and so took up a military career to establish himself. In 1355 he served the Black Prince in Gascony in a chevauchee and deserted after the expedition returned to Bordeaux. The next year he reappeared in the reinforcements raised in Cheshire and fought at Poitiers, where he got a silver salt cellar as part of the spoils, which he sold to the Black Prince, as mentioned earlier. In 1362 he was back home and had achieved some local standing, appearing in a Cheshire deed. His new standing may may have been self-made, or have come from being a member of a rising local family. But by 1376, things had gone wrong. Calling himself Jean Joudrell de Peytowe, he had to petition John of Gaunt and the council for help in raising his ransom of 1000 francs (£200 Sterling). In the petition he claims to have lost horses, men, goods, houses and rents during the campaigns in Poitou, and so could not afford his own ransom.

So over time an archer could make a position for himself, and if unlucky, lose it again. Roger succeeded to his father William's lands in 1376. This branch of the family has improved its social rank, no doubt by a mix of good land husbandry and investment of the profits of war, for Roger was a squire of the body to Richard II. He served the King against the Welsh with four archers and the Scots with six archers, by implication as a man at arms. He survived Henry Bolinbroke's seizure of the throne and in 1406 was a commissioner of array in the Macclesfield hundred.[110] He then fought in Henry V's French campaigns. His career was clearly profitable, for when he died in 1423 his estate included jewels, silver items, armour (not surprisingly) and a fishing boat.[111]

There is little evidence of archers benefiting from the land settlement in Normandy from 1417 onwards as has been noted, except for those at Verneuil. But for those that did, it proved to be a very mixed blessing. The 1420s were fairly profitable, the situation deteriorated through the 1430s and recovered slightly in the 1440s. Finally, they would lose all with the expulsion of the English from northern France in the early 1450s.

When an archer was weighing up the potential profitability of service, he had to take a view, so far as he could, on the strategic purpose of the campaigns. In the fourteenth century, particularly when Edward III and the Black Prince were at their most active between about 1340 and 1360, the chance of major financial gain for all classes of soldier was good. In these years, the chevauchee was a major strategic tool, and, initially at least, France was rich in moveable wealth. Large amounts of valuables came back to England. A magnate like Henry Duke of Lancaster was able to build the splendid palace of the Savoy in London from his war profits.[112] When the war with France was revitalised by Henry V in the fifteenth century, the strategic purpose became conquest. By the mid 1420s many fighting men had gained land or houses in France, giving them more than they had back in England. This was deliberate policy, as the English king tried to secure his hold on Northern France and to make the defence of these holdings self-financing. England felt little financial benefit from the wars of this period since the major gains, being real estate, were immobile. This lack of portable goods is behind Postan's observation that '… the social history of Wales in the fifteenth century (and surviving Welsh homesteads) bear very few traces of new wealth brought in by returning soldiers.'[113] He suggests that the Hundred Years War was a drain on the English economy. This may well be true of the whole impact of the War from beginning to end, but as to the specific benefits of military service for the mass of the soldiers, the archers, both Welsh and English, it is less accurate. By the fifteenth century, men were not coming back from the wars laden with booty as they may have done in Edward III's heyday. But it is likely they brought home the pay they had saved, which might be enough to rent more land, buy more beasts, or build a more comfortable farmstead.

From the 1420s to 1440s the English parliament regularly, if increasingly reluctantly, approved taxation to pay for the English forces in France. As a standing army, the men would tend to spend both their wages and any gains from booty and ransoms in France where they were based, rather than bringing them back to England. Men at all social levels who undertook military service inevitably became detached from the social and political structures of England, they did not become officers in towns or villages, or serve as JPs or MPs. Consequently they had no voice at home. The English political community who approved taxes, particularly the knights, merchants and gentry making up the Parliamentary Commons, no longer saw the value of subsidising what they saw as unprofitable wars in France.

Men were still prepared to serve as archers; service was attractive, offering excitement, a steady income, and the chance for windfall profits. It was less attractive for their betters. It was the retinue leaders who stood the losses arising from the Crown paying their wage bills late and in part.

Military service was a better gamble for the archers from the humblest backgrounds, those from peasant families with small landholdings and the urban and rural wage labourers, than it was for those from middling peasant families, the yeomen, and younger sons from sub gentry families. For the poorest, wages from long campaigns and regular service year by year could make a real difference. But they would also be the ones who would be hit hardest by the declarations of truce or peace. There is evidence from the 1350s of unemployed archers using their campaigning skills to make a living in the greenwood.[114] While this was not a new phenomenon, since men lived in the greenwood after civil wars in the thirteenth and early fourteenth century, '… the effect of *national* warfare on the composition of the outlaw population in England was altogether more significant.'[115]

The Treaty of Bretigny in 1360 may have been a peace agreement between the rulers of England and France, but it did not bring peace to either country. Inevitably the large numbers of professional soldiers that had grown up over the last 25 years campaigning would not just quietly go home. A number of the English archers had become completely detached from their towns and villages through military service. As a result the people of France continued to suffer from marauding bands of soldiers living off the land. These consisted of unemployed soldiers from the Low Countries, the Rhineland states, England, Britanny, Gascony and even France. Substantial companies roamed about France, killing and pillaging.[116]

Unemployed soldiery became a problem in England as well. In both 1361 and 1363 the king issued orders to the Justices of the Peace in the southern counties, particularly, Berkshire, Hampshire and Wiltshire, for them to deal with 'evildoers and disturbers of our peace, who lately lived by pillage and robbery in foreign parts, have joined up with other criminals, and, arrayed as if for war, ride through villages, markets and such places with naked weapons.'[117]

Not surprisingly, more displaced and unemployed soldiers turned to crime in the final years of the Hundred Years War. In 1450-1, Bale's Chronicle gives an account of how '… the sowdeours and such peple as wer dryven out of Fraunce and Normandy and had not whereof to lyve, but robbed.' The English government planned to send these experienced fighting men to Bordeaux to stiffen the English garrisons there, but the money for this purpose never got to the soldiers because of fraud and deceit by those who were meant to organise the expedition. As a result '… they [the soldiers] passed not out of this land and soo becam theves and manquellers [an old English word meaning murderer] in divers places of this land.'[118] These displaced soldiers were in a desperate situation. Many of those serving in Northern France had served year in year out as professional soldiers, and may well have had family and property in France. It is likely that they hadn't received all the pay due them for their service, given the collapse of the English administration. They were defrauded of promised payment and employment opportunities. So they used their skills to support themselves at the expense of the unlucky local population. Some of the soldiers made loud complaint in and around the king's household about the plight they and their families were in, and as a result Henry VI ordered that they should be given 15 days pay, 7/6d for an archer.[119] The presence of such men had a major effect on subsequent English history. Historians have long made play with the theory that 'the disorders of the last years of Henry VI's reign were intensified if not actually caused by the presence in England of large numbers of unpaid and mutinous fighting men recently expelled from France.'[120] Many of these soldiers would have been archers.

What was the chance of death or disabling injury? Unsurprisingly it varied from campaign to campaign. In the Middle Ages death was a constant companion, and the effect of the Black Death and the later plague outbreaks on the views men and women held about life and death can only be guessed at. Peter Ackroyd in *Albion* makes a point about the English people as a whole, in their reaction to the inconceivable death toll in 1349, which was surely even more true of the soldiers: 'A sense of mortality, or of dwindling numbers, may also encourage a sense of identity, threatened or otherwise.' They were not careless of life; soldiers both professional and levied, whether serving their own country or as mercenaries, must have thought about death, and felt that the chances of survival to enjoy their gains were good enough. In the Crecy campaign for example, the army consisted of about 2800 men at arms (this included bannerets, knights etc), perhaps 2800 hobelars and mounted archers and about 8000 shire levies (including 5000 archers). Of these perhaps 1000 were killed or invalided home between landing and the battle itself (a disproportionately high number probably being archers and spearmen because of their role in storming Caen), and maybe another 300 killed at Crecy.[121] So less than 10% casualties were suffered for the whole campaign. Given the booty taken on the march, this must have seemed good odds, after the event. Inevitably the archers who died are almost all nameless; Richard Whet was one of those archers whose fighting spirit made the taking of Caen possible, and was killed there.[122] Of course the gamble on making gains from military service could go wrong. A court record of 1400 outlines how the Earl of Shrewsbury recruited 16 men for his lordship of Painswick to serve abroad in the king's wars, of whom 11 were killed. Their widows were in dire poverty and were petitioning the Earl to be excused various dues, a request he granted.[123]

The army that landed in France for the Agincourt campaign was about 12,000 strong.[124] It is difficult to work out the losses from war and disease at the siege of Harfleur. Modern figures for the death rate for those suffering from untreated dysentery suggest that between 10% and 20% would die. We do not know what proportion of the army had dysentery; while it was a high enough proportion to be a problem, it was not enough to make the army ineffective. It would be an over-estimate to say 10% of the army died of dysentery, particularly given the number who were invalided home after the fall of Harfleur, but maybe half that number died at the siege of one cause or another. About 1300 were invalided home after the siege, about 1200 were left to garrison Harfleur, and a minimum of 112 were killed in the battle of Agincourt, though casualties of the battle are notoriously difficult to calculate. Given the uncertainties of how many of the sick recovered and the lack of records of battle casualties, an estimate of between 16% and 17% overall dying during the campaign seems to be reasonable. But this was not evenly spread through the whole army. Some retinues suffered worse than others, some classes of soldier suffered worse than others.[125] Sir Thomas Erpingham took 20 men at arms and 60 archers to France. Two of the archers died at Harfleur, one was invalided home, one died on the march to Calais and one, Stephen Geryng, was killed at Agincourt.[126] For the archers this adds up to just over 8% casualties, or less if the invalid recovered, and contrasts markedly with the casualty rate suffered by the Duke of York's retinue where 90 men (22.5% of the original retinue strength) were killed in the battle alone; we do not know how many were archers.

While there was a higher casualty rate in the Agincourt campaign than in the Crecy campaign it was not enough to dampen enthusiasm for war. Henry had no trouble raising armies for his subsequent campaigns. Part of this may have been his decision that the indenture holders should be paid to the accounting end of the campaign, 23rd November 1415[127] for anyone who died at Agincourt. This was not so much a payment to the deceased relatives, but a payment to the retinue leaders of wages they probably should have already dispersed to their men.

The potential of getting wounded in medieval warfare was high, whether the archer was involved in besieging or assaulting a fortification, or engaged in a melee like Agincourt. Armour both hard and soft would give him a better chance of surviving a blow, but neither form would protect him from a determined attack. By the fifteenth century most if not all the archers serving in indentured companies would own, or be supplied with a jack or brigandine and a helmet, commonly a sallet. It is no coincidence that Edward III's reign saw the guild of master surgeons established in 1368.[128] The endemic warfare of the period was one of the stimuli for the improvement of surgical skills in the fifteenth and sixteenth centuries. So it is possible that an archer would have a better chance of receiving skilled care if injured than civilians of the same social standing because of the increased experience of the medical practitioners attached to the armies. Evidence of this medical skill can be found among the individuals found in the Towton war grave; 32% show signs of 'well healed cranial trauma that most likely resulted from previous battles or armed conflicts'.[129] These include Towton 16 who suffered a serious wound to his jaw which healed with no sign of infection. One of the *Mary Rose* skulls also shows a healing wound.[130] This man had received a small penetration wound on the top of his cranium, possibly from an armour-piercing arrowhead. The fact that it was healing successfully at the time of his death suggests that he was wounded at least a year before his death on the ship in 1545.

However, despite these examples, and other cases where men survived serious wounds, infection would retain its deadly threat right up to the First World War. Another risk for the wounded was being left lying on the battlefield facing the likelihood of exposure, or being killed by those looting the bodies. This was a final peril for the defeated, victorious soldiers would rescue their own wounded colleagues, particularly in the case of companies of professionals used to serving together, and arrayed companies where neighbours served together.

If an archer was wounded and recovered, but was left so disabled that he could no longer earn enough at any kind of work, how would he survive? In this period there was no idea of it being the duty of local communities, or of Crown officers such as Sheriffs to provide relief for the poor and infirm. There are occasional references to retinue leaders giving instructions about the support of disabled soldiers. In 1482 when Sir Hugh Hastings was preparing to campaign in Scotland he left instructions that his executors had the discretion to reward anyone injured or disabled in his service.[131] The Church encouraged charity through its teachings, both by promoting it as a way of demonstrating one's faith through good works and so demonstrating to the community one's virtue, and by offering rewards in the next world, preaching that charitable activity would reduce the giver's time in Purgatory. The Church itself provided practical examples of charity through the support offered by monasteries to the poor and infirm, and by establishing hospitals and almshouses. It also collected and distributed alms in both cash and kind. There are very few references in any of the contemporary records or accounts of disabled soldiers causing problems, unlike the unemployed soldiers. So this suggests that either they were few, that is they tended not to survive injury, or that charity was able to cope with the number there were. By the time of Henry VIII, possibly because war was less endemic so that disabled veterans were less common and so more noteworthy, there are more comments about disabled beggars. Since medical care was sufficiently competent for fighting men to survive serious wounds, men must have entered this into their survivability calculations, although they may have underestimated the effects of shock and infection. Very few skeletal remains have been found which show traces of disabling damage.[132] A range of charitable activities probably provided support, including those already mentioned, plus the archer's own family; and perhaps magnates supported a few favoured men who had served them well. But the bottom line was that a disabled soldier could be reduced to beggary.

Before an archer on foreign service faced the dangers of campaigning, he had to endure the voyage to Europe. This was not a particular risk when serving in Brittany or Northern France, but going to either Gascony in the king's service or Prussia on crusade was another matter. In 1391 Thomas, Earl of Buckingham's fleet, heading to Prussia on crusade was scattered by storms, and the survivors limped back to England without reaching their destination. In 1443 an unknown number of the 238 soldiers, 230 of whom were archers, on board the *John Montrigo* were lost when it foundered on the coast of Ireland on its way to Gascony. The record, no doubt concerned with not over-paying the retinue leader for men who did not serve, notes 'some of those on board being drowned and other dispersed to divers parts so that none of them served in Aquitaine.'[133]

Service abroad outside the English armies as a mercenary, either freebooting or as part of 'approved' service was probably more risky although, as already seen, the pay rates were better than the English Crown rates. The

English king was happy for English archers to be employed by the Dukes of Burgundy in the fifteenth century. The downfall of Charles the Bold, largely at the hands of the renowned Swiss infantry, was bad for his English troops. After the battle of Nancy in 1477, in which Charles himself was killed, only 34 out of a company of 96 mounted archers led by John Turnbull survived to be paid.[134]

The final gamble an archer took while serving was with his immortal soul. Religious belief and practice pervaded medieval societies, and the soldiers were no exception. The account of the English soldiers kneeling, crossing themselves and kissing the earth before Agincourt is well known, and while Henry V was a notably devout king, there is no reason to believe that this sort of devotion was really out of the ordinary. No doubt many soldiers would go to a confessor at muster, on campaign or in preparation for a battle to ensure that they were as well prepared as they could be. Enguerrand de Monstrelet tells us that the night before Agincourt, the English troops:

> ... did not neglect to make their peace with God and tearfully to confess their sins; and many of them received the body of Our Lord, for, as many prisoners afterwards revealed, they thought they faced certain death on the next day.

The danger was not just damnation, but lingering in Purgatory where the souls of the dead are purified to become eligible for heaven. The Black Death encouraged the development of the doctrine of Purgatory and it was refined in the fifteenth century at the Council of Florence.[135] A major concern for soldiers was that since the prayers of the living could help souls in Purgatory, how could they be sure they would be prayed for? While they could always hope that their relatives and friends would remember them, the real answer was for them to be buried on consecrated ground where prayers might be offered. This was a real concern for the ordinary soldiers, since it was unlikely that anyone was going to move their bodies to consecrated ground.[136] One solution was to build a church, chapel or just a cross on the battlefield, particularly near the grave pits. One of the most prestigious of these was the Battlefield church at Shrewsbury, in part because of royal support. Surprisingly, given the scale of the battle, efforts by successive Archbishops of York to get a chapel established on the battlefield at Towton failed.[137]

FAME AND REPUTATION

Before the campaigns of the 1340s culminating in the battle of Crecy and the successful siege of Calais, the English had no particular military reputation. For the next 150 years or so, companies of English fighting men – particularly companies of archers – were highly valued as allies or mercenaries. In 1467 Commynes noted that the English archers were 'le fleur des archers du monde', his opinion formed after their involvement in the battle of Brustem in the service of Charles the Bold of Burgundy.[138] The archers in the service of Charles the Bold deserved this reputation, and recognition of their stalwart nature, since about 1000 of them served him until his death in battle,[139] despite already having been present at, or very aware of, the two heavy defeats his army had suffered in the months before. When the Duke of Brittany wrote to Richard III in 1483 asking for troops to aid him against the French king, he used the term 'archiers Dangleterre'.

At the beginning of the sixteenth century Italian commentators describe the high military reputation of the English, particularly the archers. The Venetian ambassador writes that the French tell their children that Talbot[140] is coming, to quiet them when they cry. The author of the *Italian Relation*, written slightly earlier, mentions the reputation of the English soldiers and particularly 'the fear they traditionally inspire in the French.'[141] These remarks were made despite there having been no major fighting on land between England and France for twenty years. Even a generation after the English had been expelled from Normandy and Aquitaine, their prowess, and particularly that of the archers, doesn't seem to have diminished in France.

As regards fame in England, men at arms and knights certainly gained celebrity from their presence at Crecy but, as ever, it is difficult to find contemporary evidence of archers enjoying a reputation from being there. An early sign of the development of the reputation of English archers both militarily and in popular esteem can be found in the *Eulogium Historiarum* written by a monk at Malmsbury Abbey in the 1360s. In his account of Crecy he makes clear his understanding of the value of the archers when he writes of 'a heap of over a thousand destriers, along with their riders killed and wounded by arrows.'[142] The sense of wonder that ordinary men could have this sort of effect on a battle is more explicit in the account of the defeat of the Scots at Humbledon Hill in 1402, when the Chronicler of St Albans wrote of 'victory not by the hand of nobles and lords but by means of poor men and servants. No lord, knight or esquire took a step until the archers had defeated the enemy.'[143] He evinces a sense of pride in the achievement of the archers, that ordinary men did not need any help from their betters to win a battle.

NOTES

1 Byerly, B F and C R (editors) (1977). *Records of the Wardrobe and Household*. London. HMSO p 39.
2 Sharp, M (editor) (1982). *Accounts of the Constables of Bristol Castle*. Bristol Record Society p.44.
3 See Morgan, P J (1987) for more information about service by mainly elite groups of archers before the Hundred Years War.
4 Hewitt, H J (1966) p.36. Both rates described as 'accustomed wages of war'.

5 Hewitt, H J (1966) p.16–17.
6 PRO E213/82.
7 Walker, S (1985). *Profit and Loss in the Hundred Years War: the Subcontracts of Sir John Strother, 1374*. Bulletin of the Institute of Historical Studies v.58.
8 Sherbourne, J W (1964). 'Indentured retinues and English expeditions to France 1369–80' *English Historical Review* p.743.
9 Gillespie, J L (1974) p.7–8.
10 Somerville, R (1953) p.168
11 Curry, A (2000) pp.413–14 Most indentees received the first instalment of their pay on June 6th 1415 at the Gascony rate, subsequent payments at France rate. Was this generosity, a sign of Henry still not having decided where the expedition was going, or to mislead French spies?
12 Newhall, R A (1940) p.32.
13 Dunham W H (1970). *Lord Hastings indentured retainers 1461–83.* Hamden Conn., Archon books p.53-4.
14 *Letters and Papers Foreign and Domestic* vol.1 pt 1 p.660.
15 Byerly, B F and C R (editors) (1986). *Records of the Wardrobe and the Household 1286–89.* London. HMSO. p.481.
16 (*BPR*) pt.1 p.13 and p.50.
17 Ayton, A and Preston, P (2005) p.231.
18 ibid p.224.
19 Rymer, T (1800) vol.3, pt 1. p.94.
20 Curry, A (2005) p.237.
21 Curry, A (2005) p.238-9.
22 Walker, S (1985).
23 Bennett, M (1983) p.176.
24 Devon, F (1835) p.272.
25 *POPC*.vol.5 p.19.
26 Statutes of the Realm (1816) vol.2 p.668.
27 Richard II raised his army for his expedition to Ireland in 1394–5 in a very similar way. See Lydon, J F, Richard II's expeditions to Ireland. *Journal of the Royal Society of Antiquaries of Ireland vol. 93, pt* 2 1963. p.135–49.
28 Brown, A L (1974) p.40–54.
29 Brown, A L (1974) p.45 and p.48.
30 *POPC* vol.3 p.125-6 and p.138 respectively.
31 *POPC* vol.3 p.242.
32 Goodman, A (1980) p.114-20.
33 Allmand, C (1997) p.120.
34 *Statutes of the Realm* (1816) p.549-50.
35 Cruickshank C G (1969) p.12.
36 Prince, A E (1931) p.356.
37 Morgan P J (1987) p.47.
38 Prestwich, M (1996) p.129.
39 Newhall, R A (1940) p.15–16.
40 Newhall, R A (1940) p.41n.

41 Bates, D and Curry, A eds. (1994) *England and Normandy in the Middle Ages* p.276.
42 Curry, A (1979) The First English Standing Army. *Patronage, Pedigree and Power in Later Medieval England.* C Ross. (editor). Gloucester, Alan Sutton p.213n.
43 Allmand, C J (1973) p.83.
44 Newhall, R A (1940) p.88.
45 Devon, F (editor) (1835) p.99 and p.83–4 respectively.
46 Curry, A (2005) p.56-7.
47 Ayton, A and Preston, P (2005) p.3.
48 Ayton, A and Preston, P (2005) p.65.
49 Barnie, J (1974) p.33.
50 Quoted in Barnie, J (1974) p.35.
51 Ayton, A and Preston, P (2005) p.65.
52 Morgan, P (1987) op. cit. p.134.
53 PRO E101/69/484. Translation from Curry, A (2000) p.438.
54 Curry, A (2005) p.227.
55 Palmer, J J N (1972). *England, France and Christendom 1377–99.* London. Routledge and Kegan Paul p.93.
56 Palmer, J J N (1972) p.95.
57 Allmand C J (1997). p.168.
58 Allmand, C J (1973).p.83.
59 Rowe, B J H (1931). Discipline in the Norman Garrisons under Bedford 1422–35. *English Historical Review xlvi* p.196–7.
60 Newhall, R A (1924) p.226–7.
61 Quoted in Goodman, A (2005) p.26.
62 Prestwich, M (1996) p.103.
63 Curry, A. (2000) p.438.
64 Rymer, T (editor) (1800) vol.3, pt1. p.94–101.
65 Curry, A (2000) p.432.
66 Curry, A (2000) p.433.
67 Curry, A (2005) p.243.
68 Curry, A (2005) p.271.
69 Allmand, C J (editor) (1973).p.83.
70 Sumption J (1990) p.510.
71 Ayton, A and Preston, P (2005) p.5.
72 Based on a longer extract in Sumption, J (1999) p.244–5.
73 Sumption, J (1999) p.447.
74 Sumption, J (1999) p.500.
75 Postan, M M (1964) p.50.
76 Curry, A (2005) p.245.
77 Barker, J (2005) p.343.
78 Rowe, B J H (1931) p.195.
79 For more on this final period see Jones, M K (1989). *War on the Frontier: Lancastrian Land Settlement in Eastern Normandy 1435–-50.* Nottingham Medieval Studies. xxxiii.

80 Myers, A R (editor) (1959) p.116.
81 Johnson, P A (1988). *Duke Richard of York 1411–60.* Oxford, Clarendon Press. p.234.
82 Curry, A (1979) p.211n.
83 Allmand, C T (1983). *Lancastrian Normandy.* Oxford p.192.
84 For more detail see Allmand C J (1968) p.463–5.
85 Devon, F (1835) p.25 and p.89 respectively.
86 Devon, F (1835) p.76.
87 *CCR* 1378 p.151 and p.154.
88 *CCR* 1384 p.474.
89 Ayton, A and Preston P (2005) p.224.
90 Bennett, M J (1983) p.185.
91 *BPR* vol. 4 p.206.
92 Prince, A E (1931) p.369–70.
93 Hewitt, H J (1966) p.30.
94 Ayton, A and Preston P (2005). p.195.
95 Allmand, C (1997). p.18n.
96 Figures to 1285 are averages found in Storey R, PhD dissertation. 'Technology and Military Policy in Medieval England, c1250-1350', University of Reading 2003. See <http://medievalhistory.mysite.wanadoo-members.co.uk/thesis.html>
97 Prices based on those paid in 1285 recorded in Byerly, B F and C R (editors) (1977) p 39.
98 Hewitt, H J (1966) p.66.
99 Ayton, A (1994). p.15.
100 Newhall, R A (1940) p.33.
101 Schofield, P R (2003). *Peasant and Community in Medieval England 1200–1500.* Basingstoke, Palgrave Macmillan p.171–2.
102 Schofield, P R (2003) p.173.
103 Cruickshank, C G (1969) p.64.
104 Curry, A (2005) p.163n.
105 Goodman, A (2005) p.45.
106 For currency equivalents see pp.592-3 Sumption, J (1999).
107 Walker, S (1985).
108 Curry, A (2005) p.239.
109 Ormerod, G (1818) *History of the County Palatinate and the City of Chester.* London p.784-5.
110 Ormerod, G (1818) p.785.
111 Driver, J T (1971) p.13.
112 Jones, M and Vale, M G A, (editors) (1989). *England and her Neighbours 1066–1453.* London. Hambledon p.304.
113 Postan, M M (1964) p.44.
114 Ayton, A (1992). *Military Service and the development of the Robin Hood Legend in the Fourteenth Century.* Nottingham Medieval Studies. xxxvi. p.138.
115 Ayton, A (1992) p.144.

116 See chapter 10 'Unfinished Business 1360–64' in Sumption, J (1999) for a detailed account.
117 Crump C G and Johnson C (1912) 'Powers of Justices of the Peace.' *English Historical Review* 1912. p.236.
118 Bale's Chronicle quoted in Vale, M G A (1970). *English Gascony 1399–1453.* Oxford, p.138.
119 Goodman, A (2005) p.90.
120 McFarlane K B (1963). *A Business Partnership in War and Administration.* English Historical Review lxxviii p.294.
121 Ayton, A and Preston, P (2005) p.190–1.
122 Bates, D and Curry, A (editors) (1994) p.257.
123 Rudder, S (1779). *A New History of Gloucestershire.* Tempus Publishing p.593–4.
124 Curry, A (2005) p 71.
125 It has been suggested that the archers might have been more resistant to dysentery than the more sheltered nobility and men at arms, but it is unprovable.
126 Barker, J (2005) p.121.
127 Curry, A (2005) p.237.
128 Roberts, C and Cox, M (2003) p.252.
129 Fiorato, V, Boylston, A and Knusel, C (editors) (2000) p.94.
130 Stirland, A J (2005) p.107.
131 Goodman, A (2005) p.92.
132 See Roberts, C and Cox M (2003) chapter 5.
133 *CPR* 1441–46 p.424.
134 Vaughan, R (1973) p.217.
135 For notes on the development of the doctrine see <http://www.vatican.va/archive/catechism/p123a12.htm#III>.
136 Although there is some evidence that this may have happened to some of the dead from the battle of Otterburn; see Goodman, A (2005) p.212.
137 Goodman, A (2005) p.212–13.
138 Ballard, M (1990) p.167.
139 Vaughan, R (1973) p.217.
140 John Talbot, Earl of Shrewsbury was one of the most able English commanders in the last thirty years of the Hundred Years War, meeting his death aged well over 60 at the battle of Castillon in 1453.
141 Cruickshank C G (1969) p.4–5.
142 Ayton, A and Preston, P (2005) p.296–7.
143 Goodman, A (2005) p.128.

What were an Archer's Wages Worth?

Large numbers of medieval English men and women took up some wage earning work as a normal part of their working year in the centuries under discussion.[1] These people fell into two categories, servants either skilled or unskilled who lived and worked in their masters' houses, and the labourers who took employment as they could find it, and who ranged from the completely unskilled to the craft journeymen. In 1300 only 20 per cent of the population of England and 10 per cent of that of Wales and Scotland lived in towns. Both categories of wage earner could be found equally in town and country. Rural wage earners in the first half of the fourteenth century who had little or no land were in a weak position, because the population was relatively large, keeping wage rates low, and land rentals high. The Black Death changed this so that by the fifteenth century the rural landless and small holding population had dwindled as land prices and rentals had fallen because of the shortage of potential tenants. The unskilled workers gained most from this.

After the Black Death the middle and upper classes used their influence through Parliament to pass eight pieces of legislation between 1349 and 1445 to help employers maintain their position in the labour market. This legislation began while the Black Death was still active in England with the Ordinance of Labourers 1349 and the Statute of Labourers 1351. If these and the subsequent pieces of legislation had been rigidly enforced throughout the country they would have fixed pay at pre-plague levels, enforced contracts of employment and made it compulsory for workers to accept offers of work. The craft guilds supported these efforts by developing their ordinances to control wage rates and terms of service. While control of wage rates was a major concern, the refusal of wage earners to accept annual contracts, preferring instead to agree day rates or piece work rates for work, was also seen as a problem by employers. In doing this the wage earners were trying to take control of their working lives by deciding themselves how long they would work for particular employers. The Crown and Parliament did not only attempt to control wages, at the same time there were regulations that attempted to fix the prices of a wide range of commodities to try to limit the economic pressure for higher wages.

Mobility of labour increased after the Black Death. Before 1349, when there was a surplus of labour, there seems to have been some movement of men and women seeking work, often regardless of their status as serfs. In general, because of the surplus, landlords were not greatly concerned by this. After the Black Death the wealthy elements of the population in both town and country were anxious to control and limit the mobility of the now scarce labour. The 1388 Statute of Cambridge laid down that those moving from place to place in search of work should carry documents. But people looking for opportunities for wage earning work not only moved geographically, they also changed occupation. Sons did not follow their father's craft, such as Richard Croggelyne, a fletcher, whose father had been a fisherman, and William, the son of John de Badley an arrowsmith, who became a clerk. Both these men lived in York and were registered as freemen of the city between 1395 and 1405.[2] There are some who changed their own jobs, including two ploughmen, one of whom set up as a carpenter, and the other became a sailor.[3] It is probable that both these men were trying to avoid not only long-term employment contracts but also being paid in kind, since it was customary for ploughmen to be part paid in grain and part in money.

Efforts to control mobility of labour in the second half of the fourteenth century and in the fifteenth century did not only come from government. The craft guilds made significant efforts in their ordinances to protect their trades from competition from workers outside the guild structure.

The effect of the seasons on work was of course most obvious in the agricultural year, but affected other activities as well, so that mining tended to be a summer activity to lessen the risks of flooding and shoemakers were busiest in the autumn as people prepared for the winter weather. This seasonality often led to both men and women having a range of part time work making up their working year. They might work in more than one trade or commercial activity, sometimes working for themselves, perhaps on their own land, and at other times working for wages. This approach to work left gaps in the year where military service as an archer could be fitted in if the man chose.

No work was done on Sundays, and by the fourteenth century, there were between forty and fifty other holidays, made up festivals including saints days, Plough Monday and Rogation days.[4] This meant that there were between 90 and 100 days a year when a wage earner was forbidden to work under penalty from the Church courts. While it is impossible to know how thoroughly this prohibition was obeyed and we have court records showing that there were some people caught working on the holidays, there is evidence of substantial compliance, in that work on demesne lands (the landlords' holdings) and on major building works stopped on these days. The ordinances of a number of craft guilds also included a prohibition of working on festal days. It is well known that Sundays were when men practised archery, with the Crown forbidding the pursuit of 'vain games of no great value' in 1363, an order repeated at intervals thereafter.[5] Before the Black Death, when wages were relatively low, the prohibition of work was a real difficulty, since it meant that there were between 90 and 100 days when the wage earner could neither earn, nor, if he had some land, work on it for his own benefit. After the Black Death, as wage levels improved relative to food prices this problem eased, so that wage earners seem to have altered their work patterns, deliberately seeking short term work contracts, a trend that was very noticeable by the last two decades of the fourteenth century. Dyer has described the 'work ethic' of the average man and women in this period: 'A plausible reconstruction of workers' attitudes in the period 1349–1520 is that they set themselves goals in cash or consumption needs, and worked until they achieved their aims.'[6] They seemed to look for leisure opportunities as part of their lives, and were able to enjoy them because of their relatively robust financial position. Guising, pageants and plays all become more obvious in the records in this period. This is not just because the records are fuller, but because these activities engaged larger numbers of participants, and larger audiences no doubt. This appreciation of leisure, of life having more to it than work, was a reaction to the devastation brought by the Black Death and subsequent outbreaks of plague – and was made possible by them.

How did military service fit into this attitude to work? The evidence seems to suggest that the Crown and Parliament viewed military service by men drawn from the mass of the population as a duty, rather than wage-earning labour, despite their commonly hiring servants whose main purpose was to serve as archers. It seems that the men themselves took the contrary view, thinking of military service as part of the range of wage-earning opportunities available to them. The table of comparative wage rates on page 140 shows that it was relatively well paid on a daily rate. Moreover, it seems that men were paid for all their days of service, including Sundays and feast days. As a result military service probably seemed to be an attractive choice as men looked at their work options, particularly as a part time, or short term part of their working life.

For military service to be attractive the financial rewards had to be enough for the archer to achieve his aims as effectively as he would following a more peaceful trade. Although much has been made of the increasing professionalisation of military service in this period, this did not mean necessarily that it became a full-time occupation for all the professionals involved. Military service could be a stage in a man's working life, or part-time work on a regular basis that made up part of a man's working year. As Bennett puts it 'Opportunities to profit through soldiering were never wholly, nor even predominantly confined to men with a full time commitment to arms. Military service was a part time occupation and supplementary source of income for *able bodied men from all social classes*.'[7] (my italics)

At the same time the industry supporting the archers grew. This again provided work opportunities largely for men, since there are no records of female bowyers, fletchers or arrowsmiths, although there are a very few for female stringers. Women and children were no doubt involved in the supply industry, namely looking after geese and plucking the wing feathers, preparing the hemp for bowstrings, and quite possibly harvesting poplar and ash stems and staves for arrow shafts. Again there was both a seasonal element to this work; the raw hemp would be worked in the autumn for example, and there was an often unpredictable demand for bows and arrows. In the first three decades of Edward III's reign and in Henry V's reign, it seems probable the craftsmen in the archery-related trades struggled to meet demand, while for considerable periods in the reigns of Richard II and Henry IV demand was low.

The simplest and easiest measure of the value of archers' wages is to compare them with other wage rates where we know them, as in the following table.

	1270-80	1340s	1380-1400	1415-20	1430s-40s	1460s-70s
Archers	4d (elite)	3d	6d	6d	6d	6d
Men at arms		12d		12d		
Sailors	3d		4d[8]	3d		3.8d[9]
Shipmasters	6d[10]		6d	6d[11]		6d
Agricultural Labourer[12]	2d (part of this could be food)		4d (part of this could be food)			
Carpenter[13]	3d	3¼d	4¼d	4¾d	5d	5½d
Mason[14]			4½d	5d	5¼d	5¾d
Thatcher[15]	2½d	3d	4d–4¼d	4¾d	4½d–5¼d	4¾d–5¼d

The comparison in rates between archers, masons and carpenters in the fifteenth century is particularly useful, since by that time, archers, like the other craftsmen, were expected to provide their own equipment.

After the jump in archers' pay in the late fourteenth century, when it seems that all archers were treated the same whether mounted, elite or foot, military wages were very stable. Annual indentures were an additional incentive. These were not common in the fourteenth century, being offered only to certain elite groups, such as Richard II's archers, although in the fifteenth century both service in France and garrison service in general seems to have been administered in this way. It is very unlikely that the mounted archers gained anything through the regard system which assisted soldiers with the costs of providing horses, since their very ordinary horses seem not to have been covered by it. This levelling out of archers' pay rates may be the result of the ownership of a horse, albeit a horse of no special character, becoming widespread after the Black Death. 'Workers became more mobile, and a growing number of smallholders ... acquired horses to enable them to find work at a distance.'[16]

One way society in fourteenth and fifteenth century England was categorized by the government was by level of annual income. Knights and potential knights would have a minimum income of £10 per year: '... for most people £10 represented a great fortune, and we are justified in regarding anyone receiving such a sum as being wealthy.'[17] An archer serving in France in the 1420s and 30s on an annual indenture, as many were, could expect to be paid a maximum of £9/2/6d, depending on deductions for holidays, illness or detached service. Since the royal pay clerks were very pernickety, it is unlikely many received the maximum,[18] but, with a bit of booty, or income from other sources it would be quite possible to reach £10 in a good year. This was not clear gain, an archer would have to buy his victuals and clothing out of his wages, so it could take three or four years of careful hoarding to accumulate this sort of money.

Rye, wheat, barley and oats were the main staples of the diet of all classes, especially the mass of non gentry. The amount and range of animal protein eaten was a mark of social status throughout the period. After the Black Death, there was a general rise in living standards as wages rose, rents fell in real terms and food prices were generally stable. One sign of this was the move to widespread use of wheat flour for bread and the use of more grain for brewing. After the Great Famine of 1315–18 when at least 10% of the population died,[19] poor harvests seem to have had less effect on the life expectancy of the population. In bad years prices rose and in extreme cases like the period 1437–40 wheat might cost between three and four times what it did in average years. People were able to survive by buying cheaper grains, and brewing less. The following grain prices are 10-year averages, and so show trends while smoothing the highs and lows of individual years:[20]

PRICES PER QUARTER:

	1340–47	1350–60	1380–90	1410–20	1430–40	1460–70
Wheat	4/10$^{1}/_{2}$d	7/-	5/3d	6/-	7/4d	5/7d
Rye	3/9$^{3}/_{4}$d	4/10$^{3}/_{4}$d	3/7$^{1}/_{4}$d	4/1$^{3}/_{4}$d	5/5$^{3}/_{4}$d	4/1$^{1}/_{4}$d
Barley	3/7d	5/2d	3/6d	3/10$^{3}/_{4}$d	3/10d	3/4$^{3}/_{4}$d

The cost of an archer feeding himself for a year based on these prices (below) is an approximation, based on the calorific needs of a moderately active man.[21] Assuming two quarters four bushels of wheat eaten as bread or pottage, and two quarters of barley brewed as ale (this is probably a generous amount of grain).

	1340–47	1350–60	1380–90	1410–20	1430–40	1460–70
Rate of pay	3d	3d	6d	6d	6d	6d
Number of days service needed to pay for grain for a year	78	103	41	46	52	43

These figures include nothing to feed the archer's horse.
The relatively low pay between 1340 and 1360 was balanced by the better opportunities for booty when campaigning in France at least.

Another sign of the rise in living standards was that the amount of animal protein in the diet of the mass of the population increased. This came about because of price stability, a general increase in individual land holdings, allowing more peasants to own more animals, and an increase in wage levels in general in the late fourteenth and early fifteenth century. The following table includes both working animals and food animals. The point to be drawn from it is that service as an archer for just one campaign of reasonable length could enable a man to buy one or more animals to help improve his own or his family's standard of living.

	1340–47	1350–60	1380–90	1410–20	1430–40	1460–70
Oxen	12/1$^{3}/_{4}$d	13/5d	13/9d	13./1$^{3}/_{4}$d	13/8$^{3}/_{4}$d	14/3d
Plough horses	9/5d	10/4d	13/6d	14/4$^{1}/_{2}$d	12/7$^{1}/_{2}$d	8/-
Cows	9/4d	9/9d	10/4d	8/11d	8/3d	9/3d
Wethers	1/1$^{1}/_{4}$d	1/5$^{1}/_{4}$d	1/8d	1/9$^{1}/_{2}$d	1/8d	1/8$^{1}/_{2}$d
Pigs	2/3d	2/9$^{3}/_{4}$d	2/8d	2/10$^{1}/_{4}$d	2/9$^{3}/_{4}$d	2/8d

Price per animal. All except the pig price are a purchase price; the pig price is a selling price, so any other type of full grown beast would be more expensive to buy.[22] (A wether is a castrated ram.)

Land fees and rentals varied widely at different times and both between and within counties. The picture is further complicated by there being two major forms of land tenure, free and customary or leasehold. This latter includes serfdom, which declined rapidly from the last quarter of the fourteenth century. Throughout the period there was a robust peasant market in selling the use of land rather than the ownership, since few peasants were free holders. 'Many of the transactions show small parcels of land of two acres of less being leased out for short terms, often expressed in numbers of crops or harvests.'[23] William of Edgesley, a Cheshire archer who joined Richard II's retinue of archers in 1398 was receiving pay of 6d per day. In 1403 he fell at the battle of Shrewsbury, most likely in Hotspur's army. The inquisition post mortem showed him to be landless but owning two cows and an acre of oats, so he clearly had use of some land.[24]

Increased personal mobility is revealed through transactions in the peasant land market. The fundamental nature of this land market changed after the plague. Before it, peasants often acquired small parcels of land for their own use, and on their deaths the increased holding was divided back into its original components as inheritances for their children.[25] After it, when there were so many opportunities for people to increase or change their landholdings, it became unusual for peasants to partition their accumulated holdings. But mobility became a basic fact of peasant life to such a degree that 'It was a rare family which in 1520 had been settled in the same place continuously since 1350'.[26] While there was a rise in the number of farmers in the fifteenth century, that is larger-scale cultivators who gained their name from their taking leases for demesne lands, who may not have been so accommodating to the customary rights of neighbouring peasants, there was nothing even approaching the enclosures and clearances of the eighteenth century. Dyer notes that 'Far from evicting peasants, lords used their courts in often futile attempts to prevent migration.'[27] Ironically, it could be successful peasant villagers who caused problems for their fellows by taking over several vacant tenancies, which could limit the opportunities for young people to find holdings, and disrupting the open field system with their commercial scale farming.

A few examples of entry fines (paid by leasehold/customary tenants at the start of their tenancy) and rents will show the opportunities that the wages from service in a campaign or two might open up. In the late fourteenth and early fifteenth centuries annual rents in towns could be 5/- for a cottage or 20/- for a craftsman's house that included workshop space.[28] In the West Midlands, entry fines declined to an average of less than £1 for a yardland[29] in the late fourteenth and early fifteenth centuries.[30] The annual rents in a region varied depending on demand and land quality but 'The median level of rent for the region seems to have been 20/- per yardland per annum…'[31] In Yorkshire at this time a tenant paid an annual rent of 16/4d for two oxgangs. Entry fines varied markedly in Lancashire and Yorkshire, with 3/4d being paid on two and a half oxgangs in Pendleton and 13/4d for one oxgang in Worsborough in South Yorkshire (this latter being less than the annual rent).[32] In Norfolk average rents declined from a rate of 10$^{3}/_{4}$d per acre in 1376-8 to a rate 7$^{3}/_{4}$d per acre in 1422–30.[33] The countrywide trend in the fifteenth century was for land fees and rents to fall in real terms so that '…tenants were apparently paying rents at least 20% lower than their predecessors before the Black Death'.[34]

Between 1300 and 1500, and particularly from about 1380 onwards, the quality of the housing that much of the rural population lived in improved greatly. While the quality of a lot of the building in towns also improved, overall there probably was not such progress as there was in the countryside. In the early fifteenth century a peasant could build a house or a barn of either two or three bays (much rural building in this period was done in bays of about 15 feet square) for between £2 and £3, these being the commonest house sizes in the countryside.[35] Town housing was more varied, commonly having two or three storeys. What amounted to one bay (often of slightly different dimensions than rural housing) cottages or terraced houses with two storeys were built for renting to labourers for about £2. A two or three bay two-storey house for a craftsman to live and work in would cost between £10 and £15 to build.[36]

It is very rare to find any example of a man who served as an archer renting, extending or building a house with the profits from military service. But looking at the costs of building it must have been possible. In the post Black Death land market, military service for one or two campaigns could give a man the money he needed to pay the entry fines on enough land for him to make a good living, or set himself up in a town.

It would be wrong to leave the impression that serving as an archer was a certain way for a man to establish himself financially, albeit at a modest level, in town or country. Things did not always go to plan for the archers and their attempts to make a profit from military service, as has been noted in the previous chapter. Putting to one side the risk of death, injury or capture, it was difficult for a man to be certain when he signed up for a particular campaign that it was going to be financially worthwhile since the pay periods of campaigns varied from one month, if cancelled after muster, to one year. A short campaign might not leave an archer out of pocket; but it might have a limiting effect on his income for that year. In the fifteenth century particularly, troops on annual indentures suffered from late or partial payment of wages, adding more uncertainty.

One final calculation for the archer is the debit column. There is no reason to believe that wages were insufficient to leave a man with a surplus after he had kept himself and his horse in victuals. How much he saved would depend on the man himself, and how much he avoided gambling and carousing. The strictures of the military ordinances issued by the English commanders make it reasonable to assume that an archer's personal property would be reasonably safe from his colleagues.

It is clear that with a modicum of good fortune the profits of service as an archer could provide a man and his family with security. For the waged (then as now), 'The only sure protection against the loss of earning capacity came from the acquisition of land or property, and many wage earners … were able to gain enough to keep themselves and give up working for others.'[37]

NOTES

1 This section draws on Dyer, C (1989) and Dyer, C (2003).

2 Collins, F (editor) (1897).

3 Dyer, C (2003) p.279.

4 For a full discussion of what he calls 'The Ritual Year in England' see chapter 1 of Hutton, R (1994).*The Rise and Fall of Merry England*. Oxford.

5 *CCR* 1363 p.534-5.
6 Dyer, C (1989) p.224.
7 Bennett, M (1983) p.162-3.
8 Devon, F (1835) p.272. These figures are actually for 1370–1; the sailors' pay rate was higher than standard because of the high cost of food.
9 Stevenson, J. (1861–4) vol.2 p.513 – sailors' pay rate expressed as 2/3d per week. From the rest of the record it seems likely that these men were to be a fighting crew rather than just ship handlers.
10 Prestwich, M (1996) p.275.
11 *POPC*. v.2 p.180.
12 Rogers J E T (1917). *Six Centuries of Work and Wages* 12th ed. London.
13 Dyer C (2003) p.240.
14 *Agricultural History of England and Wales* (AHEW). Cambridge University Press 1966–2000 vol.3 p.471.
15 Dyer, C (1989) p.215.
16 Dyer, C (1989). p.145.
17 Dyer, C (1989) p.18.
18 See Newall, R A (1940) for a thorough account of the administration of pay in this period.
19 Dyer, C (1989) p.267.
20 AHEW vol 3 p.444.
21 This calculation is derived from Dyer, C (1989) p.134.
22 AHEW vol 3. p.457.
23 AHEW vol2 p.671.
24 Gillespie, J L (1974) p.29.
25 Dyer, C (1989) p.123.
26 Dyer, C (2003) p.354.
27 Dyer, C (2003) p.350.
28 Dyer, C (1989) p.208.
29 Medieval land measurements varied depending on land quality and local custom. A yardland was about 30 acres, an oxgang about half the area of a yardland.
30 AHEW vol.3 p.640.
31 AHEW vol 3 p.639.
32 AHEW vol 3 p.605.
33 AHEW vol 3 p.619.
34 Dyer, C (1989) p.146–7.
35 Dyer, C (1989) p.166–7.
36 Dyer, C (1989) p.205.
37 Dyer, C (1989) p.233.

Conclusion

It is time to come back to the basic question posed at the start of this book: why did so many medieval Englishmen become military archers? They could not make this decision on a whim, since they could only be military archers by investing time in practising archery so that they could use the heavy English warbow effectively. We can only make guesses about how many years of weekly practice these men put in, informed by the experience of how long it takes modern heavy bow archers to become competent. The foundation of the English military system throughout the fourteenth, fifteenth and into the sixteenth centuries was the Statute of Winchester, which contained the ordinance that the majority of men between 16 and 60, as defined by economic status should have bows and arrows and be able to use them in defence of the kingdom. This duty was reinforced in a sequence of statutes starting in Edward III's reign which forbade men in this age group from playing 'vain games of no value' when they should have been practising their archery. It is difficult to know if these statutes were dealing with a real problem of a shortage of competent archers, or were born of the perceptions of the leaders of society at both local and national level. It certainly seems that English armies raised between about 1330 and Henry VIII's first campaigns abroad had few problems recruiting enough archers. The king who had the most problems was probably Edward III, whose successes established the reputation of the English military archer. This is no surprise since it was his military activities that led an increasing number of men to think it was worth making the effort to train. Similarly, because men did not realise the advantages of serving as an archer in Edward's armies, some of those sent by the Commissioners of Array were not really up to the job, in part because of evasion by some of those who were competent. This became less of a problem during and after his reign as much as anything because of the financial rewards his military successes brought. So in the Crecy campaign, the majority of the arrayed archers could handle the warbow and shoot together to provide devastating blanket shooting. Only the professional archers, whether serving in indentured retinues or those like parkers and foresters whose jobs relied in part on archery skills, could be expected to provide accurate individual shots at selected targets. But in the second half of the fourteenth century, as a result of both the military successes in France, and the increasing use of indentures to raise armies, men put more time and effort into becoming good archers. Accounts of men being shot through their visors follow, at the battle of Shrewsbury (the future Henry V), at Agincourt in the *Gesta Henrici Quinti* and in several battles in the Wars of the Roses. It is likely that this happened as men at arms raised their visors to breathe more easily, rather than the arrows actually penetrating the visors. The point is not that all arrows shot in battle were individually aimed, but that more men were capable of such shooting.

This leads to one of the great questions about medieval military archery: why did not more countries develop large numbers of competent military archers? In many of the countries of Western Europe local men served as archers, but only the archers in the fifteenth-century royal French armies seem to have approached the English in competence. They never won a battle against the English on their own, only as part of a combined force. The Scottish archers at Verneuil were comprehensively outshot. The Teutonic Knights and a number of Italian states supplied large quantities of bowstaves to the English market, and so clearly understood the value of the warbow, but they relied on the crossbow, or the employment of English mercenaries in their own armies. One of the commonly stated reasons, namely that the rulers in other countries did not trust the mass of their subjects to own and practise with arms, does not stand up, since the organising and use of citizen militias was commonplace. The argument that war was a proper activity only for the social elite only has any force at all in France, and even there it applies more to the conduct of battles rather than the composition of armies. The French army in the Agincourt campaign included a good number of infantry, who were not well used. In the end it seems quite possible that it was the traditions of heavy bow archery among the Welsh, and no doubt in the English marcher counties, and a legacy of Viking heavy bow archery in the north-eastern counties (archaeologists have found large yew bows in Scandinavia) that laid the foundations; foundations lacking on the Continent.

In the first half of the fourteenth century, when most archers were recruited through the array system, there was an element of compulsion, probably as much social as legal, in their service. Yet the way they fought suggests that they were fairly determined to do the job properly once they were in the army. Despite some desertions, there is very little sign of any great resentment felt by the men serving as archers in France under Edward III. It seems reasonable to regard the men serving in indentured retinues as volunteers, bearing in mind the social pressures noted below. As the use of indentures became the predominant method of recruiting armies for foreign service, military service as archers became increasingly professionalized, until, in the first half of the fifteenth century, the English forces in France contained considerable numbers that effectively made up a standing army. However they were recruited, I believe that the evidence suggests that the large majority of archers served willingly enough, no doubt with the traditional poor bloody infantry's grumbling about this or that unfairness, real or imagined.

It must be remembered that the array system continued throughout the period as the main method of raising forces to defend the kingdom against invasion. The army that fought at Flodden was in part raised in this way, although by the Tudor period the array system was metamorphosing into a more formal militia system. While legal compulsion was one part of the recruiting system, social compulsion was probably equally important. The array system in part depended on individuals not wanting to let down their friends and neighbours by evading service, since it was administered through the local leading members of society. The other side of this was that men could conspire with the local officials to evade the array, thereby letting down the larger community of the county, a problem which would not have been a major prick to conscience in those more parochial times. There are signs in both the array and indenture system of landlords calling upon their tenants and servants for military service. This was at the heart of the feudal system, and the great magnates regularly carried out their duty of military service to the king throughout the period. There is also good evidence of men serving as archers either in the companies of their personal landlord, or in the companies of the magnate in whose estates they lived. Some of these men seem to have been professional archers; some were just doing their social and military duty. The thread that links these considerations is loyalty to both friends and leaders. But it would be wrong to imply that landlords could compel their tenants to fight for them. After the Black Death tenants were relatively scarce and they would leave oppressive landlords and look for better opportunities. The pressure landlords could exert was based much more on support and favours offered, and the sense of loyalty to the community commonly felt by men and women.

Compulsion does occur, officially at least, with regard to archery practice. The statutes compelling archery practice on Sundays and feast days were re-enacted several times, in general after periods of relative peace. It is quite likely that men came to the opinion that it was not worth all the effort of regular practice if there were limited opportunities for profiting from this investment. But this was definitely not the case when Edward III first legislated in support of archery practice. It has already been noted that this act may have been part of the efforts by the governing classes to maintain the pre-Black Death economic and social status quo.

It is interesting to note that by Richard II's reign, this legislation emphasised the duty of servants and labourers to practise archery. This represented a deliberate clarification of the duties of men without the property qualifications of the Statute of Westminster. It was a reaction to the changes in society and work patterns developing after the Black Death, particularly the improved status of wage labourers. There may also have been a moralising element to these acts, since the games that were fulminated against

1. Prague archer by Hans Burgkmaier the Elder. 1473–1531 *The Life of Saint Catherine* (an old copy – original in Augsburg). Burgkmaier, who was an engraver as well as a painter, is typical of northern European artists in that he tried to produce naturalistic representations. He certainly had the opportunity to see English archers in Henry VIII's army. However, this archer is probably a hunter from the higher classes by his appearance, who was practised in the use of the heavy yew bow if his stance is any guide. (*Art Collections of Prague Castle.* © Picture Library of Prague Castle)

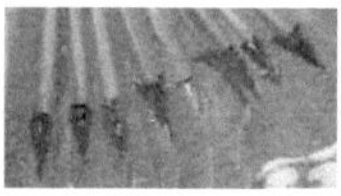

Above left: 2. Prague archer detail; fletchings and nocks. If you measure the arrows, the fletchings are about 25% the total arrow length, which makes them about 7.5 inches, if we assume the arrows are the same length as the vast majority of the *Mary Rose* arrows. The nocks appear to be horn, rather than just having horn reinforcements like the *Mary Rose* arrows.

Above right: 3. Prague archer detail; arrowheads. Smaller than the broad arrow heads that have been found in England, but effective barbed hunting arrows.

Left: 4. English archers from the Beauchamp Pageant, S. Netherlands (Bruges?) after 1483. The appearance of these archers is more true of the men of the time the artist worked, the late fifteenth century, than the time of the events portrayed, about 1419.(© British Library)

Opposite above: 5. Assault on Ribodane from Jean de Waurin. *Chronique d'Angleterre.* S. Netherlands (Bruges?) late 15th century. The archers provide covering fire for the assault. Since they don't have pavises, this was almost as dangerous as climbing a scaling ladder. (© British Library)

Opposite below: 6. Mounted Hunter with Foot Archer, the Queen Mary Psalter. English (London?) 1310-20. An early representation of an English archer. The archer is probably a man of fairly lowly status, given his lack of footware. He could have been one of the foresters or huntsmen who were sought after as military archers in the 1340s because of their skill with the bow. His bow, which is almost as tall as him and roughly finished, can be seen as a forerunner of the English warbow. The three arrows in his belt reflects common hunting practice in that a man could not afford many broad heads, and did not need to be able to shoot sustained volleys. (© British Library)

7. Detail of an illustration in the Smithfield Decretals illumination, English (London?) c.1340. Like the 'Prague Archer', this archer looks as though he is using a substantial bow for shooting animals, in this case an irritating cockerel. Though this is not of course a naturalistic painting like Burgkmaier's, it is interesting at this early date to note that the bow is coloured as though it is yew. The head on the arrow is designed for birds and small game; it could not go through the target because of the large blunt behind a small point. This would knock down the game by transferring the force of the arrow without damaging too much of the flesh. (© British Library)

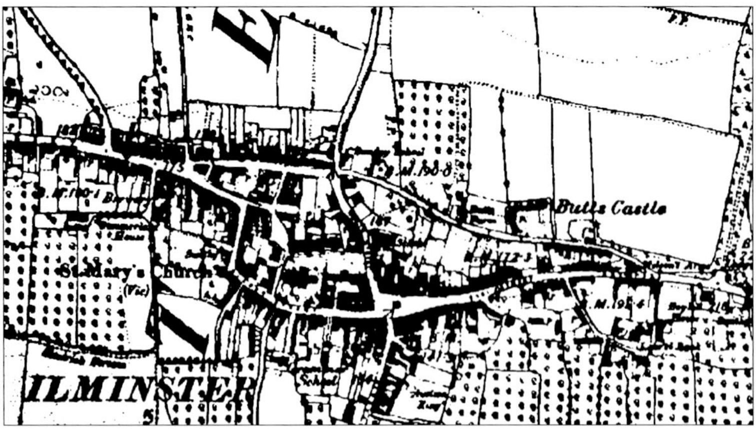

8. This Ilminster map shows how the site of the butts fitted into a town, in this case they are a separate piece of land running away from the church. Reproduced from the 1889 Ordnance Survey map. (© Crown copyright)

Right: 9. Bodrum Castle, the Hospitaller castle to which Henry FitzHugh took 13 bows, 38 sheaves of arrows and six dozen bowstrings out of England in 1409. (Thanks to gototurkey.co.uk)

Below: 10. Impression of the *Mary Rose* as she looked in 1545. Thanks to Andrew Elkington and the *Mary Rose* Trust for the use of this image. (© Mary Rose Trust)

11. Children's games among the nobility This comes from the *Weisskunig* and was engraved by Hans Burgkmaier. The *Weisskunig* (White King) is the huge autobiographical 'novel' by Emperor Maximilian I started around 1516, which contains his own and his parents' history represented by allegorical figures. Maximilian named himself *Weisskunig* after the silver-white armour he used to wear in tournaments and battle. Young princes and their companions are at play, both forms of archery practised. Modern longbow archers will be horrified by the way one youth is stringing his longbow. (© Royal Armouries)

12. Another plate from the *Weisskunig* by Hans Burgkmaier showing the young king receiving various taxes in kind. The bundle of longbows do not seem to be reflexed at all, unlike some other engravings in the same work. Did Maximilan keep the longbows for his own use or sell or gift them to his ally Henry VIII? (© Royal Armouries)

13. English archers at the Battle of Therouanne, 1513 from the *Weisskunig*. This purports to show the battle also known as the Battle of the Spurs. The English archers are shown peppering the French cavalry. Their bows are reflexed at the tips. (© Royal Armouries)

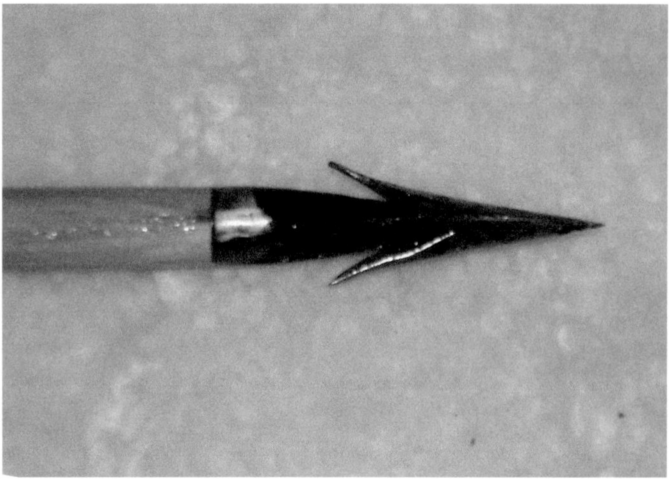

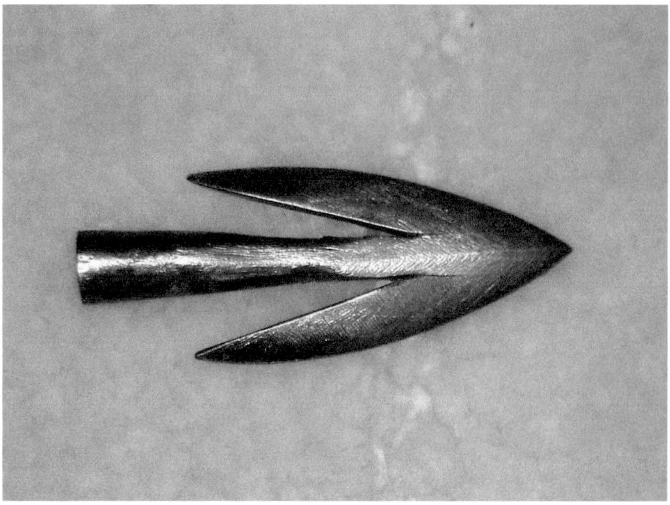

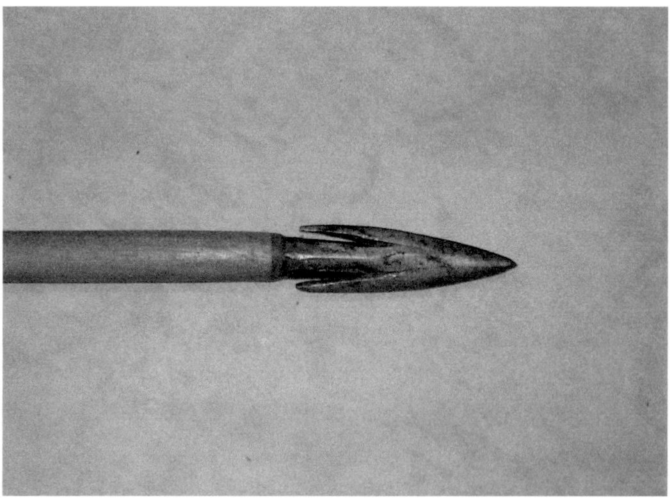

14, 15, 16. Three modern replicas of what an M4 military arrowhead of the later 14th century might have looked like. The middle one is probably too large and expensive, using more iron and steel in a single head than the crown would want to pay for. (Author's collection)

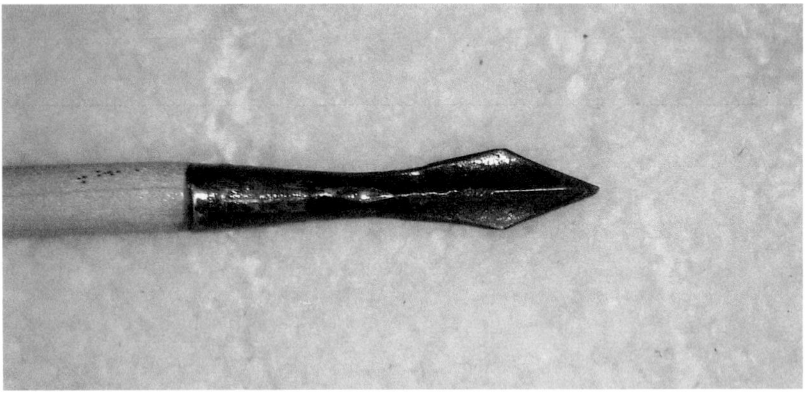

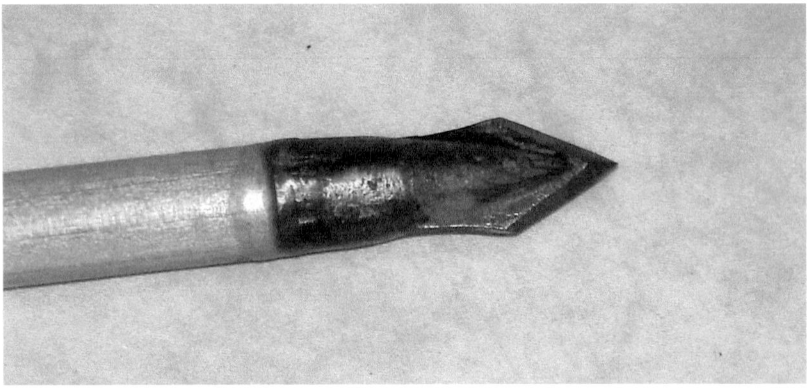

17, 18, 19. Three military arrowheads from the last third of the 15th century and the early 16th century. At the top is a replica of an armour-piercing arrowhead very like those used by the Beachamp Pageant archers. Above is a replica of a Tudor armour-piercing arrowhead. To the left is an actual arrowhead from a Wars of the Roses battlefield, which would not pierce armour. (Above, Author's collection; Left, thanks to David Starley © Royal Armouries)

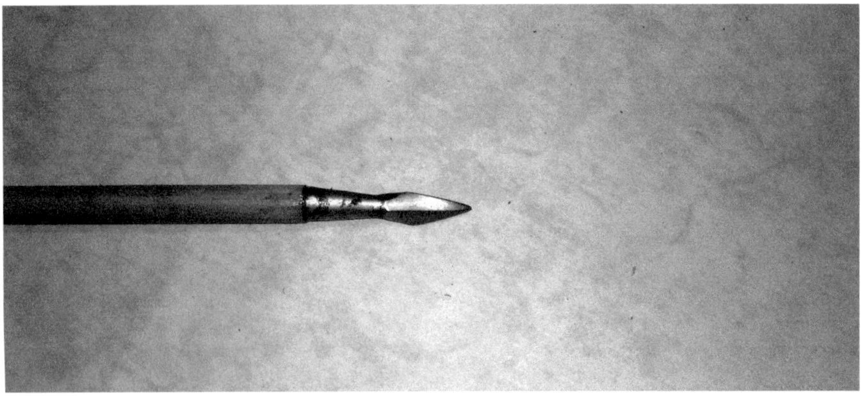

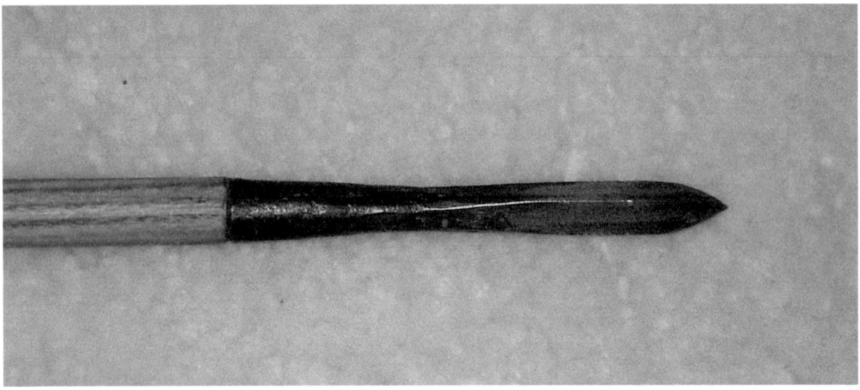

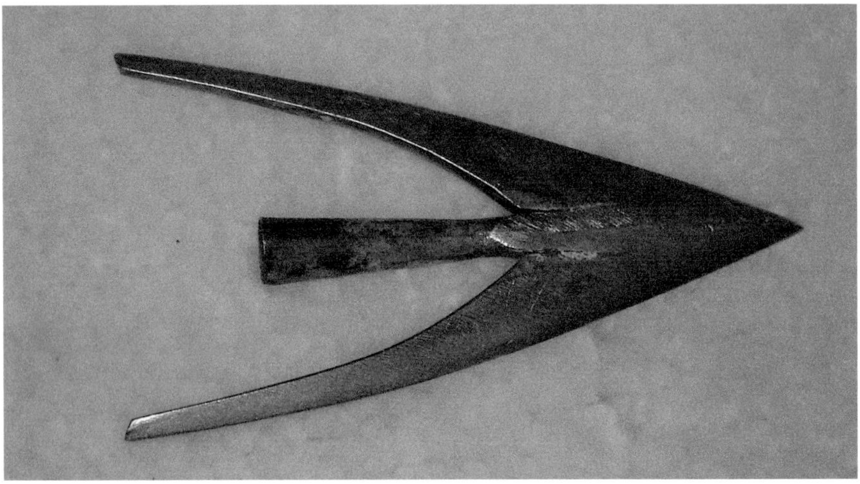

20, 21, 22. Top and middle, two interpretations of the armour-piercing arrowheads of the first half of the 15th century (M10) and bottom, a hunting broadhead (H4). As the 1435 inventory showed, H4 heads were relatively expensive to make in both time and material. Archaeologists in England find H4s in a wide range of sites, but in very small numbers on most. Without wishing to be dogmatic about the dating of the different types of military arrowhead illustrated here, since the finds of many of these designs overlap in date, I believe that these arrowheads provide evidence of the 'arms race' between arrowsmiths and armourers. (Author's collection)

23. The bow is a replica made of Italian yew by Pip Bickerstaffe and owned by Steve Stratton. It has been made to the dimensions of one of the mid-sized bows found on the *Mary Rose*. It is 82 inches long and 115 lbs draw weight at 32 inches. It shoots a replica medieval arrow as far as, or further, than many heavier bows. (Author's collection)

24. A small row of houses built in the late medieval period (altered later) on the high street of a small town. They are all single-bay with one storey and an attic, and are partially cruck-constructed. An archer could easily afford one of these after a single sustained campaign if he did not drink and gamble his wages away. (Author's collection)

25. The three-bay house in Oxfordshire, probably built in first half of the fourteenth century, is single storey with attic space, built using crucks. An archer would have to be lucky with booty or serve on two or three campaigns to afford this more substantial house, but it is quite realistic to think of a few owning a house like this. (Author's collection)

26. Two 15th-century archers practising their craft in parkland on the estates of their employer. They are using warbows (replicas of *Mary Rose* bows of between 105lb and 125lb draw weight) and each have a few military grade arrows. They are carefully nocking an arrow and preparing to shoot at a mark rather than a butt as practice for the opening volleys in a battle.

27. One archer is about to loose at the mark whilst the other begins to draw his bow. The nearer archer has a gambeson with a livery badge of his captain. The further archer has served as a mounted archer (his high buckled boots would protect his legs while riding) and wears the cross of St. George, as did all English soldiers serving in France.

28. An Indian longbow archer at the Mahabalipuram Shore Temple (Tamil Nadu, India) built at the end of the seventh century. A bas relief, weathered by the sea, showing Shiva at full draw. (Compare his stance with photographs from Badminton and other heavy bow shoots.) This is a very early representation, so it is reasonable to assume that it reflects an actual bow type in use in South India at the time, rather than just an iconographic historical representation. (Author's collection)

were associated with gambling. But can one really believe that there was no betting by archers as they practised their skills?

While acknowledging such oblique motives, these statutes can be taken at face value. They recognise that the archer was the unique component that, when used competently with other types of soldier, won battles for the English kings. A thorough study of the surviving court records may give some idea of how many men fell foul of these statutes through being lackadaisical about archery practice.

After the Black Death, a part-time work ethic, or at least a division of effort into different activities, seemed to become more common. The sustained effort that men in medieval England and Wales put into developing their archery skills could be compared with the effort they put into developing other employment-related skills, such as carpentry or tanning. Archers' wages compared favourably with those of most artisan crafts until the end of the period, when artisans' wages began to overtake them. While it is likely that artisan work offered more long-term employment, archery offered a good return from the basic wages, particularly as the men were paid for Sundays and feast days, whereas a civilian wage earner could not work on those days. And military service had an advantage over civilian work in the opportunities for 'windfall' bonuses such as booty.

It would seem obvious that the major disadvantage of being a military archer was the danger of injury and death. This risk varied depending on the circumstances; many archers fell in the English defeat at Formigny. On the Carentan-Bayeux road on April 15th, 1450, the English forces of 4000 – of whom it is estimated that three-quarters were archers – were drawn out of their prepared defensive positions behind stakes and probably hedges and farm walls by the arrival on their flank of the Breton army of Arthur de Richemont. A series of charges saw the split English force (which included at least 500 Welsh archers) overwhelmed. Deaths and serious injuries were as high as 2500, with perhaps 900 taken prisoner. The longbow did not always reign supreme on the battlefield. All that can be said is that men were not put off being archers by the risk of injury, so perhaps it did not seem much worse than what they faced in day-to-day civilian life.

As some men began to view being a military archer as a career choice, something that began as early as Edward III's reign, they were faced with the problems of what did they did in peacetime. One option for this group was to take advantage of the reputation of the English archer, and find service as mercenaries. As the trend towards increasingly professionalised service as soldiers in the English royal armies became more apparent in the fifteenth century, this led to serving archers (and other soldiers) becoming increasingly detached from English life, so that when they tried to leave soldiering they did not easily fit back into civilian society. This seems to have been a particular problem for men driven out of Northern France in the 1450s, who lost their homes and property and brought back families who may never have seen England before. This detachment from English life contributed to the Wars of the Roses, since there were plenty of experienced soldiers available who might feel the need to be part of something more organised again.

Outlaws and those indicted for committing serious offences found a particular reward in being a military archer in the king's service. If they gave satisfactory service without wages for a designated period, they could get a royal pardon. After Edward III's reign the issue of pardons in this way became less prevalent. However, on a more informal level, even for men without a serious criminal past, service in a magnate's retinue could get them heavyweight support in any court actions they became involved in afterwards.

What sort of men became military archers? This matter has been clouded by the frequent use of the term yeoman to describe them from the fifteenth century onwards. This term could describe a peasant farmer wealthy enough to be in the top half or one third of the class. It did not in itself prove that he was a free tenant rather than holding land as a serf. The term was also used to describe servants of reasonable standing. The Statute of Winchester and the subsequent statutes covering archery practice make it clear that men with lesser resources were increasingly expected to practise archery. So it seems reasonable to suggest that military archers were drawn from all tiers of the sub gentry classes, limited only by their skill and ability to afford a bow and arrows to practise with. Some members of gentry families, probably younger sons and cousins, served as archers as a sort of military apprenticeship. I believe that it was probable that the majority would be in their twenties and early thirties, although there are a good number of occasions where older men were still serving as archers. Male children matured slower in the Middle Ages than now, reaching full physical maturity in their early twenties. Henry VIII's statute of 1541–2 regards men of 24 and above as fully mature archers. But from these same statutes it seems likely that young men might start their career as an archer in their late teens, so the age profile of the archers in an army, while showing a majority in their twenties, would have a good number aged from 18 to 20. This sort of age profile fits with that of the men found on the *Mary Rose* and in the Towton grave. Stirland describes the skeletons that she feels may have been archers as belonging to fully adult men, that is in their twenties at least. The average age of the bodies from the Towton grave is maybe as old as 30, but it has been difficult to identify experienced archers among them. Two that may have been at some point in their lives are the well known Towton 16 aged between 46 and 50 at death, and Towton 11, aged between 36 and 45 at death, who shows os acromiale (a kind of shoulder damage sometimes suffered by athletes) in the left side only, but of course we have no way of knowing if they were serving as archers in their last battle.[1]

In the fifteenth century it was the English knights and gentry, rather than the archers, who were reluctant to serve in France. This often led to the indentures being adjusted with men at arms replaced by archers. Pressed men can make good fighting men, as both Frederick the Great's armies and Nelson's navy proved. But the companies that the English archers served in were neither as isolated from the rest of contemporary society, nor under such brutal discipline as was the case with both these forces.

It is very difficult to find many cases where there is a clear link between service as an archer and an improvement in the man's social or financial position. But the wage and price comparisons speak for themselves, and I believe that the number of accounts of financially successful expeditions make it probable that the archers *believed* that they would make useful financial gains. It was not only men who were ambitious to improve their lot that served as archers, no doubt many served on one campaign, at least, out of a sense of adventure. The English archer achieved a near mythic reputation in the same way that the Swiss infantry did slightly later. This would lead some men to serve simply to share in the glory.

NOTE

1 Information about the Towton bodies from Fiorato, V, Boylston, A and Knudsel, C. eds. (2000). Information about *Mary Rose* bodies and the possible significance of os acromiale from Stirland A J (2005), p.120–30.

Part 2

The Supply and Manufacture of Bows and Arrows

Introduction

The men who established the reputation of English archers in Europe at this time were only able to achieve this distinction because of the quality and quantity of the bows and arrows available to them. This section provides an outline of how it was that the archery equipment was there for the men to use. It begins with a review of the methods used by the English Royal administration to acquire military archery equipment, and some insights into the way this equipment was issued to the archers and their commanders. These methods changed over the Hundred Years War, as a result of the demands of this sustained military effort and the concomitant growth in the archery-related crafts of bowyers, fletchers, stringers and arrowsmiths. The development of the roles of these crafts is part of the discussion of the manufacturing system that produced the bows and arrows. Finally there is a consideration of the European trade system that supplied much of the raw materials. This approach starts with the archer and his concerns about getting and replacing his equipment, and ends with matters outside his immediate influence.

Archers must have met with both bowyers and fletchers in England and even had some opportunities to meet them on campaign since the larger armies in the fifteenth century at least included a few of these craftsmen among the support troops. No doubt they would have discussed the good and bad points of bows and arrows, the archers remarking on the resistance of armour to the bows and arrows they were using. But it is probable that the main influence driving any developments of both bows and arrows in this period were the officers of the Crown responsible for the ordering of the equipment, and often the organization of some of the manufacture of it as well.

As will become clear, the supply of good quality raw materials was a regular concern of the Crown, but there is little sign of royal intervention in the trade; there are few direct royal orders for the raw materials before Tudor times. In the second half of the fifteenth century royal intervention comes through legislative rather than commercial intervention. The trade system developed to meet the needs of the English archery industry without the participation of the archers, except by their disrupting it on occasion through privateering or piratical actions.

Equipping the Archers

Archers were equipped through two complementary systems. The main responsibility for an archer's initial equipment, that which he would turn up to muster with, fell on the man himself, his community if arrayed, or his employer if indentured. At the same time the royal administration acquired large numbers of bows, arrows and bowstrings, which were mainly used for re-equipping armies on campaign or providing stores in castles. Some of the Crown stocks were used to re-equip arrayed men when they came to the muster, if their communities had skimped on supplying them.

The Assize of Arms of 1242 laid the duty on the 40/- landholder to have a bow and arrows in his house, and to bring these to the array when summoned, and so formally established the archer as part of the English military system. Under Henry III and his successors, Edward I and Edward II, the recruiting and equipping system was devolved on to the counties and cities to a remarkable degree. The king would issue writs specifying the number of troops of particular types he required, often including some description of the level of equipment he expected these troops to have. Then it was the duty of the local commissioners of array to try to find them. The counties and cities were also expected to ensure that, as a minimum, the men were armed according to their station, so that arrayed archers could expect equipment provided (at the county's expense) '... [which] consisted of bows, arrows and competent arms,[1] at the time of array if their own equipment was inadequate. There were a number of occasions when the king specified a level of equipment in the writ summoning the array that went beyond what was required by statute. Edward II was particularly persistent in his attempts to increase both service and the provision of arms at local expense. Two sets of array orders from his reign required the local communities to provide armour for archers, whereas the Assizes of Arms and the Statute of Winchester both specified that the 40/- landholder served as an unarmoured archer. The writs of 1324 were not specific about the level of armour the archer was to have, but those of 1319 specified that archers from this group of landholders were to have aketons, bascinets and iron gauntlets. The mind boggles at the thought of trying to use a bow wearing iron gauntlets.

With the development of indentured military service which effectively professionalized many soldiers, archers would have their own equipment, or be supplied with it by the retinue leader. Once the campaign had started, the leader of the campaign, the king or a magnate, was largely responsible for the provision of replacement equipment while the archer was serving. Although there is evidence of retinue leaders also carrying spare equipment. John Mowbray, the Earl Marshal, for example, took chests containing bowstrings and 100 sheaves of arrows with him to support the 150 archers of his retinue during the Agincourt campaign.[2]

Edward III's expedition to Flanders and Northern France in the autumn of 1339 reveals the scale of equipment replacement necessary during a campaign. Edward led an allied army 10,000-strong, made up of English, Flemish and German troops, to besiege Cambrai. He realised that the siege was unlikely to be successful and so led the army on a broad-fronted sweep through northern France. This destructive march made the campaign a forerunner of the strategy used in the Crecy campaign. Finally, on the 21st or 22nd of October, Edward accepted the challenge of King Philip of France to meet in battle 'at a 'convenient place uncramped by rivers, walls or earthworks'[3] and so put matters to God's judgement. Edward III selected a site favourable to his army at La Flamengrie near La Capelle. In the event King Philip reconnoitred Edward's position and thought better of attacking it. The English part of this army was made up of approximately 1600 men at arms, 1500 mounted archers (mostly serving under indentures but some were arrayed), and 1650 arrayed infantry, both archers and Welsh spearmen (at least half of whom were archers). They had been involved in a fair amount of fighting, including the siege of Cambrai and various assaults on the march to La Flamengrie, and needed some re-equipping in preparation for the proposed battle. So 620 bows, 680 sheaves of arrows and 2000 bowstrings were distributed to the English archers on the eve of the battle.[4] There is no account of how these were distributed, but the most likely approach at this time, bearing in mind that the king raised the majority of the troops directly, rather than indirectly through indentures, is that they were simply available to any archer who needed them. In which case approximately a quarter of them needed a new bow and most got a spare string. But the number of arrows strongly suggests that the army must have still had supplies, since 680 sheaves, 16,320 arrows or approximately seven arrows per archer would not be enough to win a battle. This gives an idea of some of the stores thought necessary to ensure that the archers were ready for a major battle after the wear and tear on their equipment brought about in a relatively short campaign.

In 1346 one of Edward III's orders shows what he thought of as necessary to maintain his army's archery stores during his 1346 campaign: '… for the sake of our expedition of war to France, we have immediate need of a great quantity of bows and arrows.' On August 1st of that year he ordered fifteen Sheriffs to deliver 2280 bows and 5550 sheaves of arrows to the Tower of London by 15th August.[5] Assuming that Edward was realistic in his timescale for delivery, the Sheriffs must have been accumulating stocks in expectation of such requests. It is almost certain that none of these supplies reached the army before the battle of Crecy on 26th August. They would have been used to re-equip after that. This is not to suggest that Edward had a precise date in mind for his battle with the French king's armies, but he must have felt it would be sooner rather than later. While the quantity of arrows is small for an army containing about 7500 archers, the number of bows ordered allows for nearly a third of them to have a new one.

Royal supplies were not issued only to armies led by the king himself in Edward III's reign. Equipment from the royal stores in the Tower of London was issued to support allied nobles fighting in France. In 1358 William de Rothwell, Keeper of the Privy Wardrobe (at this date this was effectively the royal arsenal in the Tower) supplied Oliver de Clisson with 500 bows (200 painted and 300 white), 100 sheaves of arrows and 1500 bowstrings for his archers going to serve in Brittany.[6] Clearly it was felt that de Clisson could find arrows for himself, whereas finding English-style bows would be difficult in Brittany.

The methods of obtaining archery equipment, storing it and distributing it to the people and places that needed it developed in line with the army recruitment system. Early on in the period there is substantial evidence of a centralised system under the king's control. In the thirteenth century the king paid the fletchers directly for their work, for example. In the fourteenth century, particularly up to around 1380, the Sheriffs were the main organisers of royal supplies in response to orders from the king. After that, mirroring the Crown's reliance on contractors through the indenture system for recruiting soldiers, equipment acquisition was done through more direct links with the guilds and merchants. Regardless of how the equipment was acquired, royal castles continued to be used as distribution centres.

Large quantities of armaments could no more be acquired at short notice in the Middle Ages than they can now. The key material for both bows and arrows was of course a supply of seasoned wood, a matter which caused quality control issues at various times, as will be outlined below. The Royal administration, based up to the middle of the fourteenth century in the Wardrobe departments, had to try to predict the king's military plans at least a year in advance so that they could get equipment orders issued and hopefully fulfilled in time to resource the expeditions when they happened. By the late 1330s, the records give the impression that a continuous process of acquisition of equipment and supply to the armies went on, almost without detailed year-on-year planning of the orders. Up to about 1360 this was a practical approach for the royal officials, since campaigning was so frequent that the supplies would all be necessary. The officials were diligent and kept a keen eye on what was delivered, chasing up slow suppliers. To avoid making unachievable demands on the resources of both materials and skilled labour in any one area, the Crown would send out simultaneous orders to 20 or more counties, an approach that developed in Henry III's reign.[7] This does not mean that there were not shortages of equipment. In 1356 the Black Prince was desperate for arrows for his planned campaign that would lead to the battle of Poitiers, finding that '…no arrows can be obtained from England because the king has caused to be arrested and taken for his use all the arrows that can be found anywhere there…'[8]

This system was underpinned by a network of regional supply bases of which the Tower of London was the most important in the fourteenth century. But it is probable that these centres did not hold large stocks of equipment for long periods,[9] but acted as collection, accounting and distribution points, sending equipment on to bases near the scene of the campaign. As early as 1304, Stirling Castle is being used as a regional supply base for the Scottish wars. The Sheriff of London sent 80 crossbows, 120 bows and 200 arrowheads; the sheriff of Lincoln 36 crossbows, 286 bows, 1200 quarrels and 1200 arrows.[10] These were not large quantities when compared with the amounts ordered in the 1340s, but an indication of the developing importance of the bow rather than the crossbow. In the fourteenth century continental supply centres were established, including Antwerp, Bruges and Mechlin, with Calais becoming the most important.

The earliest examples of the expenditure of any royal revenues on bows and arrows come from the duty of all royal officials to account to the Exchequer for any expenditure. At the end of April 1285 William FitzWarren paid 35/- for 24 bows, of which 20 were given to 'Welsh archers of the king' and the other four were for the king's service, and 24 dozen arrows at 19/9d (the bows cost $17^1/_2$d each and the arrows just under 10d per dozen). The following month William bought five more bows for the King's Welshmen for 6/8d and five dozen arrows for 3/6d (this time bows cost 16d each and the arrows about $8^1/_2$d per dozen).[11] Since the arrows are bought in dozens, this suggests that at this time, a dozen arrows was the basic issue to an archer, and the use of the sheaf of 24 might have arisen later as part of the development of the English tactical system in the 1330s.

Bows of various qualities were available and used by the king's men. There is another payment in 1285 for the purchase of six bows made of auburnus (aubour)[12] at 6d each, again to equip Welsh archers. This price suggests that these were second-rate bows. Two years later, John of Helpeston, one of the king's archers, paid 2/- for a bow, a third as much again as was spent on bows for the Welsh archers in the king's service, or on bows for military use 40 years later.[13] Perhaps John had found a particularly good bow.

In 1289 Peter de la Mare, Constable of Bristol Castle, paid 11/6d for 8 bows (about 17d each) for the Queen's foresters at Feckenham.14 Although this order is not for warbows, the price is the same as those in the Fitzwarren orders, and is very similar to the prices recorded in the fourteenth century military orders. If the similarity in cost means that the bows were of similar quality to warbows, this order underlines the desirability of foresters and parkers as military archers in Edward III's armies. Not only were they skilled archers, but they were skilled using bows of similar quality to the warbows, rather than as is sometimes suggested, using hunting bows of noticeably lighter draw weight.

Not all the early royal acquisitions of archery equipment were for land forces. The accounts of Thomas de Snetesham, Clerk of the King's ships, show that having pressed ships to his service, the king was prepared to issue arms to the crews for defence.[15] Not surprisingly these are not on the scale of William de Rothwell's acquisitions to support the land war.

	1336–7	1338–9	1342–3
Sheafs of arrows	120	2072	190
Bows		241	120
Bowstrings	240	5080	712
Crossbows (1 foot)	26	256	
Quarrels (1foot)	2340	2496	
Quarrels (2 feet)	200	30844	

The large number of crossbow quarrels and crossbows suggests that the sailors were expected to do their own fighting, and that, despite crossbows being relatively expensive in comparison to longbows, these 'amateurs' were being issued with weapons that they could use more effectively. The defence of ships did not wholly rely on the sailors, as on occasion small groups of archers were employed to guard ships throughout the period.

The prices that a Sheriff might have to pay to fulfil the king's orders do vary. In 1345 the Sheriff of Somerset and Dorset had to justify his transport expenses for dispatching 300 white bows at 18d each and 400 sheaves of arrows at 16d each.[16] A little later in the fourteenth century the Sheriff of Somerset bought 120 bows at 15d each and 456 sheaves of arrows at 16d each for sending on to the Tower.[17]

The table on the following pages lists the surviving orders issued by Edward III to support his major campaigns between 1340 and 1360. It is possible that there were other Crown orders for which no record survives, and almost certain that the magnates and captains who took indentures to lead retinues ordered some equipment at their own expense.[18]

	BOWS						SHEAVES OF ARROWS					
	1341	1346	Jan 1356	Jan 1359	Nov 1359		1341	1346	Jan 1356	Jan 1359	May 1359	Nov 1359
Description in orders	white bows	bows	white bows	bows	painted bows	white bows						
Beds & Bucks	100			300			300		600	100	300	500
Bristol	1000						300					
Cambs & Hunts	200	150						250			0	600
Cheshire	300						1000					
Devon			600						400			400
Essex & Herts	300	160	500	300			1000	400	800	200	300	500
Gloucester		300	500	500	200	400	1000	500	600	200	300	700
Hants	500	100					1000	300			0	
Hereford	200						500		1000			400
Kent	300	100	400	400			1000	300	700	200	500	700
Lancs	100						1000					
Lincoln	1000		1500	800	400	200	300		600	500	500	1000
London	2500	300					1000	1000				
Middlesex		100						300				
Norfolk & Suffolk	200	200	600				300	400	700		400	900
Northants	200	100	400	300			300	200	600	200	300	600
Notts & Derby	200						500				400	800

Oxford & Berks	100	200		200			1000	400		100	300	400
Rutland	100	50					200	100				
Shropshire							1000		1000		300	500
Somerset & Dorset	300	200	300				300	500	400		300	400
Southampton												300
Stafford							see Shropshire		500	200	300	400
Surrey & Sussex	500	100					2000	500		200	400	900
Warwick & Leics	300	120	400	500			600	200	1000	300	400	600
Wilts	100						200			300	200	300
Worcs	100	100	400				500	200	1000		300	600
Yorks	500						500					600
TOTAL	**9100**	**2280**	**5600**	**3300**	**1200**		**15800**	**5550**	**9900**	**2500**	**5500**	**12100**
TOTAL NUMBER OF BOWS ORDERED: 21,480												
TOTAL NUMBER OF SHEAVES OF ARROWS ORDERED: 51,350												
TOTAL NUMBER OF ARROWS IF SHEAF = 24: 1,232,4000												

Gloucestershire 1341 order included 500 doz. bowstrings and 2000 arrowheads
Cheshire order issued in the name of Edward Earl of Chester
Shropshire and Staffordshire rated together for 1341 order for arrows
Essex and Hertfordshire 1346 order included 500 bowstrings
Essex and Oxfordshire rated on their own in Jan 1359 order

In general bowstrings are missing from these orders. Besides the exceptions noted above, there are two other orders for 500 sheaves of arrows and 1000 bowstrings, one in 1341, the other in 1345, both to the Sheriff of Staffordshire.[19] In both cases the equipment is to be sent to the Tower of London. Bearing in mind the order from the Black Prince for bowstrings from Rugeley in Staffordshire noted below, this may be evidence of specialisation in bowstring production in the area.

All these orders were issued to the Sheriffs. These may not be the quantities they sent to the Tower since, as is shown in Appendix 3, they did not always meet the royal order exactly. The 1341 orders are unusual since the order to the Sheriff of Yorkshire included prices for the equipment, white bows at 12d each, and arrows at two prices, *garbae aceratae,* at 14d per sheaf and *garbae non aceratae,* at 12d per sheaf, that is, sheaves steeled and sheaves non steeled. Comparing these prices with others recorded around this date it is quite possible that the clerk was using terms loosely, and meant arrows with or without heads, a practice recorded elsewhere. However, if the clerk was being precise, this could be an early reference to two classes of arrows, differentiated by the quality of the heads. Those in the January 1359 order are specifically described with 'the heads of which are to be hard and well steeled', in contrast to some other orders, particularly the Cheshire record below. The bows ordered in 1356 are specifically white bows.[20] The figures are thought provoking. The differing levels of orders to different counties may be a sign that those counties from which large numbers of either bows or arrows were ordered were known to have sufficient skilled labour and raw material to have a realistic chance of delivering something like the quantities, otherwise the whole system would collapse. The importance of Lincolnshire as a source of archery equipment explains the Black Prince's request. Cheshire and Cornwall do not appear in the list because they were part of the Black Prince's holdings, semi independent of the King and he had his own army to resource. It is clear from the 1346 orders that the Sheriffs were not expected to have stockpiles of equipment since they state '…you shall immediately cause to be bought and provided for us, out of the issues of your jurisdiction, [the number of bows and arrows] from whatever places may seem best to you in your counties.'[21] The hope was that the bowyers and fletchers would have built up their stocks knowing such orders were likely.

In the orders issued in November 1359 we find the Crown using direct purchase and manufacture to augment the supplies from the Sheriffs. These orders are be made on the expectation that the Sheriffs would not be able to deliver adequate supplies, since they include a clear instruction that the Sheriffs were to provide money in lieu. This money would come out of the regular royal revenues for the counties that the Sheriffs were responsible for collecting. The prices for the equipment work out at 36d for a painted bow, 18d for a white bow and 17d for a sheaf of arrows. In addition to what he would receive from the counties, William de Rothwell was instructed to buy or manufacture, no doubt using in part the money the Sheriffs sent, as follows:

> Appointment of the king's clerk William de Rothwell, keeper of the king's privy wardrobe in the Tower of London, to take in London and elsewhere as many armourers, fleccheers, smiths and other artificers and workmen as are required for the works of armour, bows, bowstrings, arrows, arrowheads and other works connected with his office, and put them to work at the king's wages to stay as long as is necessary; to buy and fell timber and wood fit for making arrows for a reasonable price to be assessed by the oath of good men of the localities where it is taken and take carriage for the same; also to buy 1000 bows, painted and white, 10,000 sheaves of good arrows and 1000 sheaves of the best arrows, with heads hard and well steeled for the archers appointed for the king's body, 100 gross of bowstrings and 24 'haucepees' for drawing crossbows, and feathers of the wings of geese and other necessaries pertaining to his office of the wardrobe and the misteries of the said flecchers and other workmen; to have armouries 'quivers' and chests in the Tower for the storing and safe keeping of the bows, arrows and strings...[22]

I have quoted this order at length because it raises a number of issues. We can see royal power exercised to conscript the necessary skilled workers for pay to achieve the required production of military equipment. Given the purpose, this power is similar to those enabling array for armies and purveyance for food supplies. We find all three powers being replaced in the late fourteenth century by reliance on more contractual arrangements, ordering equipment from the guilds or merchants, raising armies by indentures and purchasing food from merchants or the local populace.

We know from other records that William had acquired a stock of bowstaves, which is presumably why they are not mentioned in this order, but he did not have a sufficient stock of wood for making arrows. He is ordered to both buy and fell timber, which suggests that arrows might end up being made from fairly green wood. The clear expectation is that bowyers will have already made a stock of bows, both painted and white, which William can buy. There were evidently two classes of arrow, good and best, and by reading the order one way, both of which were to have hard steel heads. Presumably the difference between the classes was either quality of materials, or that best arrows were barrelled, like those found on the *Mary Rose*. With this reading, we are left with all 11,000 sheaves being for the archers appointed for the king's body, which seems excessive. Alternatively, it reads '1000 sheaves of the best arrows, with heads hard and well steeled, for the archers appointed for the king's body'. In this case we are looking at an order that includes elite equipment for an elite body of archers. I believe that this second interpretation is correct. The best arrows, which would cost more to produce, were given the king's archers, picked men who could make best use of them. These figures are a target for the delivery, giving an idea of the quantities required. A follow up to this order comes in 1360, this time ordering that the equipment be sent to Henry de

Snayth who had succeeded William as keeper of the privy wardrobe.[23] This order is worded almost the same, except that no quantities are mentioned.

When William de Rothewell was succeeded by Henry de Snayth as Keeper of the Privy Wardrobe in 1360, he submitted a final account of the contents of the Privy Wardrobe. Fortunately this has survived and shows that by 1360 he had added the following to stock, either by purchase or manufacture:

4062 painted bows
11,303 white bows
4000 bowstaves
23,643 sheaves of arrows
341 gross of bowstrings.[24]

(There is a note about painted bows at the end of this section.) Although the royal supply system throughout the earlier part of the period was centralised, based around orders being sent to the Tower of London, it was not inflexible. There are occasional examples of the equipment being sent directly to the war theatre by the supplying Sheriff or City. In June 1345 the Sheriff of Gloucestershire was ordered to supply '100 bows and 600 sheaves of arrows to be brought and purveyed with all possible speed and delivered to the one supplying place, or the attorney of Ralph Baron of Stafford, Seneschal of Gascony … to be sent to Gascony for the war there.'[25] This not a very large store, possibly designed to re-arm the troops already in Gascony, since Stafford had been there since late March. It would have been an inadequate store for the Duke of Lancaster's army, stuck in Southampton awaiting favourable weather to sail to Gascony, containing 1000 archers.

There is another example from 1364, when there is a record of payment of transport costs for 600 bows, 1000 sheaves of arrows and 2000 bowstrings '… from the city of London to Lytherpole in the county of Lancashire, thence to be sent to Ireland.'[26] In the fourteenth century sending supplies direct to the campaigning area does not seem to have been as common as it became in the fifteenth century.

So far the focus has been on the Crown's acquisition and provision of archery equipment to support its military efforts. However, Edward, the Black Prince was running a separate acquisition and provision system in parallel to his father's, Edward III. This came about because the Black Prince, as well as being Prince of Wales was also Earl of Chester and Duke of Cornwall and later Prince of Aquitaine. Cheshire was a county palatinate, which meant that its government was largely independent of royal government, while the Duchy of Cornwall also seems to have been more or less left alone by the royal officials. As a result, neither appears in these lists of royal orders for archery equipment and they only appear in later royal orders when the titles were held by the reigning king.

There was some confusion and competition between the two administrations, the King's and the Black Prince's, particularly when it came to the acquisition of bows and arrows. This was apparent in an order from February 1356 sent by the Black Prince to his Chamberlain of Chester, complaining that the King had bought up all the arrows in England and instructing him to support Robert Pipot to buy 1000 bows, 2000 sheaves of arrows and 400 gross of bowstrings. This order includes the instruction '… to arrest the fletchers themselves to continue working their craft for the Prince until his need is satisfied … and pay the fletchers from time to time such sums as he thinks will serve to encourage them in their work.'[27] A second order from the Prince to Little John of Berkhamstede in March 1356 instructs 'Touching the bows arrows and bowstrings purveyed in the county of Lincoln the Prince sends him commission under the King's seal to take carriage for them to Plymmuth.'[28] We cannot tell whether the Black Prince was being allowed some of the equipment ordered through the Sheriffs in the royal orders of January 1356, or whether his officials had managed to acquire bows and arrows in addition to the royal orders.

In 1359 the Prince was relying on his domains for supplies of archery equipment in preparation for a substantial expedition to France. In April an order went to John de Kendale the Receiver of Cornwall and John Dabernon, Steward and Sheriff of Cornwall, that de Kendale 'was to make purveyance out of the issues of his bailiwick … of 300 sheaves of arrows with heads as soon as possible and 1000 bowstrings.'[29] By August, Dabernon had managed to send 189 sheaves and 30 dozen strings to the Prince, because he was authorised to take £20/15/4d to cover the costs of acquisition and carriage.[30] Comparing this figure with the costs of bows and strings in the period, either Dabernon had to pay over the odds for the equipment, or his costs and the costs of carriage of the equipment to the prince amounted to nearly a third of the money he received. Again, this second order demonstrates the difficulty officials had in meeting demands for archery equipment. Dabernon and de Kendale's difficulties were added to when the Prince sent them another order in November of the same year for 600 sheaves of arrows 'to be made and purveyed in their bailiwick as profitably as possible and have them sent to the Prince's wardrobe in London with all speed'. Soon afterwards they received another order that they should have as many bows made and purveyed as they can, and send them with the arrows in the previous order by sea to Southampton.[31] The change of delivery destination to the likely departure port for an expedition to France emphasises the Prince's urgency. Finally in 1360, de Kendale was allowed to reclaim monies he had spent acquiring and despatching 60 bows, 355 sheaves of arrows and 2600 arrowheads to the Prince from Cornwall (this time the carriage costs amount to one fifth of what he received at most).[32] At a local level these orders suggest that archery, and its supporting crafts, were not well developed in Cornwall at this time given the quantities of equipment the Black Prince received from his officials. This had changed by the fifteenth century.

At the same time the Black Prince also sent orders to his officials in Cheshire for equipment. In June 1359 1000 sheaves and 3000 bowstrings were despatched to Sandwich, while in December of the same year John de Brunham, the Chamberlain of Chester, was 'ordered to purvey for the Prince's use 1000 sheaves of arrows wherever he can most profitably do so, whether within his bailiwick or without, and 5000 bowstrings in the towns of Bilterwas [Buildwas, Shropshire] and Ruggeley [Rugeley, Staffordshire]. The bowstrings are to be a little bigger than the last ones purveyed by him.' In February 1360 delivery of this last order was being chased up.[33]

There are no orders for specific bows here. A small number are delivered from Cornwall, although none are mentioned in any of the surviving orders. It is possible that the bows available in Cheshire were used by the Prince's officials to equip the archers he was raising from the county, at least 300 in 1346, as noted elsewhere. The difference in quantities of arrows and strings expected from the two counties reflects their difference in size and population, and Cheshire's large military community.

A record of equipment being issued from the central store accumulated by the Earl's administration comes from the accounts of the Chamberlain of Chester for 1359–60, who was providing the following equipment to three castles, Chester, Flint and Rhuddlan. The following table shows the purchases made to build up the Earl's stores after such dispersals from the following accounting year.[34]

Item	Accounts year	Quantity	Account cost	Cost each
Bows	1359–60	33	£2/4/0d	16d
	1359–60	25	£1/11/3d	15d
	1359–60	36	£1/19/0d	13d
	1359–60	42	£2/5/6d	13d
Arrows without heads	1359–60	355 sheaves	£19/4/7d	13d per sheaf
Arrows without heads	1360–61	70 sheaves	70/-	12d per sheaf
Arrowheads	1359–60	4000	£2/12/5d	2d per dozen (approx)
Arrowheads	1360–61	2624	30/6$^1/_2$d	2d per 14 heads (approx)
Arrowheads	1360–61	1000	12/6d	2d for 13 heads (approx)
Bowstrings	1359–60	5624	£7/19/0d	1d for 3 strings (approx)

The Chamberlain of Chester's accounts record from 1360–61 also tells us the level of stores that were held in the Earldom, mostly at Chester Castle, in September 1361. These comprised 148 bows, 377 sheaves of arrows, 6472 arrowheads and 5528 bowstrings.[35] The figures for both arrows and arrowheads include those purchased in the year as listed above. In these as with many other stores of archery equipment, it is difficult to see any stock management pattern. This one contains a relatively huge number of bowstrings in relation to the number of bows. There are enough arrowheads for only 70% of the arrows, although there are a good number of arrows for each bow in the store. The purchasing system within the Earldom mirrored the royal system, in that the responsibility fell on the Prince's Artiller in Cheshire and North Wales. In 1360-61 this post was held by Thomas le Parker of Denbigh who was paid the foot archers wage of 3d per day.[36] Thomas' name suggests that he was one of the skilled archers who were sought after in the armies of the day, and we know that he was a long-term servant of the Black Prince since he is recorded as receiving an extra half penny a day wages to make and repair equipment when he was in the garrison of Caernarfon Castle in 1354.

THE SHERIFFS' SUPPLY SYSTEM

These orders taken together give an indication of the scale of acquisition of bows and arrows that Edward III and the Black Prince thought necessary for their campaigns in the 1340s and 1350s. However, the surviving records are incomplete; this is particularly true for the actual deliveries made by the Sheriffs. But there are sufficient records remaining for it to be possible to get some idea of how effective this devolved method of equipment acquisition was. See Appendix 3.[37]

The Sheriff of Lincoln, for example, was particularly effective at delivering bows. In general the response to the January 1359 orders for arrows seems quite good, although some of the deliveries may have been rather late. The Sheriff of Somerset and Dorset seems to have been the kind of efficient supplier that would gladden the heart of those in the MOD acquisitions department today; except that the order took more than a year to complete. And in 1368, the order for arrows (below) still drew a blank the following year.

In the records for 1368–9 two sets of orders for arrows survive that enable us to get a much clearer idea of how efficient the Sheriffs of the various counties could be at delivering the quantities ordered. The 1368 order issued in February required delivery by Midsummer next, and is very specific about the quality of the arrows, saying 'to be made and purveyed of seasoned and not of green wood, as he will answer it before the king and to be fitted with steel heads to the pattern of the iron head which shall be delivered to him on the King's behalf.'[38] An order was issued in July 1369 to chase up the arrears from the earlier order. The figures are as follows:

County	Quantity ordered in 1368 (no. of sheaves)	Quantity outstanding in 1369 (no. of sheaves)	% outstanding
Northamptonshire	600	402	67%
Bedfordshire	600	881	73%
Buckinghamshire	600		
Lancashire	600	600	100%
Oxfordshire	600	1200	100%
Berkshire	600		
Staffordshire	600	480	80%
Essex	600	295	49%
Surrey	600	800	66%
Sussex	600		
Lincolnshire	600	218	36%
Nottinghamshire	600	407	34%
Derbyshire	600		
Herefordshire	600	360	60%
Somerset	600	1200	100%
Dorset	600		
Norfolk	600	1200	100%
Suffolk	600		
Warwickshire	600	600	100%
Shropshire	600	600	100%
Gloucestershire	600	600	100%
Leicestershire	600	600	100%
Worcestershire	600	600	100%
Yorkshire	600	600	100%
Wiltshire	600	0	0%
Hertfordshire	600	0	0%
TOTALS	**15,600**	**11,643**	**75%**

The orders for arrows were sent to the sheriff of each county individually in 1368, but in 1369 the royal clerks paired some counties when chasing up the orders, possibly because the same man was Sheriff of both counties.

Only 25% of these orders were supplied on time. While it seems that the

Sheriffs struggled to deliver the whole of any Crown order on time, the evidence from the earlier orders suggests that the 1368 level of non performance was exceptional. It may reflect war weariness, since the 1360s were a period of fewer military successes, and much reduced opportunities to profit from war for the English. Alternatively, it may be a sign that the English Crown was losing its hold over the people, with the absence of Edward the Black Prince in Spain and Edward III slipping into old age. But the King's Clerk of the Wardrobe was not put off from issuing orders for arrows by this poor performance because more were issued in October 1369 to the Sheriffs of 24 counties for 19,600 sheaves, and in February 1371 for another 16,000 sheaves.[39] All these specified seasoned wood and steel heads to match the pattern already dispatched in 1368. How many were actually delivered is uncertain, since some of the 1371 orders were cancelled in the following year. These orders included threats of the penalties which the sheriffs would suffer, in 1369 for not using seasoned wood, but in later orders for inadequate fulfilment in general. The threat in the 1371 order is more disturbing for being vague, failure will '... cause him [the Sheriff] so to be punished that his punishment shall be a terror to others negligently executing the king's commands.'[40]

Although the king's officials must have known that ordering military archery equipment through the Sheriffs was going to bring mixed results in terms of actual delivery, they continued to use the system throughout the fourteenth century. The large-scale orders for archery equipment of the 1340s and 50s are only to be expected given the scale of campaigning, but it is more surprising to find orders on a similar scale in 1383[41] when campaigning was limited. All the following were to be delivered by the Sheriffs of the counties to the Tower of London:

County	No. of bows	No. of sheaves of arrows
Bedfordshire & Buckinghamshire	300	200
Cambridgeshire & Huntingdonshire	500	300
Cornwall	200	100
Essex & Hertfordshire	400	300
Gloucestershire	400	200
Herefordshire	300	150
Lincolnshire	800	500
Norfolk & Suffolk	600	400
Northamptonshire	300	200
Nottingham & Derbyshire	600	400
Oxfordshire & Berkshire	300	200

Rutland	200	100
Shropshire	500	300
Somerset and Dorset	500	300
Staffordshire	500	300
Surrey and Sussex	300	200
Wiltshire	400	300
Worcestershire	300	200
Yorkshire	800	500
TOTAL	**8200**	**5150**
Number of arrows, assuming 24 to a sheaf		**123,600**

Cornwall is included in this list because Richard II was also Earl of Cornwall. If we compare these orders with those of Edward III above, there is a change in royal expectations in that all the counties are expected to provide both bows and arrows. In Edward III's orders, there were signs that the royal officials believed that certain counties specialised in bow or arrow production, and so could supply relatively large quantities of one or the other, while other counties could supply smaller quantities of both. There is also a different ratio of bows to arrows in the two groups of orders, with Edward III's orders requiring between 1.7 and 2.7 sheaves of arrows to be supplied for each bow, while Richard II's order require barely two thirds of a sheaf per bow.

There is no evidence of how effective Richard II's Sheriffs were in fulfilling these orders. But, in the following chapter, there is an account of how Richard II seemed to have begun the development of the alternative system of supply, working through a combination of royal officials and leading figures in the relevant misteries.

Several of the orders noted above were issued to chase up requirements for bows and arrows sent out to the Sheriffs of various counties when delivery has been slow and partial. In light of the scale of expenditure involved in these orders it is no surprise that the clerks of the wardrobe departments seem have kept close track of the supply and the issue of equipment when it was issued to other store bases, rather than to armies on campaign.

On other occasions they were aware of equipment in regional centres which was surplus to immediate local needs and so could be sent elsewhere. In 1376 Robert of Wykford, Archbishop of Dublin and Constable of Bordeaux, was ordered to send Thomas Mebburne, treasurer of the Duke of Brittany 100 bows, 200 bowstrings and 200 sheaves of arrows from the stores in Bordeaux.[42] In 1400 Henry IV ordered that a substantial assortment of arms be returned from Dublin Castle to the Tower of London, no doubt having accumulated in Dublin to support Richard II's Irish campaigns. These included '... one tun full of bows, one coffer containing 96 bows, thirty pipes and one small one full of arrows, one barrel full of bowstrings ... sixteen single canons, eight short barrels of canons, eight stokkes of canons, six barrels full of gun stones...' and tools and powder for the guns.[43] This is particularly interesting since it gives a fairly early example of the use of gunpowder weapons in small numbers, probably including handguns (the eight short barrels and eight stokkes). This development, the use of bows of both types and gunpowder artillery, becomes more apparent in orders and inventories of equipment in the fifteenth century. Another early example comes from 1404, when Robert Walys was ordered 'to take saltpetre for the king's guns and all other things necessary for the making of bows, springalds and crossbows, and for the gear and array of the guns within the castle of Pontefract.'[44]

There is no record of the royal equipment stocks being used to resource the garrisons of castles in France held by the men of the great indentured captains in the fourteenth century. Things were different in the fifteenth century, when castles and towns were held as part of the royal administration of English Normandy. In both the second half of the fourteenth and early fifteenth centuries there a sequence of orders to the collectors of customs for the south coast ports to allow bows and arrows to be taken out of the country, usually without paying customs. In 1367, John Thurston, yeoman of Sir John Chandos, with three others was allowed to take various arms including 24 bows, four dozen arrows and six crossbows '... for the munition of the town and castle of Seint Savour'.[45] This is more likely to have been a private purchase rather than royal supply because the numbers are small, more suited to a garrison than a retinue, and the castle was Chandos's main base in the Cotentin.

In the 1390s there are a group of orders to the collectors of customs for the port of London not to charge John Holand, Earl of Huntingdon and Captain of Brest any customs on equipment he is taking to Brest '... for furnishing the same'. In1390 he took 200 bows and 300 bowstrings, in 1391 he took another hundred bows there, while in 1394 William Sempyngham, servant of the Receiver of the castle, took over 108 bows, one gross of bowstrings and eight (?) sheaves of arrows with some other stores. What is uncertain in the first and third examples is the source of the bows; were they from the royal store or acquired separately by Huntingdon? The 1391 batch is specifically described as bought and purveyed by him, suggesting that he had to source armaments himself, albeit with royal authority, rather than rely on royal stocks.[46] We know that in 1415 Lord Furnival, Lieutenant of Ireland, had to equip his archers at his own cost, because there is a record of his unsuccessful attempt to get the Crown to provide their equipment.[47]

It was not only magnates with large resources who equipped their men; there are examples of lesser commanders doing the same. In 1403, John Lardener, captain of Oye castle in Picardy, took two black cloths, two red cloths, six saddles and twelve bows '...for raiment of his hired soldiers and servants and for furnishing the castle'.[48] This small retinue wearing their uniforms of red and black coats makes it look as if the Captain had ideas above his station.

The archery industry in medieval England served a number of markets. So far the evidence has been of equipment acquired for use in national military activity, but there was a great deal of equipment used in more localised or personal ways, for mercenary service and crusading, or private use in England, for hunting, brigandage and sport. Some of the accounts records have survived from when Henry Bolinbroke was preparing for his crusade to Prussia in 1390. Eighty bows were bought at 12d each, six broad bows at 24d each, 73 sheaves of arrows for a total of £4/4/4d (13.9d per sheaf) and four sheaves of broad arrows.[49] These prices for the standard bows and arrows are on the low side compared with prices mentioned in the large-scale orders of the 1340s. It was a buyer's market because of the relatively low level of military inactivity at the time. What broad bows (*arcubus latis*) were, and why they cost twice as much as ordinary bows is discussed in the note at the end of this chapter.

There are more straightforward accounts of magnates buying archery equipment for their men or their castles. In 1399–1400 the Duchy of Lancaster accounts list the purchase of 20 bows, 36 sheaves of arrows and one gross of strings for Pontefract castle at a cost of £6/6/0d.[50] These prices are much higher than Henry Bolinbroke paid ten years earlier, roughly double.

In 1413 there was an inquiry into the expenditure by the Captain of Calais and the prices charged by four victuallers. This inquiry may have been motivated by family tensions between Henry IV, and his sons, Henry of Monmouth, the future Henry V, and the Duke of Clarence, as much as concern about corrupt dealings. The inquiry recorded the prices paid by the Captain, Henry of Monmouth in the previous two years for archery equipment delivered to him. Raw materials did not seem to be a problem since 300 bowstaves had cost £9, just over 7d each or 60/- per 100, a price recorded a little later in the year as one the Exchequer would expect to pay.[51] The prices for finished equipment tell a different tale since the Captain paid 2/- for bows, 2/- per sheaf for arrows with heads and 8d per dozen for bowstrings. The inquiry cleared the Captain of any wrongdoing but the victuallers appeared to have been taking advantage, charging prices at least 33% higher for arrows and strings than those paid by the royal administration in England in the same year and 60% higher for bows (see the following chapter). The problem for the Captain of Calais in Henry IV's reign was that he was almost entirely dependent on England for supplies, whereas in the reign of more militarily successful kings he would have some opportunity for sourcing supplies in France. As a result he was at the mercy of the merchants who were prepared to risk carrying goods across the Channel. Considering that risk, maybe he was not cheated.

At the end of Henry IV's reign and more particularly in Henry V's reign, records survive which give an insight into both the level of re-equipping an expeditionary force might need and the process of how the royal administration supplied bows and arrows to the archers on campaign. In 1412 Thomas Duke of Clarence led a force of about 1000 men at arms and 3000 archers to France in support of the Armagnac faction.[52] Unfortunately for him, the Armagnacs and the Burgundians came to an agreement which left Clarence potentially without allies. However, the French king issued a safe conduct to enable the English to march to Aquitaine. In 1413 supplies were bought by the Crown to be sent to Aquitaine to supply the Earl of Dorset who had remained in Aquitaine with between a third and half of the men Clarence took to France. These supplies amounted to 500 bows, 1700 sheaves of arrows and 40 gross of bowstrings.[53] These supplies were sufficient for each archer to have at least one sheaf of arrows and three or four bowstrings, and allow at least a third to have a new bow. This may overstate the level of re-equipping necessary, since it is more generous than that noted in 1339 above; some of this equipment probably went either to local troops or into arsenals.

How were the large expeditions supplied? In 1413 John Acclane, possibly from Wiltshire, was appointed a Yeoman of the Crown on a wage of 6d per day. In July 1415 he and another man were ordered to seize all ships of over 20 tons burthen in the port of London and get to Southampton with all haste. In the same month he was ordered to 'take bows, arrows, bowstrings and other things pertaining to the office of artillery and the offices of bowyers, fletchers and stringers and carriage for the same and workmen and labourers'. In September 1417 Acclane received a similar order, this time including mention of crossbows, arbalasters and arrowsmiths.[52] In other words he was to arrange the transport of existing equipment, and some men to look after and maintain it. These workmen and labourers could not have been expected to carry out the manufacture of equipment on any scale while attached to an army on campaign. The additional equipment and skilled workers mentioned in the later order may reflect the enlargement of Henry V's ambitions after his success at Agincourt, in that he now felt conquest of France was a realistic policy and was planning larger scale expeditions.

From the 1420s to the 1440s there were no expeditions near the scale of Henry V's campaigns. Relatively small field armies were raised in England on occasion, but, in general, the forces in English-controlled France were made up of individual retinues and garrisons, from which field armies could be created as necessary. During this period the king might issue orders to create stocks of equipment, but it was the military leaders in France who were responsible for getting the equipment to their men.

The orders issued in Henry VI's name in 1430 often do not specify quantities and seem to be concerned with authorising the archery industry to produce and supply as much as possible. In 1431 Nicholas Bernardyn of Luke was licensed '... to buy 1000 bows with strings for same and 1000 sheaves of arrows in England and forward them with all speed to Rouen.'[55] Rouen was the headquarters of John, Duke of Bedford, Regent of France. Given his position it seems surprising that Bedford was not authorised to take equipment from royal stores for these troops. This is probably an example of the retinue system at work writ large, wherein the retinue leaders have a responsibility for their men's equipment. The Privy Council issued a second order in August 1432 'to do with all good haste to order and purvey 1000 bows, 2000 sheaves of arrows and three score gross bowstrings (8640) and deliver them to Stephen Flexmere',[56] who in turn would deliver them to John, Duke of Bedford in France. This order makes no mention of purchase. There is a similar order in 1435, when Alexander Learmouth esquire is instructed '… to provide carriage by land and water from London to Berwick upon Tweed for lances, bows, arrows bowstrings and other habiliment for the equipment of the said town and the king's march there.'[57] This looks like a transfer of equipment from Crown stocks, possibly housed in the Tower of London, as part of the King's duty to protect the borders of his kingdom. At this time King Henry became concerned that he was being overcharged by the suppliers of armaments, especially those in London. Writs were sent to the Sheriffs of London ordering them to make proclamations 'enjoining all makers of armour artillery [bows and arrows] and other weapons of war in the City to sell such armour etc. at a reasonable price and forbidding all armourers, bow makers and arrow makers and their servants to demand unreasonable payment for their labour.'[58]

There are two detailed records of John, Duke of Bedford's household which give an idea of the scale of military equipment he needed both for his retinue and for campaigning. In both cases these orders gave Bedford exemption from the customs due on his supplies, a relatively small concession given the cost of maintaining his household in the King's war in France. At the time of these orders, Bedford's personal retinue consisted of 100 men at arms and 300 archers and was based with him at Rouen.[59]

12th NOVEMBER 1430

4 chests filled with bows
2 casks of bowstrings
3 chests containing 200 bows.

17th NOVEMBER 1433

400 bowstaves
one coffer containing 9 dozen bows
3 gross of bowstrings
2000 feathers.[60]

Bows, bowstaves and bowstrings were evidently difficult to get in France. The household included some bowyers since staves were sent. Similarly we must assume there was a group of arrowsmiths and fletchers with no mention of arrows. While suitable wood for the shafts appears to have been obtainable locally, feathers had to be sent. The quantities of bows and bowstaves are such that these orders are clearly intended to equip more men than those in the retinue; in both cases it is reasonable to suggest that at least 500 bows (or the necessary staves) were delivered.

It is a mark of John, Duke of Bedford's importance to the English effort in France that, on his death in 1435, an inventory was made of both the amount and value of the royal military equipment held at Rouen Castle, his administrative centre. Besides detailed descriptions of gunpowder weapons and their associated equipment, there is the following list of archery equipment.[61]

Quantity	Item	Value of each
323	bows of yew without strings	34d
323	sheafs of arrows, each sheaf of two dozen, headed with iron and fletched	$19^{1}/_{4}$d per sheaf
118	sheafs of arrows, each sheaf of two dozen, headed with iron and fletched	$21^{1}/_{4}$d per sheaf
13	sheafs of arrows, each sheaf of two dozen, fletched and fitted with barbed heads	51d per sheaf
14	Sheafs of arrows fletched but without heads	$12^{3}/_{4}$d per sheaf
60	Painted bows (*arcus picturati*) without strings	$48^{1}/_{2}$d
15	bows of yew without strings	34d

These values are in English silver pence converted from Livre Tournois in the inventory. This may slightly underestimate the sterling value.

These yew bows, at about 34d, are put at just under twice the value of bows in 1420–1 noted above. Allowing for different clerks valuing things slightly differently, this is a large increase in just twenty years, given how stable the price had been up to 1420. It is no surprise to find the bows stored without strings, many of the equipment orders specify bows and strings separately. Hemp or linen strings, coated in wax or tallow, would need protecting from vermin while in storage. Specifying that the bows are made of yew may be significant; an indenture from 1475 lists both yew and wyche bows (see below). Painted bows are valued as being worth about 43% more than yew bows. It is possible that these were for the archers in his personal retinue.

We have no idea what causes the difference between the two valuations of ordinary arrows. It may be based upon the wood used for the shafts, or, as with with the arrow types in the 1475 list, it may relate to the fletchings. Given the emphasis in many previous orders on the heads of arrows being made of steel, it is likely that the clerks who recorded iron heads were more concerned to record how many arrows had heads and how many not, rather than being metallurgically accurate. Ordinary arrowheads were valued at about $3^1/_4$d per dozen. This value shows about a 60% increase in the price when compared with the Cheshire figures of 75 years earlier. The prices for complete arrows seem to have remained the most constant, showing a relatively low rise compared with bows and arrowheads. As will be made clear in the later chapters on the trade in bowstaves and the manufacture of bows, there is no reason to believe that these bows were more costly because they were yew. It may just reflect a local scarcity of good warbows. The increase in arrowhead prices could reflect an increase in the cost of iron. Arrows with barbed heads cost about two and a half times as much as ordinary arrows, and represent a very small percentage of the total. It is probable that these were not military arrows but for hunting, and, given the cost, may even have been very highly finished arrows of the kind that are found in Sir John Dynham's inventory (see page 209). Excavations at a number of English castle sites have turned up a range of arrowhead types, showing that, within castle communities at least, archery was not just a purely military occupation.

It is important to remember that the inventory is a valuation; many of the prices from the fourteenth century, particularly those for orders issued in Edward III's reign, could be purveyance prices. Purveyance was the right of the king to compulsorily purchase certain goods at a price agreed between the royal officials and the owner of the goods. Not surprisingly, it was never popular since it was felt that it was abused by royal officials. The Statutes of 1340 limited the scope of purveyance, a limitation which was regularly re-enacted through Edward III's reign.[62] The word 'purvey' appears in many of the later fourteenth century orders for bows and arrows issued to royal officials. However, as noted elsewhere, the prices are much the same as those in both the royal orders and the purchases of bows and arrows made by others. So, given the regular parliamentary activity to restrict purveyance, it seems likely that the prices in the orders reflect the market price for bows and arrows. (The kings' efforts to control the price of bows, all made in the last decades of the fifteenth century, are discussed in the following chapter.) In conclusion, prices for bows, arrows and arrowheads were fairly stable between about 1340 and 1420, but after that the prices of bows in particular began to rise.

In Henry VI's reign royal supplies of military equipment were sometimes passed on to equip troops raised by indenture, both those serving in France and the home defence forces protecting key points such as the Isle of Wight. In 1443 Gilbert Parr, the master of the king's ordinance was ordered to deliver a range of equipment to John Dawson, the master of the Duke of Somerset's ordinance, to supply an expedition the Duke was mounting to France. Besides the constituents of gunpowder this included 3000 bows, 3000 sheaves of arrows and 200 gross of strings.[63] In November 1449 Parr, now called 'keeper of our artillery in the Tower of London', was ordered to deliver supplies to Robert Whitingham or his deputy for the defence of Caen, including 1000 'long bowes', 2000 sheaves of arrows,

20 gross of strings, gunpowder, saltpetre, sulphur, iron, tar, pitch and caltrops.[64] This is one of the orders that show how badly the situation was deteriorating in English-held Normandy, with Caen under real threat. It is not clear how much of this equipment was actually delivered in either case. In February 1450 there is an order for the despatch of 600 bows, six gross of strings, gunpowder and saltpetre to Caen, again to Whitingham or his deputy, who is named this time as John Cauners. Attached to this order is a warrant to Gilbert Parr to deliver 1000 sheaves of arrows and brimstone to Caen as well.[65] This equipment may be another delivery in addition to the November 1449 order, or a record of what was actually available to be delivered. Another example of how rapidly the English hold on Normandy was collapsing comes in June 1450 in an urgent order for supplies to be sent to Cherbourg, described as standing in 'greet jupart and perille'. This included saltpetre, sulphur, 400 bows, 1000 sheaves of arrows, 20 gross of strings, wheat, malt and hops (beer must have been vital to strong defence) and two gunners.[66] Clearly the garrison had enough archers, but there were vacancies for specialist gunners to be in charge of the artillery.

Meanwhile in 1442 the Privy Council issued a slightly confusing set of orders for the equipping of troops protecting the Isle of Wight.[67] In August Sir Stephen Popham, Sir William Iver, Miles Stapilton and John Heron were ordered 'to keep the sea'. They were to muster their forces on the island, and were given 200 spears, 300 bows and 300 sheaves of arrows to equip them. Popham was authorised to take victuals for 100 archers. These orders then seem to have been reissued, except that 500 bows and sheaves of arrows, along with the spears and victuals, were to be sent in the later version. It is not clear how many men these four were expected to raise, but it was a relatively small number of arrows per bow. Later, in 1450, the defence of the Isle of Wight was was causing concern again, so the King ordered that Thomas Vaghan, 'master of our ordinance', should be given sufficient money from the Exchequer to buy eight fowlers, six serpentines, 12 ribaldequins, 24 culverins, a pipe of gunpowder, 100 'longebowes', 100 sheafs of arrows, 30 crossbows, a pipe of quarrels, pole arms and armour, mainly to furnish Carisbrooke Castle.[68] This order gives an interesting insight into Henry VI's military administration. Firstly, the Crown does not appear to have this range of equipment in storage and hopes to be able to buy at least a proportion of it quickly from commercial suppliers. Secondly, the mix of missile weapons shows a change in emphasis in the arming of a castle. The range of types of guns would cover most needs, but the longbows were not well supplied with arrows, while the small number of crossbows that were supplied seem to have had a more generous allocation of ammunition. If we compare these with the supplies mentioned above as being sent to France at this time, the guns are no surprise, since gunpowder is being sent to France as well; it is the relatively limited number of bows – and particularly arrows – and the inclusion of crossbows that is more noteworthy. Perhaps it is predicated upon the men available to defend the island, and their abilities.

What happened to the equipment ordered to be sent to the island in 1442? While there may have been orders, now missing, that requested the return of the equipment to London once the emergency was over, it may also be an early sign of the casual use or even wastage of stores of military equipment that is implied by records of Henry VIII's reign noted below.

Whenever the king's prestige was at stake, because he was leading an expedition abroad, significant efforts were made to ensure that the expedition was properly supplied. We know quite a lot about the archery equipment committed to Edward IV's expedition to France in 1475. In preparation orders were sent to the Sheriffs of 33 counties and of Canterbury, Coventry, Lincoln, London, Nottingham, Southampton and York

> ... considering that among other ordinance bows and arrows be most specially necessary, therefore our said lord commandeth that no fleccher make any manner of tackle for shooting but only sheaf arrows: and that all bowyers make their bowstaves into bows: and that the bowyers and flecchers and makers of arrow strings and heads for bows every of these as pertaineth to his occupation in all haste possible make and do to be made the same good and sufficient so that no default be found in them upon pain of the king's displeasure.[69]

It seems that by this time there is no need for precision in the orders, the military standard is well known, although, as will be apparent from the next document, the specification of a sheaf arrow varied. Later in 1475 there is an indenture, effectively a delivery note confirming the arrival of a whole range of equipment in France for the expedition. While most of it is connected with gunpowder weapons, it includes the following: 1134 yew bows, 225 wyche bows, 182 gross of bowstrings, 350 sheaves of arrows with nine-inch fletchings, 1750 sheaves of arrows with eight-inch fletchings, 7960 sheaves of arrows with seven-inch fletchings and 228 sheaves of unheaded arrows.[70] There is much of interest in this document. Firstly there is the mention of warbows made of different woods. It is unlikely that this represents something new, just that the surviving records are not specific before this. It may show that there was a shortage of yew staves of sufficient quality to make warbows. While we know that Henry VIII had to issue orders about the production of bows in lesser woods and the quality of imported bowstaves, there is no evidence of there being a crisis in the supply of staves at this time. However, there may have been, since trade between England and the Hanseatic League was at a very low level between 1470 and 1474 because of a dispute over compensation and trading rights.[71] This was significant since the ports of Holland, north Germany and the Baltic, those dominated by the Hanse, were major sources of imported bow staves. So, while the use of woods other than yew for warbows may well reflect the normal practice, it may also be the result of the temporary difficulty in gaining foreign supplies. The specification of three classes of arrows according to length of fletching is a bit of a puzzle. The quantities suggest that seven-inch fletchings were the norm, a suggestion supported by evidence from the *Mary Rose*, where the vast majority of the arrows also showed signs of having seven-inch fletchings. Eight- and nine-inch fletched arrows make up 17% and 3.5% respectively. Why were arrows supplied with such long fletches, since it would not have improved their performance? It is not laziness on the part of the fletchers, not bothering to cut down the feathers, since it left them with a longer fletch to whip. Yet again, enormous numbers of strings were supplied, over 26,000, for the number of archers involved.

Once large-scale regular military activity such as the wars in France and the Wars of the Roses were over, the Crown administrators under Henry VII became very careful about spending money to stockpile bows and arrows. In 1489 there is an order from Henry VII – who had a well earned reputation for being careful with money – delivered through the Mayor, Aldermen and Council of York concerning bows and arrows taken up at the Crown's behest for the defence of the city, but, in the event, proving unnecessary. The order stated '…that every bower and fletchers shold tak ther bowez and arrowez agane…'[72] An early example of sale or return.

A case can be made that the high point of English military archery from a purely military point of view was any of the following: the 1340s, 1350s, Henry V's reign, or the 1420s. But the apogee of equipment development was in Henry VIII's reign. Because of the sinking of the *Mary Rose*, it is the only part of the period from which actual English military bows and arrows survive.[73] Henry VIII's reign also marks the beginning of the end of archery as a major element of English military practice. Henry is well known to have taken a keen interest in archery, both personally as a sport, and as one of England's military strengths, so it is reasonable to assume that the archery equipment used in his reign was of high quality. Bows and arrows were distributed from central stores, mainly from the Tower. In 1511 Sir Sampson Norton, the Master of the Ordinance, delivered bows to various commanders in England, and in 1512 there was a more specific delivery of 100 bows and 200 sheaves of arrows to Norham Castle in preparation for trouble with the Scots.[74]

Henry VIII made determined efforts to ensure the supply of good bows and similar efforts were made in regard to other equipment. Thousands of harnesses – comprising a pair of plates, splints for the arms, gorgets and helmets – were bought for the infantry, for the bill and pikemen. Handguns were bought including 80 from a Spanish merchant for 6/- each, and harquebuses from other suppliers costing nearly twice as much.[75] It was publicly recognised in the 1540s that the skills of using the handgun needed to be encouraged and was surely understood before then. But in 1513, when Henry's army invaded France, hand guns were expensive in comparison with the English bow, and it seems that there were still sufficient skilled archers available to meet the demands of Henry's military ambitions.

The records of this army have survived in considerable detail and as a result there is a good deal of information about the 'support units' of the force. Sir Sampson Norton, the Master of the Ordinance, led a retinue of 1079 men made up of the various categories of support troops, which included gunners – a small number of men with specialist knowledge who acted as gun captains directing ordinary troops to work the guns – carters, pioneers, miners, eight bowyers, eight fletchers and bowstring makers. There were more specialists in the army to support the archers since pay records for the army when it was in France list a master bowyer and 20 bowyers, a master fletcher and 20 fletchers, and a master stringer with 4 stringers. The masters were paid 12d per day while the ordinary craftsmen were paid 8d,[76] in line with an archer's pay. Eight pence was not the 'minimum wage' in the army since the two carters who carried 'the king's bows and arrows' were paid 6d per day.[77] These figures suggest that the commanders of large English armies expected that there would be a need for a considerable amount of maintenance work on bows and arrows while on campaign. Manufacturing activities would only really be practical when the army was static, either in camp or more likely besieging somewhere. It would be difficult to get much work done at each nightly stop, even allowing for the rather leisurely rate of march of Henry's army in 1513.

The remarkable archaeological excavations of the *Mary Rose,* which sank in 1545, recovered many artefacts including 138 complete bows, parts of another 34, 3969 arrows and 18 bracers. In comparison with the inventory figures for the *Mary Rose* in the Anthony Roll, these finds represent 55% of the bows listed (70% if we include the bow pieces) and 40% of the arrows (if all the sheaves were of 24 arrows, which is far from certain, since some leather spacers for 36 arrows have been found), a remarkable proportion.[78] Not all the bows were for use in the engagement during which the *Mary Rose* sank, as 84 of them were found in two chests.[79] It is unlikely these bows were stored with strings since the practice throughout the period was to store bows and strings separately, and so these were not for immediate use. It is probable that the inventory does not list all the bows and arrows on board. It is unlikely to have included any bows and arrows brought on board by archers serving on the ship. There is some debate about how many men were on the ship when she sank since the contemporary sources are ambiguous. The consensus is that there were 200 sailors of all ranks, 185 soldiers and 30 gunners.[80] In common with the figures for the complements of other ships in Henry's navy these make no differentiation between different types of soldier. The highest likely number of archers would have been maybe 120, if the same ratio between archers and close quarters soldiers applied as did in the 1420s for sea soldiers.[81] However, if the number of archers was in the ratio to other types of soldier as in contemporary land retinues, then no more than half were archers, particularly if there were some hand gunners on board. Stirland suggests that the skeletons she identified as probably belonging to archers belonged to specialist, or professional archers.[82] Such men would be harder to find in the 1540s than they were between 1350 and 1450 when endemic warfare made it worthwhile developing military archery skills. The bow recovered in a braced shape may have belonged to one of these men who were waiting on the upper decks for a chance to shoot.

Where were the archers stationed on the *Mary Rose*? Stirland makes a strong argument against the view that archers may have been posted below decks, attached to gun crews to cover open gun ports. Looking at the reconstruction, it becomes clear that it would be difficult for a large number of archers to shoot effectively from the upper decks. On both the forecastle and after castle the field of fire is restricted by the rigging and the sails, unless they were at least part reefed. While true broadside archery would have been very difficult, fore and aft shooting, and a limited number of archers shooting in an arc to the sides would have been practicable. Anti-boarding netting would probably not have been rigged on these castles, which would have made archery easier. Contemporary archers may like to consider how attractive they find the idea of shooting a heavy bow from the fighting tops. This makes it sensible to suggest that there would have been little point in more than a third of the soldiers on the *Mary Rose* in 1545 being specialist archers, since they would have struggled to find room to ply their bows. The Fighting Instructions compiled by Sir Thomas Audley in around 1530 for use by the captains of the Royal fleet make the longbow look insignificant on naval ships by this time. Audley 'almost certainly drafted [the Instructions] from long established precedents',[83] but, since he was not a military man himself, he may have made a misleading omission when he wrote 'In case you board your enemy enter not till you see the smoke gone and then shoot of all your pieces [guns], your port pieces [(hand guns?] the pieces of hail shot and crossbow shot to beat his cage deck, and if you see his deck well ridden [cleared] then enter with your best men.'[84] No mention of the longbow, a weapon which one would have thought to be very useful for clearing enemy decks given its rate of fire and impact.

The *Mary Rose* carried twice as many bows as she did soldiers serving as archers. This seems to have been the practice throughout the ship's long career. In 1513 the crew was 200 soldiers, 160 sailors and 40 gunners while the weapons on board included 350 bows, 300 bills, 300 morrispikes, 200 stakes and 220 harnesses of armour,[85] enough weaponry to give all the soldiers and sailors a choice. The presence of stakes to defend the archers suggests that the soldiers and sailors were expected to fight on land when necessary. There are several possibilities why the ship carried more bows than archers. She could have been carrying equipment to support either a landing by the ship's company or other land-based men.[86] The bows could simply be spares. And since every ship in the Anthony Roll carried bows they could have been for the sailors to use either on land or sea.[87]

At the time of the sinking of the *Mary Rose* the bow had been developing within the English tactical system for over 200 years, so these bows show the final developments in power and limb design. Henry VIII made substantial efforts to get the best bow staves he could. And since the *Mary Rose* was one of Henry's favourite ships, it is likely that it had better than average equipment. The fact that all the bows found were yew supports this suggestion, since wyche bows were available in the Royal armouries from at least 1475[88] and supplied to some other ships earlier in Henry's reign. But there is no reason to suggest that the *Mary Rose* bows were exceptional in 1545, just that they were good quality.

Evidence of the relative decline of the importance of military archery in English land forces comes from a request made by Lord Lisle and others based at Boulogne. In January 1545 they requested that 2000 pikes, 1000 black bills, 600 bows, 12 chests of arrows, 60 gross of bowstrings and 300 Italian handguns be sent to arm the English forces based there.[89] The quantities suggest that missile weapons are subordinate to contact weapons, but bows are still regarded as highly effective when compared with handguns. While this may have been an economic decision, since bows were cheaper than guns, it was no doubt a practical decision as well.

After Henry's death in 1547, an inventory was compiled of all his possessions, both personal and those such as ships and gunpowder artillery that he held as King.[90] The number of bows and arrows regardless of condition or bow wood held on ships and in castles and equipment stores is large, comprising 18,513 bows and 55,451 sheaves of arrows. It is interesting to compare this with William de Rothwell's account of 1360, which listed 15,365 bows, 4000 bowstaves and 23,643 sheaves of arrows. Including staves, William had accumulated more bows, but fewer arrows per bow. While it is difficult to make a judgement as to whether the English where engaged more actively in warfare in 1360 or 1547, the number of bows at the later date is surprising given the scale of Henry VIII's purchases of bowstaves that we know about. It is clear in the inventory that not all the bows were in usable condition. Stocks in English castles and fortifications, even those at the front line like Carlisle, were likely to include a considerable number in poor condition; Warke Castle, for example had 24 'bowes good and badde' and Carlisle Castle 93 'bowes of eugh nothing worth'.

The stores of archery equipment in the royal castles could fluctuate wildly in both number and condition. Stores of bows and arrows were held in the North of England for use in countering the Scots. In January 1545 Thomas Scarden, the King's Bowyer and John Stoddar, the King's Fletcher, were dispatched from London to go north and 'put in order the bows and arrows'.[91] They were accompanied by three bowyers and five fletchers. We have no record of this sort of activity, the sending of royal artificers to maintain the archery equipment of royal castles, before Henry's reign, although there are a few records of such craftsmen being appointed to castles to fulfil the role. There is no indication of how many places Scarden and Stoddar and their men worked at. The inventory lists 93 bows in Carlisle castle and 92 in Carlisle Citadel as worthless, so perhaps they were not able to achieve much there at least.[92]

In April 1545, the Earl of Shrewsbury wrote a letter to the King describing the amount and readiness of the gunpowder artillery at Carlisle in both the Town and the Castle. Almost as an aside he mentions that he has 9000 bows, 1000 sheaves of arrows 180 bills and 180 moorish pikes.[93] This figure for bows is almost incredible, representing nearly half the number of bows listed in the whole inventory two years later. Even more surprising is that the inventory only lists 93 bows in Carlisle Castle and 92 in the other fortifications within the city, none of them usable. The two-year gap between Shrewsbury's letter and the compilation of the inventory in September 1547 means that the stores of equipment at Carlisle could have been used to equip the army engaged in the 'Rough Wooing' of Scotland in 1545–47. This campaigning included the English defeat at Ancrum Moor in 1545 and the much greater Scottish defeat at the Battle of Pinkie in 1547. Once bows were issued to campaigning armies, there is no evidence of them being returned to store at the end of the campaigns, so the Carlisle store could easily have been reduced to nothing by the time of the inventory.

What happened to all the bows Henry had made? Between 1510 and 1514 he ordered and probably received at least 40,000 staves from the Venetians, plus at least half as many again from the Luccan merchant Bonvix. (See Conclusion, page 240, for further discussion of this, and comments in the Afterword, page 241, on the 'arms race', part of the answer.)

CROWN SPECIFICATIONS

There is no surviving specification for an English military bow from this period, which suggests that the bowyers knew what was required. The only contemporary specification is one for a hunting bow given by Gaston Phoebus, Count of Foix in his *Book of the Hunt*, c.1388. He writes that the bow should be about 70 inches nock to nock and be braced to about $7^3/_4$ inches. He also specifies an arrow length of about 28 inches, suggesting a shorter draw than the English warbow which could be drawn to at least 30 inches based on the *Mary Rose* arrows.[94] The terms of the surviving royal orders suggest that ensuring the supply of good quality arrows presented more problems throughout the period than did the supply of good quality bows. Arrows were supplied both with and without heads. As a result we find that there are separate quality control issues for both arrows and arrowheads. We have already noted that in February 1368 orders were sent out the sheriffs of 26 counties for 600 sheaves of arrows from each, which is 374,400 arrows, to be delivered to the Tower of London by midsummer. These orders specified the use of seasoned wood not green, but, in common with bow orders, with no mention of particular woods. They were to be 'fitted with steel heads to the pattern of the iron head which shall be delivered to him on the king's behalf.'[95] This indicate that the royal officials had been advised about possible shortcomings in the arrow manufacture limiting the effectiveness of English archery. At both the Battle of Poitiers (1356) where the archers in the Earl of Warwick's battle found their arrows ineffective when shooting head-on at the advancing French cavalry (they moved out to the flank and devastated the French by shooting into their horses' flanks) and at the battle of Auray (1364) where the armour and large shields of the French men at arms frustrated the archers (who put their bows down and joined in the melee to great effect) it was demonstrated that English archery could be negated. The arrowheads were to be made of steel to improve the chances of the arrow penetrating armour.

The provision of a pattern for the arrowheads is significant. It is the only example I have found of the Crown providing a precise specification for a piece of archery equipment in this whole period. What was the pattern?. In his new typology of medieval arrowheads, Oliver Jessop[96] has suggested that the M4 type – London Museum Medieval Catalogue (LMMC) Type 16 – was introduced in the fourteenth century. 'Bodkin' type heads, M10 in his classification (LMMC 8 and 10) he finds over the whole period from the twelfth to the fifteenth century. In the examples he has seen, the size variation is less in the type M4 than it is in the type M10. This may because of the longer period of development of the type M10. However, it may be because the type M4 is a standard for a period. There has been some metallurgical analysis of medieval arrowheads, and the most recent study, by David Starley, found that of the four M4 heads he analysed, three 'were clearly of composite construction with iron socket and steel point and wings, quenched and tempered to provide optimum properties.'[97] He also examined two bodkin heads, one of which was iron and the other had some steel in it but there had been no attempt to harden it. These metallurgical results, admittedly from a very small number of archaeological finds because the analysis is destructive, could support the theory that the type M4 represents the standard of the 1368 orders. If this was the case, and this is no more than a hypothesis, Jessop's dating sees M4 superseded at some point in the fifteenth century by the M10 and/or M3, which were quicker to make, and possibly more effective against armour.

By 1405-6 it seems that things had slipped, and there was concern about the quality of arrowheads supplied. Henry IV issued the following statute:

> Because the arrowsmiths do make many faulty heads for arrows and quarrels, defective, not well, nor lawful nor defensible to the great jeopardy and deceit of the people and of the whole realm; It is ordained and established that all the heads and quarrels after this time to be made shall be well boiled or brased and hardened at the points with steel … And every arrowhead and quarrel be marked with mark of him that made the same.[98]

There were penalties of fines and confiscation for those not complying, but unlike the orders of 1368-71, the penalties fell directly on the producers of the arrows and not on the Sheriffs. There was a clear understanding at the time that arrowheads needed to be in part steel to help improve penetration of plate armour, and developments in armour would have driven the technical advance in arrowhead design. This explains the term 'well steeled arrow'.

These standards were not always maintained, and there is evidence of a decline in quality in the Wars of the Roses. Finds from the sites of the battles of Towton and Tewkesbury suggest that the M1 type, which has a light, short socket with small flat wings attached, was common.[99] Arrowheads of this type have also been found in excavations at other military sites, including Sandal and Carisbrooke Castles, dated to the fifteenth century. M1 arrowheads would have been faster and cheaper to produce than the M4 and M10, because they contained less iron and no steel. The accounts of the Duke of Norfolk support the notion of relatively cheap arrowheads commonly being used in the Wars of the Roses since he paid 25% less than the Rouen inventory prices for arrowheads in the 1460s.[100] This type of arrowhead would not pierce armour, although it would penetrate a gambeson. This may mean that 'hard' armour, both plate and brigandines, was relatively rare among the men in the armies of the Wars of the Roses. Alternatively, it may just be a sign of haste in the preparations for war. The injuries on the bodies found in the Towton war grave show that these cheaper arrowheads were not used exclusively. Towton 40 had a wound from an armour-piercing arrow, probably an M10, in one side of his forehead. Towton 21 has a wound in the back of his head which barely penetrated the skull made by a 'flesh piercing arrowhead' such as an M1 or broader MP5 or MP6.[101] The decline in quality was reversed under the Tudors when, as far as one can tell, armour-piercing heads of the M3 and M10 types became the norm, for the royal forces at least.

The lack of dimensions and specification for the bows and arrows in the English orders and inventories has already been noted. While arrowheads have been found in many archaeological sites, complete arrow shafts are exceptionally rare. The *Mary Rose* is our major source. The average length of these arrows is 30 inches, some slightly longer or shorter. Given the likely arrowhead used and the depth of the nock, this would be about the practicable draw length. The only specification of arrow length in the English royal orders I have found dates to 1338 when Nicholas Caraud, the King's Artillier, was ordered '… to buy 4000 sheaves of arrows of an ell in length with steel head'.[102] This is surprising since an English ell is 45 inches – although a Scottish ell is about 37 inches and a Flemish about 27 inches. If we assume that the English measure was being used, this contradicts all the contemporary pictorial evidence, which shows arrows being drawn to the head, impossible with a 45-inch arrow. It is difficult to know what to make of this.

COST OF BOWS AND ARROWS COMPARED WITH ARCHERS' WAGES

The following table shows that it was no financial burden for a man to buy his own basic military archery equipment throughout the period. At most times the outlay of less than a fortnight's wages would be sufficient to get both bow and arrows. Higher quality equipment such as painted bows were more of a commitment.

Date	Item	Archers' daily rate	Cost expressed in number of days pay for an archer
1345	Bow (white)	3d (for majority of foot archers)	5–6 days
	Sheaf of Arrows	3d	$5^1/_3$ days
1359	Bow (painted)	3d (for majority of foot archers)	12 days
	Bow (white)	3d	6 days
	Sheaf of Arrows	3d	$5^2/_3$ days
	Arrowheads (per doz.)	3d	$^2/_3$ of a day
	Bowstrings (for 3)	3d	$^1/_3$ of a day
1390	Bow	6d	2 days
	Sheaf of Arrows	6d	$2^1/_3$ days
1435	Bow (painted)	6d	8 days
	Bow (yew)	6d	$5^2/_3$ days
	Sheaf of Arrows	6d	$3^1/_2$ days
	Arrowheads (per doz)	6d	$^2/_3$ of a day

All price data reflects Crown payments except for 1390, which is exceptionally low.

HOW MANY ARROWS WERE USED IN A BATTLE?

The short answer is that we don't know. This chapter offers an idea of the number of arrows the Crown ordered, based on incomplete records. While there are traces of stocks of arrows being moved from one supply base to another, I have seen no reference to supplies of arrows being returned, to the Tower of London for example, by an army or retinue after a major campaign.

Archers who shoot longbows of draw weights comparable to the estimated draw weights of the *Mary Rose* bows reckon that it takes between seven and nine seconds to complete an aimed shot from nocking the arrow to loosing it.[103] So Medieval archers in battle could have loosed off between seven and nine arrows a minute each, each capable of carrying 200 yards at least. While this is much less than the figures achieved by archers using lighter bows, with shorter draw lengths, shooting a shorter distance, it still represents a daunting prospect if you were on the receiving end. A man at arms advancing at a steady walking pace would take at least one and half minutes to cover this distance, so an archer could get off between 11 and 14 arrows as he advanced; but only three arrows at a mounted knight if his horse travelled at 20 mph. This rate of fire helps to clarify how many arrows were carried by armies on campaign, and how they were supplied with arrows in battle, since, basically, they would not have the opportunity to shoot off that many arrows. At Agincourt, those archers making up the wings of the English army probably would have used most arrows. First they repelled the French cavalry charges, and then shot at the French battles as they advanced, and would have been able to keep shooting into their flanks as they began to engage the English men at arms. The archers among and in front of the English men at arms would have had to retreat in the face of the oncoming French, and so may have only been able to shoot off a sheaf of arrows at most. It would have been easier to resupply the archers on the wings, where there were no English men at arms in the way. At Crecy, if we follow Ayton and Preston's convincing arguments about the site of the battle, the archers would have shot in short bursts as each French attack came on, and then would have had to stop as they got too close to the English men at arms, or moved out of convenient range. So there would have been plenty of opportunity to get new supplies of arrows. It is clear from the accounts of the battle of Formigny that if the English archers did not have some cover – stakes, ditches or hedges for example – they could not get off enough arrows to stop a determined charge by armoured cavalry.

Does this reduced rate of fire make a nonsense of the term 'arrowstorm' which we know was recorded in the fifteenth century at least? No. Take Agincourt as an example, where between 5000 and 7000 English and Welsh archers were present.[104] The Norman chronicler Pierre Cochon tells us 'the ground was so soft that the men at arms sunk into it by at least a foot', which would have slowed down cavalry as well as infantry, so the attacking French forces could have been on the receiving end of between 70,000 and 120,000 arrows (less than a sheaf per archer), surely a terrifying arrowstorm to any observer or participant. Among the French chroniclers, the Monk of Saint-Denis is scathing about the thousand well-mounted men at arms who, 'to their eternal shame', turned and fled at the very first volley of arrows.

As to power rather than volume of fire, Fred Hageneder in his beautiful book, *Yew, A History*, quotes Giraldus Cambrensis' well-known description of the siege of Abergavenny Castle, as early as 1182, in which he declares the attacking Welsh archers drove their arrows straight through the tower's solid oak door, three or four inches thick. 360 years later, the longbows of the *Mary Rose* had a much greater draw weight, up to 80kg (185lb). Even at a range of 240m, it has been estimated that perhaps only some 16% of velocity would be lost using these fearsome weapons.

Were arrows used more than once on the the battlefield? Common sense says that the archers probably did pick up arrows for reuse, both of their own choice and under orders from their commanders keen to reduce potential supply problems. Three occasions are recorded: at Poitiers; in a fifteenth-century record of men at Rouen being detailed to pick up arrows during a sortie;[105] and at Towton the Yorkist archers are said to have shot their opponents' arrows back at them at the start of the battle.

NOTES ON PAINTED BOWS, BROAD BOWS AND BROAD ARROWS

PAINTED BOWS

It is clear from their cost that painted bows were special. In the November 1359 order, the Crown price for painted bows works out at 36d and that for white bows at 18d.[106] The order to William de Rothwell issued in 1359 just asks for 1000 bows painted and white, with no concern about quantities of each. In the 1435 inventory the difference in price between yew bows and painted bows had shrunk to 43%. In 1435 15% of the bows in the arsenal were painted bows, too many for them to be elite weapons for the Duke and his friends to use in sport; these painted bows were perhaps made from selected staves and particularly well finished for picked archers. After the 1340s and 50s, Crown orders didn't ask for painted bows, no doubt to save money. Orders and deliveries of painted bows were unusual in these decades, and, in the records I have seen, all related to Gloucestershire and Lincolnshire (except for a few delivered from Norfolk and Suffolk in1356).

The most popular explanation is that painted bows were smoothly finished and varnished. The Ordinances of the York Bowyers from 1419-20 include reference to 'polyssyng and skynnyng' as the last stage of bow production.[107] This seems to be part of the normal production process and is costed as taking just over 9% of the production time. A later amendment to the York Ordinances forbids the painting of bows before they have been inspected by the officers of the mistery.[108] So it seems that painting was an additional process, applied in addition to 'polyssyng and skynnyng'. It was probably quite time-consuming given the extra cost of painted bows, and maybe obscured the quality of the wood, or of the workmanship. There is no evidence that these parts of the ordinances related only to the production of civilian bows, nor that painted bows were made of any special type of wood. From the 1435 inventory we can see that it was some sort of process applied to them that separated them from the ordinary yew bows.

BROAD BOWS (*ARCUBUS LATIS*)

There are very few English records that use the term broad bows. The 1390 account of Henry Bolinbroke's preparations for his expedition to Prussia only tells us that broad bows cost twice as much as ordinary war bows, and were relatively uncommon.[109] There is another reference to broad bows in the Close Rolls for 1400. It is an order to the customs collectors of Dover and Sandwich to allow Ranagius, an armourer of Milan, and a King's Sergeant, to go overseas with 'six broad bows and four dozen broad arrows for the wood.'[110]

It may be a term for what we would now call a flat bow. Broad bows might cost more for three reasons. Firstly, since bowstaves of this period were mass produced by distant suppliers, who presumably tried to get as many staves as possible from each tree, staves that would produce a good broad bow may have been unusual. Secondly, these bows might take more work to produce, being out of the ordinary run of producing roundish section bows. Thirdly, the context of the surviving records suggests these bows were especially well finished for elite owners. These records make no mention of what wood was used. Wyche bows may well have been much flatter in section because of the nature of the wood. But the records of Henry VIII's reign make it clear that wyche bows were regarded as second class bows, referring to bows of 'Elme Wiche or other wood of lytell price and value'.[111] It seems very unlikely that bows of these woods would achieve a premium price in the fourteenth century.

The Ranagius order makes clear reference to the broad bow being used for hunting. It is likely that Henry Bolinbroke acquired them for the same reason. Although he was going on crusade with the Teutonic knights for the good of his soul, the quality of the hunting in Prussia was another incentive. By the mid fourteenth century the order of Teutonic knights, 'in order to attract pilgrim knights to assist in their crusading, feasted them liberally and took them on bear and elk hunts in the great German forests.'[112]

So broad bows were in all probability yew flat bows, primarily for hunting. The scarcity of references to them, and Gaston Phoebus' description of a yew or boxwood bow suitable for hunting, suggest that they were unusual even in this usage.

BROAD ARROWS

Although this study is mainly concerned with military archery, I have included several references to broad arrows, mainly in orders to customs collectors instructing them to allow bows and arrows to be taken out of the kingdom. A number of these are explicitly linked to hunting, and none of these are in an exclusively military context. Bolinbroke took four sheaves of broad arrows to Prussia in 1390, a small number compared with the 73 sheaves of ordinary arrows he also took. In 1392 Ralph Garet, a foreign monk, travelling with two servants, was allowed to take a bow and '...one sheaf of arrows called brodarwes'.[113] In 1394 the Vicomte de Meloun travelling with his entourage was allowed to take six dozen bows and twelve sheaves of broad arrows.[114] And of course there is also Ranagius. The arrows with barbed heads in the 1435 inventory sound like broad arrows under another name. In 1465 the records of the Duchy of Lancaster have a record of 'brode arrow hedes' being bought for Edward IV's 'disport'.[115] Edward greatly enjoyed hunting.

The inventory of 1435 values arrows with barbed heads at more than twice the value of ordinary arrows. This reflected the extra work and material necessary to make the heads. Greater care was probably taken in making these arrows because it was expected that they would be used a good number of times. Broad arrows can be found quite widely in England, in towns and villages as well as in castles, but that they are found in small numbers compared with other arrow head types. Despite the popularity of hunting as a sport, physical activity and source of food, the small numbers of these arrows recovered suggest that men would only own a few, perhaps only two or three, since they expected to recover and reuse them. In his discussion of arrowhead types, Ascham clarifies the definition: '…having two points or barbs looking backwards to the stele and the feathers, which surely we call in English a broad arrow head or swallow tail.'[116]

Arrowheads of this type with two proportionally large barbs come in variations of size and shape, but can be categorised into two major forms: H3, in which the socket blends into the barbs more to make a flattened diamond section, and H4, where the socket makes a central spine with the barbs being flatter in section. Jessop suggests that the H3 was developed in the latter half of the thirteenth century and the slightly more sophisticated H4 half a century later. Before these dates hunting arrows tended to be smaller, and had less exaggerated barbs.[117]

NOTES

1 Hewitt, H J (1966) p.40.
2 Curry, A (2005) p.65.
3 Sumption, J (1990) p.285.
4 Ayton, A and Preston, P (2005) p.359n.
5 Allmand C T (1973) p.65.
6 Hewitt, H J (1966) p.70.
7 Storey, R (1998). 'The Tower of London and the garderobae armorum' in *Royal Armouries Yearbook 3*. Leeds, Royal Armouries.
8 *BPR* pt.3 p.223.
9 See Storey, R (1998) for evidence of the small amounts of equipment held in the Tower of London on a regular basis.
10 Storey, R (1998).
11 Byerly, B F and C R (editors) (1977) p.39 and p.41.
12 This is usually thought to mean laburnum.
13 Byerly, B F and C R (editors) (1986) p.64.
14 Sharp, M (editor) (1982) p.27.
15 PRO E 101/20/9 quoted in Storey, R (1998).
16 Hewitt, H J (1966) Pr. p.66.
17 Prestwich, M (1996) p.140.
18 Figures from following sources: 1341 Rymer, vol.2 pt 2 p.1157; 1346 Rymer vol.3 pt.1 p.87–8; 1356 *CCR* 1354–60 p244; Jan 1359 Rymer, vol.3 pt.1 p.414; May 1359 Rymer vol.3 pt.1 p.426; Nov 1359 *CCR* 1354–60 p.601–2. Figures in

italics from Hewitt, H J (1966).
19 Wrottesley G (1887) p. 68 and p.75.
20 *CCR* 1354–60 p.224.
21 Allmand, C T (1973) p.65.
22 *CPR* 1358-61 p.323.
23 *CPR* 1358-61. p.422.
24 Hewitt, H J (1966) p.69.
25 *CCR* 1345 p.538.
26 *CCR* 1364 p.29.
27 *BPR* pt.3 p.223.
28 *BPR* pt.3 p 224.
29 *BPR* pt.2 p.155.
30 *BPR* pt.2 p.161.
31 *BPR* pt.2 p.167–8.
32 *BPR* pt.4 p.254.
33 *BPR* pt.3 p.379–80.
34 Booth, P H W and Carr, A D (1991). '*Account of Master John de Burnham the Younger, Chamberlain of Chester of the Revenues of the Counties of Chester and Flint, Michaelmas 1360 to Michaelmas 1361.*' Record Society of Lancashire and Cheshire. p.97.
35 Booth, P H W and Carr, A D (1991) p.116–7.
36 Booth, P H W and Carr, A D (1991) p.85.
37 Figures for the receipts in Appendix 3 from PRO E101/392/14, Accounts of William de Rothwell Keeper of the Privy Wardrobe. Figures for orders as above.
38 *CCR* 1368 p.414.
39 *CCR* 1369 p.41 and *CCR* 1371 p.208-9.
40 *CCR* 1371 p.208.
41 *CCR* 1383 p.284–5.
42 *CCR* 1376 p.385.
43 *CCR* 1400 p.79.
44 *CCR* 1401–05. p.433.
45 *CPR* 1367–70 p.56.
46 *CCR* 1390 p.134; *CCR* 1391 p.376 and *CCR* 1394 p.309 respectively.
47 *POPC* vol.2 p.200.
48 *CCR* 1403 p.73.
49 Toulmin Smith L (1894) p.34 and p.154 for sheaves of arrows.
50 Somerville, R (1953). p.168.
51 Wylie, J H (1914). *The Reign of Henry V. Vol 1*. Cambridge University Press, p.45 for Calais inquiry and p.159n for Exchequer price.
52 Curry, A (2005) p.26.
53 Devon, F (1837). *Issues of the Exchequer.* London. J Murray. p.318.
54 *CPR* 1413–16 p.172 and p.344 and *CPR* 1416–22 p.120 respectively.
55 *CPR* 1429–36 p.113.
56 *POPC* vol. 4 p.126.
57 *CPR* 1429–36. p.611.

58 *CLBCL* Book K p.205-6.
59 Curry, A (1994). 'English Armies in the Fifteenth Century' p.61. *Arms, Armies and Fortifications in the Hundred Years War*. Edited by A Curry and M Hughes. Woodbridge. Boydell Press.
60 *CCR* 1430 p.74 and *CCR* 1433 p.267 respectively.
61 Stevenson, J (1861–4). vol.2 p.572.
62 McKisack, M (1959) p.163.
63 *POPC*. v.5. p.281.
64 Stevenson, J (1861–4) vol.1 p.501 This may be the earliest surviving official use of the term 'long bow'.
65 Stevenson, J (1861–4) vol.1 p.513.
66 Stevenson, J (1861–4) vol.1 p.517–18.
67 *POPC* vol.5 p.198-9.
68 Stevenson, J (1861–4) vol. 2 p.475.
69 *CCR* 1468–76 p.376–7.
70 Allmand, C T (1973) p.67-8.
71 Ross, C (1974) p.366.
72 *York Civic Records* vol. 2 p.52.
73 Except of course for arrowheads and bowstrings. We have a considerable number of arrowheads from a wide range of archaeological sites, whereas none survive from the *Mary Rose* in a condition that allows us to describe them. No bowstrings survive from any site of the period as far as I am aware.
74 *Letters and Papers Foreign and Domestic 1509–19* vol.1 pt.1 p.500 and p.611.
75 Cruickshank C G (1969) p.78.
76 *Letters and Papers Foreign and Domestic 1509-19* vol.1 pt.1. p.964–5.
77 *Letters and Papers Foreign and Domestic 1509-19* vol.1 pt.2. p.1068.
78 Stirland, A J (2005) p.123. Anthony roll lists 250 bows, 400 sheaves of arrows and six gross of bow strings.
79 Strickland, M and Hardy, R (2005) p.6.
80 Stirland, A J (2005) p.54.
81 Newhall, R A (1924) p.196-9.
82 Stirland, A J (2005) chapter 8.
83 Corbett, J S (1905). *Fighting Instructions 1530–1816*. London. Navy Society p.14.
84 Corbett, J S (1905) p.15.
85 Crew figures from Spont, A (1897) *Letters and Papers relating to the war with France 1512–13*. London. Navy Records Soc. p.80; Weapons from Stirland, A J (2005). p.21.
86 Based on a comment by R. Hardy in a lecture at National Army Museum, 22nd Oct. 2005.
87 Stirland, A J (2005) p.123.
88 See the inventory for Edward IV's expedition to France in that year quoted above.
89 *Letters and Papers Foreign and Domestic*. vol.20 pt.1. p.18.
90 All references to the inventory in this discussion are from Davies, J (2001). *The Inventory of King Henry VIII.* Journal of the Society of Archer Antiquaries

Vol 44. p.31–38.

91 *Letters and Papers Foreign and Domestic* vol.20 p.35.

92 Davies, J (2001) p.34.

93 *Letters and Papers Foreign and Domestic*. vol.20 pt.1. p.236–7.

94 Quoted by Longman, C J and Walrond, Col. H (1894). *Archery*. London. Longmans and Green. p.132.

95 *CCR* 1368 p.414.

96 Jessop, O (2000). A New Artifact Typology for the Study of Medieval Arrowheads. *Medieval Archaeology* XL 2002 p.192–205.

97 Starley, D (2005) 'What's the point? A Metallurgical Insight into Medieval Arrowheads' p.214 in Bork, R. ed. (2005) *De Re Metallica: the Uses of Metal in the Middle Ages*. Aldershot. p.207–18.

98 *Statutes of England* vol 2 p.153.

99 Personal communication by David Starley, commenting on a paper he and Rachel Cubitt gave at the 4th International Fields of Conflict Conference held at the Royal Armouries at Leeds in September/October 2006.

100 Longman, C J and Walrond, Col. H (1894) p.130.

101 Fiorato, V, Boylston, A and Knudsel, C (editors) (2000) p.98.

102 *CPR* 1338–40. p.124.

103 Stretton, M (2005/6) 'Medieval Arrow Heads part 3' p.19 in *The Glade* 110. winter 2005/6 and S Stanley personal communication.

104 The size of the English army is still a matter of debate. Anne Curry after years of thorough work makes a powerful revisionist case in her 2005 book that the English army was larger than is commonly thought and contained around 7000 archers at Agincourt. Most other authors favour a smaller figure, between 5000 and 6000 archers.

105 Newhall R A (1924) p.260n.

106 *CCR* 1360 p.601.

107 *York Memorandum Book, part 1 1376–1419*. (1912) Publications of the Surtees Society vol.120 p.199.

108 Strickland M and Hardy R (2005) p.23.

109 Toulmin Smith L (1894) p.34.

110 *CCR* 1400 p.215.

111 *Statutes of the Realm*. (1817) vol. 3 p.25-6.

112 Cummins, J (1988) *The Hound and the Hawk*. London. Weidenfeld and Nicolson. p.5.

113 *CCR* 1392 p.12.

114 *CCR* 1394 p.298.

115 Somerville, R (1953). p.235.

116 Ascham, R (1985). *Toxophilus: the School of Shooting*. Manchester. Simon Archery Foundation. p.130.

117 Jessop, O (2000) p.200.

The Manufacture of Bows and Arrows

Discussions of the manufacture of medieval English bows tend to concentrate on the use of yew. This is quite understandable since it became the preferred bow wood in the period. But military bows were made from other woods from the last quarter of the fifteenth century onwards and they were not a novelty. Henry VIII's legislation seemed to establish the idea of men practising with non yew bows, so that the best wood could be saved for use as military bows. It is possible that the majority of men tended to have bows made from the cheaper, more easily obtained woods in their houses, with yew bows either being issued when men agreed to serve, or owned by the more professional archers. Alternatively, it could be just another sign of Henry's tendency to try to keep the best of things for royal use as far as possible. Pieces of an ash bowstave dating no later than 1338 were found at Southampton by archaeologists in 1966.[1] Most historians have tended to concentrate on the use of imported yew staves, dismissing the use of yew from the British Isles. While British yew may not match the best Italian yew, indeed the experience of modern archers who have Italian yew bows supports this assertion; good bows are regularly made from British yew today, and no doubt were in medieval times.[2]

The earliest traces of archery related crafts that I have found come from the thirteenth century. In Coventry John le Fleccher was a leading citizen, as he appears as a witness in a number of charters from the late 1230s to the early 1250s.[3] In the same city Henry le Bouhestrengere took up a tenancy with his wife Matilda in about 1280. In the early 1290s Matilda 'Bowestrengmakere' took up a tenancy in her own right. The earliest record of commercial bow making is from York in 1276 when John of St. Botulphs, a bowyer, was entered on the Register of Freemen for the city. Entry in the Register implies John was a mature craftsman who had probably worked in the city for a number of years. A little later there is evidence of the archery industry developing in London with the appearance of Bowyers Row in St. Martins Ludgate from about 1300.[4] The naming of a group of houses and workshops in this way suggests that the bowyers had been working there for a good number of years. It has been suggested that it was Edward II's action in allowing the Wardrobe, the section of royal administration responsible for maintaining supplies in general, to become based in London that was a major encouragement for the development of both a bow and an arrow making industry in the city. A result of settling of the Wardrobe in the capital was that the Privy Wardrobe, responsible for supplies of weaponry, came to be based at the Tower of London. The large orders issued by the royal administration proved to be a significant incentive for bowyers, fletchers and stringers to settle in London. An early example of a large-scale order for archery equipment by the Crown can be found in 1338 when Nicholas Caraud, the king's Artillier, was ordered '… to buy 1000 bows, 4000 bowstrings and 4000 sheaves of arrows of an ell in length with steel heads … and if he cannot find the full number of bows and arrows he is to buy wood for bows and arrows, feathers to wing the arrows with and iron and steel for their heads as may be required, to hire makers.'[5] While an order of this scale may not have been completed entirely in London, the London craftsmen must have made a very significant contribution. It is noteworthy that even at this early point in the development of English military archery, steel arrowheads are specified.

The role of the craftsmen of the capital must not be over-emphasised at this time, given the large royal orders sent to the county Sheriffs in the 1340s and 1350s noted in the previous chapter. However, it seems that by the late fourteenth century, the misteries were in control of the archery industry, as the Crown employed fewer artisans directly. Signs of this can be found in London, where both the bowyers and the fletchers gained ordinances and had their separate misteries recognised in 1371.[6] In York the Bowyers' mistery must have been established by that date since an apprentices indenture survives, although the earliest ordinances for the bowyers date to 1395, and for the fletchers to c.1388.[7] In Chester the misteries of bowyers, fletchers and stringers were established by 1422. The development of the Chester misteries was encouraged by the local demands of the royal Earls of both Chester and Lancaster needing bows and arrows for the large retinues they raised for service in Scotland, Ireland and overseas. The establishment of separate misteries of Bowyers and Fletchers in London in 1371 caused difficulties since a number of craftsmen had been making both bows and arrows, but membership of both misteries was prohibited. They would have finished stock and raw materials for both trades and apprentices or workmen of both trades working for them, and so it was difficult for them to choose which trade they followed. Only one man, Robert atte Verne seemed to be unwilling to choose, since he was brought before the mayor two or three times for following both trades, and each time he decided to follow a different trade. In the end he settled on being a fletcher.[8]

In 1345 the Keeper of the Wardrobe at the Tower was instructed to receive 1200 bows, 1000 sheaves of arrows and 4000 bowstrings from the Mayor and Sheriffs of London.[9] But not all the military orders were on this large scale. There are records of small scale commercial orders, such as one from around 1369, when John Yerdbergh, clerk to the wardrobe of the Duchy of

Lancaster, was ordered to get 50 bows and their appurtenances as quickly as possible form Robert Waukere, a bowyer who lived in Fleet Street in London.[10]

At the beginning of Richard II's reign we find early signs of a major change in the methods used by the Crown to order and maintain military archery equipment, in that much greater reliance is placed on the bowyers', fletchers' and stringers' misteries for direct supply. This was practical because, in London particularly, the bowyers and fletchers misteries were well established and largely controlled the trade. He did not rely on this new approach entirely since there are two orders to successive Keepers of the Privy Wardrobe concerning the making of bows and arrows using direct labour, following the practice of his grandfather Edward III. In 1385, Ranulph de Hatton was ordered 'to take and put to work there [the Tower of London] and elsewhere at the King's wages sufficient armourers, fletchers, smiths and other artificers and workmen for making armour, bows, arrows [and] arrowheads ... also to buy timber and wood fit therefore at a reasonable price.' His successor John Loderwyk received a similar order in 1396, except that this time the Sheriffs were instructed to support Loderwyk by imprisoning any who refused to comply.[11] This last instruction to the Sheriffs exemplifies what contemporaries saw as Richard II's increasingly despotic approach to kingship.

The new system was developed in parallel to the older direct labour approach, beginning in 1378 when William Biker was appointed the King's bowyer in the Tower on a wage of 6d per day and a set of clothing the same as that of the King's yeomen each year. This may well be a confirmation of an appointment by Edward III since in 1390 Biker seems to be pensioned off on the same wages as long as he remains living in the Tower, having 'served for 22 years or more'.[12] The role of the king's bowyer may well have evolved in Biker's time in office. Originally it seems to have been a craftsman's post, responsible for the care and maintenance of the king's personal bows. But by this point in the fourteenth century, while keeping the technical role, the king's bowyer seems to have got more heavily involved in organizing and managing the supply of bows for the king's military activities. His successor was Adam Okehull, described as 'bowyer', which signifies membership of the mistery of bowyers, who was made a yeoman of the King's Privy Wardrobe in 1389.[13] On his death he was succeeded in 1396 by Robert Bridford who was granted the office of keeper of the King's bows in the Tower for life on a wage of 6d per day and lodgings.[14] While there are some inconsistencies in the description of the appointments of these three, they had similar backgrounds in the bowyers' mistery and a similar role to fulfil. Bridford's role expanded in 1399 when he was granted 'the office of keeping, making and providing the King's bows for the Tower, Calais and Ireland, as well as strings for them at the King's charge.' Having received this grandiose title, he was instructed 'to take bowyers and stringers for the making of bows for the Tower, Calais and Ireland, and strings for the same and put them to work at the king's charge.'[15] He was to use his knowledge of the bow making industry to employ workers to make bows for the Crown, presumably from raw materials previously acquired. Links with the Fletchers' mistery were established in the same way when, in 1395, Stephen Sedar, Fletcher, was appointed to the office of keeping and repairing the King's arrows in the Tower, again for 6d per day. Sedar (or an older namesake) had probably been the Master of the mistery of Fletchers in 1386.[16]

Henry IV on his accession ordered the officers in post, William Byker, John Wydemar, Giles Fosse, William Morys (hauberger), Stephen Sedar and Thomas Coton 'to inspect and try all armaments, coats of arms and other stuff in the King's privy wardrobe in the Tower of London and remove such as may be unfit.'[17] Most of these men were confirmed in their posts at about the same time that they were set this task, a stock taking exercise by the new King. Thomas Coton, a London bowyer, was appointed to the office of making the king's bows at this time, in succession to Robert Bridport. William Byker's role is redefined as artiller, and his pension confirmed.[18] At this time, an artiller was probably more concerned with crossbows than hand bows, although in his case it may have been an honorific title given to a pensioner. More equipment was clearly necessary since Stephen Sedar was ordered to recruit fletchers and other workmen of the fletchers' mistery for the king's works in 1403.[19] At the same time as the appointments of all these officers were made, a succession of Keepers of the Privy Wardrobe was also appointed, John Norbury in 1399, followed by Henry Somer in 1405 and Simon Flete in 1408. The terms of their appointments allowed them to take armourers, fletchers, smiths etc for 'the works of armour, bows, arrows, arrowheads and other works' and to take raw materials. Flete's appointment recognises the importance of gunpowder artillery, since he can also take stonecutters and carpenters to support it.[20]

In December 1403 Nicholas Frost was appointed as the bowyer making the king's bows in the Tower of London with a wage of 6d per day and 'a suit of the esquires of the king's chamber'. Henry V confirmed him in his office for life in 1413.[21] In December 1416 Nicholas was sworn in as one of two masters of the Bowyers mistery.[22] No doubt this was both a reflection of his standing among the bowyers and the usefulness of his close links with the royal administration. Henry V also appointed Nicholas Mynot 'Fleccher' to the office of keeping the king's arrows within the Tower of London and mending them when required in 1413 in succession to Stephen Sedar. Not only was Mynot paid 6d per day and in receipt of a livery of a yeoman of the king's chamber, but he was also granted lodgings in the Tower.[23] This appointment again points to the close links between royal office and being a senior member of the relevant mistery since Mynot, or an older relative, was one of the Masters and Wardens of the Fletchers in 1387.[24] There was a clear hierarchy among the craftsmen appointed to make and maintain the king's military equipment, since while Frost and Mynot were paid 6d per day, Martin Pull, 'armourer of the king's body', was paid 12d per day.[25] This mirrors the Crown wage rates for soldiers, 6d per day for archers, 12d per day for men at arms. I am not sure that an armourer is so much more skilled than a bowyer. What is noticeable in Henry IV's and Henry V's reigns is that the links between the London citizens and the misteries on the one hand and the Crown and its administration on the other have become more formalised through the appointment of senior members of the misteries as royal officials. These officials probably had to carry out most of the practical activities, including recruitment of skilled labour, that ensured that the Crown built up adequate stores. The role of the Keeper of the Privy Wardrobe probably became much more one of supervising and coordinating the work of these specialist officers, and managing the distribution of the equipment in times of war.

These appointments were not merely sinecures or positions limited to the maintenance of the king's personal archery equipment. In the lead-up to the Agincourt campaign there are a few rare records of what mistery members were paid by the Crown for their work. In August 1413 Stephen Sedar was paid 18d per sheaf for 500 sheaves of arrows,[26] while in November of that year there is an Exchequer record of payments:

> To Nicholas Frost, bowyer, Stephen Sedar, Fletcher, Ralph the Stringer and divers others of the said misteries. In money paid to them, viz. to the aforesaid Nicholas and others of his mistery, for 500 bows £31/5/0d [15d each]; to the aforesaid Stephen and others of his mistery for 1700 sheaves of arrows £148/15/0d [21d per sheaf] and to the aforesaid Ralph and others of his mistery for 40 gross of bowstrings £12.[27]

In June 1415 Nicholas Mynot was paid 18d for 620 sheaves of arrows and 24d for 20 sheaves.[28] These prices are typical of prices throughout much of the fourteenth and fifteenth centuries, although arrows seem to have been getting more expensive, and in the case of Sedar's payment in November of 21d per sheaf match the best price for ordinary arrows given in the 1435 inventory made on the Duke of Bedford's death noted in the previous chapter. Why Mynot was paid 24d for 20 sheaves in 1415 is not indicated. This price is not high enough for the arrows to have been fitted with barbed heads, but they could have been better finished arrows for some favoured archers.

In 1415 both Nicholas Frost and Nicholas Mynot were important figures in Henry's efforts to acquire equipment to support the archers in the forthcoming campaign. Both were given far reaching commissions: in Frost's case he was to 'take bowyers and other workmen, artificers and labourers pertaining to the mistery of bowyers for the works of the king's bows in the City of London and elsewhere and timber called bowestaves and all other necessaries.'

Mynot's commission was very similar except that he was only authorised to take up to twelve 'fletchers and other workmen, artificers and labourers pertaining to the mistery of fletchers.'[29] Both had the power of arrest to ensure compliance with the king's commission. Mynot received another similar order in 1417, this time there was no limit put on the numbers of men he could recruit. In both cases he was also ordered to take 'timber for arrows and bolts and feathers, silk and wax and other necessities.'[30]

Not surprisingly given the scale of his ambitions, Henry V was very concerned about ensuring supplies of arrows. He appointed officials to manage the production of the arrows, and then made a number of orders aimed at ensuring that they had the raw materials necessary. The orders to Mynot mention that he could take wood and feathers, possibly by purveyance. However it is probable that he was able to draw upon stores accumulated as a result of other orders issued by the royal clerks. In 1416 Henry forbade the use of ash for clogs and shoes so that the wood could be used for arrows, making Mynot's task easier. Late in 1418 he took another unusual step towards ensuring arrow supply by ordering the Sheriffs of 28 counties to collect 1,190,000 feathers 'for making arrows for the King's use.'[31] (How would they be counted one wonders? That's quite an audit.) Some Sheriffs administered two adjacent counties so we find one third of the feathers came from four Sheriffs, those of Kent, Essex/Hertfordshire, Norfolk/Suffolk and Lincolnshire. This orders should have produced enough fletchings for over 396,600 arrows, which was only part of what was necessary given the numbers of arrows Henry went on to order: 150,000 in 1418 and 425,000 in 1421.[32]

None of these orders make mention of iron and steel for arrowheads. These were ordered from other specialists. In 1416 William Skorer of Roderham (Rotherham) was ordered to take workmen to produce 200,000 arrowheads without delay. He received another order in May 1421 for 400,000 heads. In February 1422 William Shemylde of Sheffield was also ordered to make 400,000 arrowheads for the King's use.[33] There is no mention of misteries in these orders implying that the arrowsmiths of South Yorkshire were not organised in that way. The brevity of the orders, making no mention of materials or patterns, suggests that both Skorer and Shemydle knew the specification of military arrowheads without further instruction.

Henry V's military activities increased the demand for warbows in comparison with the reigns of his two predecessors, but the price of them does not rise much in his reign. There is a record in the household accounts of Thomas, Duke of Clarence for 1420-1 in which his treasurer was instructed to account for 58 bows received at a cost of 18d each.[34] This is very much in line with the values put on bows in the royal orders of the 1340s and 1350s and payments made in preparation for the Agincourt campaign. This steadiness in the price suggests that the bowyers of England were able to produce enough bows even at times of large-scale military activity to meet demand so that prices did not rise because of scarcity. There is no evidence of royal price controls at this time.

Henry V ensured the availability of skilled labour by appointing senior members of the relevant misteries as royal officials. Then he ensured the availability of raw materials. He followed Edward III's and Richard II's practice of using the network of Sheriffs to accumulate materials from all over the country and he issued direct royal orders to prioritise the use of wood for arrows. He used specialist suppliers to produce arrowheads which could then be brought to the arrows.

The misteries made much of developing a 'quality control' role, partly to reassure their customers, particularly the officers of the royal administration. But another aspect of this was a desire to protect the financial interests and standing of their members against sharp practice and unregulated labour. They were exercised about the way their products were sold and the danger of sales at low prices undermining the business of their members. The beginnings of this latter concern can be found in 1374–5 when the members of the Bowyers mistery successfully petitioned the Mayor and Aldermen of London to forbid the selling of new bows at Cornhill.[35] In 1432 the 'Flecchers' asked that the articles of the mistery be amended to prohibit both working at night or in secret, and the substitution of green wood 'and other false stuff' for good stuff and dry wood so that unserviceable arrows were made.[36] This worry about the use of green wood echoes royal orders first issued in 1368.[37] The prohibition of night work and secret work suggests both a concern about the quality of work done by candlelight and about the use of labour unregistered or unapproved by the mistery.

The ordinances of the York Mistery of Bowyers approved in 1419–20,[38] define the 'taskewerk' done by 'taskemen', wage earning craftsmen employed by the mistery members. They lay down what the taskemen should be paid for each stage of the manufacturing process for what sounds like mass production of bows (table, opposite page). The purpose of these ordinances is to control the rates of pay and periods of employment offered to the taskemen by full members of the mistery, to stop some members monopolising all the most skilled workers by paying them higher rates.

The payments come to 18/- for making 100 bows, just over 2d each, without including the time for drilling the horn pieces for the nocks. Contemporary bowyers with experience of making yew bows say that to make a bow is a day's work (approximately 8 hours); it might take a little less if you had the level of experience medieval bowyers would build up. It would be wrong to assume all the bows being made at the time of these ordinances were of yew, but it is likely that the majority were. While it is probable that the 'taskemen' were given at least one meal a day as part of their pay, they were not well paid compared with the archers who used their bows. There is nothing in these ordinances to suggest whether the bows being made were of military standard or for general public use. Practical sense tells us that the bows were probably a mix of sorts and weights dictated by the qualities of the bowstaves. However, given the way military bows were bought up by the Crown and other large scale users, bowyers probably built up a stockpile of military weight bows to meet both those orders and a demand from professional archers buying their own equipment.

Term in Ordinances		Operation[39]	Pay rate per 100 bows
Latin	English		
	Chipping	Rough cutting the stave to shape with a hand axe	16d
	Thwyting	Whittling or scraping the back of the stave to about a single growth ring	20d
	Dressing 'by his own work'	Working down the sides and the belly to a rough finish	20d
Aptaverit	Dresse them 'at his own expense'		48d
	Bending	Tillering	60d
	Horning	Nocking	6d
Pugacione	Clensyng uppe	Final smoothing, particularly at the tips after nocking	6d
	Afterbendyng	Final tillering to check the shape	20d
	Polyssyng and Skynnyng	Honing the surface of the bow (now done with a round metal bar) and sealing with linseed oil, wax or similar	20d
Penetracione	Boryng	Drilling out horns for nocks	15d per 1000

A thwiting knife is a paring or scraping knife used by bowyers.

The only evidence of how long it actually took to make a bow is found in Elizabeth I's reign, when the London bowyers successfully lobbied to be excused making the regular quantity of bows of inferior woods, as required by the laws outlined at the end of this chapter. Instead they had to be prepared to make 50 bows of wyche elm, ash or similar woods in 20 days, a production rate of $2^1/_2$ bows a day. This would be a challenge unless the bowyer had skilled men working with him.

In 1538–9 Henry VIII paid a group of bowyers, Henry Pykeman, Thomas Bolley, William Ruckstead, John Snodin and Robert Patty, 8d per bow for making 6000 bows, and Henry Dicker 7d for 758 bows.[40] This is about four times what the Bowyers of York were paying their taskemen 120 years earlier. Even allowing for inflation and Henry's occasional extravagance, this demonstrates the difference between what a Bowyer received and what he paid his craftsmen.

The earliest surviving set of Ordinances of the London mistery of Fletchers date to 1403.[41] These allowed for the appointment of two Wardens to inspect all types of arrows and quarrels made both within and without the City of London and to seize defective work for destruction. No arrows could be sold in the City unless the Wardens had assayed them. They checked that arrows were made of seasoned wood with hardened heads and not by night working. Broad arrows and quarrels could be sold by both freemen of the City and non citizens. The mistery was concerned with the quality of all arrows, but particularly the ordinary ones, which, given the terms of these ordinances, would include military arrows as ordered by the Crown. This is understandable given the scale of orders from the Crown and other important military leaders. The lack of concern about overseeing the trade in broad arrows or quarrels suggests that the production of these was not on a large enough scale to matter to the members of the mistery when compared with military arrow sales.

Quality control problems continued. Further changes to the Ordinances were made in 1432. 'Some fletchers hired to make arrows for the king and his people frequently worked at night and changed good material and dry wood for green wood and false material making unserviceable arrows to the prejudice of the company.' Not only was the ban on night working reiterated but freemen of the mistery could only employ workmen in their own homes so that they could supervise the work.

Amendments in 1484 defined categories of arrow and set rates of pay for their making.[42] 'For the makyng of (100) beryng shaftes of seasonable tymber and clenly made cros nokked, skynned and sered 14d; for making of [100] of the best beryng shaftes well and clenly cros nokked after the best maner and skynned and sered as is aforesaid 16d; for the making of [100] merke arrow shaftes well and clenly after the forme aforesaid 20d.' These rates were for preparing shafts without fletches or heads, presumably for ease of storage, and to allow the purchaser choice of head.

Nocks are specified as being cut across the grain, but there is no mention of horn inserts. Similarly horn is not explicitly mentioned in Henry VI's orders for arrows, but it could have been included in 'other requisites for arrow making'. The Arundell archive inventory of arrows discussed below in the section on luxury equipment also suggests that not all arrows had either horn inserts or horn nocks.

The use of seasoned wood is emphasised, and the shafts are to be skinned and sered (varnished?) The different costs for each type of arrow reflects the amount of work in selecting better shafts, and possibly profiling them in the case of 'merke' arrows shafts.

The rest of the amendments are concerned with the selling of arrows: the members of the mistery are forbidden from displaying more than two sheaves of arrows in their shops or stalls, and any goods being taken out of London for sale at markets elsewhere must be inspected by the Wardens of the craft. The latter ordinance is concerned with quality control, ensuring that poor quality arrows are not dumped on markets away fom London. The purpose of the former is less clear; it may have been meant to stop any one fletcher flooding the local market, or been an early clampdown on the iniquities of advertising.

The Ordinances of the York Mistery of Fletchers were also amended, a little earlier in 1476. They refined the proscription against working on festal days: '… noman of the saide craft shall uppon the Sonday or other festival day shafe and waxe fethir nor glewe but if it be in a tyme of necessitie to fests down a fethir or two that is lowse.'[43] So running repairs if someone was going shooting, perhaps following the laws encouraging the practice of archery, were fine, but not serious commercial work. It is worth noting that the York Ordinances make no mention of skinning and sering, but do mention shafing, possibly covering the use of a drawknife or plane to make and finish shafts, and waxing, possibly rubbing the shaft with wax to seal it.

In 1488 an additional ordinance for the London mistery of bowyers forbade members of the bowyers' mistery from delivering any bows to members of the fletchers' mistery for resale, but it allowed that 'a fletcher may have three or four bows for his own use and disport'.[44]

What does 'skynned' mean in both bow and arrow manufacture? In the case of arrows it has been suggested that it refers to peeling the bark layers off the arrow shafts to make them clean and smooth, necessary when the arrows were made from coppiced wood.[45] By the 16th century at least, military arrows do not seem to have been commonly made from coppiced timber since all those found on the *Mary Rose* were made of dowels cut from planks. However, there is another explanation, which would apply equally in both manufactures, that it refers to the use of dogfish skin as an abrasive, as we use sandpaper. It was certainly used in medieval England for this purpose; there are two references to its purchase in royal accounts from the fourteenth century, one from 1355, to 'a skin called huyndysfishskyn for the carpenters'.[46] And in the customs accounts of Hull for 1401, we find part of the cargo of the *Katelyn*, a Flemish ship, was five dozen dogfish skins (hundefisheskyns) on which customs duties were paid.[47]

Judging by law-court records, the Stringers were the last of the archery trades to establish a mistery in London. In 1385 Alan Birchore, a stringer, confessed to selling false bowstrings and was condemned to stand in the pillory at Cornhill, and the strings were to be burnt beneath him.[48] In 1416 'respectable men of the trade of Stringers' petitioned the Mayor and Aldermen of London to be allowed to become a company with Wardens to maintain the quality of the strings the members of this company produced. The petition said that this was necessary because 'in the past, many had lost their lives fighting in the king's battles owing to defective bowstrings, for which the London Stringers had been blamed'.[49] The reference to men losing their lives because of poor bowstrings is the only contemporary reference to the matter. As the English warbow developed in this period, possibly gaining some draw weight to counter the improvements in armour, the string must have been under increasing strain. The issuing of extra strings was normal before a battle, which suggests that the archers restrung their bows as part of their preparations for a fight as a matter of course. This preparation could be fatally undermined by poor strings.

We hear nothing more of the Stringers until 1499 when they petitioned to amend their Ordinances in an effort to try to maintain the quality of the strings. These amendments included that stringers were to use only 'well chosen English Hemp' not tubbed (soaked or steamed?) or Coleyn (imported, possibly from Northern and Eastern Europe) hemp; they could employ no one from outside the City of London until that person had sworn to the Wardens that they would 'make true and able work'; and that they would not buy strings from outside the City and resell them within.[50]

By Henry VI's reign the London misteries were the key to supply because of their control of the manufacturing process, something demonstrated by the fact that Henry VI ordered equipment through the misteries in 1430. These orders started in February 1430 with the commissioning of Walter Middleton '... to provide the 'bowyers' and other workmen, artificers and labourers belonging to the 'bowyers' mistery required to manufacture and repair the king's bows in the City of London and elsewhere in England: also the timber called bowestaves and other requisites with carriage of same.' A similar order was issued to Nicholas Bowyer of London. Arrows were also ordered through a 'Commission to William Crane,[51] citizen and 'Fleccher' of London to provide in London and elsewhere in England the 'flecchers' and other workmen, artificers and labourers belonging to the mistery of the 'flecchers' required for the king's present voyage: also timber, feathers, silk, wax and other requisites for arrow making.' The arrowheads came through a separate commission to Robert Scot expressed in similar terms, he also was required to provide the materials, 'iron, steel and other necessaries.'

In April 1430 there was an all embracing follow up 'Commission to William Middleton to provide in London and elsewhere in England the bowyers, flecchers, stringers, arewesmythes and other workmen and labourers belonging to their misteries, required to make bows, arrows, bowstrings and arrowheads for the king, also the timber called bowestaves and other timber for arrows: as well as bows, arrows, bowstrings arrowheads, steel, hemp and other requisites of the said misteries.'[52] Both Walter and William Middleton are identified as a 'Purveyor of Bows', presumably a royal official.[53] The instructions insisted that 'bowestaves' are a special category of timber, whereas arrows could be made from ordinary timber. In William Crane's commission, silk, presumably for whipping the fletchings, and wax, possibly for lubricating the nocks or to be used like modern 'hot wax' to fit the heads, is specified. Silk would all have to be imported. But using fine silk thread would reduce drag on the arrow compared with alternatives. There is no evidence that these royal orders were for 'elite' grade equipment, with ordinary archers getting arrows with the fletchings whipped with linen thread. Arrowheads were a separate item, and the implication is that the fletchers were only expected to supply arrows without heads. William Middleton's commission implies it was the norm for warbows to have hempen strings, a practice confirmed in the amendments to the ordinances of the London Stringers' mistery made sixty years later.

In 1435 William Crane received another commission '...to provide 4000 sheaves of arrows or timber, feathers, silk and wax and other materials to make up the number'.[54] In the same year Robert Whitgreve was also given a commission '... to provide in the counties of York, Lincoln, Notyngham and Derby as many bows and sheaves of arrows as he shall judge necessary upon the information the king has given him.'[55] The vagueness of this order is intriguing. We can guess from other orders that the information the king gave Whitgreve was either a maximum sum of money to spend, or an outline of the number of soldiers who needed supplies. Walter Crane, as a leader among the London fletchers, was also prominent in ensuring supplies of arrows for the Earl of Huntingdon's expedition to Gascony in 1439.[56]

London was not the only centre of production for archery equipment, where the Crown worked with the misteries, or at the very least prominent members of the industry, to acquire military supplies. In 1436 a commission was sent to 'the sheriff of Yorkshire, the sheriffs of the city of York, Richard Fleccher and Thomas Horden of York to provide within the said county and city 100,000 goose wing feathers fit for the arrows to be made for the king's use, and to arrest sufficient workers and put them to work on the said arrows.' Similar orders were sent to the Sheriff of Lincolnshire, the Sheriffs of the city of Lincolnshire, Gilbert Fleccher and John Lyndon, and to George Fleccher of Coventry and the Sheriff of the city of Coventry.[57] It is noteworthy that this order quantifies the number of arrows to be made by the number of feathers for fletchings, rather than the number of sheaves, as is more common.

While the Crown preferred to buy finished bows and arrows, it was also prepared to accept the materials for making them. In 1459 there is an order to the Exchequer officials '...do buy and purveye 3000 bowes stafes and stufe for to make 3000 shefe (of) arowes sufficient for yomene ...to be delivered to ...Thomas Thorpe keeper of oure privy wardrobe within oure Tower of London.'[58] Presumably the Crown was able to find enough skilled workmen for this return to production through direct labour to be a realistic course of action. This may also reflect uncertainties felt by Henry VI's household about relying on the citizens of London during the Wars of the Roses.

These close links between the misteries and the royal officials responsible for the acquisition of stocks of bows and arrows remained at the heart of the supply process for the rest of the fifteenth century. Very early in his reign in January 1486, Henry VII appointed John Symson to 'the office of bowyer, surveyor of the bowyers, keeper of the bows in the Tower of London, Ireland and elsewhere, and the keeping and purveying of strings for the same'.[59] Presumably Symson is surveyor of the bowyers employed directly by the Crown, rather having any supervisory role over the mistery members. In 1489 he was ordered in company with Richard Clerk and William Huster to impress workers of the City of London to make bows for the king's service and ordered to purvey bowstaves, bowstrings and 'other stuff'.[60]

Henry VII also issued orders to a group of officials and leading citizens of

London to impress makers of arrows and barbills (probably barbed heads)[61] and for the making of arrows in the City of London for the king's service in both 1498 and 1491. The earlier order was issued to William Lovell, Simon Mott, John Curet, John Warren and Robert Holdingby, the latter to the same men, except that Holdingby was replaced by John Burdon. Again, the purveyance of materials, timber, silk, wax, feathers and 'other stuff' is mentioned.[62] An order for arrows Henry made to Gilbert Foreman in 1492 mentions the mistery directly. Foreman was 'to impress fletchers and other labourers and workmen of his said mistery as many as are necessary for the said arrows'.[63] Henry continued the practice of his predecessors, Henry IV and V, in that William Lovell, who was given the office making and keeping the king's arrows in the Tower of London in October 1485, was an important member of the fletchers' mistery.[64] We know that John Curet was also a member from note discharging him from jury service on grounds of ill health in 1479.[65]

After the relative peace of his father's reign, Henry VIII made large-scale military preparations. These relied on the existing manufacturing and supply system, so there are records both of payments to the London misteries and of royal officials going out into the shires on purchasing expeditions. In October 1510 a payment was made to the Bowyers of London of £100 in that year as part payment for making 10,000 bows. These bows could have been made from the staves that Antonio Baverin was paid for in the same month, noted in the following chapter. In December of the same year Walter Hyndy, a member of the mistery of Fletchers was paid £13/2/3d for 'the searching' of 15000 sheaves of arrows stored in 'the house of ordinance in the Tower'.[66] If this was full payment, then Walter was just inspecting all these arrows and sorting out the defective ones no doubt.

The rest of the country was involved as well. Henry's administration continued the practice developed in the fifteenth century of royal officials going into the counties to order production and obtain supplies. In 1511 William Huxley, Clerk of the Ordinances, was paid expenses for riding around Shropshire, Warwickshire, Herefordshire, Worcester and Gloucestershire to conscript bowyers for making wych hazel bows and blacksmiths for making billheads. This mention of wych hazel bows may have meant that there was a shortage of yew staves in the country, despite Henry's attempts to get staves from Venice. These wych hazel bows were delivered to the Tower, or other royal stores, since there are records of wych bows being part of the equipment of some of Henry's navy. This may in turn have stretched the supplies of wych hazel staves, since Henry issued a statute demanding the production of such bows for men to use to practise their archery skills. In 1512 John atte Wood rode out into the counties to cause bows to be made' and to fetch bowstrings and other materials back to London.[67] In 1511 arrows were being carted from centres of production in the counties at a rate of $^{1}/_{2}$d per sheaf for 50 miles.[68]

The Stringers' misteries did not gain the same status as the Bowyers' and

Fletchers' misteries in the supply system, being established later. In the late fourteenth century it seems that Bowyers were more prosperous than Fletchers. The Poll Tax of 1381, which proved to be the most unpopular of the three poll taxes granted by parliament in Richard II's reign, was a flat rate tax of one shilling per man and woman aged between 16 and 60. The poorer people were meant to be helped by their richer neighbours paying more so that they could pay less, the total number of shillings paid by each vill not exceeding the total number of tax payers in the vill.[69] Looking at the returns for the city of York, we find that the Fletchers paid the flat rate at most, with one paying a half rate of one shilling for himself and his wife. The bowyers on the other hand tended to pay over the rate, between 2/6d and 3/- per married couple.[70] So it seems that bowyers were more prosperous than fletchers. There are no stringers listed at all. Unfortunately the poll tax records for other cities, such as Lincoln and London, centres of production for bows and arrows, do not survive. As a result it is difficult to draw general conclusions about the relative prosperity of bowyers and fletchers in the main centres. However, following up on the Black Prince's orders for strings from Rugeley quoted above, we find that in 1381 there were four stringers in Rugely and one bowyer.[71] All of them paid the standard rate for themselves and their wives, suggesting that the town remained a centre of string production and that the stringers could make a reasonable living.

York became one of the major centres of production of bows, arrows and strings in the north of England because it was the organizational centre of the defence of Northern England, and had good access to the eastern ports for the import of bowstaves. The numbers of people working in the archery crafts can be gleaned from the Register of Freemen.[72] Men and women became Freemen by serving an apprenticeship, by being the child of a Freeman, or by order of the Mayor and Aldermen, often in return for a fee. The main benefit of becoming a Freeman was that only Freemen were allowed to carry out a trade in the city. The Register of Freemen does not list all the bowyers, fletchers and stringers working in York. Occasionally the Register lists a Freeman as the son of a man in the same trade who is not on the Register. It is unlikely that many of the 'taskemen' gained enough independence to enter the register.

FREEMEN OF YORK WORKING IN THE ARCHERY CRAFTS

King	Bowyers	Fletchers	Stringers
Edward II	5	0	0
Edward III	17	6	1
Richard II	24	11	3
Henry IV	16	7	0

Henry V	15	7	0
Henry VI	39	13	3
Edward IV	10	10	3
Richard III	1	0	1
Henry VII	10	5	2
Henry VIII	13	13	1

Richard III's reign was short. The relatively smaller number of stringers is noteworthy. This may be because strings were made by women working in bowyers' shops, possibly for relatives, rather than working as tradesmen themselves. If this was the case, such women would be invisible in the surviving records. (More on the involvement of women in the stringers' trade in York follows.) From Edward IV's reign onwards fletchers become more numerous in relation to bowyers, which may suggest an increasing centralisation of the military bow making craft.This was certainly something Henry VIII encouraged, stipulating where bowyers lived and worked in the statute of 1511-12 noted below.

It has already been noted that the ravages of the Black Death opened up more and better paid employment opportunities for women. However it is hard to find traces of this in the various crafts making up the archery industry. It is known that women quite often worked as smiths, including Margaret Merssh, wife of William, the king's smith, who is mentioned working with her husband at the Tower of London in 1414.[73] So some arrowsmiths might have been women, particularly among the smiths meeting the large orders issued in Henry V's reign. Women and children looked after geese, and so were no doubt involved in the 'harvesting' of feathers for fletchings. It is quite possible, given the quantities ordered, and the need for dexterity in manufacture, that women helped in both string making and fletching. The clearest proof of this comes from York where string making came to rely on women. The Ordinances of the Stringers of the city recorded in 1420 are, like those of the London mistery, concerned with quality control, but they differ from any other set of Ordinances relating to the archery trades I have seen by repeatedly using the phrase 'quod nec vir nec mulier', 'that neither man nor woman'.[74] In 1466 Elizabeth Baker, a stringer, was listed in the Register of Freemen of York. Another example can be found in the records of payments made at the behest of York City Council between 1476 and 1479, where Agnes Alleyn, a stringer, receives payment of 40d on at least two occasions. She was registered as a Freeman of the city in 1478. A little later in Richard III's reign Alicia Hunt, the daughter of Thomas Hunt, a stringer, is registered as a Freeman of York. While this is not absolute proof that Alicia followed her father's trade it is likely.

The records of the Register of Freemen from Leicester tell a different story from those of the strstegically located York.[75] Unfortunately they are very incomplete, with those from 1380 to 1465 lost. However they show that from Edward IV to Henry VIII, a sixth of the number of craftsmen registered in Leicester compared with York, and that the proportion of fletchers was much higher. This arises once again from location; imported staves would have to be carted some distance, whereas arrows could be made largely from local materials.

BESPOKE

There was a market among the gentry and nobility for more luxurious equipment. In 1285 William Fitzwarren bought six arrows at 6d each for the use of the king.[76] At the time William also bought arrows for military archers for between $8^1/_2$d and 10d per dozen. This suggests that William was either buying very well finished arrows or possibly hunting arrows with broad heads, since they cost six times as much. John of Gaunt showed his taste for high grade, even flamboyant, archery equipment in 1372 when he ordered '40 good arrows, with heads of good steel, and well and cleanly fletched with peacock feathers'[77] In1390 John Norbury received 6/8d for a bow he bought at Newark specifically as a gift for Bolinbroke's father, John of Gaunt.[78] This is a very high price for a bow, which must have been of outstanding quality and finish, and no doubt the price includes a payment to Norbury for his efforts in acquiring it. John of Gaunt greatly enjoyed hunting, and, since he was only 50 at the time of the gift, this was almost certainly a fine hunting bow. In his description of a bow suitable for nobles to use for hunting, Gaston Phoebus, Count of Foix recommends a silk string because it is stronger than hemp. It would also be much more expensive, and was probably part of the justification for the mark-up on Gaunt's bow.

The commonest way of separating high grade arrows from the ordinary was not the heads, which would be selected to match the purpose, but the use of feathers from more exotic birds than geese for the fletchings. This is particularly apparent in the inventory of archery equipment in the Arundell archive.[79] This document was compiled for Sir John Dynham in 1422, and is a carefully itemised list of over 400 complete arrows, a number of fletched shafts without heads and a few crossbow bolts. About half of the arrows are fletched with grey goose, and headed with 'duckbills'. Gendall identifies this head as probably being the type M4 (LMMC 16), which, if correct, suggests that these arrows were left over from military service since they were described as 'old and feeble'. Most of the rest were fletched with peacock, while some had swan or white goose fletchings. Among the high grade arrows are a dozen peacock arrows, newly bound in two places with gold and silk, and with white horn nocks, headed with spearheads (probably MP1 or MP3); one dozen peacock arrows, new, with white horn nocks, laid in three places with gold foil in the featherings, headed with spearheads;

four broad hooked arrows of peacock laid in the featherings all with gold foil; one dozen peacock arrows with black horn nocks, bound with gold and red and black silk, headed with duckbill; one dozen arrows of white goose, bound with gold and red and black silk headed with beaker.

The inventory describes arrows with white or black horn nocks, with unhorned nocks and arrows where the nock is not described. It is possible that 'unhorned' means the arrow had a horn nock now missing, although the simple explanation is that it means a self nock. Some arrows had horn nocks added to the wooden shafts. There is no mention of nocks with horn inserts, like those found on the *Mary Rose*. It is noticeable that the fancy finished arrows have all three types of head listed in the inventory. The explanation probably was that Sir John liked to look good whatever type of shooting he was doing, and the extra cost if he lost an arrow was unimportant. Alternatively, he posed more than he shot.

Another example of the private ownership of flamboyant arrows is found in Thomas Eme's will of 1475, where he made a specific bequest of his best sheaf of arrows fletched with black crane feathers.[80]

THE LAW AND THE MANUFACTURE OF BOWS

In the second half of the fourteenth century, the English kings made repeated efforts to control both wages and prices. However, they did not feel the need to control the prices of bows and arrows, which suggests that even in a time of regular warfare, the supply of archery equipment was generally enough to meet the demands of the market. But by the second half of the fifteenth century, things had changed. In 1482–3 Edward IV set the retail price of bows.

> Bowyers in every part of the realm do sell their bows at such a great and excessive price that the king's subjects perfectly disposed to shoot, be not of power to buy them bows whereby shooting is greatly diminished and left, and unlawful games be used … from the feast of Easter next coming, no Bowyer nor any other person using to sell or put to sale any longbow (long arke) or bows of yew shall sell any of the same bows to any of the king's liege people above the price of 3s 4d a bow and long bows of yew under the value of the same price as the seller and buyer thereof may reasonably agree and accord.[81]

This statute blames the decline in the availability of competent archers on the high price of bows. The common approach for over 100 years previous to this had been to blame the decline in archery on men playing frivolous sports and games, and Edward IV had himself issued a statute of this type five years earlier. There is no real indication of what provoked this price fixing order. It may have been advice from his own administrators who felt hard done by when buying bows, or there may have been representations from military captains. Otherwise it is difficult to see how archers could gain the king's ear in opposition to the representatives of the misteries. The price set was a week's wages for military archers and for most other craftsmen of the day and is not greatly different from cost of bows in the comparative table on page 186.

After he won the throne in 1485, Henry VII re-enacted Edward IV's statute controlling the sale price of bows with one small amendment, the fine was doubled to 40/- per bow sold above the set price.[82] The maximum price for a yew bow set by both Edward IV and Henry VII seems to have been accepted as realistic. Edward Poyning, the King's Deputy in Ireland, was paying between 2/- and 3s 4d for bows in 1496.[83]

Price rather than apathy seems to have been regarded as the major cause of the decline of archery skills in both Edward IV and Richard III's reigns. Both kings enacted statutes that laid the blame for the decline on the high price of bows, accusing foreign merchants of causing this by charging too much for the staves. (The dominance of the bowstave trade by foreign merchants is outlined in the following chapter.) Both Henry VII and Henry VIII perceived the bow supply problem to be an internal matter, laying responsibility on the bowyers for charging high prices.

Henry VIII's solution to the perceived problem of a decline in the number of competent archers available to serve him was much more all encompassing than those of his predecessors. His statute of 1511–12 covered both the practice of archery and the supply of bows.[84] Part of the statute contains strict measures to ensure the manufacture and availability of bows throughout the country. Firstly, every bowyer had to make 'for every oon bowe of ewe that he maketh to sell at lest two bowes of Elme Wiche or other wode of mean price.' This should not be taken to mean that bows had not been made from woods other than yew previously; the indenture of 1475 recorded in the previous chapter shows that about one in six of the bows in stores of a major military expedition to France were not made of yew. But it may have reflected a decline in the use of inferior wood, since it seems probable that yew bows brought bowyers higher profits. Justices of the Peace were given the power to

> ... take, assaigne and appoynt bowers in 3, 2 or more places by their discretion in every shire, city or borowe where the mos comen repare and resort is of his subgiettes and their to inhabite and make long bowes of Elme Wiche or other wood of lytell price and value to serve the comynaltie for the due exercise of shotyng.

This makes clear the role of bows made of wyche elm and other cheaper woods as practice bows for men to maintain their skills. This had a twofold benefit, reducing the outlay for the ordinary man and reducing the demand on precious imported yew staves, which the king wanted to keep as far as possible for his army's use. The other purpose of the act, to allow the control and direction of bowyers as to where they lived and worked, is an extension of the Crown's powers to conscript bowyers and fletchers when preparing for war to ensure the production of the necessary equipment, and it does seem quite oppressive. It must have seemed an attractively simple solution to the problem of availability of bows from the Crown's point of view, but it seems not to have been successful.

For the next quarter of a century Henry was distracted from archery matters by his marital and religious problems, but in 1541–2, as military matters became more pressing, he passed another statute to both promote archery and encourage the supply of bows. This act starts with a complaint from the Bowyers, Fletchers, Stringers and Arrowhead makers about the popularity of unlawful games and the consequent decline of archery. But it also outlines another cause of this decline.

> Bowyers, Fletchers and other artificers afore named from tyme to tyme resorte, repayre and come out of all places of this your realm unto the Cittie of London for lack of livinge…other citties, townes villages and places within this realm remayne and be unfurnyshed of artyficers and craftsmen before rehersed to the great decaye of the archerie of this realm.[85]

Not surprisingly, Henry's efforts to control where bowyers lived and worked were no more successful than the sequence of Statutes beginning with the Statute of Labourers of 1351 were in directing labour. But he persisted in his efforts to ensure a supply of affordable bows by amended the regulations covering their manufacture and cost. In an effort to ensure 'that every person maye have bowes of meane price' the 1511–12 law was amended so that bowyers outside the City of London had to make 'four bows of wych elme, hazill, ash or other wood apte for the same for each yew bow made', while those within the City only had to make two.

The price controls became more sophisticated, covering bows for the different age groups, so that yew bows for 8- to 14-year-olds were to cost no more than 12d, but bowyers should have a range of yew bows costing between 6d and 12d for 14 to 21-year-olds. The maximum price of 3/4d for yew bows is now limited to 'bows of yew of the tax called elke'. I have been unable to find any further information about this.

An interesting piece of elitism was introduced in the regulation that no one under the age of 17 was to shoot a yew bow unless either he himself or his parents owned or had a tenancy of land worth £10, or moveable goods worth 40 marks (£26 12/-). Does this mean that poorer people were buying their children yew bows and so possibly creating a situation where demand outstripped supply, or is it an effort to create a market for the bows of other woods? Henry was whistling in the wind with this statute, the days of the military longbowman were passing. As a result, the number of bowyers and fletchers would also decline over the following centuries. Despite the finds on the *Mary Rose* a number of English captains and military leaders no longer thought of archery as important for military success. Henry himself recognised that military practice was changing and spent heavily on building and equipment for gunpowder warfare on both land and sea.

NOTES

1 *Medieval Archaeology* vol. 11 1967 p.291 refers to the find being a bowstave. Platt, C and Coleman-Smith R (1975). *Excavations in Medieval Southampton 1953–69,* Leicester University Press vol. 2 p.231, is less specific.

2 Comments on the quality of English yew by Chris Boyton. bowyer, personal communication. 2006.

3 Coss, P R Editor (1986) *The Early Records of Medieval Coventry*. Oxford University Press. Docs 136, 297, 298, 428, 429, 434, 435, 441, 451, 452, 453, 466. Regarding John of St. Botulphs, see Collins, F (1897).

4 Megson, B (1993). *Such Goodly Company*. London, Worshipful Company of Bowyers p.12.

5 *CPR* 1338-40. p.124.

6 Unwin, G (1938). *Gilds and Companies of London*. London p.88.

7 *York Memorandum Book part 1 1376-1419*. (1912). Publications of the Surtees Society vol. 120 p.54 (bowyers) and p.110 (fletchers).

8 Oxley, J E (1968). *The Fletchers and Longbowstring Makers of London*. London. Worshipful Company of Fletchers. p.13.

9 Megson, B (1993) p.17.

10 Goodman, A (1982) p.220.

11 *CPR* 1381–85 p.574 and *CPR* 1391–96 p.667 respectively.

12 *CPR*1377–81 p.137 and *CPR*1388–92 p.390.

13 *CPR* 1388–92. p.41.

14 *CPR* 1396–99 p.35 and p.495.

15 *CPR* 1396–99 p.495 -6.

16 Oxley, J E. (1968). p.14.

17 *CPR* 1399–1402 p.214.

18 *CPR* 1399–1402. p.98, 139 and 225 respectively.

19 *CPR* 1399–1402. p.284.

20 *CPR* 1399–01 p.336, *CPR* 1401–05 p.510 and *CPR* 1405–08 p.474.

21 *CPR* 1401–05 p.330 and *CPR* 1413–16 p.49.

22 *CLBCL* Book I p.173.

23 *CPR* 1413–16 p.30.

24 Oxley, J E. (1968). p.103.

25 *CPR* 1413–16 p.72.

26 Wylie, J H (1914) vol 1 p.160n.

27 Devon F (1837) p.318.

28 Wylie, J H (1914) p.161n.
29 *CPR* 1413–16 p.329.
30 *CPR* 1416–22 p.103.
31 *CPR* 1416–22 p.178.
32 Prestwich, M (1996) p.141.
33 *CPR* 1416–22 p. 82, 344 and 391 respectively.
34 Woolgar C M (editor) (1993). *Household Accounts from Medieval England.* Oxford. University Press. p.685.
35 *CLBCL* Book H p.6.
36 *CLBCL* Book K p.141.
37 *CCR* 1368 p.414.
38 *York Memorandum Book, part 1 1376–1419.* (1912) p.199.
39 Thanks to Pip Bickerstaffe and Fred Bentley, bowyers, for advice on this.
40 Longman, C J and Walrond, Col. H (1894) p.122.
41 Oxley, J E (1968) p 14–15.
42 *CLBCL* Book L p.212-13.
43 Percy, J W (editor) (1978) *York Memorandum Book vol. 3*. Gateshead. Surtees Society vol 186 p.191.
44 CLBLC Book L p.258.
45 *CLBCL* Book L p.212-13 footnotes offer this explanation.
46 Salzman, L F (1952). *Building in England to 1540*. Oxford University Press. p.346.
47 Frost, C (1827). *Notices Relative to the Early History of the Town and Port of Hull*. London. J B Nichols. p.20.
48 *CLBCL* Book H p.272.
49 Oxley, J E. (1968) p.119.
50 Oxley, J E. (1968) p.120.
51 William Crane was a Master and Warden of the Fletchers' Guild in 1428; see Oxley, J E (1968) p.103.
52 *CPR* 1429-36 p.43–4.
53 *CPR* 1429–36 index.
54 ibid p.607.
55 ibid p.526.
56 Vale, M G A (1970). *English Gascony 1399–1453*. Oxford. p.112.
57 *CPR* 1429–36 p.600.
58 Stevenson, J (1861-4) vol.2 p.511.
59 *CPR* 1485–94 p.59.
60 *CPR* 1485–94 p.258.
61 Barbeled was used to mean barbed in 1480.
62 *CPR* 1485–94 p.258 and p.359.
63 *CPR* 1485–94 p.392.
64 *CPR* 1485–94 p.33.
65 *CLBCL* Book L p.169.
66 *Letters and Papers Foreign and Domestic.1509-19 vol 2 pt2* p.1448.
67 ibid vol 1 pt.1 p.611.

68 ibid vol 1 pt.1 p.501.
69 Fenwick, C (1998, 2001 and 2005). *The Poll Taxes of 1377. 1379 and 1381.* Oxford University Press. vol. 1 p.xvi.
70 Fenwick, C. (2005) vol.3 p.140–56.
71 Fenwick, C (2001) vol.2 p.477.
72 All references to the Freemen of York come from Collins, F (1897) (editor).
73 Barker, J (2005) p.92.
74 *York Memorandum Book* book 2. London. Surtees Society. 1915 p.122-3.
75 Hartopp, H (editor) (1927). *Register of the Freemen of Leicester 1196–1770.* Leicester. Corporation of Leicester.
76 Byerly, B F and C R (editors) (1977) p.39.
77 Lodge E C and Somerville R (1937). *John of Gaunt's Register 1372–76.* Camden 3rd series nos. 56 and 57. London p.47.
78 Toulmin Smith L (1894) p.31.
79 Gendall, J (2001). 'The Arundell Archive of Arrows and Arrowheads' p.61–2 in *Journal of the Society of Archer-Antiquaries* vol. 44.
80 Longman, C J and Walrond, Col. H (1894) p.128–9.
81 *Statutes of the Realm* vol. 2 p.472–3.
82 *Statutes of the Realm.* vol. 2 p.521.
83 Gairdner, J (editor) (1863). *Letters and Papers Illustrative of the Reigns of Richard III and Henry VII.* London. Longman Green & co. vol.2 p.314.
84 *Statutes of the Realm.* vol. 3 p.25–6.
85 *Statutes of the Realm.* vol. 3 p.837–8.

International and Domestic Trade in Bowstaves

The earliest records of international trade in bowstaves date from the late thirteenth century.[1] Spanish merchants imported yew bowstaves through Bristol in the 1280s.[2] In 1293 eleven ships from Germany and Frisia were driven into Scarborough by bad weather. Their combined cargoes included bowstaves, and while it is likely they intended to bring them to an English port, Boston for example, since there are early records of bowstaves being imported there, we do not know for certain.[3] The Oak Book of Southampton is a collection of legal and administrative documents dating to around 1300, which includes a list of the custom rates to be charged on imports. This list includes the following: 'del cent bastouns pur arcs et pur arbalstes 2d'.[4] While this gives us no firm evidence for the age or the scale of the trade at this date, it suggests that bowstaves had been an import item in sizable quantities for some years at least.

The development of the trade in its earlier stages was encouraged by large royal orders. Two of the early examples of these were one from Edward II's reign when 180 dozen bows of Spanish yew were ordered[5] and another from 1351 when a Hanse merchant from Lubeck, Johannes of Sestede, was paid by the king's officials for 5000 bowstaves[6] which were delivered through the north eastern ports. Deliveries on this scale by a single merchant were not seen again until the middle of the fifteenth century.

These early examples of the trade in bowstaves demonstrate two of the three trade routes developed by merchants, namely from the North and East of Europe and from Spain. Although Genoese galleys made trading expeditions to North Sea ports in the late thirteenth century, with the Venetians following quickly, direct import of bowstaves from Italy does not seem to have developed until the fifteenth century.[7] The Hanseatic merchants – both German and Dutch – and the Italian merchants developed trading networks within Europe to supply the staves to the northern ports for export to England.

NORTHERN AND EASTERN EUROPEAN PORTS

The network developed by the Hanseatic merchants based mainly in the German Baltic ports was probably the most extensive, the Italian and

Spanish merchants relying on sources within their own country in general, if not within their home state, given the political divisions in both Spain and Italy at this time. The Hanseatic merchants came to control the Baltic trade by the end of the fourteenth century. While the major Dutch ports were part of the Hanseatic League they seem to have acted fairly independently of the decisions made in the German Baltic ports, and bowstaves were exported from ports such as Middleburgh and Amsterdam by both English and Dutch merchants, regardless of the rulings of the Hanseatic League.[8] The Hundred Years War created the large scale demand in England for good quality bowstaves from these sources, but it also caused the disruption of the sea trade routes through privateering and piracy. Dutch and German markets and ports benefited from this because land trade routes from Italy through the Austrian and Swiss alpine passes developed as a result.[9]

The earliest traces of the bowstave trade between Europe and England come from the end of the thirteenth century and suggest that it was based around the North Sea, and to a lesser degree in the ports of Aquitaine and Spain. Howeve,it became significant in the first half of the fourteenth century, stimulated by Edward III's wars. Despite the importance of the trade in bowstaves to the military success and security of England, it became increasingly dominated by foreign merchants and ships. However, some Englishmen and some naturalised foreigners took part in the trade throughout the period. In the fourteenth and first half of the fifteenth centuries these men used English ships slightly more commonly than they used ships based in Dutch or German ports. When it is possible to trace where they lived it seems that the majority lived in England, although there are also records of some English merchants living in the Baltic ports in the fourteenth and fifteenth centuries. These latter found their activities hampered on occasion by the Hanseatic merchants not always sticking to the agreements they made with the English kings regarding equality of treatment. One example that is particularly interesting is that of John Swerd of York, a bowyer working in the city for at least ten years prior to 1373, who was given permission to set up an establishment in Prussia in that year. He sent '… four yeomen and two grooms of his craft to Prussia to stay there for four years to fashion bows there and send them to York from time to time'.[10] We do not know how successful this imaginative venture was.

Inevitably there were ups and downs in relations between the Hanseatic merchants and the English, both customs collectors and merchants. In 1392 the Hanse merchants successfully claimed against the mayor, bailiffs and customs collectors of Southampton for overcharging on a range of customs duties including those 'upon every hundred of boghstaves'.[11] By about 1400 we know that relations between English merchants and the Hanse merchants in Danzig had broken down since we have record of a complaint by Robert atte Wood and other English merchants that they were being ill-treated and imprisoned. Apparently the Burgmasters of the city were preventing the English merchants from buying bowstaves and waynscotes, and from forming trading partnerships with the Danzig merchants.[12] However, this may have been a local or personal contretemps; English merchants were still trading successfully with the Hanseatic League at this date. Customs accounts survive from Hull for 1401 that show some Englishmen were able to acquire both bowstaves and wainscots for import to England.[13] These include records of merchants with English names bringing bowstaves into Hull on ships based in both Bremen and Danzig, as well as three English ships bringing in bowstaves for English merchants. The cargoes on the German ships, which belonged no doubt to the Hanseatic League, indicate that the Englishmen had formed trading partnerships with Hanse merchants. The English ships may also reflect this practice, but are as likely to be carrying goods for English merchants living in the Baltic ports. The records of the Hanse at this time list a good number of English merchants, many probably from Yorkshire and neighbouring counties, paying dues.[14] At least a third of the English merchants mentioned in the Hull customs records as importing bowstaves in 1401 appear in the Register as Freemen of York as mercers, that is as cloth merchants. They took English cloth to Northern Europe and brought back bowstaves, wainscot and osmund (Swedish iron). These mercers of York would find a ready market for the staves in the city since bow making was booming, with 24 bowyers registered as Freemen in Richard II's reign, and bowyers' registrations continued at a similar rate in Henry IV's reign.[15] The links between the merchants importing bowstaves and the bowyers were close on occasion. William del Hill imported staves in 1401, and Laurence del Hill was a bowyer in York, both men registered as Freeman of the city in Richard II's reign.

There were clearly some problems to sort out, since Henry IV made an agreement in 1408 allowing English merchants to live and trade in Prussia. But the profits of the Baltic trade must have been good since English merchants continued to try to be part of it. In 1436 Nicholas Hisham, a well established merchant of York, was given permission to take four ships to Prussia ' ...in quest of woods for spears and bows there being a scarcity of such wood in England'.[16] This is a rare piece of evidence that the administration understood the scarcity, at a time when trade with the Hanseatic merchants was disrupted. By the second half of the fifteenth century the English merchants found their opportunities for trade with the northern and eastern ports severely limited both by Hanse restrictive practices and the enthusiasm for piracy and privateering of both English and Hanse merchants. In general the English, Dutch and German merchants tended to trade in hundreds rather than thousands of staves at a time and they never brought in single deliveries to rival the size of some of those in the Venetian carracks and galleys in the later half of the fifteenth century.

As the surviving customs records are patchy, it is difficult to discern whether any of the English, Dutch or German merchants specialised in supplying bowstaves. Examples of some who may have done follow, but even these always imported other goods with the staves. The most significant

English merchant in the records is Thomas Neleson of Hull, who imported staves over a fourteen-year period in the 1450s and 1460s using ships based in Dutch and German ports mainly, but he did use a Hull ship on at least one occasion. In 1462 he brought in 2500 staves in Dutch ships (confusingly both are recorded as being the *Kateryn* of Middleburgh, landing in August, but they have different masters), the largest single delivery recorded from an English merchant. William and Thomas Gaunte, who were part of a merchant family living in York, also brought in a substantial number of staves in 1453, using ships from Danzig and Westernschouwern. The home ports of the ships suggest that the Gauntes may have had a trading relationship with Hanseatic merchants. Two thirds were described as 'wrek' in the customs record, poor quality staves which the 1472 Statute noted below regards as being fit only for making bows for children.

Among the Hanse merchants participating in the bowstave trade with England, some were more prepared to import larger quantities more frequently, although none in the fourteenth and fifteenth centuries took the risk of specialising exclusively in bowstaves. Those who imported larger quantities included Bartholomeus Wulfe, who imported staves in the 1460s. Hans and Herman Overcamp used Danzig-based ships to bring in middling quantities of staves between 1480 and 1489. The only Hanse merchant in the fifteenth century who is recorded as importing staves in quantities that rivalled those from the Italian merchants is Hans Stagnet, who brought in just under 5000 in 1483.

In the sixteenth century the Italian merchants dominated the bowstave trade, but it would be a mistake to assume that the Hanse merchants gave up. In 1523, about ten years after Henry VIII's large-scale purchases of Italian staves described below, Sir William Skevington, Master of the King's Ordinance, signed an indenture with George Guys, a Hanse merchant for the delivery of 6000 'bowstaves of yewe' in August of that year.[17] There is no indication of the cost of these staves on the indenture.

The Hanseatic merchants' sources of bowstaves included the lands controlled by the Teutonic Order in Prussia, Lithuania and the Eastern borders between the German states and Poland. They also bought bowstaves that came from the Carpathians up the rivers to the Baltic ports, and from Norway.[18] Examples of the Teutonic Order's involvement in this trade include one from 1386 when 7600 unworked yew staves for bows (*yewenbogenholcz*) and 1150 staves for crossbows were deposited with a citizen of Danzig at the behest of the Grand Master of the Order.[19] There is also a reference to the Teutonic Order supplying bowstaves as part of the international network of the Church. When Cardinal Beaufort was making preparations for his crusade against the Hussites in 1427–8 he wrote a letter in which he expressed concern about a shortage of bows and asked his ecclesiastical colleague, the Master of the Teutonic Order, to load 'without delay two ships … with wood and materials suitable for the making of bows' and despatch them to London.[20]

VENICE, GENOA AND MILAN

Italy did not exist as a country until 1870. In the Middle Ages the Italian peninsula was home to a large number of city states. While they were all in theory independent, by the fourteenth century the Italian peninsula was dominated by a small number of states including the Venetian Republic, Milan, Florence, Genoa, The Papal States and the Kingdom of Naples. The smaller cities tended to be allies or subjects of their more powerful neighbours. In this patchwork, Venice, and to a lesser degree Genoa, were unusual in that they built up substantial maritime trading networks. Venice also built up an 'empire' in the Balkans, Greece and Ionian islands that was an integral part of her trading activities. As a result Venice became effectively the trading middle man between the Middle East and the West. Genoa added to her trading activities by being a source of mercenary galleys and crossbowmen. The latter would learn a keen appreciation of the qualities of the English archers and their bows. Italian merchant houses also became involved in banking activities. The Genoese first and then the Venetians started to send trading fleets up the Atlantic coast of Iberia and France to North Sea ports in the last quarter of the thirteenth century. Initially these seemed to concentrate on bringing Mediterranean luxury goods including wine and spices, but they came to realise the advantage of engaging in the specialist bowstave trade with England. The Italian merchants, particularly those from Venice also developed land trade routes using the Austrian and Swiss Alpine passes in response to the insecurity rising from the first four decades of the Hundred Years War. These routes finished at the Dutch and Flemish cities and ports. Since bowstaves were bulky in relation to value, it is unlikely that large quantities regularly came this way. By the fifteenth century the Italian merchants seem to have been so confident that their large, well armed merchantmen travelling in flotillas were safe in northern waters that 'in almost any year after 1421 the great Italian carracks and galleys might have been found lying up in Southampton during at least part of the winter ...'[21] In the first half of the fifteenth century, the earliest records of Italian merchants importing staves to England are of agents for Italian merchant companies in Southampton, who would have had plenty of opportunity to investigate new trading opportunities in England. These include Paul Morell who was bringing in staves in 1435 and 1440, maybe an early specialist in the trade, and Andrea Spynell in 1440. The Italian suppliers of staves, especially the Venetians, had a significant effect on the whole bowstave trade because of the quantity they brought in at any one time. Eight thousand staves were imported in one ship by Phillipo Cyny in 1464, and an almost incredible 18,656 staves were brought in three galleys of the Venetian trading fleet of 1481 by Antonio Baverin. I have seen no evidence of these large deliveries in the fifteenth century being in made in response to direct royal orders, as was the case in Henry VIII's reign. These staves were commonly landed at Southampton, no doubt to be sold by the agents of the Italian merchant companies there. In 1481 things were slightly different because Bavarin landed about 70% of his staves in Southampton and the rest in London. The galley that sailed to London temporarily detached itself from the fleet for this delivery, perhaps to meet a specific royal order.

Venetian merchants almost certainly sourced a good proportion of the staves they supplied from north-eastern Italy (very limited supplies are still available from this area), but other may have come from their trading sphere of influence in the Balkans and just possibly from further afield such as the Carpathians. The Genoese – and later in Henry VIII's time the Milanese – could draw on supplies from Northern Italy and Switzerland. They may also have sourced some in Iberia. As the fifteenth century progressed, the Venetians became the dominant Italian suppliers of staves and quite possibly supplied a higher proportion of the staves reaching England than any other group of merchants.

Very early in his reign, Henry made contact with a Venetian merchant firm, Cha de Pesaro, to arrange the supply of a large number of bowstaves.[22] In doing this, Henry chose not to rely on the regular trade in bowstaves for the raw materials for his military plans, but returned to the practice of direct royal orders for bowstaves used by the first three Edwards before the trade was fully developed. In July 1510 the Doge and Senate of Venice wrote to Andrea Badoer, their Ambassador in England, asking him to advise Henry of the progress with the order for staves that he had with the firm of Pesaro. He informed the King that while Cha de Pesaro had '... a large supply already prepared' they had no means of getting them to England since the state galleys were not going to sail for fear of French attack.[23] In September 1510, Piero, a member of the Cha de Pesaro, presented a letter to the Venetian Senate requesting permission to export 40,000 'bows' using ships of any nation. The request was agreed.[24] This was a pragmatic decision by the Venetians, attempting to meet their trading commitments with their important royal ally despite the extra cost of using shipping from other states. The Venetians hoped to transport their goods in ships from home states that were not at war the French, as Venice was at this time. The decision was also coloured by ongoing negotiations between the Venetians and Henry for a loan, which he offered in a letter sent in September. The Venetians offered to deliver to Henry's ambassador to the Pope, 'or even send to England', securities for this loan comprising jewels, bows and other goods.[25] However, Henry was impatient and pressed the firm of Pesaro to deliver.[26] Henry did receive bowstaves from Venice in 1510, because Antonio Baverin receiving £762/15/- in October of that year[27] in payment for some. While the number of staves is not mentioned, it was clearly a substantial number given the amount paid, probably not less than 15,000. This could be part of an earlier order than the one for 40,000 staves, given the date of the payment, and the certainty that the Crown did not pay absolutely promptly. If this is the case it suggests that Cha de Pesaro may have specialised in supplying bowstaves. Baverin was the name of the factor of the firm in London,[28] but it is not clear if this Antonio Baverin is the same as the one who imported so many staves in 1481. He would be in his late fifties or sixties by 1511 if he was, but it is more likely that this was his son. This is more evidence of specialization by individual merchants, and continuity over the generations within merchant families. A study of Italian records may show that Cha de Pesaro was involved in the bowstave trade before Henry VIII's reign, but at present I have found no evidence of this.

In May 1511, problems with delivery of the staves persisted since Piero of the Cha de Pesaro successfully applied to be allowed to send Candia wine with the bowstaves in the foreign ships. This looks like an attempt to ensure a profit on the delivery, perhaps the Pesaro firm had realised that there was little profit in delivering the staves alone. By June 1512 the firm of Pesaro had succeeded in delivering some of the order at least because Antonio Baverin received 'payment in full of bowstaves' then.[29] However, by December 1514, Cha de Pesaro still had not been able to complete the contract. The Doge and Senate of Venice agreed in that month that not only Cha de Pesaro but 'other Venetian noblemen' could send bows and wine to England in foreign ships.[30]

The size of this order is typical of the grand scale on which Henry made his plans. We do not know how soon he expected delivery. In Henry's mind, these orders were necessary on two counts: firstly, of course, because he had military ambitions, and as an archer himself, believed that the bow could still bring military glory to England. Secondly, since his father Henry VII had shrewdly avoided war through diplomacy, the stock piles of military equipment were probably at a low level. While the declared reason for late delivery was difficulties in shipping the staves securely to England, it is also possible that the Venetians found it difficult to obtain such a large number of staves quickly. Cha de Pesaro did not have a monopoly of the Venetian bowstave trade. Appendix 3 shows that the Venetian merchants managed to deliver at least 20,446 staves in 1481, so 40,000 staves was not an unrealistic quantity, so long as Henry did not expect all the staves in one delivery. Although given his character, he probably did. The quality of the staves would have varied whatever the delivery time, judging from purchases of Italian yew staves I have made.

It is unlikely that an order of this size could have been repeated in the following years. There is no reference to any repeat orders on this scale at any time in Henry's reign. There is a record of a payment of £966/13/4d to Laurence Bonvix, a merchant of Lucca, for bowstaves in December 1511.[31] A conservative estimate of the number of staves he supplied would be about 19,400, so Henry probably needed no more. Bonvix, or Lorenzo Bonvisi as he is known in other sources, was part of a longstanding Milanese commercial presence in England since the Duke of Milan wrote to Henry VIII in 1499 asking him to grant Bonvisi an audience.[32] These orders and payments provide clear evidence of the great importance of the Italians in the resourcing of the English war effort. Henry VIII was able to avoid dependency on one major supplier of staves because of his father's diplomatic efforts.

The Venetian state galleys last sailed to England in 1532.[33] While this did not necessarily mean the end of their dominance of the trade in Italian bowstaves in England, it would have been a setback. Although by this time there are no large-scale imports of staves.

SPAIN AND PORTUGAL

In 1627, when Michael Drayton wrote, 'The English archery struck the French horses with Spanish yew so strong…' in his *Ballad of Agincourt*, he left a powerful impression that Spain was the major source of staves for the English bowyers. There is no strong evidence for this. Most of the bowstaves that came from the Iberian Peninsula were supplied through different trade mechanisms than those from Italy or Northern and Eastern Europe, in that it was less a trade dominated by the political community of the supplier, as in Venice or the Hanseatic League. Staves were supplied through what might be called diplomatic efforts, either the English king ordering purchase, or the Spanish or Portuguese kings occasionally sending quantities of staves as part of negotiations. The other trade mechanism consisted of the efforts made by individual merchants, both English and Iberian, to buy and ship staves to English ports as a purely commercial activity outside any political considerations.

An early example of the royal orders has already been mentioned when 180 dozen bows of Spanish yew were purchased for £36 in Edward II's reign. Comparing this price with those below makes raises suggests this might have been an order for bowstaves rather than finished bows. Much later, in 1448, the King of Portugal sent 4900 quarters of yew as a gift.[34]

As an example of an individual entrepreneur, in 1404 Richard Yea, a bowyer of Plymouth, traded blankets and other cloth goods to Juan, a Spanish merchant, in exchange for a future cargo of 400 bowstaves of Spanish yew.[35] In 1480 there are examples of Iberian merchants being the prime movers in the import of some staves. The London customs records for the year include two ships from Oporto in Portugal carrying staves, the *Tres Magos* with 1036 and the *Sanctus Spiritus* with 88.[36] A late example comes from the records of a court case of 1529–32, when Robert Spacheford of London brought an action against Richard Couche who was joint owner of a ship, the *Breton Foge*. Spacheford had arranged for the ship to loaded with bowstaves and cork at Abeles in Spain but the ship was driven by storms to Beaumaris where Couche seems to have sold the cargo to Rowland Thikkons.[37] This case highlights two of the the mercantile risks of the age, bad weather and dishonest ship owners.

The records listed in Appendix 4 make it clear that the Wars of the Roses, which stretched in desultory fashion from 1455 to 1487, did not cause enough disorder to disrupt the trade in bowstaves. On the one hand the raising of armed retinues would obviously provide a market for bows, as would Edward IV's French expeditions, but on the other hand, these wars caused instability and uncertainty in England, and an increase in English piracy preying on foreign shipping.[38]

A final point on the domination of the supply of bowstaves by Hanseatic and Italian, particularly Venetian, merchants (as opposed to Iberian): the kings of England's enemies were France, Scotland and, at times, Castile. These did not pose any threat, diplomatic or military, to these suppliers. The main trade routes to England used by the Hanseatic merchants were beyond easy reach of French privateers. The Venetian state trading flotillas, both carracks and galleys, were a tough proposition for any privateer to take on. Also, the Venetians dominated the supply of luxury goods from the east, so it was not in the interests of the French and Spanish kings to disrupt their trading voyages. Having said this, by Henry VIII's time when the Venetians, the English and the Papal States were allies against the French, the Venetians were reluctant to risk their galleys on voyages to England, since they would have to brave the French royal navy as well as privateers. So, while foreign dominance of the bowstave trade left the English Crown in the power of these merchants to some degree, a fact which the Hanseatic merchants exploited, it was not a weakness that England's enemies managed to use to their advantage.

The data in Appendix 4, while incomplete, indicates that bowstaves came into England in differing quantities each year. These variations were not always caused by disputes between the English and the Hanseatic League. In some years, perhaps staves were simply unavailable, as in the period December 1448 to September 1449, when no staves are listed as imported in the Southampton customs records.[39] The ports of Plymouth and Bristol do not seem to have received any bowstaves, but that may be because of the incomplete records. While it is likely that the ports on the south and east coast of England received the bulk of the imported bowstaves, it would be surprising if these two vital ports actually received none. In the customs accounts of Chester for the fourteenth and fifteenth centuries, again there is no mention of bowstaves: even more surprising since Chester was home to misteries in all three of the archery trades in the fifteenth century.[40]

COSTS OF BOWSTAVES

The earliest evidence is Edward II's purchase of 180 dozen (2160) bowstaves of Spanish yew for £36 (4d each). In 1359–60 William de Rothwell paid £40 for 4000 bowstaves, 2.4d each, which were added to the royal stores in the Tower of London.[41] In 1380 the value of 1200 bowstaves was assessed as £12 (the same, 2.4d each) by John Dernford, the then Warden of the Company of Bowyers, as part of bankruptcy proceedings.[42] This price is low when compared with other examples from thirty years later. It is possible that the relative lack of military activity at this time kept the price low. In 1396 a customs valuation from (King's) Lynn for a cargo of bowstaves, probably from north Eastern Europe, also works out at 2.4d per stave.[43] In 1401 at Hull, the average customs valuation of three batches of bowstaves works out to between 2.4d per stave in a large delivery of 1000 staves to 2.9d per stave in two smaller deliveries of 200 staves each.[44] The difference was probably down to bulk buying rather than quality. In 1430, two deliveries of one hundred bowstaves each through Southampton by an English merchant, Morysse Flesscher, show a significant increase in price. The customs records list the value of these at 5.6d per stave for one delivery and 4.8d per stave for the other.[45] It is likely that Flesscher bought these staves at a Flanders port.

These Customs valuations and some later ones in 1467 and 1504 should not be taken as a direct record of the purchase and sale price of staves at this time. Exchequer records from 1413 include a payment of 60/- per 100 for staves, just over 7d each, without mentioning the quantity. In August of the same year John Cowbill 'an esterling' was paid £28/6/8d for 1000 staves, about $6^{3}/_{4}$d per stave, while in November £52 was paid for 1200 staves, nearly $10^{1}/_{2}$d each.[46] Given his identification as an esterling, John Cowbill probably supplied Baltic or possibly Norwegian staves. At that price, those delivered in November must have been something special.

International trade was never stable. In 1385 the Grand Master of the Teutonic Order forbade the export of timber and forest products to England. This was as part of a trade dispute wherein English merchants demanded the same rights in the Prussian ports as the Hanseatic merchants. When trade restarted after each interruption, the merchants had an opportunity to make large profits. When trade between England and Danzig restarted in 1437–8 after a series of embargoes, merchants could sell staves in England at an average price of 54 marks per great hundred (120). In 1427 the Hanseatic merchants had been buying bowstaves in Poland at 14 marks per great hundred.[47] The usual margin was selling at double the purchase price, so there were certainly killings to be made in the arms trade – as always – under the right market conditions. Although an Elizabethan statute of 1566 referred to the price of staves as having risen from £5 per 100 to £12, in 1572 the Hanse merchants who had control of the supply were able to charge £6 10/- per hundred staves, 16d each – which they did not consider a good price.

The international quasi-monopoly trade was of course an ecological disaster. Fred Hageneder points out the awful truth that a yew must grow for a hundred years to produce perhaps four bowstaves. Throughout the 17th century, there was no mention of yew in the forestry records of all of the northern Alpine countries. They had all been cut down.

LEGAL CONSTRICTIONS ON THE IMPORT OF BOWSTAVES

There has already been reference to the concerns of both the English kings and their Parliaments about the perceived decline in the practice of archery by Englishmen in their leisure time. In 1472 the Commons petitioned

Edward IV saying that 'Lordes, Knyghtes, Squyers, Gentilmen, Yomen and the Comyners have used the occupation of shotyng for their myrthes and sportes with bowes of ewe [but were] nowe usen unlawfull occupations as pleiying at cardes, dise plaiying etc'. The cause of this decline was said to be a shortage of bowstaves which in turn led to an increase in the price of bows. This is described in outraged tones:

> ... such bowstaves as be brought be sette nowe to outrageous price, that is to say 100 bowstaves at 100/- or 10 markes [133/4d] and the bier to take oon with an other, ill and goode. Whereas of oolde time they were wont to be sold for 60/- or 4 marks [53/4d] an 100 of the best bowstaves, and such as were called wrak, not goode nor able to make but childern bowes were sold for 10/- or 13/4d (I mark) at moste and the boweyers might aforthe to selle a bowe for a good Yoman some for 8d, some for 10d and the best for a Yoman 12d. it is nowe that such bowes been at such excessive price, that is to say some at 10/- some at 6/8d and some at 5/- whereby the said occupation of shotyng is thus discontynnued and almoste left.[48]

The Commons are claiming that at some point in the past, staves cost between about $6^1/_2$d and $7^1/_4$d each whereas in 1472 their price had risen to between 12d and 16d. They claim that the best bow for a yeoman only cost 12d, and that ordinary bows might be available at 8d. These prices do not add up if the bows were made from imported staves costing between $6^1/_2$d and $7^1/_4$d. If we accept the prices in this petition, and that is a big if because the price per bow is below any price paid by the Crown for bows in the last 130 years, and can only be matched in 1341, then this might be evidence for 'a bowe for a good yoman' being made of other wood than imported staves. Or they were just exaggerating for effect. Though it is fair to accept that there had been a rise in the cost of staves, and that the bowstave merchants had exacerbated the matter by insisting the staves were bought in unsorted bundles. The solution proposed in the petition and enacted by Edward IV was creative, if scattergun. In an effort to get a regular supply of good bowstaves at no cost to the Crown by decreeing a new customs duty to be paid by 'Every merchant stranger of the city or county of Venice or other city, town or country from whence any such bowstaves have been before this time brought, sent or conveyed into this land'.[49] The merchants were to provide four bowstaves for every tun weight of merchandise they brought into the country. To ensure that they did not bring poor quality staves the Mayors, Sheriffs or Bailiffs of the ports were to appoint two men to inspect the staves. This should have undercut the market for staves in England by ensuring that the Crown, the largest single customer, had a free supply. I have not been able to make any sensible calculation of how many staves this regulation might have netted, since it all hinged on which ports and states the customs officials believed had supplied staves in the past. It is possible to read this purely as a measure against the Italian merchants.

Looking at the customs records for the 1470s and 1480s there is no sign that the number of staves the Crown obtained from this customs duty had any real effect on the bowstave trade, nor on the Italians. At least 25,238 staves were imported in 1481, 80% of them by Italian merchants.

A statute of Richard III's reign again blamed the decline of archery skills and 'bowyery' on the cost of staves. In 1483–4 it claimed prices had been 60/- or 66/8d at most for 100 staves, but that 'by the seducious confederacy of the said Lombards ben nowe at so outrageous price, that is to wit at £8 per 100 ... and also they wi no suffer any garbelyng of theym to be made but selle goode and bad at so excessyf price togedyr ungarbeled.' The solution was to increase the levy set up in 1472 so that now merchants from places that had hitherto supplied staves (the merchants of Venice are specifically mentioned) must bring in 10 bowstaves 'of good and hable stuff' with every butt of wine of Malvesy [sic] or Tyre. This statute also ordered that 'no suche bowestaves be sold ungarbeled'.[50] The statute put the price rise as from between $7^1/_4$d and 8d per stave to about $19^1/_4$d. Richard III, less diplomatic than his brother, openly blames the Italian merchants for taking advantage of their dominance of the bowstave market, but restricts the duty in bowstaves to the winetrade, maybe simply because it was a bigger target. Besides the two statutes noted above there were statutes in 1482–3 and 1485 that attempted to set the maximum price for a yew bow.

In 1503–4 a statute removed the customs duties from all bowstaves $6^1/_2$ ft long and above because it was felt that insufficient good staves were being imported.[51] The customs collectors of King's Lynn do not seem to have been aware of this since they charged both Hanse and English merchants duty in the summer of 1504.

As previously described, Henry attacked the problem with his usual vigour. He tried to stop any perceived sharp practice by merchants.[52] Any merchants importing yew bowstaves had to sell them separately, not in bundles so that 'the buyers of theym may have perfite knolege of the goodnes of them'. He reiterated the controls over aliens exporting bows without a licence; with the additional limitation that aliens could not even use a longbow without a licence. In 1514–15 Henry VIII clarified Richard III's statute of 1483–4 which increased the import duty that was paid in bowstaves. Henry emphasised that this act applied only to the merchants of Venice and other merchant strangers, that is, those specifically described as aliens, and that other merchants did not have to provide these staves.[53]

In 1518 the Venetian Senate extracted a promise from Cardinal Wolsey that he would ensure the cancellation of the law requiring merchants importing Malmsey to England to bring in 10 bowstaves with each butt of wine.[54] From what we know of the value of bowstaves at this time, it is difficult to believe that this was a significant financial burden, but it was probably a nuisance. Perhaps the merchants were finding it difficult to obtain sufficient numbers of adequate staves from the lands under Venetian influence after the earlier large-scale orders.

THE INTERNAL TRADE IN BOWSTAVES

Seaports were not centres of production for bows and arrows as far as we can tell. London is the major exception to this throughout the period, while Bristol is cited in the fourteenth century, but is soon included in the orders sent to the Sheriff of Gloucestershire. Some merchants acted as wholesalers at the ports, selling on staves to specific bowyers, while other merchants no doubt brought their whole cargo to a major centre like York for sale to the bowyers. This trade provided work for the carters and packhorse men transporting the staves from the ports. We can construct some of the distribution range from the ports in the fourteenth century by looking at the royal orders sent to the county Sheriffs in the 1340s and 1350s. Looking at those orders for the sheriffs to produce large numbers of bows, at least 500, in addition to the centres noted above, Lincoln is very significant, while Devon, Norfolk and Suffolk, Hampshire, Surrey and Sussex, and Warwickshire and Leicestershire, are all expected to produce this quantity on one occasion. Lincoln must have been receiving staves through the east cost ports, particularly Boston; Norfolk and Suffolk could have done through King's Lynn; Hampshire from Southampton; Warwickshire and Leicestershire may have received staves along the old Roman roads; and Surrey and Sussex from either south coast ports or London. York only appears in the orders in 1341, although there is plenty of evidence of it being a substantial bow and arrow making industry. As a munitions base for the troops keeping the Scots at bay, perhaps the bowyers were busy enough without large Crown orders.

Some staves left Southampton and other ports by sea, probably coastal transfer to other English ports rather than export or re-export to French ports to support the English armies in Normandy and Aquitaine. In 1402 Thomas Pocoke of Calais was allowed to take seven bows and four score bowstaves there. This was a private commercial transaction rather than a government order for the garrison because Pocoke had to pay the subsidy on them.[55] Exports of archery equipment from England were rigidly banned at this time, so that even supplies going to English garrisons needed specific approval. Coastal trade between mainland English ports was not controlled in this way. In 1436 John Bawe of Newport sailed from Southampton with 100 bowstaves.[56] There are two later examples from the same port in 1510; in March the ship of John Jandes left with 300 bowstaves and other goods belonging to John Hardwyn of Coventry, while in July 6000 staves left the port in a ship *pro rege*, for the king.[57] It is likely that a quantity this high came from Italy in the Venetian galleys and unlikely that these are some of the 40,000 staves Henry ordered through the Venetian merchant firm Cha de Pesaro, given the date and the questions Henry had to raise in Venice over delays in delivery of this very large order.

Surprisingly, given the number of bowstaves imported through Southampton, there are a number of records of bowstaves being brought into Southampton by land. In April and May 1444, eight carters came into Southampton with bowstaves. They all left to go to London with various goods including wine, wool and cloth.[58] It seems likely that these staves came from London at the behest of the Crown, even from stores in the Tower of London, and that they were sent to Southampton for export to the English armies in France. Three other carters brought bowstaves into Southampton that year, but it is difficult to be certain where they brought them from. One left Southampton for Sarum with a mixed load, another for Bristol with wine and the third, who brought in a mixed load of bowstaves and wine in two carts, left for Coventry with woad. Only Bristol was a source of bowstaves, so it is impossible to locate the bowstave sources. In August 1449 William Geffrey brought 'divers bows and arrows of Thomas Daniell, armiger of our lord the King' to Southampton in his cart.[59] Frustratingly, because the king of course paid no duties, we do not know the quantities being transported. The maximum number of staves in a cart in the 1440s is 300, although in the 1470s it is 400. So the eight carters brought something between 1600 and 2000 bowstaves into Southampton.

The Brokage Books also record a number of transactions that show the quantities of bowstaves being distributed around the country. These fall into two categories, those where a general carter is carrying staves for a merchant or craftsman, and those where a man is transporting his own staves.

Bowstaves transported by carters or packhorse men					
Date	Carter or Packhorse men	No. of carts or pack-horses	Quantity of Staves	Destination	Owner of staves
5th Oct 1439	William Lambe	1 cart	$1^1/_2$ centena	Salisbury	Henry Baron[60]
24th Sept. 1444	John Walle	1 cart	200	Abingdon	William Bowyer
25th Sept 1444	John Pye	1 cart	300	Abingdon	William Bowyer[60]
5th Oct 1448	John Wodele	1 cart	200	Romsey	William Bowyer
9th May 1449	Ingram Hewet	1 cart	200	Romsey	William Bowyer
24th May 1449	Stephen King Thomas Hewet Richard Hoker	3 carts	400	Sarum	John Hall

11th July 1449	John Ede	1 cart	100	Romsey	John Lorde
23rd Aug 1449	John Hayward Stephen King	2 carts	351	London	Julian Corold[62]
13th Oct 1477	Thomas Geffrey	1 cart	400	London	Christopher Ambrose
19th Nov 1477	Henry Lange	8 pack-horses	170	Exeter	John Bowyer
17th Dec 1477	John Frankelyn	1 cart	100	Stattisbury (poss Stuckbury, Nothants)	Robert Boweer
14th Feb 1478	Thomas Swolfe	1 cart	150	Salisbury	Stephen Bowyer of Bristol
20th Feb 1478	Richard Hanger John Hange	3 carts	343	London	Christopher Ambros[e]
28th Feb 1478	William Bockett	1 'half cart'	200	Salisbury	Stephen Bowyer of Bristol
31st Mar 1478	Richard Gissege	1 cart	150	Abingdon	William Bowyer
21st April 1478	Richard Pynhorn	1 cart	150	Wherwell (Hants.)	William Bowyer
15th May 1478	John Hoggson	1 cart	100	Coventry	Robert Hurseley & Laurence Saundres
30th May 1478	Willaim Vise	1 cart	100	London?	Christopher Ambros[e]
16th June 1478	Thomas Manne	1 cart	60	Abingdon	Peter Jocobson
20th July 1478	William ?	3 pack-horses	100	Exeter	William Bower of Exeter
19th Sept. 1478	William Writtle	1 cart	100	Derby	William Bowrer of Derby[63]

'Centena' could mean a hundredweight, which would give us between about 18 and 27 staves if the weight for a stave as calculated below is accurate. A better interpretation is 'set of a hundred', so this load would be about 150 staves, or 180 if counted in long hundreds.

In general the carters carried other goods with the bowstaves to make up a load, very like contemporary haulage companies. Many of the owners of the staves have the 'Bowyer' family name or derivatives, although this may be misleading. Perhaps the carters answered the officials' question 'Whose staves are these?' with 'William the Bowyer' because that was how they knew him. While it is not surprising that the majority of staves were delivered relatively short distances, William Writtle had a journey of over 170 miles ahead of him. Christopher Ambros(e) was a significant figure in the industry in London since he ordered 843 staves, just over 40% of those listed in 1477–8. The use of packhorses for the trips to Exeter either reflects the quality of the roads to and from the city, or transport practice in the South West in general.

Men transporting their own bowstaves				
Date	Owner	No. of carts or packhorses	Quantity of Staves	Destination
26th June 1444	John Eton	1 cart	200	Ufton (Warks or Berks)[64]
26th Aug 1449	William Bawyer	1 cart	24	Sheet (Hants)[65]
2nd April 1478	William Boweer	4 packhorses	100	Shaftsbury
27th May 1478	Robert Boweer	3 packhorses	100	Shaftsbury[66]

From these tables one can estimate the weight of an individual stave. A packhorse could carry between 220lbs and 330 lbs. Since the smallest number of packhorses used to carry 100 staves was three, a stave weighed between $6^1/_2$ and 10lbs, probably tending towards the lower figure. Another sign of the decline in the trade in the sixteenth century comes from the Brokerage Books of 1527–8, which contain no records of bowstaves being carried by carters.

In the fourteenth century a system of shares was set up by the leading citizens of Hull, whereby anyone who belonged to the town could buy a share of incoming trade goods at cost price. By the late 1360s bowstaves were included among the goods that this practice covered.[67] So that this was not a disincentive to the merchants who took the risk of buying goods abroad and getting them shipped to England, minimum sizes for shares of particular goods were established at such a level that only substantial citizens would be able to afford to take advantage of the discount. It seems probable that the purpose was to prevent one person gaining control of the market for a particular commodity by importing large quantities. If this was the case, it was a similar attempt to free up the market as the ordinances of the London mistery of Bowyers that limited the number of staves a bowyer could hold.

INTERNATIONAL TRADE IN ARROW MATERIALS

The favoured woods for shafts, poplar and ash, grow rapidly and easily in England, so there was no real need for imports. However, a customs record for May 1401 from Hull records the landing of 2000 arrowshafts owned by Gerwyn Dune from the *Mary Knight* of Danzig.[68] It is likely Dune was a Hanse merchant, given the home port of the ship and the rest of the cargo. There is also reference in Flemish commercial records to the export of arrowshafts, which as yet have not been tracked down in English customs records.[69]

Osmund (a high-quality form of iron produced in Scandinavia and the Baltic regions that was still being exported to England in the 18th century), and other forms of iron were very common imports through the east coast ports. Some of these imports would have been used by arrowsmiths, particularly to meet Henry V's large scale orders to suppliers based in Rotherham and Sheffield, since transport from the east coast ports would have been easy.

INTERNATIONAL TRADE IN BOWSTRINGS

I have only found one reference to bowstrings being traded internationally. That comes from the customs records of Boston for 1391 when Gilbert de Gariga, the only foreign merchant on an English ship carrying woollen cloths for a group of English merchants, is listed as having 52 gross and 10 dozen belts (7600!) and two gross of bowstrings.[70] De Gariaga was a general merchant. There is another Boston customs record for 1403 listing him importing wine.[71] This does not point to a significant trade in bowstrings. It is much more likely that de Gariga knew of a group of archers, not necessarily English, serving abroad, and was exporting strings either to meet a commission he already had or as a small speculative venture.

LEGAL CONTROLS ON EXPORTS

It is no surprise that the English kings wanted to control the export of bows and arrows in this period, to ensure supply for their armies and to deny English archery equipment to potential enemies. In 1357 Edward III sent an order to the sheriffs and bailiffs of the east coast ports from Newcastle upon Tyne southwards that they should make a proclamation '...that no stranger or inhabitant shall take corn, wine, ale, horses, bows, arrows or other weapons out of England ... except to Bordeaux, Calais and Berwick on Tweed.' This order also went to the Sheriffs of York, Lincoln, Norfolk and Suffolk, Essex and London. At the same time the Mayors and bailiffs of the south coast ports, the sheriffs of Kent, Sussex, Southampton (ie Hampshire),

Somerset/Dorset, Devon and Cornwall and the Warden of the Cinque Ports also received the order, with one important qualification:

> But it is not the King's intention that men at arms, hobelars and archers, his subjects and adherents who are about to set out in his service with their horses and armour to the parts of Normandy and Brittany, and have taken with them corn and victuals for their maintenance, or merchants wishing to take corn and victuals to Normandy and Brittany for maintenance of those lieges shall be impeded under colour of the present order.[72]

The specific listing of each set of officials that needed to act on the king's order inevitably missed out some ports, so follow-up orders had to be sent out to plug holes in the controls, as happened to the Keeper of Rochester castle in 1360.[73] Local officials had to enforce this prohibition, particularly the collectors of Petty customs. There were clearly concerns about the effectiveness of this order. In 1369 the Mayor and Sheriffs of London were ordered to have proclamations made *monthly* forbidding the export of corn, gold and silver, and bows and arrows.[74] In 1413, Henry V trumpeted the prohibitions again, ordering the Sheriffs of London to proclaim 'No liege man of whatever estate or condition shall sell bows, arrows, armour or artillery to any man of Scotland or any other aliens, the king's enemies'.[75] One unintentional result of these orders is that we know more about men taking bows and arrows abroad for their own use, since they had to get royal licences to do so.

NOTES

1 This section uses the data of imports of bowstaves into England listed in Appendix 4.

2 Childs, W R (1978). *Anglo-Castilian Trade in the later Middle Ages*. Manchester University Press p.31.

3 Salzman, L F (1964). *English Trade in the Middle Ages*. London. p.362–3.

4 Studer, P (editor) (1910-11). *The Oak Book of Southampton. vol.2* Southampton Record Society p.6.

5 Prestwich, M (1996) p.359n.

6 *Hanserecesse und Andere Akten de Hansetage 1256-1430*. (1970-77) Leipzig vol. 1 p.87.

7 Van Houtte, J A (1977). *An Economic History of the Low Countries 800–1800*. London. Weidenfeld and Nicolson. p.47.

8 Van Houtte, J A (1977) p. 92.

9 Van Houtte, J A (1977). p.101.

10 John Swerde registered as a Freeman of York in 1362. Collins, F (1897) (editor). Prussian venture *CPR* 1370-74 p.264.

11 *CPR* 1389–92. p.250.
12 Salzman, L F (1964) p.330.
13 Frost, C (1827) Appendix p. 5–18.
14 *Hanserecesse und Andere Akten de Hansetage 1256–1430*. (1970–77) Leipzig vol.3 p.408–13.
15 Collins, F (1897) (editor).
16 A Calendar of the French Rolls in the 48th Annual Report of the Deputy Keeper of Public Records (1887). London, HMSO p.314.
17 PRO E101/58/1.
18 Lloyd, T.H (1982). *Alien Merchants in England in the High Middle Ages*. Sussex, Harvester Press p.148.
19 Ekdaht, S. 'Horses and Crossbows' p.119–52 in Nicholson, H, (editor) (1998) p.136.
20 Stirland, M and Hardy, R (2005) p.24.
21 Platt, C (1973). *Medieval Southampton*. London. Routledge and Kegan Paul. p.153.
22 The letters all refer to bows. While this is not impossible, it does seem unlikely that there were sufficient bowyers in Northern Italy practised in making English warbows. We know Henry received a lot of bows from English bowyers at this time. The letter of 1514 seems to use the terms bows and bowstaves indiscriminately. So it seems more likely that the Venetians supplied bowstaves, which also agrees with English customs records (see Appendix 3).
23 *Calendar of State Papers: Venetian 1509–19* p.33.
24 *Letters and Papers Foreign and Domestic vol.1 pt.1* p.330.
25 *Letters and Papers Foreign and Domestic vol.1 pt.1* p.348.
26 *Letters and Papers Foreign and Domestic. Vol.1. pt.1* p.348.
27 *Letters and Papers Foreign and Domestic. Vol.2 pt.2*. p.1448.
28 *Calendar of State papers; Venetian 1509–1519* p.80n.
29 *Letters and Papers Foreign and Domestic.1509-19 vol.1 pt.1* p.670.
30 *Calendar of State papers; Venetian 1509–1519* p.214.
31 *Letters and Papers Foreign and Domestic. Vol.2 pt.2* p.1453.
32 *Calendar of State Papers: Milan 1385-1618*. London. HMSO. p.378.
33 Salzman, L F (1964) p.431.
34 Longman, C J and Walrond, Col. H (1894) p.123.
35 Childs, W R (1978) p.185.
36 See Appendix 4.
37 PRO C1/618.34.
38 The Duke of Warwick when Captain of Calais in 1470–1 financed himself and his men and consolidated his hold on Calais by piracy.
39 Lewis, E A (1993). *Southampton Port and Brokage Book 1448–4*. Southampton. University Press.
40 Wilson, K P (editor) (1969). *Chester Customs Accounts 1301–1566,* Chester, Record Society of Lancashire and Cheshire, lists none.
41 Devon, F (1837) p.171.
42 Megson, B (1993) p. 28.

43 Gras, N S B (1918). *Early English Customs System*. Cambridge Mass., Harvard University Press p.436-7.
44 Frost, C (1827) Appendix pp.5–6.
45 Studer, P (1912). *The Port Books of Southampton 1427–30*. Southampton p.99, 102.
46 Wylie, J H (1914). p.159n.
47 Hirsch, T (1858). *Danzigs Handels–und Gewerbsgeschichte*. Leipzig. p.253.
48 *Rotuli Parliamentorum* vol.6 p.156.
49 *Statutes of the Realm. vol.* 2 p.432.
50 ibid vol. 2. p.494.
51 ibid vol. 2 p.649.
52 *Statutes of the Realm. vol. 3* p.25-6.
53 ibid vol. 3 p.131-2.
54 *Calendar of State papers; Venetian 1509–1519* p.441.
55 *CCR 1402* p.531.
56 Foster, B (editor) (1963). *Local Port Book for Southampton for 1435–6*. Southampton University Press. p.63.
57 James, J B (editor) (1990). *The Port Book of Southampton 1509–10*. Southampton University Press. p.126 and p.208 respectively.
58 Coleman, O (editor) (1960–1). *Brokage Books of Southampton 1443–44* Southampton. University Press p192, 205 and 207–210.
59 Lewis, E A (1993) p.203.
60 Bunyard B D M (editor) (1914). *Brokage Books of Southampton 1439–40*. Southampton. Cox & Sharland. p.11.
61 Coleman, O editor. (1960-1) p.240, 311 and 312.
62 Lewis, E A (1993) p. 94. 180, 184, 196 and 209.
63 Stevens, K P (1985). *Brokage Books of Southampton 1477–8* and *1527–8* Southampton. University Press. References between p.8 and 115.
64 Coleman, O editor. (1960–1) p.240.
65 Lewis, E A (1993) p.209.
66 Stevens, K P (1985) p.68 and 83.
67 Gillett, E and MacMahon, K A (1980) p.27.
68 Frost, C (1827) Appendix p.6–7.
69 Thanks to Gert Neelan for this information.
70 Rigby, S H (editor) (2005). *Overseas Trade of Boston in the Reign of Richard II*. Lincoln Record Society vol. 93. Woodbridge. Boydell Press. p.136.
71 Rigby, S H (editor) (2005) p.197.
72 *CCR 1356-60*. p.401.
73 *CCR 1356-60*. p.607.
74 *CLBCL Book G* p.256.
75 *CCR 1413* p.72.

Conclusion

When a man decided to serve as a military archer one of the major changes over the period of the Hundred Years War in the circumstances of his service was that he came to be regarded more as a responsible individual than as a body in a feudal host. Developments in the way archers were equipped are part of the evidence for this change. In Edward III's reign the Crown ran a centrally controlled equipment procurement and issue system. The Crown called on the Sheriffs to supply bows, arrows and bowstrings from the towns and shires under their control at a time when these same communities also had the duty to equip the men they raised through the array system. Just as the array system had a variable success rate, so did these royal orders through the Sheriffs.

As the indenture system became the major recruitment system later in the fourteenth century, the archer or his immediate employer became responsible for the necessary equipment. The indentures issued by the Crown specified that the men must be appropriately armed at the time of muster, or they would not be accepted. This meant that both the company captain and the man himself had a vested interest in ensuring that he was properly equipped, since men who were not armed to the standard in the indenture were struck out at muster and got no pay. The array system was not so clear cut, royal officials seemed to be resigned to the fact that they might have to equip some men themselves, despite the clear instruction that the town or county had to equip the men they sent. The two systems worked together to stimulate and maintain a dispersed archery equipment industry, supplying 'government standard' bows and arrows for as long as England was engaged in sustained military activity. By the beginning of the sixteenth century there was a decline in the numbers of provincial bowyers.

The main purpose of these royal orders was to re-equip troops on campaign, rather than equip bodies of troops from scratch at the beginning of an expedition. This remained the case throughout the period. There is no way of telling if equipment from royal stores was better than that issued to the arrayed archers by their community, or bows they may have owned themselves as indentured men, but it is likely that it was of a more consistent quality.

The likelihood is that archers replaced their bowstrings regularly on campaign, particularly as part of their preparations for battle. I have had personal experience of the wisdom of this when a linen string on a self bow a little lighter than the likely draw weight of medieval warbows broke after about 100 arrows.

Increasingly the royal stores of archery equipment tended to be stored near to the place of potential need, so Rouen, Calais and Carlisle all had stores at various times. The Tower of London remained the administrative centre, since it was the royal armoury for the period and many of the royal officials involved in ordering, making and maintaining military stores were based there.

While royal officials paid close attention to the quality of the arrows and arrowheads they received, to judge from the regular references to 'well steeled' arrows and the emphasis on not using green wood, there is no reference to the quality of bows being inadequate in supply records until Tudor times. This is interesting since royal officials did not formally set standards for bows, arrows or bowstrings. There is an isolated reference to arrows of an ell in length, but the most determined effort to set standards dates from the second half of the fourteenth century when a pattern for arrowheads was sent out with orders. Otherwise the minimum draw weight of the bows and the minimum length of the arrows seem to have been a given and needed no reiteration – consider the consistency of both bow and arrow size from the *Mary Rose*. Indeed, having seen the accurate measurements of some of the bows found, the bows may have been made to a size, as far as the bowstave and the tillering process would allow, and different draw weights may have arisen from the individual nature of the wood in each stave.[1] The denser staves may have been less affected by centuries underwater. But this is speculation.

Just as the dimensions of bows and arrows are not mentioned in the royal orders, specific wood types for them are mentioned only very rarely until late in the period. Ash was preserved for the use of fletchers in an order of Henry V in one of the earlier examples, while other fifteenth-century orders list other materials, particularly for arrowmaking, including silk. Henry VIII's statute requires the production of relatively large numbers of bows in woods other than yew to encourage archery practice.

Changes in the Crown supply system mirrored those in the recruitment method, in that there was a consistent move away from what might be called a feudal chain of command, whereby the king summoned resources from towns and counties, to a more commercial system of issuing contracts for the recruitment of soldiers or ordering equipment and materials from the craft groups.

The earliest signs of the development of the archery crafts on a commercial scale and of the trade in bowstaves are found in the last quarter of the thirteenth century. It would be unwise to suggest these started from nothing, stimulated by Edward I's wars, since Edward did not develop the English tactical system. The actions (or inactions) of his son encouraged the establishment of the Tower of London as the centre of royal works for the manufacture of bows and arrows. But at no time in this period can we be sure the Crown directly manufactured large quantities of bows, arrows or strings. Henry V ordered large quantities of feathers and arrowheads, but it is not known whether these were used by Crown workmen, or were distributed to fletchers' workshops to be used on arrows to meet royal orders. Again, when Henry VIII ordered large quantities of bowstaves, there is no evidence that they were all used by directly employed royal bowyers. In London in particular, the misteries came to dominate the supply of bows and arrows to the king through direct supply, and through the regular appointment of senior mistery members as royal officials. (This often seems to be the outcome for the luckier senior figures involved in today's Private Finance Initiatives.) Elsewhere in the country I have seen no evidence of such close links between the misteries and the household administrations of the king or the magnates.

The misteries cemented their position in the major cities by outlining the standards expected of their members and the workers in their workshops, and the apprenticeship system that maintained the skill base of the craft. Senior members of the misteries also acted as quality controllers for the products and prescribed where and how they may be sold. This was enlightened self-interest since they were able to stop any one member undercutting his fellow members and threatening the livelihood of the whole group, either by selling inferior products, or just pricing others out of the market. Of course they also stopped non members from taking part in the craft. As a result, the royal officials issuing the orders were confident that the bows and arrows they received would be of adequate quality. The fifteenth-century royal orders for arrows did not even include the strictures about not using green wood of the previous century.

The crafts developed and grew in the various counties and cities partly in accordance with the availability of raw materials. Those places with good access to the imported bowstaves, such as London and York, developed bowmaking, while inland counties concentrated more on the production of arrows. Southampton was an exception in that it functioned purely as a port and not a manufacturing centre.

As the royal acquisition system moved away from relying on the Sheriffs to provide bows and arrows, there was some decline in the provincial industries, although there was localised specialisation, such as arrowhead production in South Yorkshire and bowstrings in Staffordshire. By Henry VIII's reign there was a clear perception that the number of provincial bowyers had declined, since his statute of 1511–12 allowed JPs to 'appoint' bowyers to provincial centres. But even royal heavyhandedness could not stem the economic tide that meant bowyers could only make a living in larger towns and cities by the sixteenth century.

The limited surviving tax records and other commercial records suggest there was an unofficial hierarchy among the manufacturing crafts. Bowyers and Fletchers came at the top, with bowyers probably being the most prosperous, followed by stringers and finally arrowsmiths.

The English bowyers relied increasingly on imported yew bowstaves, particularly to make warbows. There is much less evidence of imported arrowshafts, but arrowsmiths must have used imported iron. Little of this import trade remained in the hands of English merchants by the second half of the fifteenth century at the latest. The English merchants were not apathetic, far from it, but significant efforts at trade protection in the Baltic markets, either by the use of force or of regulation, limited their opportunities. The Hanseatic League was the beneficiary of this. English involvement in Mediterranean trade was of course limited as much as anything by geography. English merchants had to brave French pirates and privateers, a hostile Castilian fleet and occasional Genoese mercenary flotillas in the service of France to trade in the Mediterranean. As regards southward trade, English merchants settled for maintaining the Gascon wine trade, which was hazardous enough. The Dutch and Flemish ports were fairly open, and being at the end of a land and river trade route from north Italy, were a source of luxury goods for the English market in the fourteenth century.

Fortunately for the English kings, relations with the Hanseatic League remained more or less cordial in the fourteenth century. As difficulties with the League became more common in the fifteenth century, the Italian merchants started to bring in more and more staves. In the latter part of the fifteenth century there was much diplomatic activity. Edward IV both came to terms with the Hanseatic League and encouraged the Italian merchants, while Henry VII shrewdly and effectively used diplomacy rather than war to pursue England's interests. Henry VIII built on this by entering a formal alliance with Venice and the Empire, which helped to ensure he had a good supply of bowstaves.

All through the period, bowstaves were imported in varying quantities from the Iberian Peninsula. These came in smaller numbers than from the other two sources. There is no evidence of staves from one source being preferred to another, although the scale of the Italian imports suggests they were perceived as better.

While some merchants specialised in the bowstave trade insofar as they brought in multiple shipments or large quantities, none traded exclusively in staves. Merchants hedged their bets by always importing a range of other goods along with bowstaves, and commonly used more than one ship to bring the goods to England. The trade across the North Sea, whether by Hanse or English merchants, concentrated on bulk goods, with wool and cloth being exported from England and bowstaves and other raw materials being imported. The Italian merchants tended to bring more luxury goods with the staves and return with cloth. Even the merchants trying to honour Henry VIII's huge order for staves in 1510-11 wanted to bring in wine as well to improve the profitability of the venture.

Archers also provided a market for other military equipment from abroad. There are occasional references in customs records to the import of archers' sallets from the North European workshops. These were clearly a specialist item, made to meet this particular market.

So what happened all these bows and arrows? The 1457 Bridport Muster shows that more people kept bows (and arrows) at home than was the case a century earlier. Increasing numbers of archers became professional soldiers in this period, and so would keep their own military quality bow or bows. But large numbers of bows made from prime imported bowstaves just seemed to vanish. Unlike the eighteenth century onwards, when equipment was recovered from discharged soldiers, there is no evidence of royal officials reclaiming bows from the archers when they were disbanded at the end of a campaign. This attitude was born from the expectation that the men had come to the muster properly equipped, and so could take their equipment away with them. Officials did keep account of bows and arrows in store, and captains may well have had to account for any stock of equipment they had received from the royal stores. However, the inventory of royal possessions made on Henry VIII's death does not even account clearly for bows recorded in castle stores just two years previously. It seems that, despite the increasing cost of a military standard yew bow by the later fifteenth century, no effort was made to keep track of them once they left the royal stores. They were a consumable item. No doubt the individual military archers prized particular bows and would have tried to select the best replacements. They would have taken care of bows because their lives depended on them. But, although a yew bow will remain a good bow for a number of years with basic care, they seem to have been regarded as a disposable item in military terms.

NOTE

1 Thanks to Steve Stratton, bowyer and fletcher, for this observation.

Afterword

Throughout the book I have tried to avoid getting drawn into the debate about how powerful the warbows used by the English and Welsh archers were, and how effective they were against armour. While I am a longbow archer who shoots medieval style longbows, I do not have sufficient practical experience of bowmaking or of shooting bows of comparable weight to the medieval bows to be able to make to take part in this debate with any authority. But I can make a few general comments.

Firstly, there was an arms race in this period run by the armourers and the weapon makers, stimulated by their users. Bow design and power developed as part of this, with most improvements happening in the fourteenth century. This is not to suggest that the bows used at Crecy had low draw weights, just that the design, and possibly the consistent quality of the staves used, improved. As part of this arms race I have shown that royal orders specified developments in arrowhead design on at least one occasion, although there is no evidence of specifications for warbows being issued.

Secondly, the recent availability of yew from North Italy has enabled the making of *Mary Rose* replica bows that are likely to be like the originals because the wood used is of very similar character. This is not to belittle either English or American yew, but to observe that they are likely to have different characteristics to Italian wood.

Thirdly, some contemporary accounts of battles refer to the problems archers had in penetrating armour at different times. The most sustained practical investigation of the penetrative power of the medieval warbow and medieval arrows is that carried out by Mark Stretton and his colleagues reported in *Glade* Magazine as the 'Secrets of the English Warbow'.[1] There are several battles where armour protected the wearer against lethal or disabling damage from English archery: Poitiers and Verneuil for example, and the onset of King James' battle at Flodden provides a third. When men wearing high quality armour faced English archers, how did they survive the blunt force trauma of an arrow strike?[2] Some of Mark Stretton's tests suggest that this should be lethal in many cases, yet this seems not to have been the case in battle. I do not really have an answer to this question except to suggest that the development of oblique surfaces on armour to deflect blows may have helped; the ability of a body to move in reaction to the blow certainly helps to minimise damage, and we do not know how deeply padded and quilted arming jacks were to help protect the wearer. It is often said the softer the padded jack, the better the protection was from sword or arrow.

There is always of course the debilitating effect of the heat of battle; every bullet is lethal, but it is said that it took a million of them to kill a single soldier in World War I. It is a fact of warfare that soldiers, even seasoned professionals like many of the fifteenth-century archers, do not aim at the height of battle and many shots fly high and wide. But we know from accounts of battles such Dupplin Moor, Humbledon Hill and the rout of the Earl of Lennox and Duke of Argyle's men at Flodden by the archers of Edward Stanley that archers could destroy lightly armoured opponents. Maybe the best armourers did, finally, defeat the longbow.

NOTES

1 *Glade* Magazine, see www.theglade.co.uk. Soar, H D H (2006) 'Secrets of the English War Bow.' Yardley, Penn. Westholme Pub.

2 Blunt force trauma occurs when a moving object hits the body and commonly causes bruising or damage of varying severity without penetration.

APPENDIX I

London Arrays

Looking at the place names in many of the surnames in these far from complete records, it is striking what a magnet London was to men from all over England. It is tempting to suggest that a lot of these men were comparative newcomers to London since their surnames linked them to other towns, although hereditary surnames were becoming widespread in large sections of the sub genteel strata of society in the southern half of England. So we may be looking at second or third generation Londoners. For example Hugh de Lodelowe (Ludlow) is mentioned as contributing to the Lay Subsidy of 1292, so William and John mentioned in the lists are probably descendents of this man rather than newcomers to London. There is one case where the name could tell us a story. Arnald de Bayon is in the 1338 list, and his name suggests that he may be a hireling, possibly a professional soldier from Bayonne in southern France in the area long held by the English kings. Some men from this area may well have developed archery skills to serve in the English army. This suggestion gains credence because of a court case in 1339, when a Robyn of Toulouse was imprisoned for selling the arms and equipment given him by a London citizen who was paying him to serve as a man at arms.

Evidence of some men taking part in more regular military service can be found in the 1338 list. Firstly, the Mayor, Aldermen and Commonality of London had to explain to the king why they were late in sending their men to him, saying that 'many of those chosen ... declared that they were about to cross the sea with the king in the suite of divers magnates' Though some of the men claiming this were just trying to dodge military service. Secondly, 12 of the men have the same name as men in the larger 1337 list, and another four may have. Even allowing for coincidence, this suggests up to 16% may either have been professional soldiers hired by London citizens, or Londoners who found military service attractive. There are also five men listed in 1338 who may be following relatives who served in 1337. So we can see signs of the beginning of a group of professional military archers of the type who became so important to the English military system over the next two centuries.

TABLE 1: MEN SENT TO GASCONY BY THE MAYOR, ALDERMEN AND COMMONALITY OF LONDON OF LONDON IN AUGUST 1337. BOOK F OF LONDON LETTER BOOK PP.11-14

Forename	Surname	Rank	Occupation	Place
Henry	Garland	Centenar		
Richard	Constantyn	Vintenar		
John	le King de Wodestre	Vintenar		

Nicholas	Esher	Archer		Esher?
John	Yann	Archer		
John	de Kingeswode	Archer		Kingswood (Bucks or Surrey)
William	de Bardeneye	Archer		Bardney (Lincs)
Henry	de Egynton	Archer		Eggington (Beds)
Walter	de Wylleye	Archer		Whyle (Heref)?
William	de Lenham	Archer		Lenham (Kent)
Wat	Somery	Archer		
Richard	de Whityngham	Archer		Whittingham (Northumb)?
Nicholas	de Went	Archer		
Matthew	de Went	Archer		
John	de Went	Archer		
John	de Shyngleton	Archer		Shingleton?
John Aleyn	de Shyngleton	Archer		Shingleton?
Richard	de Kynebauton	Archer		Kimbolton (Cambs)?
Roger	atte Chamber	Archer		
Adam	de Ardernee	Archer		
Richard	de Normanville	Archer		
Roger	de Caxton	Vintenar		Caxton (Cambs)
John	Burgeoys de Horsham	Archer		Horsham (W. Sussex)
William	Knight	Archer		
John	de Walton	Archer		Walton (W. Sussex or Suffolk)
John	Reulebon	Archer		
Richard	de Parys	Archer		
Thomas	Prior	Archer		
Henry	Galeys	Archer		
William	de Redham	Archer		
Thomas	de Donstable	Archer		Dunstable
John	de Somersete	Archer		Somerset
John	de Maydenstan	Archer		Maidstone
John	de Ebor'	Archer	Physician	York

John	Priour	Archer	Butcher	
John	de Blounham	Archer		
John	Robert	Archer		
Robert	Devenishe	Archer		
Bartholomew	de Ockham	Archer		Ockham (Surrey)
William	de Reding	Archer		Reading
John	de Shrouesbury	Archer	Tailor	Shrewsbury
Thomas	de Denton	Vintenar		Denton (Kent)
John	Fraunceys	Archer		
Thomas	de Wantynge	Archer		Wantage (Oxon)?
John	Wyger	Archer		
John	son of Roger le Cook	Archer		
William	Gase	Archer		
Thomas	de Westminster	Archer		Westminster
Robert	de Wardone	Archer		
Richard	Fisshe	Archer		
Richard	Cotel	Archer		
Geoffrey	de Pekham	Archer		Peckham
Thomas	Handekyn	Archer		
John	atte Cross	Archer		
William	Travers	Archer		
Thomas	de Bartone	Archer		Barton (Cambs or Oxon)
Stephen	de Newcastle	Archer		Newcastle
John	de Donewyche	Archer		Dunwich
John	le Mareschal de Aynho	Archer		Aynho
William	Smert	Archer		
Thomas	de Mynstretone	Archer		
Nicholas	de Reymes	Vintenar		Rheims is unlikely
William	de Uptone	Archer		Upton (Berks, now part of Slough)
Robert	Horn	Archer		
Benedict	atte Rothe	Archer		

William	Scot	Archer		
Richard	Vivien	Archer		
John	atte Hay	Archer		
Nicholas	Pycot	Archer		
Ralph	de Burtone	Archer	Dyer	Burton (many to choose from)
Peter	Lovel	Archer		
William	Herberd	Archer		
John	de Ebor'	Archer	Furrier	York
John	de Picheford	Archer		Pickford (Warks, now part of Coventry) or Pitchford (Shrops)
John	de Derby	Archer		Derby
John	de Bedeford	Archer	Tailor	Bedford
John	de Stuntefeld	Archer		
Thomas	de Uphill	Archer		
Laurence	Russel	Archer		
John	le Long	Archer		
Nicholas	de Leghtone	Archer		Leyton
John	le Parker	Vintenar	Parker	
Henry	le Glover	Archer	Glover	
John	de Romford	Archer		Romford
John	le Doo	Archer		
Salomon	de Laufare	Archer		
James	Wylcher	Archer		
Robert	Sergeaunt	Archer		
John	de Burgh	Archer		Burgh (Suffolk)
John	atte Lee	Archer		
John	de Gloucestre	Archer		Gloucester
Henry	de Hellyngeleye	Archer		Hellingley?
Henry	de Grenstede	Archer		Greenstead (Essex)
Thomas	de Crulfeld	Archer		
Roger	Boneye	Archer		
William	de Brynchelsee	Archer		

Richard	de Shiryngtone	Archer		
Walter	Dymmoke	Archer		
John	Gerveys	Archer		
Thomas	Hare	Archer		
John	de Aukeland	Archer		Auckland?
Thomas	Hereberd	Centenar & Vintenar		
Roger	de Herlostone	Archer		Harlestone (Northants) or Harleston (Suffolk or Norfolk)
Roland	de Colebroke	Archer		Colebrook (Devon)?
John	le Chapman	Archer	Chapman	
Thomas	de Piphurst	Archer		
Richard	Fauconer	Archer		
William	de Lodelow	Archer		Ludlow
John	de Norhamptone	Archer		Northampton
John	le Barber de Flete	Archer	Barber	presumably Fleet in London
John	de Benyngtone	Archer		
John	de Malmesbury	Archer		Malmesbury
Denny	le Cook	Archer	Cook	
John	de Billebury	Archer		
John	Cook de Berkynge	Archer		Barking?
John	de Wykendene	Archer		
William	King	Archer		
Richard	Wolf	Archer		
Richard	de Newyntone	Archer		Newington (Kent) or as in Stoke Newington
Paulin	Chaumberleyn	Archer		
Adam	Grenelef	Archer		
John	le Devenisshe	Vintenar		
Thomas	Busshons	Archer		
John	le Marechal de Croydon	Archer		Croydon

John	de Wardone	Archer		Warden (Northumb)?
William	Baudry	Archer		
John	de Ottleye	Archer		Otley (Suffolk or Yorks)
Simon	Bas	Archer		
John	de Kirkeby de Kendale	Archer		Kirkby Lonsdale (Cumbs) nearest Kirkby to Kendal?
Gilbert	Morice	Archer		
John	de Bedeford	Archer	Skinner	Bedford
Adam	de Southam	Archer		Southam (Warks or Gloucs)
John	de Grimesby	Archer		Grimsby
John	de Cornubia	Archer	Farrier? Smith?	Cornwall
John	de Bury	Archer		Bury (Cambs or W. Sussex)
John	de Bernyngham	Archer		
Richard	Dundalk	Archer		
John	Hervy	Archer		
Nicholas	Dirlande	Archer		
Robert	Kilpek	Archer		Kilpek (Heref)?
Robert	Bynde	Archer		
Richard	de Stauntone	Vintenar		Staunton (Gloucs)
William	Crips de Bockebroke	Archer		
John	de Watford	Archer	Bowyer	Watford
William	de St. Albans	Archer		St. Albans
William	de Rotland	Archer		Rutland
John	de Walshale	Archer		Walsall?
William	de Kestevene	Archer		Kesteven (Lincs)
John	de Wyndesore	Archer		Windsor
John	de Stoke	Archer		Stoke (Kent or Hants)?
Thomas	de Multone	Archer		Moulton (Northants or Suffolk)?

John	de Pedewardyn	Archer		
Roger	de Barewe	Archer		Barway in Cambs?
John	de Rokyngham	Archer		Rockingham (Northants)
John	le Coupere	Archer	Cooper?	
Henry	de Pertone	Archer		Perton (Herts or Staffs) or Purton (Gloucs or Wilts)
John	de Okthorpe	Archer	Clerk	Oakthorpe (Leics)
John	de Bradlee	Archer		Bradley (Hants or Lincs)
Alan	de Cestre	Archer		Chester
Thomas	de Mershetone	Archer		Merston (Sussex)?
William	Bataille	Archer		
John	Priour	Vintenar	Armourer	
Simon	Hunte	Archer		
Richard	Cokey	Archer		
John	de Morland	Archer		Morland (Cumb)?
Richard	de Belcham	Archer		Belchamp +suffix 3 villages (Essex)
Thomas	de Dallyngge	Archer		
Thomas	de Uske	Archer		Usk (Monmouth)
Richard	Cavenard	Archer		
William	Faunt	Archer		
John	Jordan	Archer		
Thomas	Walssheman	Archer		The Welshman?
Ralph	de Thorp	Archer		Thorpe (Surrey or Notts)
Thomas	de Stanes	Archer		Staines
Walter	de Bolneye	Archer		Bolney (Sussex)
William	Shipman	Archer		
John	de Brykleswade	Archer		
John	Peverel	Archer		
Thomas	Jordan	Archer		
Richard	Rose	Archer		

Thomas	de Landaf	Archer	Carpenter	Llandaff (Glams)
Richard	Derewent	Vintenar		
Roger	Brown	Archer		
Adam	de Wrotham	Archer		Wrotham (Kent)
John	Duraunt	Archer		
Thomas	de Melton Moubray	Archer		Melton Mowbray
Alexander	de Berdefeld	Archer		
Thomas	de Ebor'	Archer	Coppersmith	York
William	Le Bakere	Archer	Baker?	
John	de Pokelyngtone	Archer		Pocklington (Yorks)
John	atte Grove	Archer		
William	de Coventre	Archer		Coventry
Robert	Derewent	Archer		
John	Ballard de Willesdon	Archer		Willesdon
Thomas	de Pampesworth	Archer		Papworth (Cambs)?
Gilbert	de Taunton	Archer		Taunton
John	de Lincoln	Archer	Goldsmith	Lincoln
William	Dauncer	Archer		
Robert	de Wakerle	Archer		Wakerley (Nthants)
Richard	le Bakerer	Archer	Baker?	
Hugh	le Fauconer	Archer	Falconer?	

TABLE 2: MEN FROM LONDON ARRAYED AND SENT FOR SERVICE IN JUNE 1338 BY THE MAYOR, THE ALDERMEN AND THE COMMONALITY OF THE CITY						
Forename	**Surname**	**Rank**	**Occupation**	**Namesake in 1337 list**	**Notes**	**Place**
William	Hauteyn	Vintainer & Centainer				
William	de Wykham	Armed man				Wickham (Bucks or Hants)
John	de Flete	Armed man				Fleet
Ralph	de Irby	Armed man				Irby (Cheshire or Lincs)
John	de Riveshale	Armed man				
Roger	de Bathe	Armed man				Bath
Thomas	le Mazerer	Armed man	Mazer?			
Walter	Russel	Armed man				
Henry	de Hontyngdone	Archer				Huntingdon
John	de Gloucestre	Archer		Yes		Gloucester
John	de Lodelow	Archer			William de Lodelow in 1337	Ludlow
John	Poyntel	Archer				
Richard	Cotel	Archer	Kerverer	Yes		
Robert	de Meltone	Archer				Suffolk?
Robert	de Staverne	Archer				
Roger	Boneye	Archer		Yes		
Thomas	Husk	Archer				
William	de Cornewaille	Archer				Cornwall
William	de Tettesworth	Archer				Tetsworth (Oxon)
William	de Warwyk	Archer				Warwick
William	Malesheurs	Vintainer				
Henry	Pipard	Armed man				
John	son of Richard Talbot	Armed man				
John	Wrenche	Armed man				

Roger	Warde	Armed man				
Thomas	de Kymberle	Armed man				Kimberly (Norfolk or Notts.)
Walter	de Ware	Armed man				Ware
William	Herberd	Armed man		probably	William Herberd archer in 1337	
Arnald	de Bayon	Archer				Bayonne in southern Aquitaine?
Henry	de Grenstede	Archer		Yes		Greenstead (Essex)
John	de Kent	Archer				Kent
John	Devenysshe	Archer			John le Devenisshe a vintainer & Robert Devenishe archer in 1337	
John	Fraunceys	Archer		Yes		
John	Tany	Archer				
Roger	de Barwe	Archer		Probably	Roger de Barewe in 1337	Barway in Cambs?
Roger	de Herlastone	Archer		Yes		Harlestone (Northants) or Harleston (Suffolk or Norfolk)
Stephen	atte More	Archer				
Thomas	de Horselee	Archer				Horseley (Gloucs, Derbys or Northumb) or Horseley Cross (Essex)
William	Boterade	Archer				
William	de Lenham	Archer		Yes		Lenham (Kent)

William	de Pokeriche	Vintainer				Puckeridge (Herts)
John	de Bedeford	Armed man		Yes	Two John of Bedfords in 1337	Bedford
John	de Massyngham	Armed man				Massingham
Nicholas	Jolype	Armed man				
Richard	de Bretone	Armed man				Bretton (Flints)?
Robert	le Palmer	Armed man				
Roger	le Barber	Armed man	Barber?		John le Barber archer in 1337	
William	Bonefay	Armed man				
Alexander	de Poperynge	Archer				
John	de Bovyngtone	Archer				Bovingdon (Herts)?
John	Ruylbon	Archer		Probably	Spelled Reulebon in 1337	
Clement	de Stafford	Archer				Stafford
Henry	Husk	Archer				
John	atte Hethe	Archer				
John	de Bassyngburne	Archer				Bassingbourn (Cambs)?
John	Messager	Archer				
Richard	de Rose	Archer		Probably	Richard Rose in 1337	Rose (Cornwall) or Rose Green (Essex or Suffolk)
Robert	de Cestre	Archer			Alan de Cestre in 1337	Chester
Walter	de Ingelond	Archer				
William	de Dodele	Archer				Dudley?
William	de Braunfeld	Vintainer				

Gilbert	de Carletone	Armed man				Carelton (Norfolk), several villages with diff. suffixes eg Carlton Forehoe
John	atte Grene	Armed man				
John	de Ledes	Armed man				Leeds (Kent or Yorks)
John	de Wynchecombe	Armed man				Winchcombe (Gloucs)
John	Peverel	Armed man		Yes	John Peverel archer 1337	
Richard	de Wedone	Armed man				Weedon (Bucks or Northants)?
Thomas	de Lenne	Armed man				
Adam	de Pomfreyt	Archer				
Henry	Ive	Archer				
John	de Bannebury	Archer				Banbury
John	de Kyngewode	Archer		Yes		Kingswood (Bucks or Surrey)
John	de Kentissh	Archer				Kent?
Michael	de Dene	Archer				Dean (Hants or Oxon)
Richard	Giffard	Archer				
Robert	de Ingeford	Archer				
Robert	le Fourbour	Archer				
William	de Coventre	Archer		Yes		Coventry
William	de Lychefeld	Archer				Lichfield
William	de Tonebregge	Archer				Tunbridge
William	de Oxenford	Vintainer				Oxford
Adam	le Dragoner	Armed man				
John	de Multone	Armed man			Thomas de Multon archer in 1337	Moulton (Northants or Suffolk)?

Roger	de Engleby	Armed man				Ingleby (Derbs)?
Walter	Sterre	Armed man				
William	de Casewelle	Armed man				Caswell?
William	Symeon	Armed man				
William	Warman	Armed man				
John	atte Welle	Archer				
John	de Blebery	Archer				
Nicholas	Passour	Archer				
Ralph	le Chaumberleyn	Archer				
Reginald	le Sergeaunt	Archer				
Richard	de Brichesdene	Archer				Brickendon (Herts)?
Richard	de Croydon	Archer				Croydon
Richard	de Midlyngtone	Archer				Middleton (Essex, Northants and many others)
Thomas	de Alegate	Archer				Alegate was a ward of London
Thomas	de Excestre	Archer				Exeter
Thomas	de Piphurst	Archer		Yes		
Thomas	le Pybakere	Archer				

TOTALS		
	Vintainers	5
	Armed men	35
	Archers	60

APPENDIX 2

Developments in the Make Up of Retinues

This appendix contains comparative data showing the make up of a selection of typical retinues from 1330s to about 1500, with brief notes on the circumstances of the service. It has been kept separate from the main body of the book both to make it a more comfortable read, by drawing conclusions in the book based on this information, without bogging the reader down in detail, and to give the reader the choice as to whether they read lots of figures or not. The intention is for it to be a representative selection of typical retinues for the period, rather than an exhaustive list, and as a result it will show up some of the English military practices of the period. I have concentrated on retinues since this became the dominant method of raising troops for foreign service. In the fifteenth century it was also a common method of raising troops for use within the British Isles, and has long been regarded as an enabling factor, rather than a cause, in the Wars of the Roses.

TABLE 1

Date	**Leader**	**Composition**		**Comments**
		Men at arms	**Archers**	
1346	Earl of Northampton	160	141	All archers mounted[1]
1346	Sir Thomas Haukeston	161	554 (313 mounted)	These men were reinforcements raised in August, and included both indentured and arrayed troops[2]
1359	Earl of Northampton	160	200	Mounted archers[3]
1361	Lionel, Earl of Ulster, Lieutenant of Ireland	97	100	All archers mounted[4]
1370	Sir Robert Knollys	199	200	Archers probably all mounted[5]
1385	John of Gaunt	800	1200	Shows the resources of the Duchy of Lancaster. Array system used in part for this expedition to Scotland[6]
1389	Sir John Stanley, Justiciar of Ireland	50	400	Does the ratio reflect the nature of warfare in Ireland?[7]

1400	William, Lord Willoughby	29	163	Muster figures for an abortive campaign against the Scots[8]
1415	Duke of Gloucester	190	610	Muster figures. Gloucester had indentures for 200 men at arms and 600 archers
1415	John Mowbray, Earl Marshal, Earl of Nottingham and Norfolk	47	171	Again, muster figures. Mowbray had indentures for 50 men at arms and 150 archers[9]
1416	John, Duke of Bedford	200	400	Indenture figures for a naval retinue. Bedford led the English fleet to victory off Harfleur[10]
1420	Earl of Devon	240	480	Part of a larger force charged with guardianship of the seas under Devon's command[11]
1428	Sir John Radclyff	100	700	For service in France[12]
1439	Earl of Huntingdon	301	2009	Muster figures for an expedition to Gascony[13]
1443	Edmund Duke of Somerset	43	3400	These figures are from Issue rolls for paying wages and are well below indenture especially for men at arms[14]
1449	Edmund Duke of Somerset. Lieutenant of France	100	1200	PRO E101/71/4/923 Muster Portsmouth 11th June
1453	John Viscount Lisle	77	800	Mustered in Feb/March and probably involved in Castillon campaign
1453	William Lord Saye	50	468	Mustered August
1453	Ellis Longworth esquire	20	187	Mustered August[15]

TABLE 2

Date	Leader	Number of troops of different types		
		Men at arms	Armed men[16]	Foot Archers
1341	Walter Mauny	80	30	100
1341	Earl of Derby	200	100	200
1341	Earl of Northampton	250	100	200[17]
These retinues were ordered for an abortive campaign. By including 'Armed men' these companies resemble in composition some of the forces raised by Edward II and even Edward I, rather than the forces that were common in the 1340s and later.				

These figures demonstrate that the types of soldier in a retinue, and the proportion made up by each type varied over the period. We can see two things from these figures. Firstly the differentiation between foot and mounted archers goes; and secondly while up to the 1380s the normal ratio between men at arms and archers in a retinue was 1:1 by the time of the Agincourt campaign it had shifted to 1:3. Retinues for sea service always tended to have proportionally more men at arms, than contemporary land forces.

The ratio of men at arms to archers of 1:5.6 found in Lord Willoughby's retinue of 1400 is slightly below that for the whole force. This is an unusually high proportion of archers for the armies of this date and may reflect three things. Firstly the army was raised by the king appealing directly to the magnates and men with personal indentures with him, who raised their forces from tenants and, no doubt, unemployed professionals. Secondly, campaigning in Scotland was unprofitable. Finally, and perhaps most importantly, Henry IV had only just seized the throne from Richard II. These factors could have led men who were wealthy enough to have the equipment to serve as men at arms to hold back, rather than put their goods at risk.

The *consistent* change in the ratio of archers to men at arms occurred from the 1420s onwards. In part this may have been a deliberate decision by the military administrators because archers represented excellent value for money, but it also reflected the reluctance of the more wealthy to serve. One unlooked for consequence of this was that in a set-piece action some of the English armies would not have enough men at arms to form a robust battle line. The outcome of the battle of Formigny was probably heavily influenced by this imbalance, since accounts of the battle make clear the fighting spirit of the archers. In Tudor times, following practice developed in the Wars of the Roses, this problem was resolved by reducing the number of archers and replacing them with billmen who could form a battle line.

NOTES

1 Ayton, A and Preston, P (2005) p.205
2 Ayton, A and Preston, P (2005) p.239
3 Ayton, A (1994) p.10
4 Wrottesley, G (1887) p.104
5 Fowler, K (2001) p.290
6 Goodman, A (1992) p.212
7 Bennett, M (1983) p.167
8 Brown, A L (1974)
9 Curry, A (2000) p.436
10 Allmand, C (1997) p.107
11 Newhall, R A (1924) p.199
12 POPC vol. 3 p.295

13 Vale, M G A (1970) p.110
14 Vale, M G A (1970) p.129
15 All 1453 retinues from Vale, M G A (1970) pp.232–3
16 Prestwich (1996) p.108. These were heavily armed infantry, probably carrying large spears. They were paid 6d a day, the same as hobelars and mounted archers. They did not become an established feature of the English armies because of their relative immobility as the concept of the chevauchee developed.
17 All figures from Prestwich, M (1996) pp.111–12

APPENDIX 3

Bows and Arrows received at the Tower of London January 1355–February 1360

The devolved system of equipment acquisition through the Sheriffs. The surviving records are incomplete. The Sheriff of Lincoln was a particularly important source of bows. See page 167 for a fuller commentary on these figures.

	Date rec'd	Painted Bows	White Bows	Ordered	When	Sheaves	Ordered	When
Beds & Bucks	Oct 1356					260	600	Jan 1356
	July 1359					300	100	Jan 1359
	Aug 1359					200	300	May 1359
Gloucester	Oct 1355					116		
	June 1356		230	500	Jan 1356	446	600	Jan 1356
	Aug 1359					300	300	May 1359
Hereford	Oct 1356					363	1000	Jan 1356
Kent	May 1356					112	700	Jan 1356
	Aug 1356					120		
	May 1359					346	200	Jan 1359
	June 1359					300	500	May 1359
Lincoln	June 1355	217	755					
	July 1355	141	285					
	Oct 1355					334		
	May 1356	96	550	1500	Jan 1356 (white bows)	266		
	Aug 1356		832			258		
	May 1357		139		Rest of above order?	133	600?	Part of Jan 1356 order?
	May 1359					416	500	Jan 1359
	Feb 1360					499	1000	Nov 1359
Norfolk & Suffolk	May 1356	66	164	600	Jan 1356 (white bows)			
	July 1359					400	400	May 1359

	Feb 1360					900	900	Nov 1359
Notts & Derby	July 1356		118			202		
	Aug 1359					428	400	May 1359
Somerset & Dorset	Feb 1357		300	300	Jan 1356	400	400	Jan 1356
	July 1359					300	300	1359
Stafford	June 1356		113		?	186	500	Jan 1356
	Aug 1359					240	300	May 1359
Worcs	Feb 1357		50	400	Jan 1356			
Wilts	May 1359					207	300	
Camb & Hunts	July 1359					400		
	Oct 1359					400		
	Dec 1359					200	600	
Warks & Leics	Oct 1356					179	1000	Poss earlier deliveries not listed
	Aug 1359					367	400	
Northants	No year					200		
Southampton	No year					100		
Surrey & Sussex	No year					300		
Essex & Herts	1359					235	300	

APPENDIX 4

Customs records of bowstaves imported in this period

Year	Date	English Port	Ship	Home Port
1293		Scarborough	11 ships of Germany and Frisia	
1303	1st Sept	Boston	Ship of Folcard Fresus	
1303	23rd Aug	Boston	Ship of Arnald Blank	
1303	23rd Aug	Boston	Ship of Arnald Blank	
1303	23rd Aug	Boston	Ship of Arnald Blank	
1303	23rd Aug	Boston	Ship of Arnald Blank	
1303	23rd Aug	Boston	Ship of Arnald Blank	
1324		Bristol	*St. Blasius*	Bayonne
1390		Newcastle u Tyne	*Christopher*	Edinburgh
1390	20th June	Boston	Ship of Ludekin Wangmeistre	
1390	26th June	Boston	Ship of Frederic van Farlen	
1390	26th June	Boston	Ship of Frederic van Farlen	
1390	26th June	Boston	Ship of Frederic van Farlen	

Merchant		status	Quantity of staves	Notes	source
		alien?	300	A report of cargoes of 11 ships driven into Scarborough by bad weather	salzman
Henry	of Holdefar	alien		cargo & names suggest Baltic or North European port of origin	gras
Henry	Swerfar	alien		cargo & names suggest Baltic or North European port of origin	gras
Arnold	Blank	alien		cargo & names suggest Baltic or North European port of origin	gras
ohn	of Holdefar	alien		cargo & names suggest Baltic or North European port of origin	gras
Conrad	of Maideburgh	alien		cargo & names suggest Baltic or North European port of origin	gras
ohn	Greue	alien		cargo & names suggest Baltic or North European port of origin	gras
ohannes	Farnur	alien		quantity not clear	cw
			1200	Although Scottish ship, Salzman suggests that cargo comes from northern or eastern ports as trade for wool	salzman
aderus	Pierson	alien?	700	cargo & names suggest Baltic or North European port of origin	rigby
ohn	Sharp	native?	400	Baltic or North European port of origin likely for cargo	rigby
rederic	de Flete	native?	200	Baltic or North European port of origin likely for cargo	rigby
William	Stephenson	native?	200	Baltic or North European port of origin likely for cargo	rigby

1390	26th June	Boston	Ship of Johannes Papengode	
1390	26th June	Boston	Ship of Henricus Covenste	
1390	26th June	Boston	Ship of Arnaldus Eylgeit	
1390	26th June	Boston	Ship of Arnaldus Eylgeit	
1390	26th June	Boston	Ship of Arnaldus Eylgeit	
1390	26th June	Boston	Ship of Arnaldus Eylgeit	
1390	4th July	Boston	Ship of Gerardus Ferkynsteer	
1390	20th Aug	Boston	Ship of Johannes Moleman	
1396	3rd May	Lynn	Ship of Arnold van Tiliight	
1401	22nd May	Hull	*Maryknight*	Bremen
1401	22nd May	Hull	*Maryknight*	Bremen
1401	22nd May	Hull	*Maryknight*	Bremen
1401	22nd May	Hull	*Maryknight*	Bremen
1401	25th May	Hull	*Maryknight*	Danzig
1401	25th May	Hull	*Chistopher*	York
1401	25th May	Hull	*Chistopher*	York
1401	25th May	Hull	*Chistopher*	York
1401	25th May	Hull	*Chistopher*	York
1401	25th May	Hull	*Chistopher*	York
1401	8th June	Hull	*Elyn*	Hull
1401	27th June	Hull	*Maryknight*	Danzig
1401	27th June	Hull	*Maryknight*	Danzig
1401	27th June	Hull	*Maryknight*	Danzig

John	Barfoot	native?	600	Baltic or North European port of origin likely for cargo	rigby
Richard	Broune	native?	300	Baltic or North European port of origin likely for cargo	rigby
Robert	Gybon	native?	600	Baltic or North European port of origin likely for cargo	rigby
Thomas	Porter	native?	400	Baltic or North European port of origin likely for cargo	rigby
Bartholomew	Walsoken		300	Baltic or North European port of origin likely for cargo	rigby
William	Kempe	native?	600	Baltic or North European port of origin likely for cargo	rigby
Roger	Broune	native?	600	Baltic or North European port of origin likely for cargo	rigby
William	Holden	native?	600	Baltic or North European port of origin likely for cargo	rigby
John	Lancowe	hanse?	600	Baltic or North European port of origin likely for cargo	gras
Henry	Preston	native?	1000		frost
John	Crisacre	native?	700		frost
Robert	Warde	native?	200		frost
Robert	Louthe	native?	200		frost
Bernard	Boweman	hanse?	480		frost
Richard	Thoresby	native?	900	Baltic or North European port of origin likely for cargo	frost
Robert	Louthe	native?	600	Baltic or North European port of origin likely for cargo	frost
Laurence	atte Hull	native?	400	Baltic or North European port of origin likely for cargo	frost
Richard	Russell	native?	200	Baltic or North European port of origin likely for cargo	frost
John	Percehay	native?	600	Baltic or North European port of origin likely for cargo	frost
John	Bolton	native?	200	Baltic or North European port of origin likely for cargo	frost
John	Brotherton	native?	800		frost
William	del Hill	native?	200		frost
Richard	Soureby	native?	600		frost

1401	1st July	Hull	*Saint Maryshipp*	Hull
1401	1st July	Hull	*Saint Maryshipp*	Hull
1401	1st July	Hull	*Saint Maryshipp*	Hull
1430	30th May	Southampton	*Gost*	(Sout)Hampton
1430	10th July	Southampton	*Marie*	Shoreham
1435	18th Nov	Southampton	Carrack of Pier Vent	Venice
1437	18th Aug	Bristol	*Trinite*	Minehead
1439	23rd Nov	Southampton	Boat of John Cornysshe	Plymouth
1440	25th June	Southampton	Genoese Carrack	Genoa
1440	8th Feb	Southampton	Ship of Camffer	Vere
1440	8th Feb	Southampton	Ship of Camffer	Vere
1440	9th Dec	Southampton	Carrack of Jacobus Erian	Venice ?
1440	9th Dec	Southampton	Carrack of Jacobus Erian	Venice ?
1453	10th April	Hull	*Maryknight*	Westernschouwen
1453	15th Aug	Hull	*Trynyte*	Vere
1453	15th Aug	Hull	*Cristofre*	Newcastle
1453	15th May	Hull	*Jacob*	Danzig
1453	15th May	Hull	*George*	Danzig
1454	30th Jan	Newcastle u Tyne	*Cristofur*	Newcastle
1454	30th Jan	Newcastle u Tyne	*Cristofur*	Newcastle
1461	14th Dec	Newcastle u Tyne	*John*	Dordrecht
1461	6th Aug	Hull	*Jacob*	Danzig
1461	6th Aug	Hull	*Jacob*	Danzig
1461	6th Aug	Hull	*Jacob*	Danzig

ohn	Whitgift	native?	200	Baltic or North European port of origin likely for cargo	frost
William	del Hill	native?	200	Baltic or North European port of origin likely for cargo	frost
Ienry	Moreton	native?	200	Baltic or North European port of origin likely for cargo	frost
Iorysse	Flesscher	native	100	valued at 46/8d by customs	studer
Iorysse	Flesscher	native	100	valued at 40/- by customs	studer
'aul	Morel	alien	1240		frostb
Jicholas	Sawyer	native	3 quarters	from Ireland	cw
ohn	Pecott	native	200	cargo items suggest northern or eastern port of origin but no proof	ruddock
Andrea	Spynell	alien ?	100	Agent for Genoese firm Spinola in Southampton	ruddock
Jicholas	Persyssson	hanse ?	100		ruddock
acob	Williamysson (of Middleburgh)	hanse ?	100		ruddock
'aulus	Morell	alien ?	550	Florentine agent in Southampton	ruddock
homas	Jaye		100		ruddock
homas	Gaunte	native	600	bowstaves described as 'wrek'	child
homas	Neleson	native	200		child
Villiam	Stockton	native	400		child
Villiam	Gaunte	native	600	bowstaves described as 'wrek'	child
Villiam	Gaunte	native	600		child
ohn	Byrd	native	84	recorded as 7 doz. probably from Dutch ports but could be internal trade	wade
obert	Penrethe	native	100	probably from Dutch ports but could be internal trade	wade
mon	Frithland	alien	300		wade
Ians	Gronhawe	hanse	100		child
eorge	Skeke	hanse	260		child
Ierman	Jerman	hanse	260		child

1461		Southampton	Galley of Georgius Redmondus	Venice
1462	18th Aug	Hull	*Kateryn*	Middleburgh
1462	18th Aug	Hull	*Kateryn*	Middleburgh
1463	10th Jan	Hull	*Jacob*	Middleburgh
1463	19th Jul	Southampton	Carrack of Johannes Solego	Venice?
1463	19th Jul	Southampton	Carrack of Johannes Solego	Venice?
1463	19th Jul	Southampton	Carrack of Johannes Solego	Venice?
1463	19th Jul	Southampton	Carrack of Johannes Solego	Venice?
1463	20th Oct	Southampton	Galley of Lodowicus Gradenegro	Venice?
1463	20th Oct	Southampton	Galley of Dominicus Travisan	Venice?
1463	20th Oct	Southampton	Galley of Paul George	Venice?
1463	21st Aug	Hull	*Maryknight*	Selice
1463	22nd Aug	Hull	*Mareknyght*	Danzig
1463	22nd Aug	Hull	*Mareknyght*	Danzig
1463	22nd Aug	Hull	*Mareknyght*	Danzig
1463	24th Aug	Hull	*Mare*	Danzig
1463	24th Aug	Hull	*Mare*	Danzig
1464	12th Jun	Southampton	Carrack of Christoforus Solego	Venice?
1464	12th Jun	Southampton	Carrack of Christoforus Solego	Venice?
1464	12th Jun	Southampton	Carrack of Christoforus Solego	Venice?
1465	10th May	Hull	*Christofer*	Danzig
1465	21st May	Hull	*John*	Danzig
1465	21st May	Hull	*John*	Danzig
1466	14th Oct	Hull	*Trinite*	Hull
1466	14th Oct	Hull	*Trinite*	Hull
1466	31st Oct	Hull	*Andrewe*	Middleburgh
1467	10th Mar	Lynn	Ship of Thomas Wadnowe	

Georgius	Redmondus	alien	2000		quinn
Thomas	Neleson	native	2000	Copyn Lambe master	child
Thomas	Neleson	native	500	Petrus van Toll master	child
Thomas	Dalhouse	native	300		child
acobe	de Stephano	alien?	3850		quinn
Nicholao	de Candea	alien?	138		quinn
Luco	de Flowr	alien?	1250		quinn
Bease	Corore	alien?	318		quinn
Paulo	de Garba	alien?	100		quinn
Dominicus	Travisan	alien?	1000	also recorded as 1500 staves	quinn
Baldino	Negro	alien?	300		quinn
Antony	Antonius	alien	400		child
Court	Knope	hanse	1200		child
acobus	Plubb	hanse	300		child
Andreas	Harder	hanse	300		child
Hans	Wynrick	hanse	500		child
arthlomeus	Wulfe	hanse	84		child
Maragono	de Coyr	alien?	336		quinn
Phillipo	Cyny	alien?	8000		quinn
Nicholao artholomeo Dominico	de Nicholo Calessa de Gersa	aliens?	300		quinn
ermyan	Vanrode	hanse	800		child
Simon	Luneyenk	hanse	450	1 last of bowstaves (see note above)	child
oger	Vinger	hanse	50		child
William	Butler	native	100		child
Thomas	Neleson	native	200		child
etrus	Brokke	hanse?	2 bunches		child
ohn	Gaunse	native	200	cargo & names suggest northern or eastern port of origin	gras

1467	17th June	Hull	*George*	Danzig
1467	17th June	Hull	*George*	Danzig
1467	17th June	Lynn	Ship of Paul Rode	
1467	3rd Aug	Hull	*Christoffre*	Hamburg
1471	2nd Dec	Southampton	Carrack of Baltizar Scorcifficus	Venice?
1471	9th Nov	Hull	*Mare*	Westernschouwen
1472	13th Jan	Hull	*Cristofur*	Vere
1472	27th Jan	Hull	*Hilda*	Hull
1472	3rd Nov	Southampton	Galley of Francisco Deodo	Venice
1477	30th Sept	Southampton	Galley of Cristoforo Deodo	Venice
1477	30th Sept	Southampton	Galley of Cristoforo Deodo	Venice
1477	30th Sept	Southampton	Galley of Powle Moasse	Venice?
1478	13th Jan	Southampton	Galley 'Capitano' of Petrus Priole	Venice
1478	13th Jan	Southampton	Galley 'Capitano' of Petrus Priole	Venice
1478	28th Apr	Southampton	Galley of Pero Cownteryn	Venice
1478	28th Apr	Southampton	Galley of Pero Balbe	Venice
1478	28th Apr	Southampton	Galley of Pero Balbe	Venice
1480	13th Nov	London	*Maria*	Danzig
1480	13th Nov	London	*Maria*	Danzig
1480	6th Nov	London	*Tres Magos*	Oporto
1480	6th Nov	London	*Tres Magos*	Oporto
1480	6th Nov	London	*Tres Magos*	Oporto

Hansse	Durecope	hanse	230	half last of bowstaves (see note above)	child
Thomas	Neleson	native	400		child
Mathias	Fynkynbergh	hanse	300		gras
Barthlomeus	Wulfe	hanse	2250	5 lasts of bowstaves (see note above) BW only merchant on ship	child
Aungell	Corore	alien?	50		quinn
Petrus	Jacobson	alien	200		child
Thomas	Phelipp	hanse?	100		child
ohn	Whytfeld	native	100		child
ohannes	de Nicholo	alien?	32		quinn
ero	de Crayne	alien?	18	galley listed as from Flanders for last port of call	quinn
owle	Tepill	alien?	810? recorded as bows	galley listed as from Flanders for last port of call	quinn
ado	de Castilnuovo	alien?	4 recorded as bows		quinn
ichaell	Stalk	alien?	274 recorded as bows	galley listed as from Flanders for last port of call	quinn
achomo	Lawrenci	alien?	150 recorded as bows	galley listed as from Flanders for last port of call	quinn
	Comytt de Galea Cownteryn	alien	150 recorded as bows		quinn
ichaell	de Skorpett	alien	100 recorded as bows		quinn
eorge	Dentin	alien	20 recorded as bows		quinn
ans	Overcamp	hanse	900		cobb
ans	Stutte	hanse	300		cobb
lexanderndér	Portinarius	alien	shared 929		cobb
eter	Vase	alien	shared 929		
eter	Andrewe	alien	shared 929		

1480	6th Nov	London	*Tres Magos*	Oporto
1480	6th Nov	London	*Tres Magos*	Oporto
1480	7th Nov	London	*Sanctus Spiritus*	Oporto
1481	12th Feb	Southampton	Galley of Petrus Surans	Venice
1481	12th Feb	Southampton	Galley of Petrus Surans	Venice
1481	12th Feb	Southampton	Galley of Petrus Surans	Venice
1481	12th Feb	Southampton	Galley of Petrus Surans	Venice
1481	12th Feb	Southampton	Galley of Alowisus George	Venice
1481	12th Feb	Southampton	Galley of Alowisus George	Venice
1481	12th Feb	Southampton	Galley of Bernard Bondymer	Venice
1481	14th Jun	London	Galley of Bernard Bondymer	Venice
1481	14th Jun	London	Galley of Bernard Bondymer	Venice
1481	16th June	Newcastle u Tyne	*Playtt*	Danzig
1481	21st Jul	London	*George*	Danzig
1481	21st Jul	London	*George*	Danzig
1481	21st Jul	London	*George*	Danzig
1481	21st Jul	London	*George*	Danzig
1481	21st Jul	London	*Mighell*	Danzig
1481	21st Jul	London	*Mighell*	Danzig
1481	25th Feb	London	*Trego*	Arnemuiden
1481	28th Aug	London	*Reynold*	Danzig
1481	2nd Jan	London	*George*	Middleburg
1481	3rd Sept	London	*Santa Maria*	Cadiz
1483	16th July	Hull	*George*	Danzig
1483	16th July	Hull	*Trenyte*	Danzig
1483	16th July	Hull	*Trenyte*	Danzig

ygo	Yenes	alien	shared 929		
erald	Yenes	alien	16		
aptista	de Aurea	alien	88		cobb
	Admirall	alien	250	galley listed as from Flanders for last port of call	quinn
tephano	Cateryn	alien	400	galley listed as from Flanders for last port of call	quinn
nthonio	Baveryn	alien	5600	galley listed as from Flanders for last port of call	quinn
eronimo	Typolo	alien	700	galley listed as from Flanders for last port of call	quinn
amiso	Peron Jurato	alien	100		quinn
nthonio	Bavaryn	alien	7200		quinn
amise	de Georgeo	alien	150		quinn
amyan	de Catero	alien	190		
nthony	Bavaryn	alien	5856	a state galley, part of a flotilla of 3 recorded at Southampton	cobb
artholamur	Rawyn	alien	200		wade
eter	Eksted	hanse	560	record says '1 Last' of bowstaves. Number estimated on an unprepared stave weighing c.8lb	cobb
erman	Overcamp	hanse	600		cobb
ans	Stut	hanse	924		cobb
ylman	Barkys	hanse	408		cobb
ans	Rutyng	hanse	300		cobb
ans	Stut	hanse	632		
lbright	Falland	hanse	600		cobb
ans	Stut	hanse	308		cobb
erard	Lesbern	hanse	400		cobb
hn	Ambros de Nigron	alien	268		cobb
ans	Stagnet	hanse	2000		child
ndreas	Hartwich	hanse	1	Is this figure right? Poss. error in original or v. accurate customs	child
ans	Stagnet	hanse	2972		child

1483	16th July	Hull	*Trenyte*	Danzig
1483	9th June	Hull	*Nicholas*	Danzig
1488	15th April	Newcastle u Tyne	*Cristofur*	Amsterdam
1488	9th Mar	Newcastle u Tyne	Anne	Danzig
1489	12th Apr	Hull	*Mare*	Danzig
1489	21st June	Hull	*Mary*	Danzig
1489	3rd Sept	Hull	*Cristofer*	Danzig
1489	3rd Sept	Hull	*Cristofer*	Danzig
1490	31st Mar	Hull	*Cristofer*	Amsterdam
1504	27th Aug	Lynn	*Anne*	Danzig
1504	30th May	Lynn	*George*	Danzig
1504	31st July	Lynn	*John*	Lynn

KEY FOR SOURCE COLUMN

child	Childs, W R editor (1986) *Customs accounts of Hull 1453–1490*. Leeds. Yorks Archaelogical Soc.
cobb	HS Cobb editor (1990) Petty Customs Accounts: Imports PRO E122/194/25 from *Overseas trade of London: Exchequer and Customs accounts 1480–81* London. Record Soc.
cw	Carus Wilson, EM (1937) *Overseas trade of Bristol in the later Middle Ages.* Bristol Record Soc.
frost	Frost, C (1827) *Notices Relative to the Early History of the Town and Port of Hull.* Beverley. J B Nicholls
frostb	Frost, B (1963) *Local Port Book for Southampton.* Southampton. University Press.
gras	Gras NSB (1918) *Early English Customs System.* Oxford University Press

Petrus	Nygyerbur	hanse	1	Is this figure right? Poss. error in original or v. accurate customs	child
Nicholas	Molner	hanse	90		child
ohannes	Arlsom	alien	400		wade
Thomas	Kempe	hanse	816		wade
Mathias	Vynckenbere	hanse	123	Poss same ship as below since Laurence Shoemaker is master	child
Matheus	Martrius	hanse	150	Poss same ship as above since Laurence Shoemaker is master	child
Herman	Overkamp	hanse	1000		child
ohannes	Stangnel	hanse	25 bunches		child
ohanes	Menson	alien	30		child
Hans	Lutkeher	hanse	c1650 + 8 bundellis	3 lasts (see note above) + bundles	gras
Hans	Lutkeher	hanse	800	recorded as 60 bunches containing 800 staves. Each bunch would weigh c.1 cwt	gras
homas	Greneway	native	100		gras

uinn	Quinn, D B and Ruddock A A editors (1937-8) *Port Books or Local Customs Accounts of Southampton for the reign of Edward IV.* Southampton. Cox & Sharland.
gby	Rigby, S H (2005) *Overseas Trade of Boston in the Reign of Richard II.* Woodbridge. Boydell Press.
uddock	Ruddock, A A (1951) *Italian Merchants and Shipping in Southampton 1270–1600.* Southampton University Press.
alzman	Salzman, L F (1964) *English Trade in the Middle Ages*. London. H. Pordes
uder	Studer, P (1913) *Port Books of Southampton 1427–30*. Southampton. Cox & Sharland
ade	Wade, J F (1995) *Customs Accounts for Newcastle upon Tyne*. Gateshead. Surtees Soc.

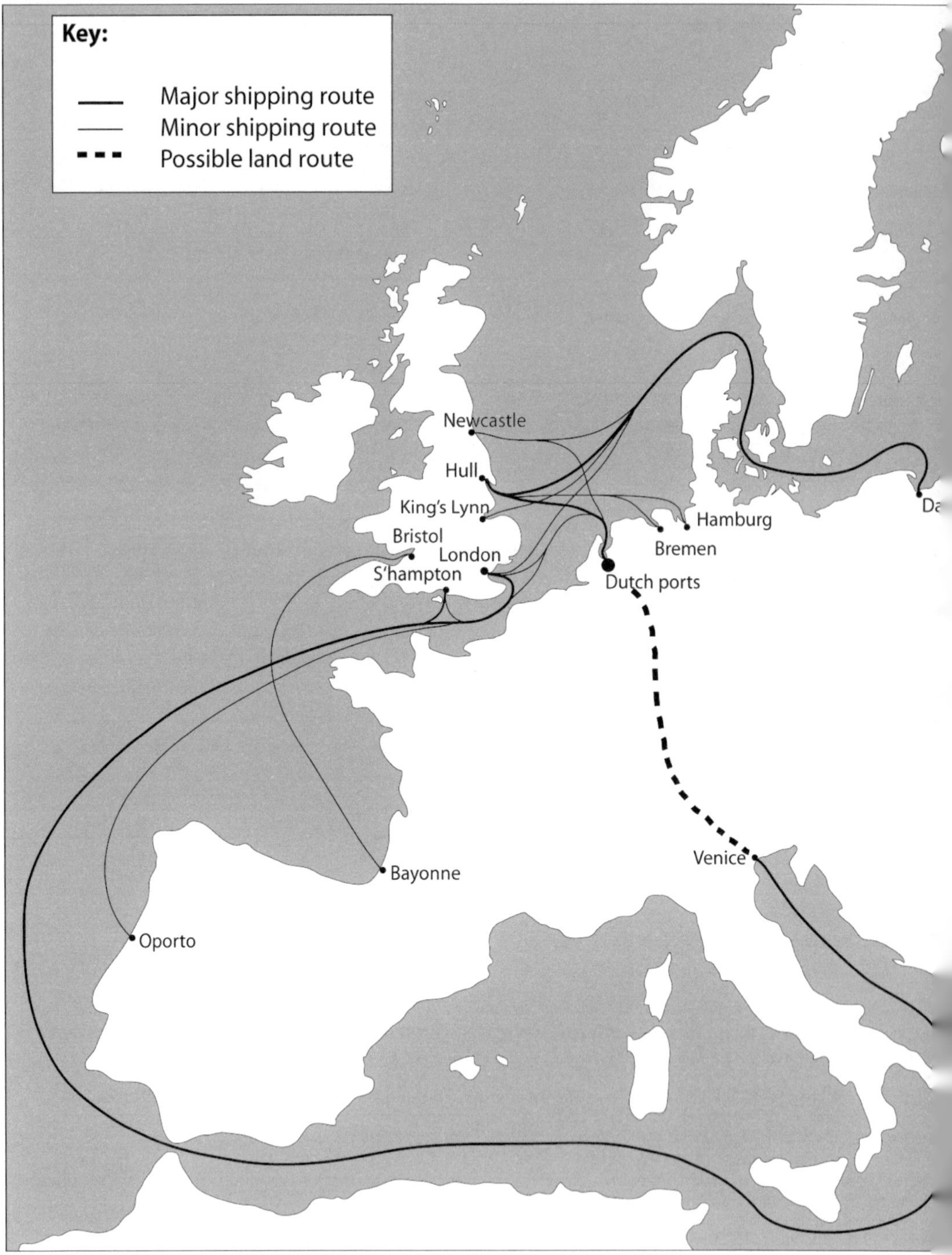

Trade routes for importing bowstaves.

Bibliography

Printed and Manuscript Sources

Ascham, R (1985). *Toxophilus: the School of Shooting*. Manchester, Simon Archery Foundation.

Attreed, L C (editor) (1991). *York House Books*. Stroud, Sutton Publishing.

Booth, P H W and Carr, A D (editors) (1991). *Account of Master John de Burnham the Younger, Chamberlain of Chester of the Revenues of the Counties of Chester and Flint, Michaelmas 1360 to Michaelmas 1361*. Manchester, Record Society of Lancashire and Cheshire.

Bunyard B D M (editor) (1914). *Brokage Books of Southampton 1439–40*. Southampton, Cox & Sharland.

Byerly, B F and C R (editors) (1977). *Records of the Wardrobe and Household*. London, HMSO.

Byerly, B F and C R (editors) (1986).*Records of the Wardrobe and the Household 1286–89*. London, HMSO.

Calendar of Close Rolls (CCR) (1900–63). London, HMSO.

Calendar of French Rolls; 48th Annual Report of the Deputy Keeper of Public Records. (1887). London, HMSO.

Calendar of Patent Rolls (CPR) 1893–1916). London, HMSO.

Calendar of State Papers and manuscripts relating in archives and collections of Milan 1385–1618 (1912). London, HMSO.

Calendar of State Papers and manuscripts relating to English affairs in archives and collections of Venice 1202–1519 (1864-1947). London, Longman Green.

Roll A 3: 1338–41, Calendar of the plea and memoranda rolls of the city of London: volume 1 1323–1364 (1926). URL: http://www.british-history.ac.uk

Childs, W R (editor) (1986). *Customs accounts of Hull 1453–1490*. Leeds, Yorkshire Archaeological Society.

Cobb H S (editor) (1990). *Petty Customs Accounts: Imports PRO E122/194/25 from Overseas trade of London: Exchequer and Customs accounts 1480–81*. London, Record Society.

Coleman, O (editor). (1960-1). *Brokage Books of Southampton 1443–44*. Southampton University Press.

Collins, F (editor) (1897). *Register of the Freemen of the City of York: Vol. 1: 1272–1558*. Gateshead, Publications of the Surtees Society no. 96.

Coss, P R (editor) (1986). *The Early Records of Medieval Coventry*. Oxford University Press for the British Academy.

Devon, F (editor) (1837). *Issues of the Exchequer*. London, John Murray.

Devon, F (editor) (1835). *The Issue Roll of Thomas de Brantingham*. London, J. Rodwell.

Ekwall, E (1951).*Two Early London Subsidy Rolls*. Lund .CWK Gleerup.

Foster, B (editor) (1963). *Local Port Book for Southampton for 1435–6*. Southampton University Press.

Gairdner, J (editor) (1863). *Letters and Papers Illustrative of the Reigns of Richard III and Henry VII*. London, Longman Green & Co.

Hanserecesse und Andere Akten de Hansetage 1256–1430. (1870–1970) Leipzig, Dunker & Humblot.

Hartopp, H (editor) (1927). *Register of the Freemen of Leicester 1196–1770*. Leicester, Corporation of Leicester.

Hopkinson, A M (editor) (2000). *The Rolls of the Derbyshire Eyre*. Derbyshire Record Society vol. XXVII.

James, J B (editor) (1990). *The Port book of Southampton 1509–10*. Southampton University Press.

Letters and Papers Foreign and Domestic of the reign of Henry VIII (1965). Vaduz, Kraus reprints.

Lewis, E A (editor) (1993). *Southampton Port and Brokage Book 1448–4*. Southampton University Press.

Lodge E C and Somerville R (1937). *John of Gaunt's Register 1372–76*. Camden 3rd series, nos. 56 and 57.

Percy, J W (editor) (1978). *York Memorandum Book vol. 3*. Gateshead, Surtees Society.

Proceedings and Ordinances of the Privy Council of England (POPC) (1834–7) London, Eyre & Spottiswoode.

Public Record Office, PRO C1/618.34

Public Record Office, PRO E101/392/14
Public Record Office, PRO E101/69/484
Public Record Office, PRO E213/82
Quinn, D B and Ruddock A A (editors) (1937–8). *Port books or local customs accounts of Southampton for the reign of Edward IV.* Southampton, Cox & Sharland.
The Register of Edward the Black Prince (BPR) (1930–33). London, HMSO.
Raine, A (editor) (1939). *York Civic Records.* Wakefield, Yorkshire Archaeological Society.
*Rotuli Parliamentorum…(*1767–77). London.
Rymer, T (editor) (1800). *Foedera, conventiones, litterae.* London
Statutes of the Realm (1810–28). London.
Sharp, M (editor) (1982). *Accounts of the Constables of Bristol Castle.* Bristol Record Society.
Sharpe R R (editor) (1899–1912) *Calendar of Letter Book preserved among the archives of the City of London at the Guildhall (CLBCL).* London Guildhall Corporation.
Spont, A (editor) (1897). *Letters and Papers relating to the war with France 1512–13.* London, Navy Records Society.
Stevenson, J. (editor) (1861–4). *Letters and Papers illustrative of the wars of the English in France in the reign of King Henry VI.* London.
Studer, P (editor) (1910–11). *The Oak Book of Southampton.* Southampton Record Society.
Studer, P (editor) (1913) .*The Port books of Southampton 1427–30.* Southampton, Cox & Sharland.
Wade, J F (editor) (1995). *Customs accounts for Newcastle upon Tyne.* Gateshead, Surtees Society.
Willis Chapman, A.B (editor) (1912–15). *The Black Book of Southampton.* Southampton, Cox & Sharland.
Wilson, K P (editor). (1969). *Chester Customs Accounts 1301–1566.* Chester, Records Society.
Woolgar C M (editor) (1993). *Household accounts from Medieval England.* Oxford University Press.
York Memorandum Book, book 2 (1915).Gateshead, Surtees Society.
York Memorandum Book, book 1 1376–1419 (1912). Gateshead, Surtees Society.

Secondary Literature

Ackroyd, P (2002) *Albion: The Origins of the English Imagination.* London, Chatto & Windus.
Agricultural History of England and Wales (AHEW) (1966–2000). Cambridge University Press.
Allmand, C T (1968). *The Lancastrian Land Settlement in Normandy 1417–50.* Economic History Review XXI 1968.
Allmand, C T (editor) (1973). *Society at War; the Experience of England and France during the 100 Years War.* Edinburgh, Oliver & Boyd.
Allmand, C T (1997) *Henry V.* New Haven, Yale University Press.
Allmand, C T (1983). *Lancastrian Normandy.* Oxford, Clarendon Press.
Archer, R E and Walker, S (editors) (1995). *Rulers and Ruled in Late Medieval England.* London, Hambledon Press.
Armstrong, C (1983). *England, France and Burgundy.* London, Hambledon Press.
Ayton, A (1994). *Knights and Warhorses.* Woodbridge, Boydell Press.
Ayton, A and Preston, P (2005). *The Battle of Crecy 1346.* Woodbridge, Boydell Press.
Ballard, M (1990). *An Expedition of English Archers to Liege in 1467 and the Anglo Burgundian marriage alliance.* Nottingham Medieval Studies. XXXIV 1990.
Barker, J (2005). *Agincourt: the King, the campaign, the battle.* London, Little Brown.
Barnie, J. (1974). *War in medieval society; social values and the Hundred Years War 1337 -1453.* London, Weidenfeld & Nicolson
Bartlett, C (1997). *English Longbowman 1330–1515.* London, Osprey.
Bates, D and Curry, A (editors) (1994). *England and Normandy in the Middle Ages.* London, Weidenfeld & Nicolson.
Beardwood, A (1931). *Alien merchants in England; their legal and economic position.* Medieval Academy of America, Cambridge, Mass.
Bennett, M J (1983). *Community, Class and Careerism.* Cambridge University Press.
Bork, R (editor) (2005). *De Re Metallica:the Uses of metal in the Middle Ages.* Aldershot
Bridge, J S C (1921). *History of France from the Death of Louis XI.* Oxford, Clarendon Press.
Brown T (1997). *English Martial Arts.* Hockwold cum Wilton, Anglo Saxon Books.
Burne, Col. A H (1956). *The Agincourt War.* London, Eyre & Spottiswoode.
Carus Wilson, E M (1937). *Overseas trade of Bristol in the later Middle Ages.* Bristol Record Society.
Castor, H (2000). *The King, the Crown and the Duchy of Lancaster.* Oxford University Press.
Childs, W R (1978). *Anglo-Castilian Trade in the later Middle Ages.* Manchester University Press.
Corbett, J S (1905). *Fighting Instructions 1530–1816.* London, Navy Society.
Cruickshank C G (1969). *Army Royal: Henry VIII's Invasion of France 1513.* Oxford, Clarendon Press

Crump C G and Johnson C (1912). *Powers of Justices of the Peace.* English Historical Review 1912.
Cummins, J (1988). *The Hound and the Hawk.* London, Weidenfeld and Nicolson.
Curry, A and Hughes M (editors) (1994). *Arms, Armies and Fortifications in the Hundred Years War.* Woodbridge, Boydell Press.
Curry, A. (2000). *The Battle of Agincourt; sources and interpretations,* Woodbridge, Boydell Press.
Curry, A. (2005). *Agincourt; a new history.* Stroud. Tempus Publishing.
Davies, J (2001). *The Inventory of King Henry VIII.* Journal of the Society of Archer Antiquaries vol 44.
Driver, J T (1971). *Cheshire in the later Middle Ages 1399–1450.* Chester, Cheshire Community Council.
Duffy, S (1997). *Ireland in the Middle Ages.* London, Macmillan.
Dunham, W H (1970). *Lord Hastings indentured retainers 1461–83.* Hamden, Conn., Archon books.
Dunn, A (2002). *The Great Rising of 1381.* Stroud, Tempus Publishing.
Dyer, C (2003). *Making a Living in the Middle Ages: The People of Britain 850–1520.* London, Penguin.
Dyer, C (1989). *Standards of Living in the later Middle Ages.* Cambridge University Press.
Fenwick, C (1998, 2001 and 2005). *The Poll Taxes of 1377, 1379 and 1381.* Oxford University Press.
Fiorato, V, Boylston, A and Knusel, C (editors) (2000). *Blood Red Roses: the archaeology of a mass grave from the Battle of Towton AD 1461.* Oxford, Oxbow Books.
Fowler, K (2001). *Medieval Mercenaries vol. 1, The Great Companies.* Oxford, Blackwell.
Frost, C (1827). *Notices Relative to the Early History of the Town and Port of Hull.* London, J B Nichols.
Gendall, J (2001). *The Arundell Archive of Arrows and Arrowheads.* Journal of the Society of Archer-Antiquaries vol. 44.
Gillespie, J L(1974). *Richard II's Cheshire Archers.* Transactions of the Historical Society of Lancashire and Cheshire CXXV.
Gillett, E and MacMahon, K A (1980). *A History of Hull.* Hull University Press.
Gillett, E (1970). *History of Grimsby.* Oxford University Press.
Given-Wilson C and Beriac, F (2001). *Edward III's prisoners of war: the battle of Poitiers and its context.* English Historical Review CXVI, 2001.
Goodman, A (1980). *Military sub contracts of Sir Hugh Hastings 1380.* English Historical Review XCV 1980
Goodman, A (1981). *The Wars of the Roses: Military Activity and English Society.* London. Routledge and Kegan Paul.
Goodman, A (1992). *John of Gaunt; an Exercise in Princely Power.* Harlow, Longman.
Goodman, A (2005). *The Wars of the Roses: the Soldiers' Experience.* Stroud, Tempus Publishing.
Gras, N S B (1918). *Early English Customs System.* Cambridge Mass., Harvard University Press
Hageneder, F (2007). *Yew, a History.* Stroud, Sutton Publishing.
Hardy, R (1992). *Longbow; a Social and Military History,* 3rd ed. Yeovil, Patrick Stephens Ltd.
Haigh, P A (1995). *The Military Campaigns of the Wars of the Roses.* Stroud, Sutton Publishing.
Hearder, H and Loyn H R (editors) (1974). *British government and administration.* Cardiff, University of Wales Press.
Hewitt, H J (1966). *The Organization of War under Edward III.* Manchester University Press.
Hirsch, T (1858). *Danzigs Handels – und Gewerbsgeschichte.* Leipzig.
Hudson, W (1900). *The Norwich Militia in the Fourteenth Century.* Norfolk and Norwich Archaeological Society. vol. XIV.
Hunt, R W, Pantin, W A and Southern, R W (editors) (1948), *Studies in Medieval History presented to F M Powicke.* Oxford, Clarendon Press.
Hutton, R (1996). *The Rise and Fall of Merry England.* Oxford University Pres.
Jessop, O (2000). *A New Artefact Typology for the Study of Medieval Arrowheads.* Medieval Archaeology XL 2002.
Johnson, P A (1988). *Duke Richard of York 1411–60.* Oxford, Clarendon Press.
Jones, M K (1989). *War on the Frontier: Lancastrian Land Settlement in Eastern Normandy 1435–50.* Nottingham Medieval Studies. XXXIII.
Jones, M K (2002). *The Battle of Verneuil 17th August 1424.* War in History vol. IX.
Jones, M (1970). *Ducal Brittany 1364–99.* Oxford University Press.
Jones, M and Vale, M (editors) (1989). *England and her Neighbours 1066–1453.* London, Hambledon Press.
Jones, T (1980). *Chaucer's Knight; the Portrait of a Medieval Mercenary.* London, Weidenfeld and Nicolson.
Kerling, N J M (1954). *Commercial relations of Holland and Zeeland.* Leiden, E J Brill.
Koczy, L (1936). *The Baltic Policy of the Teutonic Order.* Torun, The Baltic Institute.
Labarge M W (1980). *Gascony England's First Colony.* London, Hamish Hamilton.
Lane F C (1966). *Venice and History.* Baltimore, John Hopkins University Press.
Lloyd, T H (1982). *Alien Merchants in England in the High Middle Ages.* Sussex, Harvester Press
Longman, C J and Walrond, Col. H (1894). *Archery.* London, Longmans and Green.
Lucas, H S (1929). *The Low Countries and the Hundred Years War 1329–47.* Ann Arbor, University of Michigan Press.

Lydon, J F (1963). *Richard II's Expeditions to Ireland.* Journal of the Royal Society of Antiquaries of Ireland, Vol. 93 pt2.
Mallett, M (1974). *Mercenaries and their Masters*. London, Bodley Head.
McFarlane K B (1963). *A Business partnership in war and administration.* English Historical Review LXXVIII 1963
McKisack, M (1959). *The Fourteenth Century.* Oxford University Press.
McNiven, P (1975). *The Men of Cheshire and the Rebellion of 1403.* Transactions of the Historical Society of Lancashire and Cheshire vol. 129.
Meek, E L (2001). *The Career of Sir Thomas Everingham 'Knight of the North' in the service of Maximilian Duke of Austria.* Historical Research vol. 74.
Megson, B (1993). *Such Goodly Company.* London, Worshipful Company of Bowyers.
Morgan, P J (1987). *War and Society in Medieval Cheshire 1277–1403.* Manchester University Press.
Morris J E (1901). *The Welsh Wars of Edward I.* Oxford, Clarendon Press.
Myers, A R (editor) (1959). *The Household of Edward IV.* Manchester University Press.
Newhall, R A (1924). *English Conquest of Normandy 1416–1424.* New Haven, Yale University Press.
Newhall, R A (1940). *Muster and Review; a Problem of English Military Administration. 1420–40.* Cambridge mass., Harvard University Press.
Nicholson, H (editor) (1998). *Military Orders volume 2, Welfare and warfare.* Aldershot, Ashgate
Ormerod, G (1818). *History of the County Palatinate and the City of Chester.* London, Lackington, Hughes, Harding, Mavor and Jones.
Orpen, G H (1911–20). *Ireland under the Normans.* Oxford, Clarendon Press.
Oxley, J E (1968). *The Fletchers and Longbowstring Makers of London.* London, Worshipful Company of Fletchers.
Palmer, J J N (1972). *England, France and Christendom 1377–99.* London, Routledge and Kegan Paul.
Platt, C (1997), *King Death; the Black Death and its Aftermath in Late Medieval England,* London, UCL Press,
Platt, C and Coleman-Smith R (1975). *Excavations in Medieval Southampton 1953– 69.* Leicester University Press
Platt, C (1973). *Medieval Southampton.* London, Routledge and Kegan Paul.
Pollard, A J (1983). *John Talbot and the War in France 1427–53.* London, Royal Historical Society.
Postan M M and Miller E (1987). *Cambridge Economic History of Europe, volume 2 Trade and Industry in the Middle Ages.* Cambridge University Press.
Postan, M M (1964), *The Costs of the Hundred Years War.* Past and Present 27.
Postan, M M (1973). *Medieval Trade and Finance.* Cambridge University Press.
Powicke, M (1962). *Military Obligation in Medieval England.* Oxford, Clarendon Press.
Prestwich, M (1996). *Armies and Warfare in the Middle Ages: the English Experience.* New Haven. Yale University Press.
Prince, A E (1931). *The Strength of English armies in the reign of Edward III.* English Historical Review XLVI 1931
Richardson, T (1998). *The Bridport muster roll of 1457.* Royal Armouries Yearbook 2 1997. Leeds, Royal Armouries Museum.
Rigby, S H (editor) (2005). *Overseas Trade of Boston in the Reign of Richard II.* Lincoln Record Society vol. 93. Woodbridge, Boydell Press.
Roberts, C and Cox M (2003). *Health and Disease in Britain.* Stroud, Sutton Publishing.
Rogers J E T (1917). *Six Centuries of Work and Wages.* 12th ed, London.
Ross, C (1974). *Edward IV.* New Haven, Yale University Press.
Ross, C (editor) (1979). *Patronage, Pedigree and Power in Later Medieval England.* Gloucester, Alan Sutton.
Rowe, B J H (1931). *Discipline in the Norman garrisons under Bedford 1422–35.* English Historical Review XLVI.
Rowe, B J H (1926). *A Contemporary account of the 100 years War from 1415–29.* English Historical Review.
Rudder, S (1779, 2006). *A New History of Gloucestershire.* Stroud, Nonsuch Publishing.
Ruddock, A A (1951). *Italian Merchants and Shipping in Southampton 1270–1600.* Southampton. University Press.
Russell, P E (1955). *English Intervention in Spain and Portugal.* Oxford, Clarendon Press.
Salzman, L F (1964). *English Trade in the Middle Ages.* London, H Pordes.
Salzman, L F (1952). *Building in England to 1540.* Oxford University Press.
Schofield, P R (2003). *Peasant and Community in Medieval England 1200-1500.* Basingstoke. Palgrave Macmillan.
Searle, E and Burghart, R (1972). *Defence of England and the Peasants' Revolt.* Viator vol. 3 1972.
Sherbourne, J W (1964). *Indentured retinues and English expeditions to France 1369– 80,* English Historical Review, Oct. 1964.
Sherborne J W (1965).*The Port of Bristol in the Middle Ages.* Bristol, Historical Association.
Soar, H D H (2006). *Secrets of the English War Bow.* Yardley, Penn., Westholme Publishing.

Somerville, R (1953). *History of the Duchy of Lancaster, vol. 1 1265–1603.* London, Chancellor and the Council of the Duchy of Lancaster.
Stirland, A J (2005). *The Men of the* Mary Rose. Stroud, Sutton Publishing.
Stonor Saunders, F (2004). *Hawkwood: the Diabolical Englishman.* London, Faber.
Storey R, PhD dissertation. *Technology and Military Policy in Medieval England, c1250-1350* University of Reading 2003, http://medievalhistory.mysite.wanadoo-members.co.uk/thesis.html.
Storey, R (1998). *The Tower of London and the Garderobae Armorum.* Royal Armouries Yearbook 3 1998.
Stretton, M (2005/6). *Medieval Arrow Heads part 3,* The Glade 110, winter 2005/6.
Strickland, M and Hardy, R (2005). *The Great Warbow.* Stroud. Sutton Publishing.
Sumption, J (1999). *The Hundred Years War, vol. 2, Trial by Fire.* London, Faber.
Sumption, J (1990). *The Hundred Years War, vol. 1, Trial by Battle.* London, Faber.
Toulmin Smith L (1894). *Expeditions to Prussia and the Holy Land made by Henry Earl of Derby.* London, Camden Society.
Tout, T F (1920–33). *Chapters in the Administrative History of Medieval England.* Manchester University Press.
Tyreman, C (1988). *England and the Crusades.* Chicago, University of Chicago Press.
Unwin, G (1938). *Gilds and Companies of London.* London, George Allen and Unwin.
Vale, M G A (1970). *English Gascony 1399 – 1453.* Oxford University Press.
Van der Wee, H (1963). *Growth of the Antwerp market.* The Hague, Nijhoff.
Van Houtte, J A (1977). *An Economic History of the Low Countries 800–1800.* London, Weidenfeld and Nicolson
Vaughan, R (1966). *John the Fearless.* London, Longman.
Vaughan, R (1970). *Philip the Good.* Harlow, Longman.
Vaughan, R (1973). *Charles the Bold.* London, Longman.
Vaughan, R (1975). *Valois Burgundy.* London, Allen Lane.
Walker, S (1985). *Profit and Loss in the Hundred Years War.* Bulletin of the Institute of Historical Studies v.58 (1985).
Warner, M (1998). *Chivalry in Action: Thomas Montagu and the War in France, 1417–28.* Nottingham Medieval Studies XLII.
Wolffe, B (1981). *Henry VI.* London, Eyre Methuen.
Wrottesley, C (1887). *Collections for a History of Staffordshire vol. 8.* London, Harrison and Sons.
Wylie, J H (1914). *The Reign of Henry V, vol 1.* Cambridge University Press.

Index

INDEX

INDEX